The Sixties······

The **6**

Sixties . . . .

From

Memory

to

History

Edited by David Farber

The University of North Carolina Press   *Chapel Hill & London*

The paper in this book meets the guidelines for
permanence and durability of the Committee on
Production Guidelines for Book Longevity of
the Council on Library Resources.

Library of Congress
Cataloging-in-Publication Data
The Sixties : from memory to history /
edited by David Farber.

   p. cm.
Includes bibliographical references
(p.) and index.
ISBN 0-8078-2153-5 (cloth : alk. paper).—
ISBN 0-8078-4462-4 (paper : alk. paper)
1. United States—History—1961–1969. I. Farber,
David R.
E841.S54   1994
973.92—dc20   93-40102
                  CIP

04   9 8 7 6

Contents

• • • • • •

The Sixties⋯⋯

Introduction

• • • • • •

DAVID FARBER

Americans cannot seem to let the sixties go gently into the night. While the 1970s disappeared before they even ended and the 1950s succumbed to a nostalgic fog, the 1960s stay hot. We make politicians take a decades-old drug test and scrutinize their position on the Vietnam War—though few of us are sure what makes for a passing grade in either case. We wonder if black power marked the end of a great man's dream of a color-blind nation or the beginning of a multicultural society. And of less profound importance, but harder to miss, songs and images of the sixties flood the mass media and the marketplace—in homage to that pig in the demographic python, the baby boomers.

To a large extent, memories of the sixties shadow both the public realm and the private lives of tens of millions of Americans. So far, many of the most popular books and movies about the 1960s—Oliver Stone's *JFK*, Todd Gitlin's *The Sixties*, Neil Sheehan's *A Bright Shining Lie*—have been powerful acts of memory wrestling with history in an effort to bring some order to the rush of still vivid experiences. The history of America in the 1960s has admirably resisted becoming just another dryasdust subject of scholarly inquiry. Yet, hard as it is for a generation that still sees itself as "the young people" to admit, the 1960s were a long time ago: it is many more than twenty years ago today that Sgt. Pepper and his friends taught America how to play.

The original essays in this book represent, I believe, some of the most exciting ways in which historians are beginning to paint those times onto the larger canvas of American history. In this collection we, the essayists, ask fundamental questions about how much America changed in the 1960s and why it changed. Our answers center on two related concepts: cultural authority and political legitimacy. The separate chapters analyze the ways in which the great issues of the sixties—the war in Vietnam, race relations, the role of the federal government, youth culture, the status of women, the private enterprise system, the fabric of the good life—are shaped and contested through the changing nature of cultural authority and political legitimacy. We argue (as historians tend to do) that the set of events and problems we call the sixties can be understood only in the context of the larger history of Americans in the post–World War II decades.

In postwar America the shape of political and cultural life was in flux. After the depression of the 1930s and the market scarcities of the war years, the majority of Americans had achieved by the early 1960s a level of material comfort unprecedented in world history. Tom Wolfe, one of the most perceptive contemporary cultural critics in the sixties, claimed that American affluence had created a "Happiness Explosion!" that offered nearly unlimited opportunity for people to find "novel ways of . . . *enjoying*, extending their egos way out on the best terms available, namely their own."[1] Many believed that the old rules of scarcity and the traditional values of thrift and delayed gratification no longer held. John F. Kennedy, in his 1961 inaugural address, seemed to agree that a new age of limitless possibilities—for better or for worse—had arrived. "Man holds in his mortal hands," the doomed president orated, "the power to abolish all forms of human poverty and all forms of human life." In such a boundless universe, to whom did one listen for guidance and for ordering principles? Cultural authority—the power to set the rules of proper conduct and behavior—was up for grabs in the midst of the Happiness Explosion and the nuclear age.

America's brand new international role also contributed to the flux. No longer a relatively isolated, second-rate military power, the United States in 1960 stood as colossus of the free world, the mightiest nation on Earth. Americans were thrilled when their young leader, continuing his inaugural address, trumpeted America's world mission: "We shall pay any price, bear any burden, meet any hardship, support any friend, oppose any foe, in order to assure the survival and the success of liberty. This much we pledge—and more." But what did such overheated rhetoric really mean? On what political ground would the United States "pay any price . . . and more" to intervene in the affairs of every country in the world? How did the Constitution mesh with the arsenal of democracy's national security state? How would the American people decide these questions? In the 1960s Americans felt so very much was possible. At the same time, however, many shared the feeling that the possibilities were by no means all good ones.

By the sixties local customs and local power elites were being challenged and often radically subverted by national and international forces. Huge corporations that depended on a national mass market pushed Americans to develop different kinds of social relations and cultural iden-

David Farber

tities than did small-town banks, family businesses, or small farms. Cold war Democratic president John F. Kennedy, trying to win decolonizing nations in Africa and Asia to the American side, understood that he needed a different kind of relationship (or at least the appearance of a different kind of relationship) with people of color than did old-time southern Democratic party leaders.[2] Television executives operating out of New York City produced a different kind of news and thus a different kind of informed citizenry than did newspaper editors in homogeneous communities in the prairie states. New kinds of authorities like macroeconomists, public policy analysts, foreign area experts, marketing specialists, and education consultants—a whole class of professional people that exploded after World War II—entered the corridors of power and rethought the capacities of the federal government, as well as those of universities, business corporations, and other large-scale institutions, in order to shape daily life in America and the world.[3]

Though national in scope, these changes had different impacts on different communities within the United States. For African Americans living in the South, the new national politics was a godsend—it offered a structure in which their struggles could be more successful.[4] For others, like Christian fundamentalists, who insisted that public school children in their local communities start each day with a prayer, the new expansive but intrusive national politics, built on an increasingly national culture and international economics, seemed to threaten their way of life.[5] Many Americans, from the self-consciously radical young people who founded the Students for a Democratic Society in the early 1960s to the proudly traditional Irish American parents in Boston who opposed busing children to end racial segregation in the schools in the late 1960s, feared the centralized, expert-oriented, and bureaucratized kind of society that America was becoming.[6]

Young radicals in America in the 1960s, their numbers greatly expanded by a cold war struggle gone very sour in Vietnam, tended to see all of life's chances as infiltrated and even determined by the binds of the political. By politics they meant not simply the overt positions taken by elected officials or the partisan battles of Democrats and Republicans, but the elaborate structures used by all authorities—school administrators, corporate executives, doctors, members of the clergy, television producers—to shape what was legitimate and what was deviant, what was debatable and what was not of collective concern. Their investigations of the ideological bulwarks of American society led them to argue that more than individual opportunity needed to be unblocked to create a more just and fair system. They challenged the integrity and virtue of basic institutions and values that had taken on the cover of American tradition, like the nuclear family, anticommunism, the economic bottom line, and material progress. They questioned just how natural feminine and masculine behaviors were and how much individual merit really determined one's status in America. Some challenged the system; others rejected it and tried to create an alternative culture.[7] They tested American common sense.[8] As the essays in this book will argue, some directly, others more implicitly, these challenges resonated because American common sense had been subverted and hollowed out by the radical political, cultural, and economic changes of the postwar era.

In the last few years, most historical accounts, memoirs, and movies about the sixties have focused on the liberal, leftist, and liberationist impulses of that time. That focus is, in the main, appropriate. The many and different people who fought to make the United States a more inclusive society and a more permissive society, who challenged the foreign policy of the federal government and questioned the meaning and reach of American democracy, *were* the central agents of change during the 1960s.

Still, if the sixties constituted a period when liberalism briefly shaped the agenda of the federal government and leftist-oriented activists challenged established cultural and political authorities, they were also the seed time of conservative populism and religious fundamentalism. The nomination of arch-conservative Senator Barry Goldwater of Arizona as the Republican presidential candidate in 1964 marked not, as many thought then, the last gasps of a parochial and fragmented band of zealots, but the first, partial victory of a powerful movement that would capture the White House by 1980.

Those who will write the history of the 1970s and 1980s would do well to see the 1960s as a key chapter in the organizational history of a many-faceted, reanimated, right-wing political and cultural movement. In an historical irony, it was the Right, not the Left, that first publicly charged the dominant elites in America with being, in Barry Goldwater's telling phrase, "false prophets." Tens of millions of Americans who called on their religious faith as their guarantor of virtue, and on their families as the repository of bedrock values, scorned the bureaucratic mentality of big government, distrusted the distant merchants of national culture, and feared the managers of international corporate capitalism. They rightfully saw that these rigidly secular agents of centralized power challenged the meaning and the security of their lives. The radical political and cultural outbreaks of the sixties only deepened the certainty of these Americans that their country was losing its moral and spiritual soul.[9]

In the 1960s public life erupted out of the narrow confines within which some Americans thought it belonged. As public life expanded, power relations that had been seen as either privately negotiated areas of life (like to whom you could and could not sell your home) or simply unquestionable traditional roles (like men's domination over women) were challenged and taken up by people who defined them as political issues that the nation needed to address. In the 1960s and early 1970s, many Americans from both the Left and the Right, and often from a populist perspective, reinvigorated by redefining political life in America.

As a result of what America did in the sixties, the United States changed dramatically. Equal opportunity became far more possible, foreign policy again was openly debated, freedom of expression exploded, America became a far more inclusive society, and social justice became a national priority (though an increasingly partisan cause). What Americans accomplished in the sixties put to rest one long era, a dark era for many citizens, and began another.

Our problems in the 1990s are different from theirs, sometimes because their solutions became a part of our problems. If Americans of the sixties emphasized the freeing of individual expression, we worry about the meaning of virtue in an unanchored marketplace of ideas and values. While they properly learned to be skeptical of their leaders, we consider how to make politics vital to a nation grown cynical about all government. While they struggled to figure out what just role the world's most affluent people should play globally, we search for ways to keep our workers internationally competitive. And fundamentally, in part because of what people did in the 1960s, just exactly who "we" signifies in our public life has become an explosive question.[10]

This collection of essays is not a call for another sixties. It serves instead—like much history—as a cautionary tale. But unlike right-wing politicians or conservative social critics who summon the 1960s as a kind of catchall bogeyman, useful for scaring up customers, this work reanimates that period for subtler purposes. It is hoped that, by stripping away some of the veils that cover the sixties, we can gain some clarity in thinking through who we were back then, who we might have become, and who we wish to be.

Robert Collins, in "Growth Liberalism in the Sixties: Great Societies at Home and Grand Designs Abroad," argues that liberals' embracing of federal economic growth policies allowed the capacity of government to expand rapidly. The linked phenomena of economic growth and government expansion undergirded much of the political fervor of the 1960s.

Mary Sheila McMahon, in "The American State and the Vietnam War: A Genealogy of Power," reasons that the failure of foreign policy elites to create the ground for their own legitimacy set the ideological and political scene for America's difficulties in Vietnam. Chester Pach, in "And That's the Way It Was: The Vietnam War on the Network Nightly News," writes of a different group of experts involved in the foreign policy process—the television news community. Like McMahon's "systems knowledge" experts who formulated foreign policy, the TV professionals who interpreted the war in Vietnam for Americans back home were masters of a process in which content had become less important than form.

David Colburn and George Pozzetta, in "Race, Ethnicity, and the Evolution of Political Legitimacy," address the ways in which a majority of Americans redefined their relationship with national culture and politics as they reinvented their racial and ethnic identities in the sixties. The authors examine how the civil rights movement and African American struggles for social justice became deeply enmeshed with a great many Americans' uncertainty about the meaning and utility of individual and collective *power* in the United States.

Alice Echols, in "Nothing Distant about It: Women's Liberation and Sixties Radicalism," demonstrates that 1960s radicals did, in general, develop a critique of liberal concepts of the boundaries of public life and political action. Focusing on the women's movement, she contends that radicals increasingly differed from liberals inasmuch as they sought to politicize issues—for feminists, the issue of family life in particular—that liberals thought were outside the domain of public life.

Terry Anderson, in "The New American Revolution: The Movement and Business," argues that the vast majority of protesters in the sixties were not dedicated to a radical critique of liberalism or capitalism. In his examination of activists' protests against American business corporations, he shows that activists were driven by local and immediate concerns. But he also reveals that most of the protests against business in the 1960s and early 1970s contained a powerful, if inchoate, critique of the narrowly market-driven concerns of the corporate community. Private enterprise, the protesters maintained, was a public affair.

George Lipsitz, in "Who'll Stop the Rain?: Youth Culture, Rock 'n' Roll, and Social Crises," further explores the contradictory and contested terrain of market-based culture in America. Lipsitz suggests that young people saw in their music the possibility of a cross-class and cross-racial community. Beth Bailey, in "Sexual Revolution(s)," also analyzes how some young people—and some not-so-young people—used cultural claims to make arguments about social relations and political authority in the sixties. Bailey concludes that the sexual revolution in America in the sixties was much more about the legitimacy and meaning of both gender roles and sexuality than it was simply about more sex.

Kenneth Cmiel, in "The Politics of Civility," charts the shift within the United States during the sixties from one understanding of social order to another. Cmiel holds that a broad "informalization" of society was legally sanctioned by the late 1960s and early 1970s through a series of Supreme Court rulings that responded to social pressures by rebalancing the weight of freedom and order in American public life.

In my contribution to the book, "The Silent Majority and Talk about Revolution," I build on the essay by Colburn and Pozzetta. Many Americans in the 1960s found themselves uncomfortably caught in a national culture that little praised the value of their productive labor and that increasingly gave voice to critics of their newly developed life-styles.

To some extent the sixties ended, or at least mutated, when the realm of the public imploded in the Watergate scandals, expanded with the immense growth of "inside-the beltway" interest groups, and was challenged by a variety of interests that fought to subdue federal power. Probably as we move into the twenty-first century the clean line between the sixties and the years that followed will seem less certain. That, however, is a story yet to be written.

In this collective story, the essayists bring different political perspectives to the history of the 1960s, and I, at least, disagree with some of my colleagues' conclusions. But we have tried to formulate the historical issues in similar terms. We are most interested in how Americans in the 1960s came to reconsider the boundaries and grounding of political life and how they debated the meaning and the underlying premises of the "good life." Our collective account emphasizes Americans' struggles during that period to connect their moral vision with their collective public life.

NOTES

1. Tom Wolfe, *The Pump House Gang* (New York: Bantam, 1968), 9.

2. For an outstanding critical overview of the liberal Democratic party

agenda in the 1960s and its discontents, see Allen Matusow, *The Unraveling of America: A History of Liberalism in the 1960s* (New York: Harper and

Row, 1984). For a more positive appraisal of Lyndon Johnson's Great Society and a short but rich biography of the president, see Paul Conkin, *Big Daddy from the Pedernales: Lyndon Baines Johnson* (Boston: Twayne, 1986); see also Robert Divine, *The Johnson Years* (Lawrence: University Press of Kansas, 1987). The main biographers of Lyndon Johnson, Robert Caro and Robert Dallek, have not yet written about the presidential years but their biographies should be consulted for their differing interpretations of Johnson's character. A new and more positive history of President Kennedy's domestic record is given by Irving Bernstein, *Promises Kept: John F. Kennedy's New Frontier* (New York: Oxford University Press, 1991). Hugh Graham, *Civil Rights and the Presidency: Race and Gender in American Politics* (New York: Oxford University Press, 1990), provides a masterful narrative of federal civil rights policy in the 1960s and early 1970s.

3. A general history of these changes has yet to be written. For an excellent beginning, see James Gilbert, *Another Chance: Postwar America, 1945–1985* (Chicago: Dorsey, 1986).

4. Though there are many fine books about the African American struggle for social justice in the sixties, no single work adequately describes American race relations during that era. A fine start in this direction is offered by David R. Goldfield, *Black, White, and Southern: Race Relations and Southern Culture, 1940 to the Present* (Baton Rouge: Louisiana State University Press, 1990), and Jack Bloom, *Class, Race, and the Civil Rights Movement* (Bloomington: Indiana University Press, 1987). The most influential group of black militants, the Student Nonviolent Coordinating Committee (SNCC), is covered by Clayborne Carson, *In Struggle: SNCC and the Black Awakening of the 1960s* (Cambridge: Harvard University Press, 1981). Riots and uprisings in African American communities in the 1960s have also not yet received much historical attention, though a great deal was written about them at the time they occurred. For a painstaking account of the major uprising in Detroit in 1967, see Sidney Fine, *Violence in the Model City: The Cavanagh Administration, Race Relations, and the Detroit Riot of 1967* (Ann Arbor: University of Michigan Press, 1989). Other important books include Taylor Branch, *Parting the Waters: America in the King Years, 1954–1963* (New York: Simon and Schuster, 1988), William Chafe, *Civilities and Civil Rights: Greensboro, North Carolina, and the Black Struggle for Freedom* (New York: Oxford University Press, 1980), Steven Lawson, *Running for Freedom: Civil Rights and Black Politics in America since 1941* (New York: McGraw-Hill, 1991), Neil McMillen, *The Citizens' Council: Organized Resistance to the Second Reconstruction, 1954–1964* (Urbana: University of Illinois Press, 1971), Michael Belknap, *Federal Law and Southern Order: Racial Violence and Constitutional Conflict in the Post-Brown South* (Athens: University of Georgia Press, 1987), Robert Norrell, *Reaping the Whirlwind: The Civil Rights Movement in Tuskegee* (New York: Vintage, 1985), Nicholas

Lemann, *The Promised Land: The Great Black Migration and How It Changed America* (New York: Knopf, 1991), and the excellent overview offered in Robert Weisbrot, *Freedom Bound: A History of the American Civil Rights Movement* (New York: Norton, 1990). For an insightful summary of white working-class and lower-middle-class perceptions of black revolt, see Jon Reider, *Canarsie: The Jews and Italians of Brooklyn against Liberalism* (Cambridge: Harvard University Press, 1985).

5. In 1962 the Supreme Court ruled that prayer in the schools was unconstitutional. For a superb history of religion in postwar America, see Robert Wuthnow, *The Restructuring of American Religion: Society and Faith since World War II* (Princeton: Princeton University Press, 1988).

6. For masterful accounts of busing in Boston, see Ronald P. Formisano, *Boston Against Busing: Race, Class, and Ethnicity in the 1960s and 1970s* (Chapel Hill: University of North Carolina Press, 1991), and Anthony Lukas, *Common Ground: A Turbulent Decade in the Lives of Three American Families* (New York: Knopf, 1985).

7. Little sound writing has been done on sex and drugs and rock 'n' roll in the 1960s. The drug culture, not surprisingly, has yet to find its historian. Jay Stevens, in *Storming Heaven: LSD and the American Dream* (New York: Atlantic Monthly Press, 1987), has come the closest in his highly recommended and mind-expanding study of LSD celebrities and advocates. For the emblematic leaders of the counterculture, see Tom

Wolfe, *The Electric Kool Aid Acid Test* (New York: Bantam, 1968). For the counterculture in San Francisco, see Charles Perry, *The Haight-Ashbury: A History* (New York: Vintage, 1985). For an evocative account of the counterculture in Kansas, see David Ohle, Roger Martin, and Susan Broussea, eds., *Cows Are Freaky When They Look at You: An Oral History of the Kaw Valley Hemp Pickers* (Wichita: Watermark Press, 1991). For a perceptive and inside account of the underground press, see Abe Peck, *Uncovering the Sixties: The Life and Times of the Underground Press* (New York: Pantheon, 1985). In general, see Matusow, *The Unraveling of America*.

8. White student radicals enjoy a rich historical literature, though one narrowly focused on the early leaders of the Students for a Democratic Society: James Miller, *Democracy Is in the Streets* (New York: Simon and Schuster, 1987), Todd Gitlin, *The Sixties: Years of Hope, Days of Rage* (New York: Bantam, 1987), and Tom Hayden, *Reunion: A Memoir* (New York: Random House, 1988). For an excellent analysis of the main premises of the student New Left, see Wini Breines, *Community and Organization in the New Left, 1962–1968* (New York: Praeger, 1982). For an oral history of the international student movement, see Ron Fraser, ed., *1968: A Student Generation in Revolt* (New York: Pantheon, 1988). In Sara Evans, *Personal Politics: The Origins of Women's Liberation in the Civil Rights Movement of the Sixties* (New York: Vintage, 1980), the evolution of the women's movement—made up over-

whelmingly of women under thirty—from the student New Left and civil rights movement is ably documented. For a fuller description of the creation of the women's liberation movement out of the radical politics of the 1960s, see Alice Echols, *Daring to Be Bad: Radical Feminism in America, 1967–75* (Minneapolis: University of Minnesota Press, 1989).

9. A scholarly history of right-wing populism and conservative religious reaction to social change in the 1960s has not been written. James Davidson Hunter, *Culture Wars: The Struggle to Define America* (New York: Basic Books, 1991), gives a good account of the outcomes but is weak on the historical development. Wuthnow, in *The Restructuring of American Religion*, brilliantly analyzes the changing role of religious belief and religious organization in American society since World War II; for the 1960s, see chapters 7 and 8. He writes convincingly about the tensions that grew in America between those who participated in America's higher education boom in the sixties and those who did not and the way in which that tension figured in Americans' view of social and cultural changes during the period. Bruce Shulman has written an outstanding account of the large-scale changes in the South that contributed to Barry Goldwater's electoral breakthrough in the region and the subsequent Republican shift—see Shulman, *From Cotton Belt to Sunbelt: Federal Policy, Economic Development, and the Transformation of the South, 1938–1980* (New York: Oxford University Press, 1991). Also useful are the astute, if at times polemical, writings of Kevin Phillips—for example, *The Emerging Republican Majority* (New Rochelle: Arlington Books, 1969). A thoughtful book on the larger history of nativism and anticosmopolitan political movements is David H. Bennet, *The Party of Fear: From Nativist Movements to the New Right in American History* (New York: Vintage, 1990).

10. For histories that try to pay attention to the struggle over the contested nature of accounts of the 1960s, see David Farber, *Chicago '68* (Chicago: University of Chicago Press, 1988) and *The Age of Great Dreams: America in the 1960s* (New York: Hill and Wang, 1994), and W. J. Rorabaugh, *Berkeley At War: The 1960s* (Berkeley: University of California Press, 1989).

ROBERT M. COLLINS

1 · · · · · ·

Growth Liberalism in the Sixties

Great Societies at Home and Grand Designs Abroad

Economic growth—as an idea, as a policy goal, and as a social reality—helps to define the sixties. John F. Kennedy's New Frontier and Lyndon B. Johnson's Great Society were built on a faith in economic growth, both as an end in itself and as a tool for achieving other goals. Conservatives viewed economic growth as a validation of the free enterprise system. The seeming dependability of growth during much of the sixties shaped the dreams and nightmares of a good many political and cultural radicals. To examine the issue of economic growth in the sixties is to understand why so many believed so much was possible during those years and how events forced Americans to wrestle with the fact that the nation's reach had exceeded its grasp. The specific ways American policymakers envisioned, pursued, and reacted to economic growth help to explain what made the sixties distinctive and also how the central themes of the era make sense in a larger historical frame.

To appreciate the place of economic growth in the sixties, one must begin, paradoxically, with a consideration of its opposite, stagnation. The Great Depression introduced a strong note of pessimism into the discussion of economic affairs in the 1930s, a fear that the United States now constituted a mature, indeed sclerotic, economy and faced a static rather than dynamic future.[1] It was against this backdrop of hopelessness that economic growth would take on its exceedingly powerful allure in the years after World War II.

During the depression, with economic pessimism nearly endemic, a full-blown school of economic analysis known as stagnationism emerged. Harvard economist Alvin Hansen gave the stagnationist theory its clearest formulation in his presidential address to the American Economic Association in December 1938. The economy, he told his colleagues, had previously depended for its dynamism on three crucial forces: population growth, the frontier, and technological innovation. In the modern, mature economy, however, these engines of growth simply did not work any longer. Population growth, on the decline throughout the 1920s because of a secular trend toward lower birth rates and diminished immigration due to legislative restriction, plummeted under the pressures of the depression. The territorial expansion of the frontier era was past. Technological innovation, such as the automobile, could not be counted upon to appear with sufficient regularity to propel the economy forward. Slack was now a natural condition of the economic system, and only large-scale government investment could prevent "sick recoveries which die in their infancy and depressions which feed on themselves and leave a hard and seemingly immovable core of unemployment."[2]

World War II proved that the stagnationists had underestimated the fundamental strength of the economy. Jump-started by the demands of war and sustained—to just what degree would become the subject of heated debate—by the subsequent mobilization for a cold war, the economy moved into a period of unparalleled affluence that would last until the early 1970s, an era that appears in retrospect to have been America's economic golden age.

Where had the stagnationists gone wrong? The answer is that the engines of economic progress that Hansen had identified in 1938 had not expired but merely stalled. Population growth rebounded dramatically, as the vaunted baby boom in the years 1946–64 gave America the largest absolute population increase in its history.[3] The frontier experience was replicated in the explosive growth of the crabgrass frontier of suburbia and in the emergence of the Sunbelt. Innovation continued to exert a healthy influence as the auto boom continued into the postwar years, with nearly 8 million passenger cars produced in 1955 (the prewar high had been 4.5 million in 1929).[4] The chemical industry—as Benjamin Braddock learned in the sixties anthem movie *The Graduate*: "Just one word. . . . Are you listening? . . . *Plastics*"—joined electronics and other defense-related industries to move the economy forward. In other words, on each specific count of their analysis the pessimists were undone by events.

The postwar affluence took hold of the American imagination. Writers found new metaphors for the American experience in the visible institutions of abundance: the supermarket was especially favored. *Life* magazine rhapsodized about shoppers whose market carts "became cornucopias filled with an abundance that no other country in the world has ever known."[5] In his poem "Superman," John Updike archly reported, "I drive my car to supermarket, / The way I take is superhigh, / A superlot is where I park it, / and Super Suds are what I buy."[6] And Norman Mailer heralded the political triumph of John F. Kennedy in 1960 in an essay entitled "Superman Comes to the Supermart."[7]

The economic reality that underlay the imagery of abundance was striking. The gross national product (GNP), measured in constant 1954 dollars, rose from $181.8 billion in 1929 to $282.3 billion in 1947. By 1960 the GNP had increased by a further 56 percent, reaching $439.9 billion. Spending on personal consumption, measured in constant 1954 dollars, increased from $128.1 billion in 1929 to $195.6 billion in 1947, and to $298.1 billion in 1960.[8]

Admittedly, hidden beneath such rosy statistics was a more disquieting aspect of the postwar economic order. By any standard, either comparative or absolute, the income distribution in the United States remained skewed.[9] In 1970 Paul Samuelson stated the matter picturesquely: "If we made an income pyramid out of a child's blocks, with each layer portraying $1,000 of income, the peak would be far higher than the Eiffel Tower, but almost all of us would be within a yard of the ground."[10] Clearly, not all Americans shared fully in the postwar boom. Blacks, Hispanics, Native Americans, and the elderly remained less well-off than others. Nevertheless, income distribution in the United States, however skewed, became slightly more equal during the postwar boom. The bottom 40 percent of American families received 12.5 percent of aggregate family personal income in 1929, 16.0 percent in 1947, and 16.1 percent in 1957; the top 20 percent of families received 54.4 percent of all income in 1929, 46.0 percent in 1947, and 45.3 percent in 1957.[11]

In a similar way, although blacks did not share as fully as whites in the postwar bounty, their position did improve. In 1960 black males received 67 percent of the salary or wage income of whites; the figure for black females was only marginally better, 70 percent. Yet before the war the situation had been even worse, with black males and females receiving only 41 and 36 percent respectively of the income earned by their white counterparts.[12] Economic growth did not end discrimination or eliminate its ravages, but it did significantly lessen the existing economic disparities.

In mid-1955, George Meany, president of the AFL-CIO, observed that "American labor has never had it so good."[13] The same could be said for the majority of Americans. On one important point, however, the stagnationists had been prescient: The postwar affluence was accompanied by the emergence of a governmental presence in the economy that dwarfed even that of the New Deal. Federal spending, which during the Great Depression had crested at 10.5 percent of GNP in 1936, averaged 17.3 percent over the period 1947–60.[14] The Employment Act of 1946 made formal the federal government's responsibility to foster maximum employment, production, and purchasing power. The law also created a new institution, the Council of Economic Advisers (CEA), to provide the president with expert economic advice on a routine basis.

The Council of Economic Advisers moved from an emphasis on stability and full employment as the chief ends of federal economic policy at the end of the war to a new emphasis by 1949 on economic growth as the overriding goal. Much of the impetus for the shift came from the formidable influence of CEA member and later chairman Leon H. Keyserling. The emphasis both contributed to the postwar boom and reflected its influence. The council's 1949 report stressed that "the doctrine of secular stagnation no longer finds place in any important public circle with which we are familiar." In its place, the council presented "the firm conviction that our business system and with it our whole economy can and should continue to grow."[15]

The council's emphasis on growth as the overriding goal of economic policy did not last, however. The return of the Republicans to presidential power in 1953 brought a renewed emphasis on the other elements in the constellation of concerns guiding policymakers, notably stability and inflation; growth was not completely dismissed but it was subordinated to these other concerns.[16] Regarding inflation, President Dwight D. Eisenhower considered the battle "never-ending."[17] When asked at a press conference whether the administration had worried "a little too much about inflation . . . and perhaps not enough about the slow rate of growth of our economy," Ike responded that "economic growth in the long run cannot be soundly brought about except with stability in your price structure."[18]

The administration's stance helped make economic growth a matter of controversy in Eisenhower's second term. The growth of the early postwar years slowed distinctly. Real GNP increased at a yearly rate of 3.8 percent from 1947 to 1954, but at a lower 3.2 percent rate from 1954 to 1960. Potential GNP (a calculation based on the assumption of full employment) grew at an average of 4.4 percent per year in the earlier period (1947–54) and at only 3.5 percent per year for the years 1954–60.[19] Of course, from a more recent perspective the economic performance of the Eisenhower years appears highly satisfactory in most respects. But the loss of economic momentum was sufficient for the question of economic growth to become a major public controversy and a staple of partisan politics before the 1950s were over.

In the mid-1950s, cold war competition raised the stakes of partisan political sniping to a new, higher level. In May 1957 Nikita Khrushchev predicted that the Soviet Union would "soon catch up to the U.S. level of per capita output of meat, milk, and butter; then, we shall have shot a highly powerful torpedo at the underpinnings of capitalism."[20] With the threat of mutual nuclear destruction still overhanging the world, the cold war took on the additional dimension of economic competition. The development of a Soviet nuclear capability and the launching of Sputnik were hard proofs, in the eyes of Walter Lippmann, that "the prevailing picture of the Soviet economy as primitive and grossly inefficient was false."[21]

The economic contest between the superpowers focused especially on the matter of growth. Again, Khrushchev made the point with frightening directness: "Growth of industrial and agricultural production is the battering ram with which we shall smash the capitalist system, enhance the influence of the ideas of Marxism-Leninism, strengthen the Socialist camp and contribute to the victory of the cause of peace throughout the world."[22] To American listeners, the threat was clear.

Allen Dulles, head of the Central Intelligence Agency (CIA), underlined the threat when he testified before the Joint Economic Committee of Congress in late 1959. Soviet industrial production, he reported, "has been growing at a rate at least twice as rapidly as that of the United States since 1950." The Soviet GNP "has also been growing twice as rapidly as that of the United States over the past 8 years." Dulles's generally scholarly and judicious analysis avoided cold war hysterics, but he noted ominously, "If the Soviet industrial growth rate persists at 8 or 9 percent per annum over the next decade, as is forecast, the gap between our two economies by 1970 will be dangerously narrowed unless our own industrial growth rate is substantially increased from the present pace."[23]

Observers reacted to the emergence of an economic cold war in a variety of ways. To some, the matter was nothing but a numbers game.[24] Others, including the outstanding growth theorist Evsey D. Domar, an MIT economist, believed the Soviet growth rate worrisome; he warned that "the influence played by a country in world affairs is related to its economic size." Jay Lovestone of the AFL-CIO believed that America's own domestic well-being required more rapid growth, and that the Soviet threat made the need all the more urgent. Howard C. Peterson of the Committee for Economic Development, a corporate-liberal business group, was less troubled: "Surely we wish to progress as rapidly as in the past, and to do better if we can—but not at any cost." Members of the business community such as Peterson generally worried that an increase in the nation's growth rate might be obtained at the price of increased government intervention and perhaps higher taxes. Clearly, responses to the Soviet Union's economic challenge were colored by fundamental beliefs as well as immediate cold war fears.[25]

While the controversy over economic growth reflected both partisan politics and cold war pressures, it was fueled as well by a generalized anxiety that seemed to come over the nation in the late 1950s. "Woe to them that are at ease in Zion," the Bible warns, and during the latter part of the Ike Age Americans grew increasingly fearful that the nation had lost its way in the blaze of its own prosperity. The result was an outburst of public soul-searching and numerous attempts to articulate an agenda of national goals that would be worthy of history's most powerful democracy. One such undertaking was the Special Studies Project of the Rockefeller Brothers Fund, organized in 1956.

The Rockefeller project set up panels in six broad areas to define major national problems and "clarify the national purposes and objectives that must inspire and direct the meeting of such great challenges." Behind the effort lay the concern that "our achievements and our strengths, because of their very magnitude, appeared in some ways to have outrun our goals." The overall Rockefeller panel of thirty notable Americans then published the individual reports as they were concluded one by one between January 1958 and September 1960. The economic policy panel report appeared in April 1958. Its message was unambiguous: "We must accelerate our rate of growth." The report viewed growth as the essential means to whatever ends U.S. society would aspire to, and it specified that a

5 percent growth rate was necessary to provide the public and private expenditures needed to achieve the nation's goals of freedom, abundance, and security.[26]

The discussion of national goals continued with the publication in *Life* magazine in 1960 of a series of articles on the theme of "the national purpose." Time-Life publisher Henry R. Luce caught perfectly the paradoxical amalgam of confidence and anxiety that pervaded the search for national goals: "But what now shall Americans *do* with the greatness of their nation?" he asked. "And is it great enough? And is it great in the right way?" James Reston called attention to "all this concern in the nation among serious men about the higher rate of growth in the U.S.S.R." But "it isn't just the Russians now," Archibald MacLeish noted, "it's ourselves. . . . We feel that we've lost our way in the woods, that we don't know where we are going—if anywhere." For Walter Lippmann, at least, the way was clear: "To use increments of our growing wealth wisely and prudently for public and immaterial ends: that is the goal, so I believe, toward which our national purpose will now be directed."[27]

Even President Eisenhower joined in the search for purpose, appointing a President's Commission on National Goals. The commission's report, publicly transmitted to the president in mid-November 1960, underscored the importance of growth while straddling most of the issues connected with it.[28] What the president's commission was unable to decide— just what a national commitment to economic growth entailed—became in 1960 one of the crucial issues of the presidential campaign.

John F. Kennedy embraced the goal of faster growth from the outset of the 1960 campaign. He called the resumption of economic progress "the number one domestic problem which the next President of the United States will have to meet" and fitted the growth issue into his basic campaign theme—the promise to get the country moving again.[29] Stiffening such rhetoric was the Democratic party platform, which committed the party to a 5 percent annual growth rate. For the party as well as for the candidate, growth would provide the means to great ends. As the platform explained, "Economic growth is the means whereby we improve the American standard of living and produce added tax resources for national security and essential public services."[30]

The Democratic onslaught left the Republican candidate in a difficult position. During the campaign, Republican nominee Richard M. Nixon found himself caught between the need to defend Eisenhower's record and the desire to identify with a more vigorous growth position. He attempted to edge closer to Kennedy's expansive position on growth while distinguishing the Republican version of such progress. "I would say that my goal," he announced, "and I think the only proper goal, for those who do not buy the theory of government manipulated growth, the only proper goal is a maximum growth rate. It might, in some instances be 3 percent, in some instances 4, in some instances 5."[31] Such efforts failed, however, to dislodge the connection in the public mind between the goal of accelerated growth and JFK's most powerful appeal, his call for action and his promise of greatness. Kennedy was the growth candidate; Nixon was not. And Kennedy won, if but narrowly.

Of course, making promises and winning elections is easier than governing a vast nation and delivering on commitments. Kennedy knew as much, even in the heat of the campaign. When he first met Walter Heller, an economist at the University of Minnesota, on a campaign swing through Minneapolis in October 1960, his initial question was: "Do you really think we can make good on that 5 percent growth promise in the Democratic platform?"[32] The commitment to increased growth was unshakable, but the political path was unclear and the consequences of the commitment unknowable. What was palpable was the political scent in the air. Richard Goodwin, a Kennedy speech writer, later recalled "the almost sensual thrill of victory—not a culminating triumph, but the promise, almost limitless in dimensions, of enormous possibilities yet to come."[33] Economic growth would be the engine to drive such expansive visions and deeds.

The problem of growth remained central as campaigning gave way to governing. Less than two weeks after his inauguration, Kennedy sent to the Congress a special message on economic recovery and growth. Cautioning that "we cannot expect to make good in a day or even a year the accumulated deficiencies of several years," he proposed that the nation aim in 1961 to bring production up to existing capacity—economists call this expansion—and in 1962 and 1963 to achieve genuine economic growth, the enlargement of productive capacity.[34] As Heller later characterized the policy reorientation, "Gone is the countercyclical syndrome of the 1950s. Policy now centers on gap closing and growth, on realizing and enlarging the economy's non-inflationary potential."[35]

The new policy of what Heller called "Keynes-cum-growth" proceeded along three major lines into the mid-1960s.[36] First, to narrow the gap between current production and existing capacity, the government expanded demand by means of a massive tax reduction—the famous Kennedy-Johnson tax cut, which was first discussed in 1962, formally proposed in 1963, and signed into law in February 1964. Second, to provide cost-price stability, the administration developed wage-price guideposts in 1962 and initiated a policy of "jawboning" business and labor into acquiescence. Finally, to increase the output potential of the economy—to achieve true growth—the Kennedy and Johnson administrations encouraged business investment by liberalizing depreciation allowances in July 1962; by instituting a 7 percent tax credit for capital outlays on machinery and equipment in October 1962; by introducing beginning in 1961 a host of manpower development, education, and retraining programs to increase the quality and ultimately the output of the labor force; and by initiating the so-called monetary twist to hold down long-term interest rates for investment purposes.[37]

The results through mid-decade were impressive. Between 1961 and 1965, real GNP increased at a rate above 5 percent per year. Employment grew by 2.5 percent per year, and in January 1966 the unemployment rate sank to 3.9 percent. The percentage of Americans mired in poverty, according to official estimates, dropped from 22.4 percent in 1960 to 14.7 percent in 1966. As these advances unfolded, the rate of inflation remained below 2 percent per year through 1965. By all the usual measures, the economic policies of the early sixties were an unambiguous success.[38]

The spectacular economic expansion and growth of the Kennedy and early Johnson years made possible the emergence of a strikingly expansive view of national possibilities. Theodore White caught the mood when he identified the rise of "a new generation of Americans who saw the world differently from their fathers. [They were] brought up to believe, either at home or abroad, that whatever Americans wished to make happen, would happen." The new expansiveness was underpinned by the belief that economic growth was not merely possible but practically inevitable given the proper policies.[39] In 1964 President Johnson expressed the point in his own way, telling an aide: "I'm sick of all the people who talk about the things we can't do. Hell, we're the richest country in the world, the most powerful. We can do it all. . . . We can do it if we believe it."[40]

The economic policy of Keynes-cum-growth had become the engine driving U.S. public policy. As CEA chief Walter Heller—with the exception of the presidents he served, as important a figure as worked in government during his time—wrote in 1966, prosperity and rapid growth put at the president's "disposal, as nothing else can, the resources needed to achieve great societies at home and grand designs abroad."[41] Growthmanship made possible a host of new undertakings in the vastness of outer space, in the jungles of Southeast Asia, and in the streets of America's inner cities. Freed for the moment from the discipline of stringency, policymakers redefined what was possible and in the bargain purchased both triumph and tragedy for the nation.

One such new frontier was that of space and science. In May 1961 Kennedy dramatically reversed Eisenhower's space policy by committing the nation "to achieving the goal, before this decade is out, of landing a man on the moon and returning him safely to the earth."[42] The contrast could not be clearer. Eisenhower had vetoed the Apollo manned-moon-shot program in 1960. When told that supporters of the venture likened it to the voyages of Columbus, Ike retorted that he was "not about to hock his jewels."[43]

The promise of a growing economy allowed Kennedy to view the space race more expansively than his predecessor. As Walter A. McDougall has pointed out, the Democratic administration thought of space exploration "in terms of ends (were they desirable?) rather than means (can we afford it?)." The NASA payroll grew tenfold under the Apollo program. By 1965 the agency and its private contractors employed 411,000. NASA appropriations rocketed from less than a billion dollars in fiscal year 1961 to $5.1 billion in fiscal year 1964. Bound only loosely by the budgetary constraints that had so fettered Eisenhower, first Kennedy and then Johnson made the space program, in McDougall's words, "a model for a society without limits, an ebullient and liberal technocracy."[44]

A similar pattern unfolded in the area of national security affairs, but one that ended far less satisfactorily for the United States. Again, the story begins with the Eisenhower presidency. As John Lewis Gaddis has argued compellingly, the Eisenhower administration had moved away from Harry S. Truman's brand of "symmetrical" containment as embodied in a National Security Council document, NSC-68. The basic reason for the change was Eisenhower's belief that the means available for national security purposes were limited; the national economy might be bankrupted if driven too hard, or its free enterprise character might be fatally compromised by a regimented cold war mobilization. Republican defense policy emphasized not the indivisibility of interests à la NSC-68 but rather the pitting of U.S. strengths against adversary weaknesses, at times and in locations of American choosing—what Gaddis labels "asymmetrical containment."[45] The trick, as Ike saw it, was "to figure out a preparedness program that will give us a respectable position without bankrupting the nation."[46] The resulting policy was called the "New Look," a defense posture that relied on the threat of massive nuclear retaliation at the top end of the ladder of confrontation and on the use of covert action through the CIA at the bottom rungs.[47] It was a doctrine, James Tobin observed at the time, "made as much in Treasury as in State."[48]

That the New Look strategy wore a dollar sign attracted critics as well as admirers. Henry A. Kissinger identified three major influences on military strategy—military doctrine, technology, and fiscal concerns—and concluded that fiscal and technological considerations had outweighed military doctrine in the formulation of U.S. policy.[49] The Democrats saw in Ike's fiscally driven asymmetrical defense policy an opportunity for political advantage. JFK and LBJ slammed home a partisan message that U.S. national security interests were indivisible. As Lyndon Johnson put it in 1964, "Surrender anywhere threatens defeat everywhere."[50] The Democratic platform in 1960 promised that a new Democratic administration would "recast our military capacity in order to provide forces and weapons of a diversity, balance, and mobility sufficient in quantity and quality to deter both limited and general aggressions." The candidate put an even finer point on the matter: "We must regain the ability to intervene effectively and swiftly in any limited war anywhere in the world."[51]

Once in office, Kennedy moved energetically to implement a policy of "flexible response." The new approach promised, in the words of its powerful champion Maxwell D. Taylor, the former army chief of staff, "a capability to react across the entire spectrum of possible challenge, for coping with anything from general atomic war to infiltrations."[52] Over the next three years there ensued what Theodore Sorensen called a "build-up of the most powerful military force in human history—the largest and swiftest build-up in this country's peacetime history, at a cost of some $17 billion in additional appropriations."[53] Kennedy's Department of Defense reported the implementation of all levels of the flexible response posture "in accordance with the President's directive that military requirements should be considered without regard to arbitrary budget ceilings."[54] The revolution at the Pentagon and the growth revolution at the White House were intertwined from the beginning.

These intertwined revolutions set the stage for tragedy in Southeast Asia. As John Lewis Gaddis has argued, it is budgetary constraint that has "most often forced the consideration of unpalatable options" in postwar foreign policy: "When one knows one has only limited resources to work with, then distinctions between what is vital and peripheral, between the feasible and unfeasible, come more easily."[55] Both the perception and the reality of limits had constrained U.S. policy toward Vietnam in the 1950s. Those economic limits would operate only weakly as the Kennedy and Johnson administrations moved toward war in Vietnam.

Southeast Asia provided immediate proof to the incoming Kennedy administration of the correctness of its complaints about Eisenhower's economically restrained New Look posture. According to Arthur M. Schlesinger, Jr., a presidential assistant, "Kennedy was appalled to discover a few weeks after the inauguration that, if he sent 10,000 men to southeast Asia, he would deplete the strategic reserve and have virtually nothing left for emergencies elsewhere." The nation's airlift capacity was such that "it would have taken nearly two months to carry an infantry division and its equipment to southeast Asia."[56] It was these findings that fueled Defense Secretary Robert S. McNamara's pursuit of what he called "usable power," power in being that could be applied to the variety of tasks Kennedy's symmetrical containment policy would find at hand. Of course, one problem with usable power is that its very existence tempts its use. As Walt Rostow observed to Kennedy in March 1961: "We must somehow bring to bear our unexploited counter-guerrilla assets on the Viet-Nam problem: armed helicopters; other Research and Development possibilities; our Special Forces units. It is somehow wrong to be developing these capabilities but not applying them in a crucially active theater. In Knute Rockne's old phrase, we are not saving them for the Junior Prom."[57]

The abundance of usable power generated by growth economics freed America's Vietnam policy from earlier logistical and fiscal constraints. By the time of Kennedy's assassination in November 1963, the United States had nearly 16,000 military personnel stationed in Vietnam and had helped overthrow the regime of Ngo Dinh Diem. When the subsequent South Vietnamese governments proved even more vulnerable to communist pressure than Diem's regime, the temptation to apply America's "usable force" directly to save the south proved irresistible. Two days after signing the Gulf of Tonkin Resolution, which authorized the use of force to assist the government of South Vietnam, President Lyndon Johnson warned, "Let no one doubt for a moment that we have the resources and we have the will to follow this course as long as it may take."[58] His administration and the nation would come to grief in learning that he was, in that statement, wrong on every count.

While economic growth supported grand designs in Asia, it undergirded a massive liberal enterprise at home as well. As with other matters, the effort began slowly and shakily under Kennedy, and emerged full-blown, perhaps overblown, under Johnson. Domestic reform ran along many lines in the superheated optimism of the early and mid-1960s. The political labels of the day seem in retrospect curiously appropriate. All along the New Frontier there appeared rough, exploratory federal efforts on civil rights, manpower training, area development, education, health care, and poverty. Upon Kennedy's death, Johnson tried to accelerate the pace of innovation and embody the results in a welter of legislative achievements that would cumulatively build a Great Society. LBJ embarked on his domestic crusade in January 1964, when he committed the nation to an "unconditional war on poverty"; the full, utopian character of the undertaking became clear later in the year when he began to invoke the phrase *Great Society* to describe his goal: "a society of success without squalor, beauty without barrenness, works of genius without the wretchedness of poverty."[59] The label quickly stuck and came to describe several hundred legislative initiatives that aimed at achieving civil rights for blacks, victory in the War on Poverty, enhanced educational opportunity, improved health care for the elderly, a more acceptable quality of urban life, better environmental protection, and improved protection for consumers. Because of such efforts, between 1964 and 1972 social welfare expenditures rose from 25.4 percent of the federal budget to 41.3 percent, and from 4.3 percent of GNP to 8.8 percent.[60]

As with the adventure in space and the engagement in Vietnam, economic growth played a significant role in liberalism's domestic program. First, it fueled the basic optimism that made the grandiose conception of the Great Society appear reasonable. "Hell," LBJ told aides in April 1964, "we've barely begun to solve our problems. And we can do it all. We've got the wherewithal."[61] Second, growth really did provide the wherewithal of which Johnson spoke. James Tobin has estimated that of the total increase in GNP over the 1961–65 period, roughly one-quarter represented the result of cyclical recovery (especially the reduction of unemployment) and the remainder was attributable to growth in the economy's capacity to produce.[62] The creators of the Great Society assumed that a portion of this growth could be redirected to support the most ambitious liberal program in U.S. history. Joseph Califano, an LBJ aide, recalled that the president "considered a robust, noninflationary economy so critical to his domestic program that he spent more time on economic matters than on any other subject."[63]

Growth influenced the Great Society in a third way through its impact on the content of that Great Society centerpiece, the War on Poverty. The War on Poverty was based on the promise and reality of economic growth, as Walter Lippmann observed in March 1964: "A generation ago it would have been taken for granted that a war on poverty meant taxing money away from the haves and turning it over to the havenots. . . . But in this generation . . . a revolutionary idea has taken hold. The size of the pie can be increased by invention, organization, capital investment, and fiscal policy, and then a whole society, not just one part of it, will grow richer."[64] But the influence of growth ideas went beyond the belief that the annual increment in GNP could be used to combat poverty.

The Johnson administration's attack on poverty was dictated by both politics and broader conceptions of political economy. As the CEA observed in its 1964 annual report, the affluent majority could conceivably just transfer money to the poor via taxes and income supplements, which would bring all poor families up to an acceptable minimum income level—for less than one-fifth the annual cost of the defense budget.[65] But as Johnson saw it, any such redistributive scheme would fail on three counts. First, it would run counter to his own work-ethic puritanism, which had little use for simple government giveaways. Second, any such redistributive plan would invite precisely the political controversy and division that LBJ's positive sum politics sought to avoid. Finally, simple redistributive proposals ran counter to the growth idea. As Carl Brauer has observed, "To growth- and efficiency-oriented economists, increasing the productivity of the poor was intrinsically preferable to paying them not to work."[66] Lester Thurow, an economist who served as a CEA consultant in the early sixties, has recalled, "The national desire to accelerate the rate of growth and stay ahead of the Russians meant that nearly all of the early Great Society and war on poverty programs were manpower training programs and not income-maintenance programs."[67]

The goal of the War on Poverty was not simply to enrich the poor but rather to change them so that they too could then contribute to the national goal of increased growth. Joseph A. Kershaw, the assistant director of the Office of Economic Opportunity, in February 1965 made the point directly: "Most income transfers simply result in different ways of slicing the income pie. . . . What we need in the longer run are ways to increase the productivity of the poor, ways to make them valuable in jobs and ways of getting them from where they are to where the jobs are. Measures that do this increase the size of the pie, not just the way it is sliced."[68] Such investment in human resources would, Kershaw concluded, enable the poor to be "generating themselves the resources which will help eliminate poverty, not only this year but for all those years to come."[69] Only later, as the sixties tailed into another era, did the political mainstream begin to reconceive the problem of poverty as a problem of inequality. Both Richard Nixon, with his Family Assistance Plan, and George McGovern, with his Demogrants, would discover the political difficulty of shifting welfare policy from the channels carved by the confluence of growth economics and liberal politics in the heady days of the New Frontier and the Great Society.

Thus did economic growth help underwrite and define the central public undertakings of the sixties. The interpenetration of growth economics and liberal politics produced a defining feature of public life in the sixties—the ascendancy of what might be labeled "growth liberalism." Growth liberalism linked together two of the most disparate presidents in American history, giving their combined leadership a distinctive identity. Joining other forces for social change that emanated from outside the established political system, growth liberalism imparted to the sixties an optimism and energy that loom large in both our social memory and our historical understanding of the era. But such was not the whole of the sixties. If growth liberalism was at its most robust in America's grand public enterprises in space, abroad, and at home in the years 1960–68, it was accompanied almost from the outset by a noteworthy ambivalence and uncertainty, by the need somehow to match its quantitative achievements with attention both to the *quality* of life and to the *ravages* that growth itself visited upon society and the environment.

By the middle of the sixties growth liberalism's complexity came more clearly into view. Growth liberals stressed production and quantitative change. Yet alongside the quantitative drive of growth liberalism there coexisted two related but hardly coincident impulses. The first was the desire to transcend the attachment to growth by means of a new emphasis on the pursuit of quality in American life. The second, developing steadily as the decade wore on, sought to cushion and repair some of the apparent consequences of growth, especially the despoliation of the environment.

The notion that material growth represented neither the apotheosis of American civilization nor an adequate basis for public policy was not at all new. There has been a long and notable strain of antimaterialist thought in the United States, running from the Puritans through the transcendentalists to the beats of the 1950s and the counterculture hippies of the sixties.[70] Moreover, doubt about the wisdom of growth as an end in itself has never been the monopoly of those on the fringes of the political culture. Eisenhower refused to view growth as an overriding goal. His former CEA chairman, Arthur Burns, observed in 1967 that "the economic growth of a nation is a blind concept unless we consider what is produced as well as the rate of growth of what happened to be produced."[71]

More striking, however, was the emergence among growth liberalism's own advocates and within its own constituency of a profound ambivalence about the relationship between quantity and quality in American life. The tension surfaced first in the 1950s, when Arthur M. Schlesinger, Jr., and John Kenneth Galbraith sought to chart a new path for American liberals. They approached the task from slightly different angles, but their arguments overlapped in important regards. Writing in 1957, Schlesinger urged liberals to reorient their creed, to move from a New Dealish concern "with establishing the economic conditions which make individual dignity conceivable—a job, a square meal, a living wage, a shirt on one's back and a roof over one's head" to a new concentration on "enlarging the individual's opportunity for moral growth and self-fulfillment." The shift would move the focus of liberalism "from economics and politics to the general style and quality of our civilization."[72] The enemy was no longer mass deprivation but rather mass culture.

John Kenneth Galbraith set forth a similar idea. The result was a best-seller, *The Affluent Society*. In it he wrote, "Liberal economic policy is still deeply preoccupied with production. . . . Platforms, manifestos, and speeches develop the vision of a growing, ever more productive America." But, he warned, the emphasis on aggregate output needed now to be replaced by a new attention to the distribution of the product, to the uses to which production was put. The United States needed to pay less attention to the production of private goods and more to the meeting of public needs.[73]

Predictably, Leon Keyserling found such views heretical, and, characteristically, he attacked them. The controversy unfolded in the pages of the *New Republic* and in private correspondence. Keyserling accused both Schlesinger and Galbraith of underestimating the extent of still-massive private poverty. He agreed on the need for a substantial, sustained increase in public spending but maintained that "to attempt to do this primarily by redistribution of expenditures—from private consumption to public needs—rather than primarily through high economic growth, defies history and reason."[74] For Keyserling, the issues of growth and social balance as between the private and public use of resources were thoroughly intertwined. Both sides to the dispute were on to something: Keyserling was correct in maintaining that quantity and quality could not be neatly compartmentalized, Schlesinger and Galbraith in pointing to the tension that existed between the quantitative and qualitative orientations.

The tension between quantity and quality remained a hallmark of growth liberalism during its ascendancy in the early and mid-1960s. Intellectuals and ideologues were more troubled by the tension than politicians, yet politicians were not immune. Schlesinger has written of Kennedy that "despite his support of economic growth and his concern over persisting privation, the thrust of his preoccupation was less with the economic machine and its quantitative results than with the quality of life in a society which, in the main, had achieved abundance."[75]

The vision of a Great Society illuminated the tension vividly. Richard Goodwin, the speech writer who coined the phrase, contended in 1965 that "the Great Society looks beyond the prospects of abundance to the problems of abundance. . . . Thus the Great Society is concerned not with how much, but how good—not with the quantity of our goods but the quality of our lives."[76] Not surprisingly, LBJ's speeches articulated the same objectives. In first announcing the Great Society at the University of Michigan in May 1964, Johnson proclaimed: "For half a century we called upon unbounded invention and untiring industry to create an order of plenty for all of our people. The challenge of the next half century is whether we have the wisdom to use that wealth to enrich and elevate our national life, and to advance the quality of our American civilization." Americans had the opportunity to choose between "a society where progress is the servant of our needs, or a society where old values and new visions are buried under unbridled growth."[77]

The tension between quantity and quality affected more than political rhetoric. By the early sixties, administrators in the Department of Health, Education, and Welfare (HEW) searched for a system of social bookkeeping that would measure quality the way that the federal government already tracked quantitative economic change. In March 1966 LBJ pushed further and requested HEW "to develop the necessary social statistics and indicators to supplement those prepared by the Bureau of Labor Statistics and the Council of Economic Advisers."[78] As a result of this charge, the secretary of HEW forwarded a report on social indicators, entitled *Toward a Social Report*, to Johnson just before he left the White House.[79] Social reporting would remain in its infancy long after the sixties had passed, but its forward movement was noteworthy, both in its own right and as testimony to a current of ambivalence that constituted the underside of growth liberalism.

Additional evidence of the complexity of attitudes regarding growth appeared in the mid-1960s, with an increasing number of people in government and out adopting an environmental sensibility and with the federal government gradually implementing measures to protect the environment from several of the worst ravages of economic growth. Although some commentators date the onset of the ecological age from the 1962 publication of Rachel Carson's *Silent Spring*, Samuel P. Hays argues persuasively that the development of environmental action was too evolutionary to be pinned to one event. According to Hays's stage analysis, between 1957 and 1965 environmentally minded people were most concerned about outdoor recreation, wildlands, and open space; from 1965 to 1972 environmental activists and policymakers focused on the adverse effects of industrial growth.[80] The shift from a conservationist to an ecological orientation marks the sixties as a crucial turning point in the man-nature relationship.

As in so many areas, Kennedy moved in the new environmental direction only tentatively. He could urge Americans to "expand the concept of conservation to meet the imperious problems of the new age," but his effort was more rhetorical than substantive and his posture more reactive than trailblazing. As Secretary of the Interior Stewart Udall reported to Arthur M. Schlesinger, Jr., "Intellectually he is fine. He knows the issues and recognizes their importance. When the problems are brought to him, his response is excellent. But he doesn't raise them himself."[81]

Johnson responded to the nascent ecological sensibility more forcefully and effectively. His rhetoric moved beyond Kennedy's both in its urgency and in the perception that economic growth—the central, guiding, and driving force behind his programs—exacted costs even as it bestowed benefits. "Ours is a nation of affluence," he stated in November 1965, "but the technology that has permitted our affluence spews out vast quantities of wastes and spent products that pollute our air, poison our waters, and even impair our ability to feed ourselves. . . . Pollution now is one of the most pervasive problems of our society."[82]

Johnson worked energetically to incorporate the emergent environmental sensibility into his Great Society framework. He signed into law almost three hundred conservation and beautification measures entailing outlays of over $12 billion. His landmark legislation included the Clean Air Act in 1963, the Water Quality Act in 1965, the Endangered Species Act in 1966, and the Air Quality Act and National Emissions Standards Act in 1967. Meanwhile, Lady Bird Johnson operated as a formidable political force in her own right on behalf of beautification. Udall captured the impact of these developments when in 1968 he wrote to Johnson: "No longer is peripheral action—the 'saving' of a forest, a park, a refuge for wildlife—isolated from the mainstream. The total environment is now the concern. . . . The quality of life is now the perspective and purpose of the new conservation."[83]

The concern with quality represented growth liberalism at its richest and most complex. The desire of liberals to use economic growth to transcend economic growth was as noble as it was chimerical, and the attention to growth's environmental consequences was as responsible as it was ironic. Still the driving optimism remained: Growth would make the chimerical and the ironic possible. On the horizon, however, lay a confrontation with national mortality, with limits, with Vietnam. Not even the supreme politician Lyndon Johnson could avoid this confrontation, and not even growth liberalism could finesse it.

In 1965, as LBJ subsequently observed, "two great streams in our national life converged—the dream of a Great Society at home and the inescapable demands of our obligations halfway around the world."[84] On the home front, more than one thousand projects had been initiated since the start of the War on Poverty.[85] In 1965 President Johnson signed into law Medicare, a federal-aid-to-education act, and the Housing and Urban Development Act of 1965. Total federal social welfare expenditures (measured in real dollars to correct for inflation) increased a stunning 18 percent in fiscal year 1965.[86]

Halfway around the world, America's grand design in Asia in 1965 became the Vietnam War. The United States began a sustained air offensive against North Vietnam in March, and a week later the first regular U.S. combat troops arrived in South Vietnam. Initially limited to defensive operations, the U.S. forces were soon allowed to go on the offensive, and in late June they executed their first search-and-destroy mission in War Zone D northwest of Saigon. In late July Johnson ordered the commitment of up to 175,000 troops in 1965, with an additional 100,000 in 1966; the United States was, in the president's words, "going off the diving board" into "a new war."[87]

The remainder of Johnson's administration would be marked by the confluence of these "two great streams": a major, if not total, commitment in Vietnam and an unparalleled attack on social problems at home. The two endeavors rested on a common economic foundation. In both cases, the administration depended on a constantly expanding economy to provide the wherewithal for the effort, in a fashion that would avoid extensive debate, harsh conflict, and the necessity of painful choices—in short, the discipline of stringency. It followed that the Great Society and the Vietnam War would be connected as well by the threat that an overacceleration of either one would inevitably endanger the progress of the other.

Johnson addressed the tension between the defining enterprises of his presidency by denying it and pursuing a policy of guns *and* butter. In January 1966 he observed that the nation continued to enjoy the longest sustained economic expansion of the postwar era: "We are a rich nation and can afford to make progress at home while meeting obligations abroad. . . . For this reason, I have not halted progress in the new and vital Great Society programs in order to finance the costs of our efforts in Southeast Asia."[88] The two crusades were as different as life and death; the one was a cause LBJ embraced enthusiastically, the other a burden he shouldered regretfully; but he wanted to prevail in both. As he later told Doris Kearns, "I was determined to be a leader of war *and* a leader of peace. I refused to let my critics push me into choosing one or the other. I wanted both, I believed in both, and I believed America had the resources to provide for both."[89]

Johnson's guns-and-butter policy began to unravel in 1965. The expansionary impact of the 1964 tax cut was now compounded by the stimulus of increased federal spending, most notably for the Vietnam War. In the fourth quarter of the year, the GNP rose by the largest amount in U.S. history. The resulting demand-pull inflation caused the economy in 1966 to suffer its most rapid price inflation since the Korean War. Thus began the great inflation of the 1960s and 1970s, which twisted the economy out of shape with consequences that would still be felt in the last decade of the twentieth century.[90]

Johnson stuck to his guns-and-butter approach and refused to push for a major tax hike throughout 1966, despite pressure from his economists and other advisers. In September, he relented sufficiently to announce a spending cut of $1.5 billion in fiscal year 1967 and the suspension of the 7 percent investment tax credit. In his January 1967 budget message, the president finally proposed a temporary 6 percent surcharge on corporate and individual income taxes; but it was not until August 1967—more than a year and a half after Gardner Ackley, chairman of the Council of Economic Advisers, had advised the president of the compelling need for a tax increase—that the administration presented a concrete plan for a temporary 10 percent surcharge on both corporate and individual income taxes to deal with what Johnson now called "the hard and inescapable facts."[91]

Johnson's long inaction on the tax front allowed the inflationary spiral to take hold. In his published memoirs, LBJ underscored the lack of support for a tax increase, either in Congress, the business community, organized labor, or his own cabinet. As Arthur Okun of the CEA recalled, "Anybody who wanted to slow things down was a killjoy." In 1966 and 1967 both the *New York Times* and the *Washington Post* opposed a major tax increase. As late as January 1968, a Gallup poll found 79 percent of the public opposed to raising taxes.[92]

Yet the difficulty of the task does not fully explain LBJ's reluctance to go all out for a tax hike. There is little doubt that Johnson realized the seriousness of the problem. Gardner Ackley believes that "from the fall of 1965 on . . . [Johnson] had no question in his mind that the failure to raise taxes would have very serious results. He never questioned that."[93] But on this issue the president was playing for the highest of stakes: the fate of his Great Society vision. To force the issue on the question of a tax hike would allow critics of the Vietnam War to savage the administration; it would also encourage conservatives to demand that the Great Society be cut back lest it interfere with the financing of the war. Johnson's acumen in such matters was validated when his long-delayed tax bill was immediately bottled up in Congress by those who wished to force the administration to trim its domestic spending.

Growth liberalism's great undertakings at home and abroad were outrunning the growth dividend. The economy could no longer finance both without an increase in taxes, but an increase in taxes threatened a political scrutiny that in turn endangered both the administration's Vietnam policy and its domestic reforms. "I knew the Congress as well as I know Lady Bird," Johnson recalled later, "and I knew that the day it exploded into a major debate on the war, that day would be the beginning of the end of the Great Society."[94] And so the president hesitated on taxes and fudged on the cost of the war, hoping against hope that the conflict could somehow be ended in a politically acceptable fashion. Vice-president Hubert H. Humphrey has described well the process that evolved: "Each year when the budget would go up to the Hill, the amount requested for Vietnam was obviously smaller than the cost would be. Later, the Administration would ask for a supplemental budget, and it was in these supplementals that the appropriation grew larger and larger. . . . Either the President was not leveling with the Congress as to what the cost of Vietnam was going to be, or he just didn't know and really had no plan as to the degree and duration of our involvement. . . . I think it was a little of both."[95] Awash in a powerful mixture of vision, ambition, delusion, fear, and duplicity, the Johnson presidency by the beginning of 1968 had stretched the U.S. political economy close to the breaking point.

The shocks of early 1968 brought an end to LBJ's guns-and-butter approach. The crises in question were two, one military and the other economic, both interrelated and heavily tinged with political implications. In Vietnam, the communists snatched a huge political and psychological victory from the jaws of military defeat in their Tet Offensive in late January and early February 1968. The Americans and South Vietnamese inflicted heavy losses on the communists, especially on the irregulars of the Vietcong. But the scale of the offensive and the communists' initial gains shocked both policymakers and U.S. public opinion. The war was far from over; any light at the end of the tunnel was far dimmer than optimistic official assessments had suggested. As if to punctuate this message, General William C. Westmoreland, the U.S. commander in Vietnam, and General Earle Wheeler, the chairman of the Joint Chiefs of Staff, in February requested the raising of an additional 206,000 troops.[96]

The second shock to LBJ's guns-and-butter policy came on the economic front. The problem centered on the complex relationships between the dollar, the balance of payments, and the international gold market. In the summer of 1967 the weak British pound came under assault by speculators, and in November the British government devalued its currency. Secretary of the Treasury Henry Fowler warned, "Now the dollar is in the front line," and the administration braced for a speculative onslaught.[97] The threat to the dollar was compounded by the deteriorating balance-of-payments problem. In 1965 the balance-of-payments deficit had been the lowest since 1957, but the Vietnam War increased the amount of direct military outlays overseas and, by overheating and inflating the economy, reduced exports, increased the demand for imports, and caused an outflow of dollars and gold. In the last quarter of 1967, the balance of payments worsened dramatically.

The administration resolved to keep the dollar convertible at $35 an ounce. To devalue the dollar (in other words, to raise the price of gold) would drive up the overseas expenses connected with the Vietnam War and quite possibly, it was feared, endanger the entire international monetary system. On New Year's Day, 1968, Johnson announced a new tougher balance-of-payments program to protect the dollar. Soon thereafter he asked Congress to remove the legal requirement that Federal Reserve notes be backed by a 25 percent gold cover. In a sardonic understatement, the economic report of the president in February concluded, "A strong and sustained advance of production surely does not mean we have solved all economic problems."[98]

Despite the administration's efforts, the speculation in gold continued, increasing dramatically in early March. Between 11 and 14 March, the London gold pool of central banks on which the United States relied to order the gold market lost about $1 billion. Johnson warned the leaders of Britain, Italy, and West Germany that prompt action was needed to prevent a financial crisis that might "set in motion forces like those which disintegrated the Western world in 1929 and 1933."[99] The London gold market was promptly shut down on Friday, 15 March, and the financial leaders of the Western alliance gathered in Washington over the weekend to avert a financial collapse. They forestalled disaster by creating a two-tiered gold system. The new arrangement separated official gold transactions from private speculative purchases, and it managed to stave off the immediate threat of financial chaos.

The convergence of problems in early 1968 marked the end of growth liberalism's ascendancy. Johnson's guns-and-butter policy had brought the economy to the verge of financial collapse; the war in Vietnam had become a national nightmare, and the Great Society's promises had outrun its resources. LBJ's presidency lay in ruin, and Eugene McCarthy's strong showing in the New Hampshire primary in mid-March underscored the president's political vulnerability. Contrary to the optimism so widely shared just a few short years before, the world was not without limits. The United States seemed to be pressing up against them everywhere. The realization that resources were indeed limited finally in 1968 forced hard choices that had been long avoided and postponed. The passage of time had not made them any easier.

In March 1968 Johnson finally acted to cap U.S. escalation in the Vietnam War. The president and his advisers knew that the nation's problems were intertwined. Johnson's new secretary of defense, Clark Clifford, undertook a sweeping reappraisal of U.S. policy and found the prospects troubling. "I was more conscious each day," he later recorded, "of domestic unrest. . . . Just as disturbing to me were the economic implications of a struggle to be indefinitely continued at ever-increasing cost. The dollar was already in trouble, prices were escalating far too fast and emergency controls on foreign investment imposed on New Year's Day would be only a prelude to more stringent controls, if we were to add another $12 billion to Viet Nam spending—with perhaps more to follow."[100]

Late in March, LBJ convened a group of elder statesmen known as the "Wise Men" to help him assess U.S. options in Vietnam. A key member was McGeorge Bundy, the former national security adviser to both Kennedy and Johnson. Bundy, too, sensed the connection between the economic and the political. "I now understand," he wrote Johnson, " . . . that the really tough problem you have is the interlock between the bad turn in the war, the critical need for a tax increase, and the crisis of public confidence at home."[101] The matter of resources and of limits had now become critical. Secretary of State Dean Rusk, contemplating the call for additional military measures in Vietnam, said, "If we do this without a tax bill we are dead."[102] Johnson agreed, recalling that "these monetary and budgetary problems were constantly before us as we considered whether we should or could do more in Vietnam. It was clear that calling up a large number of troops, sending additional men overseas, and increasing military expenditures would complicate our problems and put greater pressure on the dollar."[103]

On 31 March Johnson announced that the new troop commitment to Vietnam would be limited to 13,500 additional support troops to bolster the 11,000 combat troops airlifted to Vietnam immediately after the Tet attack. He reported that new emphasis would be placed on expanding South Vietnam's role in its own defense. Although American forces would remain in combat in Vietnam for nearly five more years, the long, gradual escalation of U.S. involvement was at last capped. In his televised address, Johnson referred to the nation's "infinite resources" and "boundless wealth," but the true substance of his message lay in the observation that "these times call for prudence in this land of plenty."[104] In truth, the decision to halt the escalation of the war was as much economic as it was political or military.

Meanwhile, the administration continued the struggle for a tax increase. Having hesitated on the tax issue for a disastrously long time, Johnson now found himself stymied by the determination of Wilbur Mills, chairman of the House Ways and Means Committee, to exact cuts in domestic spending as the price for congressional action on the administration's tax proposal. It was a clash of legislative titans. Kennedy had once said of Mills: "Wilbur Mills knows that he was chairman of Ways and Means before I got here and that he'll still be chairman after I've gone—and he knows I know it. I don't have any hold on him."[105] In the end, Mills triumphed. Johnson ended the long struggle by signing the Revenue and Expenditure Control Act of 1968 into law on 28 June 1968—two and a half years after CEA chairman Gardner Ackley had first warned of economic overheating. The administration won a retroactive 10 percent surcharge on individual and corporate income taxes but at the price of agreeing to $6 billion in immediate spending cuts and an additional reduction of $8 billion in unspent appropriations authority.

Bill Moyers, one of Johnson's closest aides, has called the delay in seeking a tax increase "the single most devastating decision in the Johnson administration. It was the beginning of the end, a time when he lost control of the administration, lost control of events."[106] The delay had been an integral part of Johnson's guns-and-butter policy, and in the end that policy destroyed his presidency. The guns-and-butter approach encouraged Johnson to avoid a national mobilization and to make war by degrees—an approach not without merit in a world of dangerous superpower confrontation, but one that ultimately left Johnson unable to achieve his purposes with the resources at hand in Vietnam. The dissembling required by the guns-and-butter policy contributed mightily to the credibility gap that plagued Johnson and that made governance markedly more difficult for his successors as well. Finally, the failure to act on taxes began a spiral of inflation that would, when compounded by other long-running problems and short-term events, haunt the U.S. economy for a generation.

Moreover, Johnson's guns-and-butter policy found itself unable to deliver fully either the guns or the butter. As noted, the policy encouraged military incrementalism. And in the end, Johnson's worst fears about the war devouring his Great Society visions came true; the tax hike struggle forced Johnson to sacrifice the Great Society to pay for the Vietnam War. It was, to be sure, not the only force at work against the Great Society— administrative difficulties, hardening racial attitudes on all sides, and the apparent intractability of problems such as poverty all contributed to the slowing of the reform surge—but the war was a singularly significant influence. Thus when the Kerner commission investigating the racial disorders of the previous summer issued its report in February 1968, calling for a massive stepping up of Great Society programs, Johnson found himself unable to comply. The problem, he recalled, was "money." "I will never understand," he wrote, "how the commission expected me to get this same Congress to turn 180 degrees overnight and appropriate an additional $30 billion for the same programs that it was demanding I cut by $6 billion."[107] In fiscal year 1969 federal social welfare expenditures (in constant dollars) grew at a rate less than half that of 1965. The story was much the same on the frontier of space, where, as Robert A. Divine has observed, "the course of events, especially the Vietnam War, forced [Johnson] . . . to impose some very real limits on the American effort."[108] In the end, Johnson saved the Apollo moon-landing program but sacrificed post-Apollo projects to Vietnam-related budget cuts. The new universe of limits extended, it now seemed, to the very heavens.

The Nixon presidency continued the eclipse of growth liberalism and the transit into a new era of limits and choices. Richard Nixon self-consciously pulled back from what he considered to be America's over-extension both abroad and at home. In Vietnam, he followed LBJ's capping of U.S. escalation with a painfully slow and costly withdrawal of American forces. More broadly, the Nixon administration retreated from the two-and-a-half-war readiness goal established by McNamara to a one-and-a-half-war standard; the so-called Nixon Doctrine of 1969 phased down U.S. commitments around the world by specifying that other nations would henceforth be expected to assume primary responsibility for their own defense; and Nixon moved away from "superiority" as the goal for nuclear deterrence policy toward the more austere concept of "sufficiency."[109] At home, Nixon proposed some notable initiatives, such as the Family Assistance Plan, continued many of the Great Society programs already under way, and brought to domestic policy a note of "benign neglect" that contrasted sharply with the passionate, chaotic activism of his predecessor.

Nixon thus served as a transitional figure, standing between the ascendancy of growth liberalism in the 1960s and the rise of a new regime of balance and scarcity in the 1970s. The allure of growth remained strong. In July 1969 William Safire sent the president a long memorandum on ideas and slogans for the administration's economic policy. The key term Safire invoked was *growth economics*; his focus was how to fix the program in the public mind. "An excellent idea—one of the best I've seen in Administration," noted Nixon in the margin.[110] In another example, late the next year the Department of Commerce erected an appropriately outsized tote board to record the achievement of a $1 trillion gross national product. By prearrangement, the numbers on the board were to flash the $1 trillion figure at noon on a day in mid-December 1970, at which time Nixon was to make a few celebratory remarks. When the president's arrival by car was delayed, technicians scrambled to turn the machine back. The board seemed to take on a life of its own, however, and despite their best efforts it flashed the $1 trillion figure at 12:02 P.M. By the time Nixon arrived at 12:07 P.M., $2.3 million more had been added as the machine began calculating the GNP at a wildly accelerating rate. Nixon struck a defiant note: "I think that rather than apologizing for our great, strong private enterprise economy, we should recognize that we are very fortunate to have it. . . . That's the way to look at it. Don't look at it simply in terms of a great group of selfish people, money-grubbing."[111]

Nixon's State of the Union address that year showed clearly how far the ambivalence about growth had proceeded over the course of the sixties. Nixon observed proudly that the GNP would increase by $500 billion over the next decade, an increase that alone would be greater than the total growth of the economy from 1790 to 1950. He noted, however, that "the critical question is not whether we will grow but how we will use that growth." Speaking of the nation's need for "the lift of a driving dream," Nixon proposed that "the time has come for a new quest—a quest not for a greater quantity of what we have but for a new quality of life in America." The president neither dismissed growthmanship out of hand (as he had done, rather defensively, during the 1960 campaign) nor did he mindlessly embrace the cult of production. Instead, he sought, as had the growth liberals who preceded him, a way to use growth to transcend growth, to shift society's focus from quantity to quality. "The answer," he asserted, "is not to abandon growth but to redirect it."[112]

The disparate elements of the new driving dream were illuminated again when Nixon's National Goals Research Staff issued on 4 July 1970 a study entitled *Toward Balanced Growth: Quantity with Quality*.[113] The extraordinary balancing act of the title, the exquisite tension between the concepts of balance and growth, quantity and quality, reflected well both the complexity and the evolution of ideas about growth as the era of growth liberalism drew to a close. Soon small would be beautiful, but not quite yet.

The 1970s brought the eclipse of growth liberalism, and that shift helps denote the end of a distinctive era. A new epoch took shape as the nation retreated from the Great Society at home and shrank from its grand designs abroad. Democratic presidential aspirants began to suffer a generation-long electoral retribution for growth liberalism's overreach. The oil embargo of 1973, the economic recession of 1974–75, and the subsequent onset of stagflation together marked a distinct weakening of the great postwar economic expansion that had run for nearly three decades. As economic growth became more difficult, so too did it become more controversial. The earlier uncertainty and ambivalence that had in the sixties run as an undercurrent now took on a new scope and stridency. The furor surrounding the Club of Rome's 1972 report on *The Limits to Growth* popularized the idea that population pressure, resource depletion, and the dangers of pollution made future economic growth either undesirable or impossible.[114] The accompanying loss of optimism was palpable; it reached to the center of the political culture as the expansiveness of the Kennedy-Johnson years faded into the malaise politics of Jimmy Carter and the ecosensibility of California's Jerry Brown.

The frustration of the politics of growth in the 1960s and its subsequent decline in the 1970s had long-range consequences. The appeal and legitimacy of liberalism during its postwar ascendancy rested on the exploitation of economic growth. Growth promised that reform would be a positive sum game, from which all parties would emerge winners. The rising tide would lift all boats. The vision of an expansive future served as the linchpin that held together the varied elements of the liberal worldview. In this sense, economic growth played the same central, energizing role for sixties liberalism that the discovery of corruption had played for progressivism early in the century and that the pursuit of security had played for the New Deal.[115] The collapse of LBJ's guns-and-butter policy therefore not only fatally wounded his presidency but also brought low the ideological foundation on which it rested. The reassertion of scarcity economics in the 1970s completed liberalism's unraveling, and the inability of liberals to reconfigure their doctrine contributed mightily to the conservative tenor of U.S. politics in the decades that followed the sixties. Growth liberalism's heady conflation of hope and hubris in the Kennedy-Johnson years echoes still.

NOTES

1. Regarding the centrality of mature economy ideas, see Theodore Rosenof, *Dogma, Depression, and the New Deal* (Port Washington, N.Y.: Kennikat Press, 1975).

2. Alvin H. Hansen, "Economic Progress and Declining Population Growth," *American Economic Review* 29 (March 1939): 1–15 (quotation, p. 4).

3. Andrew Hacker, ed., *U/S: A Statistical Portrait of the American People* (New York: Penguin, 1983), 13–14.

4. *The Statistical History of the United States from Colonial Times to the Present* (Stamford, Conn.: Fairfield, 1965), 462.

5. Quoted from William Leuchtenburg, *A Troubled Feast: American Society since 1945*, rev. ed. (Boston: Little, Brown, 1979), 55.

6. John Updike, *Verse* (Greenwich, Conn.: Fawcett, 1965), 55.

7. Norman Mailer, "Superman Comes to the Supermart," *Esquire*, November 1960, 119–27.

8. *Statistical History of the United States*, 143, 158.

9. Using a complicated semidecile ratio, Peter John de la Fosse Wiles has found that for the late sixties, the measure of income inequality stood at 3.0 for Sweden, 5.9 for the United Kingdom, 6.0 for the USSR, and 13.3 for the United States. Wiles, *Distribution of Income: East and West* (Amsterdam: North Holland Publishing Co., 1974), xiv, 48.

10. Paul Samuelson, *Economics*, 8th ed. (New York: McGraw-Hill, 1970), 110.

11. *Statistical History of the United States*, 166.

12. Ibid., 168.

13. Quoted from Stephen E. Ambrose, *Eisenhower: The President* (New York: Simon and Schuster, 1984), 249.

14. Calculated from statistics in Herbert Stein, *Presidential Economics: The Making of Economic Policy from Roosevelt to Reagan and Beyond* (New York: Simon and Schuster, 1984), 381.

15. Quoted from Robert M. Collins, "The Emergence of Economic Growthmanship in the United States: Federal Policy and Economic Knowledge in the Truman Years," in *The State and Economic Knowledge: The American and British Experiences*, ed-

ited by Mary O. Furner and Barry Supple (New York: Cambridge University Press, 1990), 149.

16. For a succinct summary, see Erwin C. Hargrove and Samuel A. Morley, eds., *The President and the Council of Economic Advisers: Interviews with CEA Chairmen* (Boulder, Colo.: Westview Press, 1984), 89–94, 123–26.

17. Dwight D. Eisenhower, *The White House Years: Waging Peace, 1956–1961* (Garden City, N.Y.: Doubleday, 1965), 462.

18. *Public Papers of the Presidents of the United States: Dwight D. Eisenhower, 1959* (Washington, D.C.: GPO, 1960), 125.

19. *Economic Report of the President, 1962* (Washington, D.C.: GPO, 1962), 113.

20. Quoted from U.S. Congress, Joint Economic Committee, *Comparisons of the United States and Soviet Economies: Papers Submitted by Panelists Appearing before the Subcommittee on Economic Statistics, Pts. 1–3* (Washington, D.C.: GPO, 1959), 549.

21. Walter Lippmann, "America Must Grow," *Saturday Evening Post*, 5 November 1960, 92.

22. Quoted from U.S. Congress, Joint Economic Committee, *Comparisons of the United States and Soviet Economies: Papers*, 549.

23. U.S. Congress, Joint Economic Committee, *Comparisons of the United States and Soviet Economies: Hearings before the Joint Economic Committee*, 86th Cong., 1st sess., 1959, 6, 11.

24. "Russian v. U.S. Growth," *Time*, 14 December 1959, 90.

25. Evsey Domar quoted from U.S. Congress, Joint Economic Committee, *Comparisons of the United States and Soviet Economies: Hearings*, 247; Lovestone paraphrased and Peterson quoted from U.S. Congress, Joint Economic Committee, *Comparisons of the United States and Soviet Economies: Papers*, 567, 525.

26. *Prospect for America: The Rockefeller Panel Reports* (Garden City, N.Y.: Doubleday, 1961), xv, 251–333 passim.

27. *The National Purpose* (New York: Holt, Rinehart and Winston, 1960), v, 120, 38, 133.

28. *Goals for Americans: The Report of the President's Commission on National Goals* (New York: Prentice-Hall, 1960), 10–11.

29. Quoted from Arthur M. Schlesinger, Jr., *A Thousand Days: John F. Kennedy in the White House* (Boston: Houghton Mifflin, 1965), 625. See also U.S. Congress, Senate, Committee on Commerce, *Freedom of Communications*, pt. 1: The Speeches, Remarks, Press Conferences, and Statements of Senator John F. Kennedy, 1 August through 7 November 1960, 87th Cong., 1st sess., 1961, passim.

30. The Democratic platform is reprinted in Arthur M. Schlesinger, Jr., ed., *History of American Presidential Elections, 1789–1968* (New York: Chelsea House, 1971), 4:3482.

31. "Statements of the Candidates on Growth," *New Republic*, 10 October 1960, 16.

32. Walter Heller, ed., *Perspectives on Economic Growth* (New York: Random House, 1968), ix.

33. Richard Goodwin, *Remembering*

America: A Voice from the Sixties (Boston: Little, Brown, 1988), 132.

34. *Public Papers of the Presidents of the United States: John F. Kennedy, 1961* (Washington, D.C.: GPO, 1962), 41.

35. Walter Heller, *New Dimensions of Political Economy* (Cambridge: Harvard University Press, 1966), vii–viii.

36. The phrase is from Heller, *New Dimensions*, 70.

37. The "monetary twist" was a policy begun in 1961 that raised short-term interest rates in order to minimize the outflow of volatile funds to other countries while holding down long-term interest rates to encourage investment.

38. James Tobin, "The Political Economy of the 1960s," in *Toward New Human Rights: The Social Policies of the Kennedy and Johnson Administrations*, edited by David C. Warner (Austin: Lyndon B. Johnson School of Public Affairs, 1977), 35.

39. Theodore H. White, *In Search of History* (New York: Harper and Row, 1978), 492–93. See also Michael Barone, *Our Country: The Shaping of America from Roosevelt to Reagan* (New York: Free Press, 1990), 388.

40. Johnson quoted from Goodwin, *Remembering America*, 258.

41. Heller, *New Dimensions*, 11.

42. *Public Papers of . . . Kennedy, 1961*, 404.

43. Walter A. McDougall, *. . . The Heavens and the Earth: A Political History of the Space Age* (New York: Basic Books, 1985), 225.

44. Ibid., 308, 362.

45. John Lewis Gaddis, *Strategies of Containment: A Critical Appraisal of Postwar American National Security Policy* (New York: Oxford University Press, 1982), 134, 147. See also Richard A. Melanson, "The Foundations of Eisenhower's Foreign Policy: Continuity, Community, and Consensus," in *Reevaluating Eisenhower: American Foreign Policy in the 1950s*, edited by Melanson and David Mayers (Urbana: University of Illinois Press, 1987), 31–64.

46. U.S. Department of State, *Foreign Relations of the United States, 1952–1954*, Diplomatic Papers, vol. 2, pt. 1, *National Security Affairs* (Washington, D.C.: GPO, 1984), 236.

47. On the New Look policy, see Russell F. Weigley, *The American Way of War: A History of United States Military Strategy and Policy* (New York: Macmillan, 1973), chap. 17; Glenn H. Snyder, "The 'New Look' of 1953," in *Strategy, Politics, and Defense Budgets*, by Warner R. Schilling, Paul Y. Hammond, and Glenn H. Snyder (New York: Columbia University Press, 1962); and Stephen E. Ambrose with Richard H. Immerman, *Ike's Spies: Eisenhower and the Espionage Establishment* (New York: Macmillan, 1981).

48. James Tobin, "Defense, Dollars, and Doctrines," *Yale Review* 47 (March 1958): 324–25.

49. Henry A. Kissinger, "Strategy and Organization," *Foreign Affairs* 35 (April 1957): 379–94.

50. *Public Papers of the Presidents of the United States: Lyndon B. Johnson, 1963–64* (Washington, D.C.: GPO, 1965), 1:494.

51. Schlesinger, *History of Presidential Elections*, 4:3471; John F. Kennedy, *A Compendium of Speeches*,

Statements, and Remarks Delivered during His Service in the Congress of the United States, S. Doc. 79, 88th Cong., 2d sess. (Washington, D.C.: GPO, 1964), 929.

52. Maxwell D. Taylor, *The Uncertain Trumpet* (New York: Harper, 1960), 6.

53. Theodore Sorensen, *Kennedy* (New York: Harper and Row, 1965), 608. Yet, because the economy was growing at a 4 percent annual rate, the percentage of GNP allocated to national defense actually decreased slightly, from 9.1 percent in fiscal year 1961 to 8.5 percent in fiscal year 1964. Gaddis, *Strategies of Containment*, 226.

54. U.S. Department of Defense, *Annual Report for Fiscal Year 1962* (Washington, D.C.: GPO, 1963), 3.

55. Gaddis, *Strategies of Containment*, 261.

56. Schlesinger, *A Thousand Days*, 315–16.

57. Rostow to Kennedy, memorandum, 29 March 1961, quoted from George McT. Kahin, *Intervention: How America Became Involved in Vietnam* (New York: Knopf, 1986), 131.

58. *Public Papers of . . . Johnson, 1963–64*, 2:953.

59. Ibid., 1:114, 822.

60. Robert H. Haveman, ed., *A Decade of Federal Antipoverty Programs: Achievements, Failures, and Lessons* (New York: Academic Press, 1977), 11.

61. Goodwin, *Remembering America*, 270.

62. Tobin, "Political Economy of the 1960s," 35.

63. Joseph A. Califano, Jr., *The Triumph and Tragedy of Lyndon Johnson:*

The White House Years (New York: Simon and Schuster, 1991), 75. See also Sar A. Levitan and Robert Taggart, *The Promise of Greatness* (Cambridge: Harvard University Press, 1976), 29.

64. Walter Lippmann, column, *Washington Post*, 19 March 1964, sec. A.

65. U.S. Council of Economic Advisers, *Economic Report of the President, 1964* (Washington, D.C.: GPO, 1964), 77.

66. Carl M. Brauer, "Kennedy, Johnson, and the War on Poverty," *Journal of American History* 69 (June 1982): 108.

67. Lester C. Thurow, "Discussion," in *Decade of Federal Antipoverty Programs*, edited by Haveman, 118.

68. Joseph A. Kershaw, "The Attack on Poverty," in *Poverty in America*, edited by Margaret S. Gordon (San Francisco: Chandler Publishing, 1965), 56.

69. Ibid., 57.

70. See, for example, David E. Shi, *The Simple Life: Plain Living and High Thinking in American Culture* (New York: Oxford University Press, 1985).

71. Burns quoted from Walter P. Reuther, "Goals for America," in *National Priorities: Military, Economic, and Social*, by Kenneth E. Boulding et al. (Washington, D.C.: Public Affairs Press, 1969), 66.

72. Arthur M. Schlesinger, Jr., "Where Does the Liberal Go from Here?," *New York Times Magazine*, 4 August 1957, 7, 38.

73. John Kenneth Galbraith, *The Affluent Society* (New York: Mentor Books, 1958), 152–53.

74. Leon Keyserling, "Eggheads

and Politics," *New Republic*, 27 October 1958, 13–17 (quotation, p. 16). See also "Galbraith and Schlesinger Reply to Leon Keyserling," ibid., 10 November 1958, 14–15; Keyserling, "Leon Keyserling on Economic Expansion: A Communication," ibid., 17 November 1958, 16–17; and correspondence among the principals in box 38, John Kenneth Galbraith Papers, John F. Kennedy Presidential Library, Boston.

75. Schlesinger, *A Thousand Days*, 657.

76. Quoted from Raymond A. Bauer, ed., *Social Indicators* (Cambridge: MIT Press, 1966), xii.

77. *Public Papers of . . . Johnson, 1963–64*, 1:704.

78. *Public Papers of . . . Johnson, 1966* (Washington, D.C.: GPO, 1967), 1:246–47. See also Bertram M. Gross, "Preface: A Historical Note on Social Indicators," in *Social Indicators*, edited by Raymond A. Bauer, ix–xviii, and Otis Graham, Jr., *Toward a Planned Society: From Roosevelt to Nixon* (New York: Oxford University Press, 1976), chap. 4.

79. U.S. Department of Health, Education, and Welfare, *Toward a Social Report* (Ann Arbor: University of Michigan Press, 1970).

80. Samuel P. Hays, *Beauty, Health, and Permanence: Environmental Politics in the United States, 1955–1985* (New York: Cambridge University Press, 1987), 54–55.

81. John F. Kennedy, Preface to *The Quiet Crisis*, by Stewart Udall (New York: Holt, Rinehart and Winston, 1963), xiii; Schlesinger, *A Thousand Days*, 659.

82. *Public Papers of . . . Johnson, 1965* (Washington, D.C.: GPO, 1966), 2:1101.

83. Quoted from Martin V. Melosi, "Lyndon Johnson and Environmental Policy," in *The Johnson Years: Volume Two*, edited by Robert A. Divine (Lawrence: University Press of Kansas, 1987), 117. On Lady Bird Johnson's role, see Lewis L. Gould, *Lady Bird Johnson and the Environment* (Lawrence: University Press of Kansas, 1988).

84. Lyndon Baines Johnson, *The Vantage Point: Perspectives of the Presidency, 1963–1969* (New York: Holt, Rinehart and Winston, 1971), 324.

85. *Public Papers of . . . Johnson, 1965*, 1:199–201.

86. Levitan and Taggart, *Promise of Greatness*, 21.

87. Johnson quoted from Jack Valenti, *A Very Human President* (New York: Norton, 1975), 345. On the crucial July 1965 troop commitment, see Larry Berman, *Planning a Tragedy: The Americanization of the War in Vietnam* (New York: Norton, 1982), and Kahin, *Intervention*, 347–401.

88. *Public Papers of . . . Johnson, 1966*, 1:48. Regarding LBJ's guns-and-butter policy, see Donald F. Kettl, "The Economic Education of Lyndon B. Johnson: Guns, Butter, and Taxes," in *The Johnson Years: Volume Two*, edited by Divine. Kettl's superb essay has informed my discussion throughout.

89. Doris Kearns, *Lyndon Johnson and the American Dream* (New York: Signet, 1976), 296.

90. Arthur M. Okun, *The Political Economy of Prosperity* (Washington, D.C.: The Brookings Institution, 1970), 66–79; Robert A. Gordon, *Eco-*

nomic Instability and Growth: The American Record (New York: Harper and Row, 1974), 155–57; Herbert Y. Schandler, The Unmaking of a President: Lyndon Johnson and Vietnam (Princeton: Princeton University Press, 1977), 226.

91. Public Papers of . . . Johnson, 1967 (Washington, D.C.: GPO, 1968), 2:733. For a good discussion of LBJ's struggle in 1966 to control inflation without a tax hike, see Califano, Lyndon Johnson, 137–48.

92. Johnson, Vantage Point, 440–44; Okun, Political Economy of Prosperity, 71.

93. Quoted from Hargrove and Morley, Interviews with CEA Chairmen, 254.

94. Quoted from Kearns, Lyndon Johnson and the American Dream, 296.

95. Hubert H. Humphrey, The Education of a Public Man: My Life and Politics (Garden City, N.Y.: Doubleday, 1976), 340.

96. Schandler, Unmaking of a President, 74–120.

97. Quoted from Burton I. Kaufman, "Foreign Aid and the Balance-of-Payments Problem: Vietnam and Johnson's Foreign Economic Policy," in The Johnson Years: Volume Two, edited by Divine, 93. The discussion that follows draws heavily on Kaufman's excellent analysis and on the discussion in Johnson, Vantage Point, 314–21.

98. The 1968 balance-of-payments program is discussed in Public Papers of . . . Johnson, 1968–69 (Washington, D.C.: GPO, 1969), 1:133–37, 144 (quotation).

99. Johnson, Vantage Point, 319.

100. Clark Clifford, "A Viet Nam Reappraisal: The Personal History of One Man's View and How It Evolved," Foreign Affairs 47 (July 1969): 612.

101. Quoted from Larry Berman, Lyndon Johnson's War: The Road to Stalemate in Vietnam (New York: Norton, 1989), 193.

102. Quoted from Johnson, Vantage Point, 407.

103. Ibid., 406.

104. Public Papers of . . . Johnson, 1968–69, 1:469–76.

105. Quoted from Sorensen, Kennedy, 426.

106. Quoted from Kettl, "Guns, Butter, and Taxes," 54.

107. Johnson, Vantage Point, 173.

108. Robert A. Divine, "Lyndon B. Johnson and the Politics of Space," in The Johnson Years: Volume Two, edited by Divine, 233.

109. Weigley, American Way of War, 470–71; Gaddis, Strategies of Containment, 274–308; Richard Nixon, RN: The Memoirs of Richard Nixon (New York: Grosset and Dunlap, 1978), 415.

110. Stephen E. Ambrose, Nixon: The Triumph of a Politician, 1962–1972 (New York: Simon and Schuster, 1989), 296–97.

111. Public Papers of the Presidents of the United States: Richard M. Nixon, 1970 (Washington, D.C.: GPO, 1971), 1135–36.

112. Ibid., 10, 15.

113. U.S. National Goals Research Staff, Toward Balanced Growth: Quantity with Quality (Washington, D.C.: GPO, 1970).

114. Donella H. Meadows et al., The Limits to Growth: A Report for the

Club of Rome's Project on the Predicament of Mankind (New York: Universe Books, 1972).

115. See, for example, Richard L. McCormick, "The Discovery That Business Corrupts Politics: A Reappraisal of the Origins of Progressivism," *American Historical Review* 86 (April 1981): 247–74, and Robert M. Collins, "The New Deal," in *Encyclopedia of American Political History: Studies of the Principal Movements and Ideas*, edited by Jack P. Greene (New York: Scribner, 1984), 2:878–89.

The American State and the Vietnam War

A Genealogy of Power

Between 1945 and 1968 Americans witnessed a fundamental change in their government. Though historically and philosophically Americans long had been opposed to a centralized state, in the postwar years many in the governmental elite looked to the problems and possibilities of the new world and argued, publicly, that the United States had to take on new political roles in order to preserve old political ideals. In the postwar era, Americans accepted a major shift in the country's political culture—toward a more activist and outward-looking state—as necessary to strengthen and defend traditional political values. This paradoxical understanding permitted the United States, through a newly powerful state apparatus, to redefine the world: to introduce, as an alternative to the chaos left by World War II, global economic and military security

45

systems designed to increase world prosperity and maintain the stability that American state makers believed vital to the national interest.

Foreign policy was the engine of that major transformation in the role and capacity of the American state. Under the cold war paradox, foreign policy became, simultaneously, both a *process* by which the state could achieve and manage its international ambitions and a *site* on which the United States could display and articulate distinctly American cultural virtues.

In the sixties, however, under the strain of a foreign policy adventure gone wrong, many began to question the legitimacy of the activist state—not because it failed, in its processual function, to protect the national interests of overall prosperity and stability, but because it failed to embody the ideals and historical images American state makers had used to justify its very existence. Incessant reports of brutal (yet nonetheless ineffective) efforts in Vietnam exposed a gap between this form of state activism and the traditional ideals of American political culture. By the mid-1960s, any pretension to an American policy consensus had crumbled, not only along generational lines, but also across the stratum of those claiming power to make and execute foreign policy. More and more openly, establishment voices criticized the Johnson administration and urged disengagement from the equation of Vietnam and essential American ideals.

Yet throughout the decade and into the 1970s, state makers continued trying to force the war to fit the mold—activism in defense of values—that had sustained the postwar transformation. They held onto this model despite its obvious inadequacies, as though to admit that these were in-compatibilities between the cultural justification of the state and its geo-political behavior would trigger worse consequences than the unrest the war itself was causing. Put another way, American policy-making elites acted as though the existence of the American state itself rested on the outcome of a rebellion in a small, remote country that (almost everyone in the government agreed) was peripheral to the core material interests of the United States.

This legitimation crisis did not derive from policy questions per se. It reflected a problem of metapolicy: how a state capable of managing a Vietnam could come to exist within the terms of American political culture. That is, the crisis of state authority in the sixties grew out of an enduring difficulty about defining legitimate state powers at all.

This difficulty is as old as the Constitution. It was created when the Constitution eschewed a specific governmental center of sovereignty in favor of the deliberately ambiguous authority of "the People."[1] Subsequent arguments about national policy—from questions of Western expansion in the nineteenth century to the League of Nations fight in 1919 to the fiercely personal battles over isolationism in the 1930s—were embedded in the deep structure of this tension between allegiance to a central political symbol and organizing document and the need for clarity on who is authorized to manage and speak for national interests.

In one sense, the architects of the postwar state engaged in time-honored elite practices when they co-opted the rhetoric and imagery of American history to justify policy changes. But until the early twentieth century, state reformers had been successful largely when they could demonstrate that the growth of governmental powers was not change, but an organic by-product of the *spread* of American political ideals. Beginning in the 1930s and continuing into the postwar national security state, change was justified instead as a means of *protecting* original values. That is, state makers believed that, given the developing configuration of the international system, the United States could not continue to operate within the boundaries of eighteenth-century concepts of government; to endure (let alone dominate), the country had to adopt "modern" methods of organization and administration. At the same time, they insisted that these innovations were merely functional, not essential. The new state would defend the core of American values, not replace it. It would have a hybrid vocabulary: neither new nor original, but one that operated under a certain set of principles in the name of a different historical heritage.[2]

The critical point for understanding the state that could conceive and manage a Vietnam War, then, is not the 1960s, or even the 1940s. We must begin a decade or so earlier, at the moment when political and economic elites recognized that the shifting geopolitical structure of international politics was creating opportunities for American society and problems for American government.[3]

After World War I, U.S. policymakers understood that the country's industrial and financial might could make America—at least theoretically—the world's dominant economic power.[4] Through the interwar period, however, appearances never quite meshed with reality. Government elites were not able to translate that economic power into political dominance because, into the 1920s, three ideological structures competed for power to define and direct America's international role: presidential nationalism, congressional party politics, and corporate internationalism. Elite "players" from each structure pursued distinct approaches to foreign policy that only occasionally or informally overlapped the others. Corporate internationalists, like Owen Young or the managers of the Rockefeller Foundation, extended economic and cultural networks that were practically unregulated by politics. Presidential nationalists sought, through the Foreign Service and military staffs, to maintain a consistent national policy; presidents also asserted an interest in (though not yet an ability to dominate) multilateral conferences on economics and arms control. Simultaneously, congressional leaders insisted on presiding over an ornery foreign policy in which every decision—from tariffs to battleships—was open to renegotiation because congressional party politics controlled the appropriations process.[5]

Into the 1920s, however, no domestic elite was willing to disavow its own rules of behavior, its own measures of authority, in order to cooperate on a sustained national—military and economic—policy. Instead, the intersection of government and corporate axes produced a stalemate in which no elite institution—Congress, the presidency, corporations—was powerful enough to dominate policy, yet in which each was powerful enough to prevent either of the others from gaining ascendance. Hence the coordination of power and the face that power showed to the world remained logically unstable.[6]

The 1930s witnessed the most concerted effort to find a state management system that was in concord with American political ideals. Although Franklin D. Roosevelt in some ways followed his immediate predecessors in trying simply to coordinate competing institutional interests in order to encourage stability among elites, he also understood that as long as U.S. policy-making remained entwined in a framework of competition for legitimacy, it would remain inadequate to the task of providing comprehensive oversight and guidance of public policy. Therefore, with the New Deal, he attempted to break into American culture and gain the power needed to maneuver between legitimacy and necessity: mediating between what was necessary for public order in a modern society and what was possible in a constitutional one.[7]

Specifically, President Roosevelt tried to make the case for unobstructed executive power by shifting the characterization of the presidency from a legal, constitutional one, in which its main relations were with Congress and the Supreme Court, to a frankly historicist and plebiscitary one, in which the president was more a representative of an evolving "nation."[8] FDR blurred the differences between the constitutional "People," treated as the sovereign arbiter and limiter of political behavior, and "the people" in the more organic sense of voters with legitimate needs and claims on national resources. He tacitly admitted that continuity with the past was impossible, and then he suggested that it was not important anyway because the United States had a cultural heritage in which charismatic leaders periodically interposed themselves between the creative disorder of inevitable change and the democratic dispositions of an established people.[9]

This cultural break encouraged a type of presidential managerialism that effectively treated domestic and foreign policy in similar ways. FDR envisioned the president as a kind of chief executive officer and the White House as an executive management center. With a small staff, this center could observe, classify, and map problems; define groups and agencies interested in those problems; and get people aligned with each other in an effort to facilitate both policy discipline and policy progress. Without replacing the American political culture's structures or symbols and, equally significant, without creating a European-style bureaucracy in which central decisions were imposed irrespective of local or regional concerns, FDR tried to direct American political culture away from a rigorous constitutional focus to an open, fluid, frankly synthetic system that could develop over time and be responsive to both dramatic needs and the more placid rhythms of stability.[10]

FDR's approach to both domestic and international policy management redefined the landscape of the postwar state, but not in the way intended. Under pressure of the Great Depression, Congress created administrative agencies on an unprecedented scale and delegated to them some of its information-gathering and decision-making powers. In this way, it recognized the authority of the federal government in general policy areas. But Congress consistently refused to cede to the president the budgetary or planning authority to control those agencies. Indeed, when FDR tried, during his second term, to establish an executive management system in the White House, congressional opponents successfully used constitutional imagery of checks and balances to block these "un-American" ambitions. Control of a now vastly expanded administrative government would continue to involve a tug-of-war between a president capable of defining but not controlling policy and a Congress capable of funding but not managing it.

Moreover, the character of World War II warped Roosevelt's use of the term *stability*. During the conflict, both Congress and FDR reverted to a language of "national emergency" that tacitly permitted the president to exercise exclusive decision-making power "for the duration." But mindful of the hazards of articulating specific national goals, FDR consistently maintained that the war was being fought primarily to restore order. American strategy would center on fighting an alliance war, with coordinated military strategies, rather than on satisfying particular national ambitions. In that way, he hoped to keep the focus on the *process* of maintaining peace rather than on specific goals such as had undermined the peace of World War I.[11]

Yet World War II occurred precisely because there was no order, no international status quo to be restored. In the aftermath of the depression, dissatisfied powers, like Germany and Japan, and ambitious colonial nationalists concluded that their interests were better achieved outside the interwar cooperative framework that effectively froze existing power relations. In that context, "stability" shifted definitions. Rather than a process—a means of organizing relations—the term came to be treated as a goal, a basic national interest. This shift did not occur all at once; expectations lingered that prewar powers would reassert themselves. But a new consciousness emerged with the American victory (which, by expanding the geographic boundaries of American engagement, clearly demonstrated that the United States now militarily as well as economically was a Great Power). It urged upon the public and policymakers alike the need to embrace America's "real" national identity—as a defender of order, a global "super-power"—as the only hope of maintaining stability in the postwar world.[12]

This consciousness represented a substantial, although subtle, break from previous elite understandings of state management. The most economical way to describe this new consciousness is to look at the changing discourse within the nonelite, policy-advising community. Before World War II, academics—a knowledge class—who advised the State Department and the White House spoke in an economic language of interests. Convinced that World War I had been caused by "irrational" nationalism, and that the war had disrupted economic stability for a generation, they hoped to forge a postwar peace through the "rational" techniques of cooperation. In that way, they anticipated a more harmonious international relations, presumably because it would be based on the common objectives of all concerned: economic stability and security.[13]

By 1945 these advisers had compiled a solid record of success, most notably the Bretton Woods monetary agreement, in which they were able to persuade the British and (briefly) the Soviets to participate. To economic foreign policy managers, this was a clear and positive reassertion of the prewar cooperative diplomacy. As Dean Acheson declared to a group of businessmen at the end of the European war, Bretton Woods rested on the basic assumption that "peace is a possibility only if countries work together and prosper together."[14]

However, by 1945 these arguments had not been challenged so much as marginalized by new voices clamoring for admission to the advising community. These voices reflected an eclectic group of academics and professionals: émigré scholars like Arnold Wolfers, Hans J. Morgenthau, and Hans Vagts (Charles Beard's son-in-law); older nationalists like Nicholas Spykman and Edwin Montefiore at Yale; career foreign service and military officers like George Kennan, George A. Lincoln, and Herman Beukema of West Point; and young political scientists like Frederick S. Dunn, William Fox, and Bernard Brodie, many of whom found their first real jobs as military and naval intelligence officers. Not part of the academic community interested in problems of public administration, these individuals had labored in what, in the 1930s, had been the very peripheral field of strategy. But during the war, they used popular magazines like *Time* and their employment by fringe agencies such as the Office of Strategic Services (OSS) to mount a public and private campaign, not against stability itself, but against cooperation and compromise as a means to stability.[15]

Specifically, these outriders were interested in issues of national identity as a key to defining national interests. They saw identity as largely determined by a combination of geographic position and historically conditioned cultural traits. For example, Spykman and Dunn argued that America was surrounded, essentially, by the "rimlands" of Europe and Asia; because of that, it had to be concerned with the stability of those regions. In 1917 and 1941, they continued, the United States belatedly entered wars to avoid having those regions controlled by hostile forces. In the postwar world, the country ought to take its "rightful place in world affairs" to prevent future threats from arising in the same locations.[16]

This understanding was not based on a detailed study of geography or on a historical chronology that linked the present, step by step, to the past. Moreover, it downplayed the issues that concerned economic planners, especially the argument that, industrialism having remade all social relations, the problem was to make a new inter-national culture—a problem that entailed structural reform. Rather, these theorists bundled environmental factors into an almost literary reading of the general character of various national leaders; states that had satisfactory geographic security (like Britain, for instance) had different psychological profiles than others in less secure geographic positions.[17] Though vague, these arguments offered a sense of coherence and continuity, for they effectively encoded states with recognizable personalities. This method of analysis had the cachet of explaining long-term trends while neatly sliding over more recent global developments or existing domestic political conditions.[18] Not least, from the standpoint of public opinion and policy-making, the dramatic prose of this "realist" approach minimized the need for the extensive structural reforms anticipated by the economic perspective. In the realist view, the United States had to be concerned with "fitting in," not reconstruction.[19]

Still, both economic policy adherents and national identity proponents meant to define a policy that kept the United States involved in world affairs yet also prescribed effective limits to that involvement. The national identity proponents assumed that the country had to defend specific geographic positions—Western Europe, Japan, the Western Hemisphere—precisely because the United States was like other powers: struggling within limits not wholly defined by itself. What happened in other areas—Asia, Africa, even Eastern Europe—might be tragic or triumphal, but it was somebody else's concern, somebody else's history. Without denying the importance of Europe or Japan, economic internationalists evaluated them less from geographic than economic considerations. They assumed that there would be a few dominant economic powers and anticipated that policy would be handled pragmatically, on a case by case basis, since most postwar problems would involve so many interconnected interests that only compromise could lead to stable solutions. Whereas the economic approach assumed that clear-cut identities and overt definitions of interests would limit conflict by demarcating boundaries that should not be crossed by others, the geographic approach assumed that bargaining could yield innovative solutions for emerging conditions precisely because boundaries and historical interests were discounted as valuable.

Ironically, the commingling of these two discourses produced the sensibility of limitlessness that characterized American foreign policy into the 1960s. This combination first played out in Europe between 1947 and 1949 when American policymakers, casting about for a means to break the deadlock in international negotiations over Germany and eager to strengthen European governments' wills to maintain anti-inflationary policies, embarked on a performative strategy that packaged economic stability in the broad terms of cultural character. In 1947, policy-making elites—financiers and corporate elites like John McCloy, Averell Harriman, Robert Lovett, Dean Acheson, David Bruce, and Lew Douglas—had concluded privately that no agreement on Germany was possible on Soviet terms. They also had decided (with the tacit encouragement of Europeans such as Jean Monnet and Ernest Bevin) that the United States had to act more imperially toward Europe, dictating the economic terms under which European states had to operate in order to sustain long-term economic growth. But while the Americans believed that German integration into the West European orbit would provide a useful economic and psychological boost, they did not want to cut off arbitrarily all hopes of compromise with the Soviets. Furthermore, they feared that Congress would refuse to fund any kind of multilateral program intended merely to solidify economic ties with Europe.[20]

With the Marshall Plan, policymakers made an exhilarating and crafty effort to use national identity as a great power to package an economic agenda, and then to turn both into an argument for the executive management of foreign policy. The Truman administration asserted that economic assistance to Western Europe was necessary because the "national security" interests of the United States would be damaged if the country failed to stabilize the democracies of Europe. A variety of administration spokesmen solemnly assured Congress that without the Marshall Plan democracy would lose its credibility as a social system, thus paving the way for Soviet expansion. But they not only presented a stark alternative: restore economic stability in the present or station American troops in Europe again. More significantly, they treated the opportunity offered by the Marshall Plan as a metahistorical miracle, a moment in which American history was again brushed by the course of Divine Providence and Americans were again offered the chance to "be" what Americans had been intended to be.[21]

In the short term of the 1940s, this argument made it easier for policymakers to concentrate directly on the problems at hand. By making things "clearer than truth" to a Congress they despised as (and surely was) parochial, administration spokesmen like Acheson avoided having to dress foreign policy in ritual forms. Instead, they produced bold, creative policies like the European Recovery Program (ERP).[22] Moreover, under the force of Marshall Plan rhetoric, the Truman administration was able to achieve a portion of the executive coordinating system that Roosevelt had sought. The National Security Act, passed in July 1947, created a Central Intelligence Agency (CIA) to provide information and advice on international situations, formed a National Security Council (NSC) to coordinate policy, and consolidated the armed services into a single Department of Defense in order to bring military strategy more directly under the purview of the president.[23] In the context of the 1940s, the Marshall Plan was an unprecedented success in its ability to signify a "state" in both senses of the term: as an institutional order of regulation that accepted responsibility for managing foreign policy, and as a condition of being, a solid sense that such international responsibilities were integral to the state of "being American."

Initially, however, the Marshall Plan was not intended to "fight" communism, that is, to define an extensive campaign requiring the full powers of the state. Although the Truman administration clearly did not want communists in the governments of Western Europe, its primary interest was to modernize and stabilize national economies quickly so as to create an international circuit of economic management, one that theoretically would minimize the role of national governments altogether.[24] The use of national identity was intended to be a creative fillip that signified a moment in which cosmological schema met pragmatic necessity, but the national identity itself was intended to be functional, not essential or determinative. Without derailing great power negotiations, policy managers wanted to use the character issue much as FDR had pragmatically accepted any policy that helped the war effort: that is, quite instrumentally, to scare Congress into ceding broad enabling power to manage foreign policy. In addition, they wanted to use this performative identity to impress Europeans (including the Soviets) by investing American foreign policy with an aura of firmness and dependability.

To an extent, this instrumentality worked. Yet the new executive mechanisms did not replace the existing political structure. Congress still controlled the appropriations power. It jealously vetted every subsequent foreign policy program or budget just as it had examined the Marshall Plan: for evidence that it was serving the national identity by furthering "anti-Communist" or "pro-democratic" interests (especially if those interests redounded to local district benefits). Moreover, by making the Marshall Plan a character issue, albeit now as an external perimeter of identity, the Truman administration reopened the old, troublesome issue of cultural legitimacy. In doing so, it permitted two problems associated with authenticity to extend into the realm of foreign policy.

First, since every elite—congressional, presidential, corporate—claimed eighteenth-century sources, all demanded that their pet policies be supported lest the U.S. "reputation" suffer abroad. By the late 1940s, reputation had become an extremely flexible tool for different political vocabularies. It was used, variously, by the military to acquire supplementary appropriations from Congress even against the wishes of President Truman; by modernization enthusiasts like Nelson Rockefeller to support foreign economic assistance programs in the underdeveloped world even against the wishes of the State and Defense departments; and, eventually, even by client states outside the United States that clamored for military assistance against communist insurgencies and that, if thwarted by the administration, merely cultivated congressional, bureaucratic, or journalistic champions.[25] In the process, government machinery began to expand far beyond the intentions of the international lawyers and financiers who ostensibly ran the administration.[26]

Second, and ironically in light of its capacity to accommodate a virtual thesaurus of programs all claiming to support Americanism, a foreign policy reflective of an "authentic" American character allowed no space for cultural innovation or invention such as FDR had attempted. Its logic enveloped everything *except* sovereignty, that is, the ability to define limits to American interests, the ability to prioritize and maintain restrictions on what foreign policy should be about. In the short term, the Marshall Plan expanded managerial power regarding foreign policy. Over the longer term, however, the convergence of elite policy with national identity, once transposed into practice, made the control of foreign policy all but impossible.

The ironies in this managerial situation (in which the apparent harmony between practice and identity led to struggles without end) already were apparent in 1948. Having acquiring the ERP by means of a not-subtle appeal to anticommunism, policymakers felt emboldened to declare that Western governments that admitted communists to power would forfeit American aid.[27] The subsequent breakdown in American-Soviet relations during 1948 probably reflected Stalin's intention to use a show of force to encourage the Allies to return to the negotiating table.[28] But if that was the case, the Americans missed the signals completely, for they responded truculently as if, having told a scary story, they suddenly had become frightened that their make-believe monster had come to life. By 1949 the administration had concluded that the economic alliance could be stabilized only if Americans participated in a European defense pact. With NATO, the United States broke national tradition by expressing direct responsibility for maintaining the European balance of power.

Still, policymakers recognized that in Europe this framework—that of the United States being put to a test, of having to measure up to the standards of a great power—was a game, a performance that they had devised. Even throughout the Berlin airlift crisis, the Truman administration cut the defense budget, suggesting that the elite remained aware that its *primary* goal was economic stability and that this goal required the United States to avoid inflationary practices.[29] But although they recognized it as a game in Europe, policymakers were less sure that in Asia they controlled the rules that distinguished between real interests and rhetorical tactics.

By 1949 policymakers believed that Japan had to be part of the Atlantic trade and financial network, a belief that, in itself, hardly was distinguishable from that of prewar internationalism.[30] Yet if the United States was to rebuild the "workshop" economy of Japan by restoring its economic ties with Asia, it needed terms different from the imperialist ones that Japan had used in the 1930s and 1940s lest America be accused of providing for Japan what it had just spent a long, terrible war trying to prevent Japan from taking on its own.[31] Here, the Joint Chiefs of Staff insistence that Japan was "*the* key strategic position in East Asia for the United States" (because military bases there "would force the Soviets to think about a two-front war") became a convenient reinforcement for the economic plans.[32] However, the Asia policy clouded the priorities between two sets of interests—economic and strategic—whose compatibility was by no means clear. Was Asia, especially Southeast Asia, primarily an economic perimeter for Europe and Japan? Was it part of a bulwark against Soviet and Chinese expansion that eventually would threaten Japan (and hence American strategy in the Pacific)? And if, as most agreed, it was both, which framework—economic stability or political legitimacy—should have pride of place in organizing American policy?[33]

Nonelite, knowledge class advisers seemed both aware of and puzzled by the ambiguity connecting American economic and security concerns on the defense perimeter. At a Policy Planning Staff (PPS) meeting in the State Department in June 1949, policy analysts argued that stabilization was possible without U.S. militarization, with most embracing some kind of informal assistance to neocolonialists as a pragmatic way of enforcing order without committing American resources or prestige to messy little revolutions that were sure to be black holes of imperialism, communism, and anti-Western nationalism.[34] By contrast, Secretary of State Acheson and High Commissioner of Germany McCloy argued strenuously that communism had to be defeated so that Western Europe and Japan could find markets there. They asserted that the United States should be prepared to provide financial and military assistance to integrate Southeast Asia into the Western orbit.[35]

The disagreement, seemingly small, encompassed a cultural world of difference. Whereas both positions reflected a sense of urgency about stabilization and accepted the need for interdependent economic relations between Asia and Europe and Japan, Acheson's brushed over the complexity of the regional conditions: the sources of disorder, the interests involved, the balance sheet that calculated what types of order would be acceptable, and what the United States should be willing to expend. Instead, the secretary of state packaged support in terms that flirted with an equation between stability and American legitimacy. By suggesting that security rested on communism's defeat, every revolution potentially became a reflection on or a test of American self-worth.

Less than a year later, this flirtation had become outright seduction. In October, George Kennan, the PPS director, criticized Acheson's acceptance of the "irreconcilable" argument that rejected all attempts to negotiate with the Soviets. Without a commitment to negotiation, Kennan feared, the United States would freeze existing divisions in Europe and Asia.[36] In early 1950 Kennan rejected the argument that all communist incursions were of equal weight by arguing that not all American interests were equally important. The United States could afford to ignore some maneuvers, he argued, since "world realities have greater tolerances than we commonly suppose against ambitious schemes for world domination."[37] But Acheson dismissed Kennan's argument that economic recovery in Europe would be a sufficient deterrent to Soviet influence. In 1950 Kennan departed, replaced as director of the PPS by financier Paul Nitze, someone much more attuned to Acheson's uncompromising view. Nitze summarized the emerging elite consensus in a report drafted by a joint State-Defense group. It virtually abandoned Kennan's containment doctrine in the course of requesting vastly expanded military capabilities to keep the doctrine from being merely "a policy of bluff."[38]

The new report—NSC-68—centered foreign policy squarely on the issue of legitimacy. Without declaring outright that containment had failed to persuade allies of the desirability of the American perspective, it took as a given that the United States had to confront any further communist incursions—crucially, even if those occurred in areas of little direct economic or security interest to the country—or risk losing its future capacity to persuade others to accept American cultural hegemony. Breaking with Kennan's argument that U.S. security could be satisfied by defending selected geographic strong points, NSC-68 declared that "the defeat of free institutions anywhere is a defeat everywhere" since the Soviets were guided by the ambition of demonstrating that democracies lacked the "will" to fight because they were "decadent and doomed."[39]

This was a profound policy shift. Rather than measuring strategy on the basis of economic capacity, military potential, or even cultural evaluations of the behavior and possible intentions of other powers, and, crucially, rather than measuring strategy on the basis of the nation's own interests,

NSC-68 assumed that American behavior alone was the linchpin of global stability. John McCloy made the point directly in a State Department meeting in early 1950. "European integration," he asserted, "is connected with our policy in Asia, for Soviet success in the East would make the Allied position in Europe untenable."[40]

At the risk of reducing explanation to psychobabble, this sensitivity to the perceptions of others abandoned all attempt at self-definition, at psychological boundary maintenance. Instead of trying to maintain a sense of proportion, NSC-68 linked U.S. policy to what the Soviets, Europeans, and Japanese thought about the United States. Effectively, it transferred control over U.S. interests to outside arbiters of behavior.[41]

Of course, behind psychological conditions, cultural preconditions always exist. In this case, NSC-68 reflected as much the habits and political fortunes of a social class as it did specific policy differences. For example, compared with someone like Kennan, elites like McCloy and Acheson were narrow, even mediocre thinkers. But they were completely self-assured men, accustomed to working at the top of every system, indeed, to identifying systemic interests with their own. This sense of privilege had been ingrained by the prep school ethos in which they had been raised, an ethos that accustomed them to claiming power as their right, based on who they were rather than what they thought.[42] However, this sense of privilege was far less "Established" than it was individualized. Largely because until the war there was no "state" to speak of, American elites constituted a ruling class that largely lacked an institutionalized locus of power. As a result, they were trained less to articulate a broad vision or to manage a national government than to display their legitimacy by adopting a public "character" of courage, rectitude, and resoluteness that ostensibly imitated that of the Founding Fathers.[43]

Because of such training, elites were accustomed to looking for outer yardsticks of behavior. Hence, the approbation of fellow elites in Europe counted for more than the geographically or economically based warnings of their (socially subordinate) academic advisers; their own views on foreign policy had more salience than any material (that is, delimiting) national interests. More important, this experience of placeless legitimacy left the elites with a sense of insecurity—less a feeling of self-doubt than a resentment against a system that did not unequivocally recognize their superiority and an inability to appreciate the irony of trying to maintain a unified national self-image within a political society that sustained a variety of interests. NSC-68 quite self-consciously represented a power play by the elites: an effort to institutionalize their interests quickly and ruthlessly before their power could be snatched away. "The purpose of NSC-68," as Acheson wrote later, "was to so bludgeon the mass mind of 'government' that not only could the President make a decision but that the decision could be carried out."[44] To do that, though, elites had to deny rhetorically, and limit in practice, the diversity and competition at the center of American political life.

In articulating what Quentin Anderson called "an imperial self," in which the term *America* became bound up with the nation and Western civilization and freedom, NSC-68's drafters eradicated through omission the vocabulary of competition and self-interest that historically characterized middle-class society in the United States and Europe.[45] Effectively, they denied the split between legitimacy and stability in the United States by translating it as an external division between those who defended the notion of Western community and those (communists) who presumably were bent on destroying communal values.[46] In a superficial way, this attempt to deny the significance of traditional markers of national difference mimicked FDR's attempt to expand governmental authority to deal with emerging situations not contained within historically defined national interests. However, NSC-68 rejected precisely the commitment to pragmatic compromise that FDR had seen as the basis of stability. Its claim for unlimited power was purposive, not open-ended. It had to prevent the Kremlin from initiating a "descending spiral" that ultimately would leave the United States alone and defenseless.[47]

Theoretically, this rhetoric was directed outward. It analyzed Soviet tactics and declared that, to combat communism, the United States must be prepared to adopt similar means. "The necessity of conducting ourselves so as to affirm our values in action as well as words," Nitze wrote, "[does not] forbid such measures, covert or overt, violent or non-violent, which serve the purposes of frustrating the Kremlin design . . . provided only that they are appropriately calculated to that end, and are not so excessive or misdirected as to make us enemies of the people."[48]

However, NSC-68 also anticipated a domestic and intragovernmental power play. Essentially, it adapted for an American elite Max Weber's and Carl Schmitt's theories of a strong, plebiscitary president who, under certain circumstances dictated by himself alone, could be authorized to act beyond constitutional limits for the purpose of defending the notion of constitutional government.[49] In that sense, it was a doctrine of exception, not exceptionalism. NSC-68 did not deny the worth of democratic culture; indeed, democracy became the ideal, the emblem of American policy. Nevertheless, NSC-68 proposed that at least in foreign policy, *the state stood outside of, and was unregulated by, the values of that culture.* Rather than trying to fit a state into an American system, it effectively asserted that the state could maintain the integrity of the nation only by employing practices shunned by the political culture.[50]

Thus beyond its symbolic uses, the demonization of the Soviet Union had a very practical purpose in 1950. Nitze and the Policy Review group were eager to do two things: first, build up existing military capacity in order to achieve a rough approximation between existing power and diplomatic commitments, and second, acquire the more general authority to control budget allocations. The latter reflected the perennial constitutional battle between legislature and executive. Succinctly, administration elites meant to assert the power to calibrate policy with resources by taking foreign policy budgets out of the sphere of party interest. By avoiding the miasma of the congressional committee system, they hoped to implement a more flexible and responsive diplomatic and military system.[51]

The expansion of military capacity involved creative accounting. Nitze used alarmist language partly to make President Truman understand that military expansion did not have to be a zero-sum game, that security did not need to be limited by the existing capacities captured in an annual budget. NSC-68 suggested a "half-way point" (between business as usual and all-out preparation for world war) on which the U.S. government could stimulate higher levels of economic activity that, over time, could pay for civilian goods *and* national security. As John Lewis Gaddis has noted, NSC-68 not only asserted that there *should* not be distinctions between peripheral and vital interests. By adroit reference to the virtues of Keynesian macroeconomic management, it demonstrated "with seductive logic that there *need* not be."[52]

Seemingly without realizing it, though, NSC-68's description of a limitless Soviet threat established a linguistic trap in which elite class interests were capable of being disrupted regularly by bureaucratic "reasons of state." Undoubtedly, its drafters appreciated that, by connecting economics and security, the Marshall Plan had produced a brilliantly flexible way of breaking through America's historically conditioned reluctance to sustain international responsibility. The Marshall Plan, however, had used the connection as a platitude, a way of naturalizing a specific elite goal. In comparison, when NSC-68 thrust together economics and security, it actually weakened the political claims of an economic elite. Declaring that the Soviet Union was incapable of being restrained by negotiations and compromise clearly deepened public convictions that the United States needed a state powerful enough to restrain Soviet ambitions. Yet to the extent that NSC-68 dismissed a propensity to negotiate as weak, it limited the space in which elites could maneuver between "real" economic interests and "rhetorical" national interest justifications: space in which elites could declare allegiance to political ideals without adopting them. While economic dominance did not vanish as a goal, NSC-68's grim conclusion, that "budgetary considerations will need to be subordinated to the stark fact that our very independence as a nation may be at stake," hardly suggested John Maynard Keynes's optimistic and econo-centric view that *occasional* state interventions could contribute to long-term stability and growth. Rather, in subordinating economic to military policy (even though it was directed to maintaining the global economic system, even though the military came to be linked to employment and technological innovation), NSC-68 pushed for the kind of *staatsraison* that, Keynes had believed, endangered capitalism itself: a political system in which concern for economics shifted to concern for prestige and honor.[53]

The Korean War provided the first hint that the chiasmic system that elites had constructed could become an enclosure rather than a passageway to more clear-cut authority. Most senior policymakers agreed that Korea represented exactly the case that NSC-68 had outlined: a situation in which the communists, by expanding into a region of negligible military and economic value to the United States, challenged American prestige and resolve in the eyes of the American public and European allies.[54] Administration officials framed the U.S. response in an exceedingly clever way. By working through the auspices of the United Nations, the United States ostensibly became part of a multilateral resistance to aggression, thus simultaneously satisfying the criteria of legitimacy and stability.

But Truman's decision in Autumn 1950 to authorize troops to cross the Thirty-eighth Parallel swiftly changed the nature of the campaign from one of defending the status quo (reestablishing the dividing line established jointly by the Soviets and Americans in 1945) to one that could be interpreted as an American effort to "win" the cold war.[55] The subsequent entry of the People's Republic of China into the war reinforced the rhetoric that this was a fight between communists and "the West" and offered the president a stark choice. He could support the rhetoric of victory by waging all-out war (which effectively would have introduced nuclear weapons into battle), or he could back away from the goal of victory. Ultimately, Truman chose the latter, but he never rejected the *ideal* of victory; he only accepted the Joint Chiefs' conclusion that Korea was "the wrong place" in which to confront the Soviets. This ambiguous position—neither seeking victory nor declaring an interest solely in stability—led the administration to engage in two more years of a terrible war of attrition whose result finally was a stalemate that simply reaffirmed the Thirty-eighth Parallel demarcation. But the war effort alone was insufficient to maintain elite credibility. From 1950 on, domestic anticommunists savaged the administration, accusing it of irresolution and denouncing "treadmill policies" that "devour[ed American] economic, political and moral vitals."[56]

It is possible to argue that from the Korean truce into the 1970s, American presidents accepted in fact, if not always in rhetoric, that the United States had to make practical accommodations with the Soviets (and less directly, the Chinese).[57] From this perspective, anticommunist rhetoric became the pragmatic means of getting things done in Washington. Clearly, this rhetoric did endure partly because it was politically useful. Policymakers found that they could overcome congressional resistance to national projects ranging from highway construction to higher education by arguing that they were needed to fight communist aggression.

Such rhetoric was not unidirectional, however. Having once committed themselves to this argument, administrations found it very difficult to achieve their entire policy agenda precisely because administration speakers lacked a monopoly on the language of foreign policy. Indeed, from the 1950s administrations found that resolving the problems of modern state management created new postmodern problems of legitimation.

Up until the cold war, administration elites wrestled with the dilemma of producing an activist state that was commensurate with the United States's economic role in the world yet that did not violate cultural claims of American exceptionalism, of its difference from European empires. FDR, for example, argued that he could not manage a modern society under the existing loose systems of power. Yet in the 1930s, he was rebuffed by the congressional logic that power requires administration, administration requires executive bureaucracy, executive power threatens legislative autonomy, and anything that threatens Congress threatens the American Constitution's ideal of democracy.

By comparison, NSC-68 reconfigured the entire constitutional argument. Its ambiguous rationale for a "national security state" asserted that "democracy" could not survive unless the United States supported a sustained administrative capacity to resist the Soviet Union, a particular but amorphous enemy. To that end, a permanent security bureaucracy—military, diplomatic, surveillance—not only was not un-American. It became the *precondition* of American integrity.

Of course, NSC-68's drafters had intended that this bureaucracy be controlled by the presidency. Instead, by identifying the American state with an overall (outer-directed) purpose, the drafters made it much more difficult for elites to define the terms of foreign policy in ways that could be linked to specific elite interests or class needs. In the context of a hybrid governing system in which the legislature accepted the bureaucracy on the terms of anticommunism, administrations were vulnerable to charges of insufficient dedication to the goals of "Americanism." While elites no longer faced a problem of producing a powerful state, they still had little control over the definition—that is, the limits—of state authority. Anyone who criticized the administration in terms of anticommunism— members of Congress, advocates for specific agencies, academic experts— acquired meaning and value in the public discourse because in Baudrillardian terms, anticommunism became the common code of the system. It invested any commentary—regardless of its logic or content—with surplus value, with evanescent but disruptive legitimacy that an administration could ignore only at risk of its own reputation.[58]

In consequence, cold war presidents found themselves encased in a postmodern conundrum: a double-entry system in which policy became divorced from material intention as the latter moved across the political landscape. For the first time in American history, presidents had enough administrative capacity to envision integrated programs, with policies tailored to address discrete issues, but they lacked a precise managerial authority and vocabulary to impose such agendas on the state bureaucracy. In the 1930s, Roosevelt forthrightly had called for "planning."[59] In the 1950s, "planning," even "management" were far too loaded—too "pink"—as terms for an American lexicon. Instead, policymakers began to use the subdued vocabulary of "the budget" to carve out a role for presidential authority to rein in the bureaucracy's appetite for congressional appropriations.

At the same time, in order to acquire the political authority to achieve and manage their own administration goals—that is, to acquire the requisite congressional support—presidents first had to demonstrate political legitimacy by measuring up to standards of leadership that above all consisted of "standing up to" the Soviets. As a result, presidents often found themselves pulled toward foreign policy situations (Dwight Eisenhower with Quemoy-Matsu or Sputnik, John F. Kennedy with the Bay of Pigs, Lyndon Johnson with Vietnam) whose only material value to their administrations was a capacity to reflect American resolve or principles. If they dismissed such situations as inconsequential to national interests, they often found their domestic capacity to shape and manage government (not to mention their chances for reelection) greatly diminished. Yet if they accepted such challenges, presidents risked entropy: overcommitting the United States abroad in ways that expanded state power but opened policy-making to a variety of power bases over which the White House had little control.[60]

The history of executive management in the 1950s and early 1960s is an arrhythmic record of fluctuations as presidents alternately sought to limit and to legitimize state power. President Dwight D. Eisenhower, for example, entered office declaring that he would cut government excess. Most directly, that meant the military, which as a result of the Korean War had swollen to almost 60 percent of the annual budget. He reconfigured military strategy, focusing on "cost-effective" nuclear weapons and surveillance systems in order to cut deeply into conventional forces and maintain a heavy-handed control over weapons and satellite development. Additionally, he cut back or eliminated "soft" programs such as foreign economic assistance to relatively wealthy nations and public information/cultural exchange programs. His rationale was concise, even blunt. Since the United States was de facto the dominant economic and military power in the world, no nation could afford permanently to ignore or antagonize it. Because of that, America did not need to "attract" nations to its side. It would maintain its military assistance obligations. But it would make the best argument for democratic capitalism by permitting private enterprise to work without government intervention.[61]

Eisenhower quickly discovered that this argument encountered two problems. First, in permitting other nations to see who else reasonably could provide economic and social services, the United States risked allowing socialist experiments, or leaving unmanaged some issues that over time could require larger, more expensive intervention in order to maintain U.S. dominance.[62] Second, by 1957 Eisenhower understood that wholesale government cuts were all but impossible. Much of the nonmilitary budget went to programs like Social Security, veterans' benefits, and unemployment insurance, which were too useful and broad-based to be cut. Equally, the administration was caught in its own ideological trap, for if democratic capitalism was the superior system, if Americans had to showcase democratic "vigor," then economic slumps and attendant unemployment hardly could be treated as "natural" or inevitable. In spite of his anti-Keynesian bent, Eisenhower in fact ran five budget deficits during eight years in office in order to avoid having people doubt the virtues of "free enterprise."[63]

As a former bureaucrat himself, Eisenhower seemed to understand how easy it was to lose sight of a singular purpose in the temptation to respond fully to immediate problems. He kept one purpose in mind: upholding the liberal boundaries of American identity. A management strategy grew from that purpose: use his personal popularity to centralize executive power in order to limit government.

In his public persona, Ike became an allegory of middle-class American life: a life so placid and banal in its beliefs and self-contained in its activities that change could hardly be conceived, let alone internalized, as desirable.[64] This hardly meant that he held himself to those limits, but he left little room for others to expand those boundaries. Sitting atop the blooming, buzzing confusion of government, Eisenhower used the surveillance capacity of the Oval Office as much as any president. Under him, for example, the National Security Council became a model of continuous policy planning, gathering and coordinating information on every conceivable policy question. Eisenhower also appointed numerous committees to consider major policy questions ranging from weapons development to the more general "purposes" of the United States. But while he controlled information and kept abreast of developments, he framed foreign policy so carefully (either as "crises" or through "plausible deniability") that he seemed to resist the expansion of government responsibility or capacity.[65] It was a public relations rather than a democratic solution, but in a negative way it did ensure that government capacity was contained within the bounds of *presidential* manageability.[66]

For progressive critics in both political parties, though, this ruthless enforcement of the status quo seemed less like sober fiscal responsibility or principled liberalism than a morally cramped policy that pushed the United States to the economic and ideological periphery of world affairs. Liberal Republicans like Nelson Rockefeller and various Democrats from Adlai Stevenson and Chester Bowles to John Kennedy saw domestic and world problems both intensifying and converging in the late 1950s in areas like racism, poverty, and technological innovation. They hardly were naive about the problems of executive management. Yet critics also saw in government much untapped capacity that could be used to meet growing domestic and foreign responsibilities.[67]

Nelson Rockefeller made the most deliberate attempt to address government management when he initiated a Special Studies Project in late 1956. Developing and publishing its results over the next four years in anticipation of a Rockefeller presidential campaign in 1960, the project tried to define and prioritize a national policy agenda. And very self-consciously, Rockefeller turned to the members of a new generation of the knowledge class—young, brilliant, and voraciously ambitious "policy scientists" like Henry Kissinger, Max Millikan, Walt Rostow, and Thomas Schelling—to create a nascent advisory and managerial staff, a "presidential government," whose primary loyalty would be to him rather than to specific policy subjects or to the bureaucracy's "permanent government."[68]

The men and women who were part of this new generation had crafted careers by moving in and out of (and thus tracing intricate, informal networks of information and influence between) academic research institutes, foundations, the White House, the Defense Department, and (by virtue of their being expert witnesses) congressional committees.[69] In ethnographic terms, the knowledge class was *liminoid*. It was not elite in the sense that its members were not responsible for standing on the threshold between past and present and articulating the relationship between current policy and an enduring cultural identity. Members of this class were useful to elites in more technical ways, as mediators among competing elite positions. Policy scientists identified themselves as people who both understood how government operated as a functioning whole *and* how government needed to act in order to continue operating smoothly. From those claims, they created vocabulary bridges between conflicting views—within administrations or parties, or between the White House, Congress, and agencies—with the immediate intention of maintaining social order, of ensuring the continuity of governance (exclusive of any value judgments about the cultural legitimacy of that governance).[70]

In their opinions for the Rockefeller project, policy scientists argued generally that the government was doing far too little to provide positive reasons for people at home and abroad to accept American leadership. Without backing away from the cold war emphasis on defense, the project reports argued that Eisenhower's "budget conscious" strategy of nuclear retaliation hampered American ability to react to "brushfires" on the perimeter. Beyond defense, the reports argued that economic and social development (or modernization, a term much in academic vogue) had to be the paradigm of American identity. "Development" defined a means of connecting American largess with the Third World as a real place with markets and resources. More important, it defined a way of thinking about the future: a means of both winning and existing beyond the cold war.[71]

Although these policy analysts provided grand overviews, Rockefeller and his personal advisers quietly recognized that few faced the contradictions between economic and security goals.[72] Walt Rostow unwittingly expressed the dilemma in a memorandum on leadership. The purpose of the Special Studies Project, he noted, was to "transform ourselves from a democracy in which leadership on national issues is only sporadically invoked . . . to one where it is steadily exercised." What that meant exactly was difficult for Rostow to say; it did not mean "an American elite, freed . . . from public opinion and pressure," but something that had to derive from the nature of American society itself, something that Rostow termed "consensus."[73] Domestically, he cheerfully declared, the United States was close to achieving complete agreement. In foreign affairs, however, this consensus sadly was missing, in large part because there was no easy way to put "our real ideological and our real power interests . . . into an orderly relationship, and lead directly to well-balanced, well-articulated lines of action." What leadership had to do, therefore, was to develop "a consensus on the character of our national interest. . . . Our institutions of leadership from the President down can not efficiently function until that consensus is established."[74]

After a careful reading of that paragraph, one must conclude that Rostow was arguing simultaneously that leadership was necessary to get consensus and yet that leadership really could not function until it achieved consensus. Rostow slipped out of the knot neatly by stating that it would be "inappropriate" for him (as a mere analyst) to do more than identify the problem and stress the urgency of it.[75] But if Rockefeller became president, nothing—no clever staff, no agencies, no plans—would be really effective until he defined and internalized a national unity.

Of course, Nelson Rockefeller did not become president. In 1960 it was John Kennedy who adopted the platform of the Special Studies Project, Kennedy who attracted policy scientists like Rostow to his administration, and Kennedy who promised to get the country moving again.[76] But if Kennedy was more politically adept than Rockefeller, he was much less clear on how to prioritize a government agenda. Indeed, entering office as a cold warrior committed to the largest military buildup in peacetime history, he spent his first year as president trying to avoid being swamped by the swells of the cold war: first by the Bay of Pigs debacle, then by the incipient bloodbath in the Congo, and, most disturbingly, by his summit with Nikita Khrushchev in Vienna, from which Kennedy emerged chastened and goaded by the Soviets and weakened in the eyes of European leaders.[77]

Only in 1962 did the young president indicate publicly how he intended to achieve his ambitious agenda. In both domestic and foreign affairs, his operative term was "expansion": expansion of the domestic economy to create full employment and greater resources for new social and military spending, and expansion of foreign policy to promote political and economic ties with emerging nations. But these policies never were intended to be just substantive. In evoking expansion in both spheres, Kennedy offhandedly—but quite consciously—used the language of planning and executive management. The bright world he envisioned was supposed to rest on a basis of quiet procedural changes in governance.

For example, the magic potion of domestic economic expansion—the elixir that would permit more spending without concomitant tax burdens—was the same NSC-68 view that budget deficits were tactical weapons in the management of a national economy. JFK made this point in an address at Yale University in mid-1962. The problems of modern government were so intricate and far-reaching, he chided, that people who worried about the dangers of "big government" or "budget deficits" were fretting about myths or goblins. These clichés sounded like "old records, long-playing, left over from the middle thirties." Governments could not be cramped into an accountant's ledger without damaging long-term investments in the basic strengths of a society, such as education or research and technology.[78]

Then, seemingly casually, Kennedy offered the methodological theme upon which his "new economics" rested. The United States, he argued, was so dominant, so essential in world affairs that it had to have some kind of "indicative planning" that was coordinated and implemented by the executive branch. After all, although economic expansion redounded to the benefit of the American public, it was not just a matter of satisfying domestic desires. American success in satisfying the broad public with a capitalist economy paid ideological dividends, too. Thus executive authority was not a constitutional problem because it was not intended just to create contemporary political advantages. Executive planning had extranational significance; as Kennedy concluded, "the safety of the world—the very future of freedom—depends . . . upon sensible and clear-headed management."[79]

Here again is this linguistic trap. Kennedy's plans rested on a presumption that the goals were so desirable that Congress, corporate America, and the voting public would agree to any methods in order to achieve them; indeed, the degree to which JFK was overt about the need for planning suggests an enormous self-confidence about his capacity to label opposition as vestigial. At the same time, what held the argument together was Kennedy's insistence that executive management was necessary primarily because the United States was responsible for *world* order. Essentially, this is the same limitless, unstable argument offered by NSC-68 on behalf of elite control. Presidents ought to be authorized to manage state bureaucracy not just because modern governments faced myriad interests unforeseen in the eighteenth century, or because governments (like corporations) run more efficiently if managed as a wholistic system with overt assumptions, specific goals, and performance evaluations, but precisely because the United States was unique in its role in the world.

From that standpoint, Kennedy's success in achieving domestic planning absolutely required the presumption that the United States could command world affairs if only the president could gain control of the American bureaucracy. By 1962, though, the administration was scrambling to rectify conditions that seemed to be leading toward a relative decline in American political and economic power vis-à-vis Europe. That is, by 1962 the United States not only faced uncertainty in the Third World related to the dissolution of colonial ties and the resultant problems of political and economic development. Equally, Kennedy acknowledged strains and tensions within the Atlantic alliance, stemming in particular from potential trade barriers created by the new Common Market, resurgent nationalism in France and Germany that resented America's nuclear monopoly in NATO, and the troublesome persistence of a balance of payments deficit with Western Europe. Thus even as Kennedy directed public attention to the "new frontiers" of Asia and Africa, his administration was constrained by the need to think as well about how to maintain the status quo with its traditional allies.

In the Grand Design (as this thinking has come to be known with regard to Europe), the Kennedy administration sought to alleviate regional grievances through integrated policies that expanded trade areas and acquiesced in more multilateral consultations and to cooperate on defense matters. Nevertheless, this "partnership" still existed under the umbrella of American predominance: America as the last word on strategic decisions. Rethinking the basis or scope of the alliance was hardly contemplated. The Kennedy administration maintained that tensions could be alleviated if the United States simply was more clear and consistent in its planning.[80]

In a memorable article in the January 1963 *Foreign Affairs*, Dean Acheson summed up the administration outlook in the course of reviewing the history of the Atlantic alliance. Acheson reaffirmed the centrality of the alliance to American foreign policy, but he also admitted that, in the past, it had had no long-term purpose; its "so-called strategic concepts . . . were largely rationalizations of what was thought practicable" at the time.[81] The "Alice in Wonderland" quality of these defense "metaphors," Acheson argued, had contributed to the current confusion because such "slogans" permitted cynicism and loose thinking to cloud the alliance's central tenet: that Europe and the United States needed each other to resist domination by a "Communist system embracing Eurasia, Africa and South America."[82] In a remarkable statement from the man who used anticommunism to "scare the hell out of Congress" and pass the Marshall Plan, Acheson now asserted that a "sound strategic plan . . . should not be designed, like the monstrous giants who guard the entrance to the temples at Nikko, to deter . . . the ill-intentioned from entering the sacred precincts, even though they scare the daylights out of the faithful as well." Instead, the United States had to develop a "master plan," followed by civilians and military alike in the American government. Once the Americans were united on what they wanted, Acheson insisted, this strategy could be proposed and fitted to Europe.[83]

Acheson's article in brief form reflected the intellectual clarity *and* the obtuseness of the Kennedy administration. Forthright in recognizing that it needed something more than the hoary slogans of the early cold war, the administration still underestimated the dispersive tendencies in world affairs. Because its focus, ultimately, was inward—on gaining control of the American government—administration policymakers had to believe that more flexible and sophisticated management of essentially the same cold war policies would be sufficient reform; the world those policies conjured had to exist if they were to have a chance to pummel the U.S. government into changing its behavior. In comparison, Europeans like Charles de Gaulle saw the economic strains in the alliance and the emergence of the Third World as long-term structural changes whose push toward multilateral centers of power portended the gradual end of the cold war. From this perspective, the American initiatives were both arrogant and outmoded. But when Europe rejected the American proposals, in January 1963, the Kennedy administration was left clinging to a rock at high tide. It could admit the hollowness of the cold war claims and find other means to justify its policies. Alternately, it could continue to paper over the contradictions and continue to use the same rationalizations in order to protect its own (domestic) claims for power.

The Vietnamese had the grave and grotesque misfortune to be present at this conjuncture. Vietnam in the early sixties became important not because it had anything to do with the European rejection of American aspirations, or because it figured heavily into Kennedy's plans, but because it offered a means by which to avoid dealing with historically structured conflicts in the elites' own ambitions and management tactics. In maintaining existing cold war commitments in Vietnam, Kennedy continued to use habitual anticommunism in order to justify elite management of foreign policy even as he tried to articulate a new language of authority.

Into the 1960s Vietnam was of minor concern to the elite community.[84] It existed on a symbolic terrain that elites had created in their cold war rhetoric, a terrain beyond the reality of most Americans on which elites could justify their privileges and prove their authority to manage foreign affairs. This landscape encouraged an expansive, even aristocratic sensibility of honor, or prestige, in which commitment to anticommunist cultural ideals was expressed by grandiosity, by the enlargement of military and financial aid with no concern for "bourgeois" considerations of economics or boundaries.[85] On a symbolic level, the assistance the United States showered on Vietnam between 1950 and 1963 served these lyrical purposes.

Still, the very visibility of this support implied more traditional, realpolitik roles of protection and responsibility as well. Indeed, these different levels almost had collided in 1954, when the impending communist victory over the French at Dienbienphu called into question both U.S. reliability as an ally and its willingness to resist communism. President Eisenhower had concluded at the time that victory was not troublesome enough to European allies to risk American prestige, and he had refused to countenance direct intervention although he continued the flow of material aid.[86]

Had the Grand Design worked, Kennedy might have been in a better position to justify an expanded political role in resolving the troubles in Vietnam against the pressure of the U.S. military bureaucracy to support the war. Instead, in 1963 the administration suddenly faced a radically restricted arena for action. As in 1954, it could not count on Allied support. Yet technical military assistance alone was not enough either to defeat the Vietminh or to push South Vietnam leaders toward "liberal" reforms.

Some American elites—such as Averell Harriman, John Kenneth Galbraith, and George Ball—urged Kennedy to pursue a negotiated settlement with North Vietnam that would have saved face, fit into new paradigms of "peaceful development," and prevented the United States from becoming distracted from real (that is, European) interests.[87] Kennedy equivocated, privately questioning the wisdom of commitment while publicly reaffirming the significance of Vietnam to the United States. In doing so, he did nothing other than what his predecessors had done on Vietnam, namely, react to problems as they arose and improvise responses to crises rather than plot out American strategy and define Vietnam's value to the United States. But in 1963 this equivocation unbearably blurred the lines between Vietnam in its cold war uses as a metonymic extension of American prestige and Vietnam in its uncertain role in a post–cold war order.

Had Kennedy lived, he might have been able to finess the disjuncture that seemed to be coming, for his political persona, as David Halberstam wrote, was one that jarred the nerves, taking Americans places that caused division and pain but framing that pain as the consequence of a great quest for purpose.[88] Kennedy telegraphed a social identity that was existentially mobile—infinitely sympathetic, yet committed to no one group or set of values, and capable, perhaps, of justifying radical switches of policy as quintessentially "American." But Kennedy never framed Vietnam as a political problem of identity. And then he died and his successor, Lyndon B. Johnson, at first was concerned with other things and then was inclined to rely on Kennedy advisers like Robert McNamara and Dean Rusk and McGeorge Bundy to define Vietnam for him. They, in turn, relied on policy scientists like Walt Rostow and Harvard Law School's John McNaughton and felt bureaucratic pressure from the Joint Chiefs of Staff, who had staked out an early policy position in favor of escalating the war. What got lost in the shuffle about what to do with Vietnam were the managerial questions of what Vietnam was, whose interests it served, and what those interests suggested about American cultural identity.[89]

In 1964 a new chapter rightly began, for Vietnam ceased being exclusively a useful place in which elites could pursue interests that had little to do with Vietnam per se. Elite influence hardly vanished. Indeed, with the Gulf of Tonkin Resolution that year, Congress gave Lyndon Johnson what presidents long had dreamed of having: broad, unquestioned power to manage foreign affairs. The irony is that, from 1964 elites found that, in using this power, their interests—particularly things connected with the management of international economics—increasingly could be elbowed aside by the interests of administrative agencies and their own policy advisers as well as by the more long-standing claims of Congress.[90]

This is not to say that the sixties' foreign policy advanced the fortunes of a new "merit class" or improved the legitimacy of Congress as articulator or manager of policy. *The failures of Vietnam corroded all claims to authority.* Instead, the American experience in Vietnam crystallizes the basic problem of state management in the United States. One can articulate a purpose, and one can pursue policy, but it is well nigh impossible to integrate one with the other, to align means with ends.

Despite the image of the establishment that contemporaneously gained academic and journalistic vogue, from 1964, Vietnam policy emerged from a loose figuration of power—a shifting system of rivalries, tensions, and alliances that consistently foiled any elite intention to control foreign policy in the interests of domestic stability. In part, that figuration derived from the structure of the government itself, in particular from the long-standing division between congressional parties (with their emphasis on negotiation and local interests) and presidential politics (with its pretensions to prioritize national issues). In part, though, that figuration also derived from attempts to sidestep those structural idiosyncrasies.[91]

Especially since the 1940s, policy-making elites tried to avoid explaining the necessity of structural change, in no small measure to avoid justifying themselves *as* elites in a presumably democratic society. Instead, they sought out policy advisers from the liminoid knowledge classes: creative lawyers and college professors trained to manage and organize information. For a while, elites profited from this arrangement for policy advisers kept public attention directed toward the "meaning" of America in an abstract sense: for what it presumably stood for rather than what the United States was in a historico-constitutional sense or was doing concretely in any contemporary situation abroad. By finessing the fact that the cold war represented a serious break in political patterns of governance, policy advisers allowed elites to be silent about that break and to act as if they were behaving in culturally authentic ways.

Over time, however, this ability to allow elites to avoid constitutional clashes with Congress created an illusion that the American political system did not have to change, that it could be made to operate effectively just as it was.[92] When the bureaucracy proved that it could stage a limitless, culturally sanctioned war against communism that hardly served elite economic or domestic status interests at all, Vietnam caught elites in a bind between rhetorical commitment to prestige and a socioeconomic interest in stability. Then the inherent tensions between elites and policy scientists became an additional structural difficulty, for what elites had not anticipated was the degree to which policy advisers would discover a status interest in this idea-creation process itself: that they could make careers out of describing *how* a policy could be accomplished, not whether it should be pursued. With Vietnam, these tensions produced a situation in which few elites dared to say that the war served no hard national interests and few advisers would admit that it could not be won. The alternative most chose—continued support of the war—eroded government and cultural authority while exacerbating the larger problem of politics: focusing on the pain and the costs of defying national limits.

For a brief time, Richard Nixon seemed set to enforce such limits. Elites and the public reluctantly swallowed Nixon because he promised to end the war and, more quietly, because he was determined to establish control over the bureaucracy. He repackaged Vietnam. Away from anticommunism or the existential dilemma of liberation and imperialism, he treated it as an irritating footnote to efforts to forge great power détente. Moreover, in domestic politics Nixon seemed to return to the limited, middleclass nationalism of the 1950s that preserved as ideal (if never practice) political management's basis in democratic representation. But ultimately when Nixon resigned, it was not because he kept the war going for five more agonizing years, and not because he could not control the bureaucracy, but because he too used the executive management system to aggrandize executive power.

Since Vietnam, first Watergate, then the Reagan Revolution and Iran-contra, and more recently Iraq-gate have become ways of talking about what is wrong with American government without challenging the larger structures of dominant class power. However, when these scandals are publicly aired, they tend to become so personalized—Nixon against the Constitution, for example—or so legalistic—Oliver North in the Court of Appeals—as to obscure that what is at issue is less the "excesses of the system" than excesses that exist because of the absence of any sustained, responsible system. Yet as the distance grows between the present and the constitutional battles of the 1930s, it becomes more difficult to explain what the central problems are, or to muster the political consensus necessary to publicly define and administer the pain of structural change.[93]

In fact, the larger problem for the post–Vietnam era may well be that American society cannot sustain the form of tragedy, although the term often is applied to Vietnam. The hallmark of tragedy is an act of assertion—the articulation of a specific great ambition—that triggers an inexorable, implacable fate. In tragedy, the hero's flaw has to lead to the hero's death; yet the significance of tragedy is not the death itself (in tragedy, nothing is pointless) but that the community derives knowledge about the consequences of tempting fate. As a mode of expression, tragedy reaffirms the limits, the bounded identity, of society, although containing enormous compassion for the human condition that must assert ambition and must fail. In the United States in the sixties there were no heroes among the elite, no one who really could articulate the meaning of Vietnam to a specific American community. And since the general public seems to hold a hazy view of the Constitution as an emblem of identity rather than as a monitor of behavior, and since it regularly expresses its disgust of all political authority, there seem fewer and fewer reasons to address the procedural problem amid ever greater pressures for quick fixes to "make the government work." Planning policy in secret or relying on de facto a-constitutional networks of influence seem to be our only options. But living with the consequences of the absence of a widely agreed-upon definition of a common political culture is the post–Vietnam story.

NOTES

1. Gordon S. Wood, *The Creation of the American Republic, 1776–1787* (Chapel Hill: Published for the Institute of Early American History and Culture at Williamsburg, Va., by the University of North Carolina Press, 1969).

2. The discussion here is informed by the recent works of Paul Kennedy, E. J. Hobsbawm, and Simon Schama. Each author (albeit in differing ways) raises these problems about articulating national identity in the context of international relations: how do national systems come to accept (or decline) power, and what cost does this choice extract from internal views about national identity? These go to the point that nation states exist in a world of other nation states, and that they establish external power relationships that are more or less separate from internal social hierarchies. Ambitions for geopolitical dominance are thus difficult to separate from concerns about rationales that are domestically stabilizing and culturally legitimate. See Paul M. Kennedy, *The Rise and Fall of the Great Powers: Economic Change and Military Conflict from 1500 to 2000* (New York: Random House, 1987); E. J. Hobsbawm, *The Age of Empire, 1875–1914* (New

York: Pantheon, 1987), chaps. 2–3, 6, and *Nations and Nationalism since 1780* (New York: Cambridge University Press, 1990); and Simon Schama, *The Embarrassment of Riches: An Interpretation of Dutch Culture in the Golden Age* (New York: Knopf, 1987). See also John Boli-Bennett, "Global Integration and the Universal Increase of State Dominance, 1910–1970," in *Studies of the Modern World System,* edited by Albert Bergesen (New York: Academic Press, 1980), 77–107, who argues that increases in the importance of transnational economic flows in the twentieth century have been accompanied by increases in the size and role of the state.

3. This is the point to which my Foucauldian subtitle–"A Genealogy of Power"–refers. Traditionally, diplomatic historians have seen Vietnam in the context of the cold war. The central controversy involves whether the cold war was something "essential" to American cultural character (imprinted by the origins of the political culture) or "imposed" on American society at some later date (as an outgrowth of industrial capitalism, for instance). By contrast to both, I am arguing that postwar foreign policy as a subject has no such secure boundaries.

Cold war foreign policy was produced as much in response to other intentions and changes—most specifically, an elite desire to create and control a stable management system for domestic policy—as it was an unreflexive cultural response or a calculated reaction to Soviet behavior. The Vietnam War, then, did not grow out of some simple worldview. It was a by-product of increasingly frazzled attempts to subjugate loose methods of governing into a more coherent and policy-sensitive (less legislative/party) structure. The merits or ethics of this may be argued elsewhere. My point here is that in the 1920s and 1930s there was a fairly self-conscious attempt to construct a unified system of state management by forging a political discourse commensurate with existing social conditions. The failure of this attempt unintentionally laid the groundwork for subsequent policy practices that resulted in the legitimation of 1960s foreign policy.

4. Frank Costigliola, *Awkward Dominion: American Political, Economic, and Cultural Relations with Europe, 1919–1933* (Ithaca, N.Y.: Cornell University Press, 1984); Melvyn Leffler, *Elusive Quest: American Pursuit of European Stability and French Security, 1919–1923* (Chapel Hill: University of North Carolina Press, 1979); Werner Link, *Die amerikanische Stabilisierungspolitik in Deutschland, 1921–1932* (Dusseldorf: Droste, 1970).

5. Ellis Hawley, *The Great War and the Search for a Modern Order* (New York: St. Martin's, 1979); Michael J. Hogan, *Informal Entente: The Private Structure of Cooperation in Anglo-*

American Diplomacy (Columbia: University of Missouri Press, 1977); Lawrence Gelfand, ed., *Herbert Hoover: The Great War and Its Aftermath* (Iowa City: University of Iowa Press, 1979); Marc Trachtenberg, *Reparations in World Politics: France and European Economic Diplomacy, 1916–23* (New York: Columbia University Press, 1980); Dan Silverman, *Reconstructing Europe after the Great War* (Cambridge: Harvard University Press, 1982); Stephen Skowronek, *Building a New American State: The Expansion of National Administrative Capacities, 1877–1920* (New York: Cambridge University Press, 1982); Robert Schulzinger, *The Making of the Diplomatic Mind: The Training, Outlook, and Style of U.S. Foreign Service Officers, 1908–31* (Middletown, Conn.: Wesleyan University Press, 1975); Martin Weil, *A Pretty Good Club: The Founding Fathers of the U.S. Foreign Service* (New York: Norton, 1978); David Burner, *The Politics of Provincialism: The Democratic Party in Transition, 1918–32* (1970; reprint, Westwood, Conn.: Greenwood Press, 1981); Charles W. Eagles, *Democracy Delayed: Congressional Reapportionment and Urban-Rural Conflict in the 1920s* (Athens: University of Georgia Press, 1990).

6. International historians have sketched out the repercussions of this. See Donald Cameron Watt, *Succeeding John Bull: America in Britain's Place, 1900–75* (Cambridge: Cambridge University Press, 1984); Brian J. C. McKercher, "Wealth, Power, and the New International Order: Britain and the American Challenge in the 1920s,"

Diplomatic History 12 (Fall 1988): 411–41, and McKercher, ed., *Anglo-American Relations in the 1920s: The Struggle for Supremacy* (London: Macmillan, 1991); and Roberta Allbert Dayer, *Bankers and Diplomats in China, 1917–25: The Anglo-American Relationship* (London: F. Cass, 1981).

7. Numerous works set FDR in the context of a long history of presidential efforts to develop a competent planning and management system. See Barry D. Karl, "Presidential Planning and Social Science Research: Mr. Hoover's Experts," *Perspectives in American History* 3 (1969): 347–409, and "Executive Reorganization and Presidential Power," *Supreme Court Review* (1977): 1–37; Otis L. Graham, Jr., *Toward a Planned Society: From FDR to Nixon* (New York: Oxford University Press, 1976); and John Milton Cooper, *The Warrior and the Priest: Woodrow Wilson and Theodore Roosevelt* (Cambridge: Belknap Press of Harvard University Press, 1983), last chapter, which argues that FDR represented a synthesis of Theodore Roosevelt and Woodrow Wilson, the two twentieth-century presidents who wrestled intellectually as well as practically with the relation between political culture and government management.

8. See the enormously suggestive argument in Pierre Clastres, *Society against the State: Essays in Political Anthropology*, translated by Robert Hurley (New York: Zone Books, 1987).

9. Alfred Haworth Jones, *Roosevelt's Image Brokers* (Port Washington, N.Y.: Kennikat Press, 1974); Betty Houchin Winfield, *FDR and the News Media* (Urbana: University of Illinois Press, 1990); Cornelis A. van Minnen, ed., *The Roosevelts: Nationalism, Democracy, and Internationalism* (Middleburg, Netherlands: Roosevelt Study Center, 1987); Edward Mortimer, *The World That FDR Built: Vision and Reality* (New York: Scribner, 1988); Halford Ross Ryan, *FDR's Rhetorical Presidency* (Westport, Conn.: Greenwood Press, 1988).

10. Barry D. Karl, *Executive Reorganization and Reform in the New Deal* (Chicago: University of Chicago Press, 1963); Richard Polenberg, *Reorganizing Roosevelt's Government: The Controversy over Executive Reorganization, 1936–1939* (Cambridge: Harvard University Press, 1966); A. J. Wann, *President as Chief Administrator: A Study of FDR* (Washington: Public Affairs Press, 1968); Marion Clawson, *New Deal Planning: The National Resources Planning Board* (Published for Resources for the Future by Johns Hopkins University Press, 1981); Peri Arnold, *Making the Managerial Presidency: Comprehensive Reorganization Planning, 1905–1980* (Princeton: Princeton University Press, 1986).

11. See generally Robert Dallek, *FDR and American Foreign Policy, 1932–45* (New York: Oxford University Press, 1979); David Keith Adams, *FDR, the New Deal, and Europe* (Keele: University of Keele, 1974); J. Garry Clifford, "Both Ends of the Telescope: New Perspectives on FDR and American Entry into World War II," *Diplomatic History* 13 (Spring 1989): 213–30.

12. William T. R. Fox is credited with coining the term in *The Super-*

Powers (New York: Harcourt, Brace, 1944).

13. Robert Divine, *Second Chance: The Triumph of Inter-nationalism in America during World War II* (New York: Atheneum, 1967). More specifically, see Leo Pasvolsky and Harold G. Moulton, *World War Debt Settlements* (New York: Macmillan, 1926) and *Current Monetary Issues* (Minneapolis: University of Minnesota Press, 1933); Isaiah Bowman, *The New World: Problems in Political Geography* (Yonkers-on-Hudson: World Book, 1928); Geoffrey Martin, *The Life and Thought of Isaiah Bowman* (Hamden, Conn.: Archon Books, 1980); Jacob Viner, *International Trade and Economic Development* (Glencoe, Ill.: Free Press, 1952); James T. Shotwell, *War as an Instrument of National Policy* (New York: Harcourt, Brace, 1929) and *On the Rim of the Abyss* (New York: Macmillan, 1936); Harold Josephson, *James T. Shotwell and the Rise of Internationalism in America* (Rutherford, N.J.: Fairleigh Dickinson University Press, 1974); Quincy Wright, *A Study of War*, 2d ed. (Chicago: University of Chicago Press, 1964), and Wright, ed., *Public Opinion and World Politics* (1933; reprint, New York: Arno, 1972); and Alfred E. Zimmern, ed., *Neutrality and Collective Security* (Chicago: University of Chicago Press, 1936).

14. Dean G. Acheson, "Bretton Woods: A Monetary Basis for Trade," Address before the Economic Club of New York (16 April 1945), in *Department of State Bulletin* 12 (22 April 1945): 738. See also Russell Leffingwell, "Managing Our Economy," *Yale Review* 34 (Summer 1945): 616. On

Bretton Woods, see Alfred Eckes, *A Search for Solvency: Bretton Woods and the International Monetary System, 1941–1971* (Austin: University of Texas Press, 1975), and Fred L. Block, *Origins of International Economic Disorder: A Study of U.S. International Monetary Policy from World War II to the Present* (Berkeley and Los Angeles: University of California Press, 1977).

15. Bernard Brodie, *Sea Power in the Machine Age* (Princeton, N.J.: Princeton University Press, 1943) and Brodie, ed., *The Absolute Weapon: Atomic Power and World Order* (1946; reprint, Freeport, N.Y.: Books for Libraries, 1972); Frederick S. Dunn, *War and the Minds of Men* (New York: Harper, 1950); Edward Mead Earle, ed., *Makers of Modern Strategy: Military Thought from Machiavelli to Hitler* (Princeton: Princeton University Press, 1943); William T. R. Fox, *Anglo-American Relations in the Post-War World* (New Haven: Yale University Press, 1943) and *The Super-Powers*; George A. Lincoln and Norman J. Padelford, *Dynamics of International Politics* (New York: Macmillan, 1962); Hans J. Morgenthau, ed., *Peace, Security, and the United Nations* (1946; reprint, Freeport, N.Y.: Books for Libraries, 1973); Hans J. Morgenthau, *Politics Among Nations: The Struggle for Power and Peace* (New York: Knopf, 1948) and *In Defense of the National Interest* (New York: Knopf, 1951); Harold Sprout and Margaret Sprout, *Foundations of National Power* (Princeton: Princeton University Press, 1945); Nicholas J. Spykman, *America's Strategy in World Politics: U.S. and the Bal-*

ance of Power (1942; reprint, Hamden, Conn.: Archon Books, 1970) and *The Geography of the Peace*, edited by Helen Nicholl (1944; reprint, Hamden, Conn.: Archon Books, 1969); Arnold Wolfers and Lawrence Martin, eds., *The Anglo-American Tradition in Foreign Affairs* (New Haven: Yale University Press, 1956). For strategic thinking from the 1950s, see Barry Steiner, *Bernard Brodie and the Foundations of American Nuclear Strategy* (Lawrence: University Press of Kansas, 1991), and Gregg Herken, *Counsels of War* (New York: Oxford University Press, 1987).

16. Frederick S. Dunn, Introduction to *The Geography of the Peace*, by Nicholas J. Spykman (New York: Harcourt, Brace, 1944), ix–x.

17. Arnold Wolfers, "Actors in International Politics," in *Theoretical Aspects of International Relations*, edited by William T. R. Fox (South Bend, Ind.: University of Notre Dame Press, 1959), 99–100. This approach acknowledges the influence of "psychological thinkers" like Harold Lasswell. See, for example, Lasswell, *Power and Personality* (New York: Norton, 1976).

18. National identity adherents offered a surrogate for historical analysis by using modernist forms of expression—juxtaposition, aphorism, ellipsis, metaphor, and above all the poetic concept of the self-reflexive image through which authors jolt audiences back to "real" experiences—to create aesthetic connections between the different value systems and packaged these within a cultural-practical orientation. See Herman Broch, *Hugo von Hofmannstall and His Time: The Euro-pean Imagination, 1860–1920*, translated by M. P. Steinberg (Chicago: University of Chicago Press, 1984); Matei Calinescu, *Faces of Modernity: Avant-garde, Decadence, Kitsch* (Bloomington: Indiana University Press, 1977); Sanford Schwartz, *The Matrix of Modernism: Pound, Eliot, and Early Twentieth-Century Thought* (Princeton: Princeton University Press, 1985); Paul Ricoeur, *The Rule of Metaphor: Multi-Disciplinary Studies of the Creation of Meaning in Language*, translated by Robert Czerny (Toronto: University of Toronto Press, 1977); Stephen Spender, *The Struggle of the Modern* (Berkeley: University of California Press, 1963); and Raymond Williams: Against the New Conformists, *The Politics of Modernism* (London: Verso, 1989).

19. The general differences within the contemporary policy debates were used to interesting effect by two people who had little philosophically in common. See Walter Lippmann, *U.S. Foreign Policy: Shield of the Republic* (Boston: Little, Brown, 1943), *U.S. War Aims* (Boston: Little, Brown, 1944), and *The Cold War* (New York: Harper and Row, 1972); and Charles A. Beard, *The Republic: Conversations on Fundamentals* (1943; reprint, Westport, Conn.: Greenwood Press, 1980), which originally ran as a series of articles in *Life* magazine. Both writers made a concerted effort to bring "realism" into the American political heritage, Lippmann to justify a more interventionist postwar role and Beard to condemn efforts to rewrite the United States as a conventional (read, European) great power.

20. Michael J. Hogan, *The Marshall Plan: America, Britain, and the Reconstruction of Western Europe, 1947–52* (New York: Cambridge University Press, 1987); Alan S. Milward, *The Reconstruction of Western Europe, 1945–51* (London: Methuen, 1984); Stanley Hoffman and Charles Maier, eds., *The Marshall Plan: A Retrospective* (Boulder, Colo.: Westview Press, 1984). William Burr, "Marshall Planners and the Politics of Empire," *Diplomatic History* 15 (Fall 1991): 495–522, offers examples of the ways that Europeans encouraged American involvement in order to disperse the responsibility for economic policies that postponed consumer relief. See also William C. Cromwell, "The Marshall Plan, Britain, and the Cold War," *Review of International Studies* 8 (October 1982): 237–45, and Allan Bullock, *Ernest Bevin: Foreign Secretary, 1945–51* (New York: Oxford University Press, 1983), esp. 409–19.

21. Presidential Committee on Foreign Aid (Harriman Committee), *European Recovery and Foreign Aid* (Washington, D.C.: GPO, 1947), 19–22; U.S. Congress, House Committee on Foreign Affairs, *Emergency Foreign Aid, Hearings*, 80th Cong., 1st sess. (Washington, D.C.: GPO, 1947), 3–10. The most famous expression of this argument is George F. Kennan, "The Sources of Soviet Conduct," *Foreign Affairs* 25 (July 1947): 566–82, esp. 581–82.

22. Walter Isaacson and Evan Thomas, *The Wise Men: Six Friends and the World They Made* (London: Faber and Faber, 1986), 476; Dean G. Acheson, *Present at the Creation: My Years in the State Department* (London: Hamilton, 1970).

23. Daniel Yergin, *Shattered Peace: The Origins of the Cold War and the National Security State* (Boston: Houghton Mifflin, 1977); John Prados, *Keepers of the Keys: History of the National Security Council from Truman to Bush* (New York: Morrow, 1991); Jeffery Dorwart, *Eberstadt and Forrestal: A National Security Partnership, 1909–1949* (College Station: Texas A & M University Press, 1991); Robert C. Perez, *The Will to Win: A Biography of Ferdinand Eberstadt* (New York: Greenwood, 1989); Townsend Hoopes, *Driven Patriot* (New York: Knopf, 1992); Demetrius Caraley, *The Politics of Military Unification: A Study of Conflict and the Policy Process* (New York: Columbia University Press, 1966). Compare the relatively swift passage of the National Security Act with Stephen K. Bailey, *Congress Makes a Law: The Story behind the Employment Act* [of 1946] (New York: Columbia University Press, 1950).

24. Melvyn Leffler, "The United States and the Strategic Dimensions of the Marshall Plan," *Diplomatic History* 12 (Summer 1988): 277–79, and, more generally, Leffler, *A Preponderance of Power: National Security, the Truman Administration, and the Cold War* (Palo Alto: Stanford University Press, 1992).

25. See Truman's threat to impound the supplemental appropriations that the military had sought outside of administration approval in Walter Millis, ed., *The Forrestal Diaries* (New York: Viking, 1951), 435–38. See also Nelson Rockefeller's testimony on behalf of

the Institute of Inter-American Affairs in U.S. Congress, House, *Hearings: Appropriations Committee: National War Agencies Appropriation Bill, 1944* (Washington, D.C.: GPO, 1945), 250, and discussion of the "China Lobby" in Gary May, *China Scapegoat: The Diplomatic Ordeal of John Carter Vincent* (Washington, D.C.: New Republic Books, 1979).

26. For a contemporary analysis that shrewdly recognized that the political management of society was antithetical to corporate or other elite control, see Daniel Bell, "America's Un-Marxist Revolution: Mr. Truman Embarks on a Politically Managed Economy," *Commentary* (March 1949): 207–12, and "Has America a Ruling Class?," Review of *Strategy for Liberals: the Politics of the Mixed Economy*, by Irwin Ross, in *Commentary* (December 1949): 603–7.

27. Dean G. Acheson, "Speech to the Delta Council, Cleveland, Mississippi," *Department of State Bulletin* 16 (18 May 1947): 993–94; Ambassador Jefferson Caffery to Secretary of State George C. Marshall, 2 October 1948, in *Foreign Relations of the United States* (hereafter cited as *FRUS*), *1948* (Washington, D.C.: GPO, 1974), 3:661, 857.

28. Adam Ulam, *The Rivals: America and Russia since World War II* (New York: Viking, 1971), 124–51; William C. Taubman, *Stalin's American Policy: From Entente to Detente to Cold War* (New York: Norton, 1982), 171–92.

29. Lynn Eden, "Capitalist Conflict and the State: The Making of U.S. Military Policy in 1948," in *Statemaking and Social Movements: Essays in History and Theory*, edited by Susan Harding and Charles Bright (Ann Arbor: University of Michigan Press, 1984), 235–42; Millis, *Forrestal Diaries*, 492–95, 498–99, 501–5, 508–11; Warner Schilling, "The Politics of National Defense: Fiscal 1950," in *Strategy, Politics, and Defense Budgets*, edited by Warner Schilling, Paul Y. Hammond, and Glenn H. Snyder (New York: Columbia University Press, 1962), 100–266; David Alan Rosenberg, ed., *The Atomic Bomb and War Planning: Concepts and Capabilities* (New York: Garland, 1989); Gregg Herken, *The Winning Weapon: The Atomic Bomb in the Cold War, 1945–1950* (New York: Oxford University Press, 1987).

30. Michael Schaller, *The American Occupation of Japan: Origins of the Cold War in Asia* (New York: Oxford University Press, 1985); William S. Borden, *Pacific Alliance: U.S. Foreign Economic Policy and Japanese Trade Recovery, 1945–55* (Madison: University of Wisconsin Press, 1984); Robert M. Blum, *Drawing the Line: Origins of American Containment Policy in East Asia* (New York: Norton, 1982).

31. Borden, *Pacific Alliance*, 8.

32. Roger Dingman, "The U.S. Navy and the Cold War: The Japan Case," *New Aspects of Naval History*, edited by Craig L. Symonds (Annapolis, Md.: Naval Institute Press, 1981), 299; Dingman, "Strategic Planning and the Policy Process: America Plans for War in East Asia, 1945–50," *Naval War College Review* 32 (November–December 1979): 4–21.

33. Harriman Committee, *European*

Recovery and Foreign Aid, 133–35; Lew Douglas to Dean Acheson, 27 June 1947, in *FRUS, 1947*, 3:32; Andrew Rotter, "Triangular Route: U.S., Great Britain, and Southeast Asia, 1945–50," *International History Review* 6 (August 1984): 404–23.

34. PPS meetings, 6, 13 June 1949, Department of State, PPS Records, Record Group (RG) 59, B.27, B.32, National Archives, Washington, D.C. See also George Kennan, "U.S. Policy toward Southeast Asia," PPS Records, RG 51, in *The State Department Policy Planning Staff Papers, 1947–1949*, vol. 3, edited by Anna K. Nelson (New York: Garland, 1983), 38–52, and Minutes of the 148th Meeting of PPS, 11 October 1949, in *FRUS, 1949*, 1:401–2. For general Foreign Service views, see May, *China Scapegoat*; Marilyn Blatt Young, *The Vietnam Wars, 1945–90* (New York: Harper Collins, 1991), chap. 1; and Robert McMahon, *Colonialism and Cold War: The United States and the Struggle for Indonesian Independence, 1945–49* (Ithaca: Cornell University Press, 1981).

35. See McCloy's comments at PPS meeting, 13 June 1949, Department of State, PPS Records, RG 59, B.27; Acheson's comments in 148th Meeting of PPS, ibid., p. 402. See also Acheson, "Agreed Tripartite Minutes on Southeast Asia," 22 May 1950, in *FRUS, 1950*, 3:1011–84.

36. Minutes of 148th Meeting of PPS, 11 October 1949, in *FRUS, 1949*, 1:401–2. See also Kennan to Acheson, 19 February 1950, in *FRUS, 1950*, 1:160–67.

37. Kennan to Acheson, 6 January 1950, in *FRUS, 1950*, 1:132.

38. NSC-68, 14 April 1950, in *FRUS, 1950*, 1:261.

39. Ibid., 1:237–92 (quotations, pp. 238, 240, 263–64). Good overviews are available in John Lewis Gaddis, *Strategies of Containment: A Critical Appraisal of Postwar American National Security Policy* (New York: Oxford University Press, 1982), 89–126; Paul Y. Hammond, "NSC-68: Prologue to Rearmament," in Schilling, Hammond, and Snyder, *Strategy, Politics, and Defense Budgets*, 267–378; and Samuel F. Wells, Jr., "Sounding the Tocsin: NSC-68 and the Soviet Threat," *International Security* 4 (Fall 1979): 116–38.

40. Quoted from John W. Auchincloss memorandum, 9 February 1950, in *FRUS, 1950*, 4:591.

41. Deborah Welch Larson, in *Origins of Containment: A Psychological Explanation* (Princeton: Princeton University Press, 1985), does a nice reading of the psychological influences on specific cold warriors but treats each as a separate entity rather than as a member of a specific social class.

42. See Richard Sklar, "Postimperialism: A Class Analysis of Multinational Corporate Expansion," in *Postimperialism: International Capitalism and Development in the Late Twentieth Century*, edited by David G. Becker (Boulder, Colo.: L. Rienner, 1987), 19–40; Priscilla M. Roberts, "The American 'Eastern Establishment' and Foreign Affairs: A Challenge for Historians," SHAFR *Newsletter* 14 (December 1983): 9–27, 15 (March 1984): 8–18; E. Digby Baltzell, *The Protestant Establishment: Aristocracy and Caste in America* (1964; reprint,

New Haven: Yale University Press, 1987); Kai Bird, *The Chairman* (New York: Simon and Schuster, 1992); and Douglas Brinkley, *Dean Acheson: Cold War Years, 1953–1971* (New Haven: Yale University Press, 1992).

43. Richard Rovere, *The American Establishment and Other Reports, Opinions, and Speculations* (1962; reprint, Westport, Conn.: Greenwood Press, 1980).

44. Acheson, *Present at the Creation*, 374.

45. Quentin Anderson, *The Imperial Self: An Essay in American Literary and Cultural History* (New York: Knopf, 1971).

46. In doing so, of course, they performed the not inconsiderable feat of reading Marx and the historical origins of communism out of "Western civilization." NSC-68's own description of the American institutions deemed vulnerable to creeping communist infiltration—liberal churches, universities, civil rights groups, labor— is chilling.

47. NSC-68, p. 290.

48. Ibid., p. 244.

49. Wolfgang Mommsen, *Max Weber and German Politics, 1890–1920*, translated by Michael S. Steinberg (Chicago: University of Chicago Press, 1984); Carl Schmitt, *The Crisis of Parliamentary Democracy*, translated by Ellen Kennedy (Cambridge: MIT Press, 1985), and *Diktatur, von den Angangen des modernen Souveranitatsgedanken bis zum proletarischen Klassenkampf* (Munich: Duncker and Humblot, 1921).

50. The fallacy of this perspective was addressed by Schmitt's British contemporary, Michael Oakeshott, in *Experience and Its Modes* (Cambridge: Cambridge University Press, 1933), 98.

51. The descendant of this fight exists today in battles over the line-item veto.

52. Gaddis, *Strategies of Containment*, 93–94. See also Leon Keyserling [chair, CEA], memorandum [Annex to NSC 68/3], 8 December 1950, in *FRUS, 1950*, 1:430: "These programs . . . fall about half way between 'business as usual' and a really large-scale dedication of our enormous economic resources . . . even when defining this large-scale dedication as something far short of an all-out . . . mobilization for war purposes"; and Paul Nitze, "The Development of NSC-68," *International Security* 4 (Spring 1980): 169: "Keyserling and I discussed these matters frequently; though he wanted to spend the money on other programs, he was convinced that the country could afford $40 billion for defense if necessary."

53. Norbert Elias, *The Court Society*, translated by Edmund Jephcott (New York: Pantheon, 1983), limns the difference between economics and honor. See also Karl Polanyi, *The Great Transformation* (Boston: Beacon, 1944). On Keynes and his American interpreters, see Hyman Minsky, *Stabilizing an Unstable Economy* (New Haven: Yale University Press, 1986), 102.

54. See Acheson, *Present at the Creation*, 528. A State Department Intelligence estimate (25 June 1950, in *FRUS, 1950*, 7:154) notes that Soviet success in Korea would cause "significant damage to US prestige in Western Europe. The capacity of a small Soviet satellite to engage in a military adven-

ture challenging, as many Europeans will see it, the might and will of the US, can only lead to serious questioning of that might and that will." For excellent overviews of the Korean War, see Bruce Cumings, *The Origins of the Korean War* (Princeton: Princeton University Press, 1981) and *Korea: The Unknown War* (New York: Pantheon, 1988).

55. James I. Matray, "Truman's Plan for Victory: National Self-Determination and the Thirty-eighth Parallel Decision in Korea," *Journal of American History* 66 (September 1979): 314–33.

56. The quotations are from John Foster Dulles, "A Policy of Boldness," *Life*, 19 May 1952, 146–60.

57. See, for example, John Lewis Gaddis, *The Long Peace: Inquiries into the History of the Cold War* (New York: Oxford University Press, 1987).

58. Jean Baudrillard, *The Mirror of Production*, translated by Mark Poster (St. Louis, Mo.: Telos Press, 1973), and *For a Critique of the Political Economy of the Sign*, translated by Charles Levin (St. Louis, Mo.: Telos Press, 1981). This is not to say that the Soviet Union never presented clear threats or that American elites were gullible about all uses of the rhetoric.

59. In a speech at a conference on regional planning, FDR noted first the public and business interest in Russia's Five-Year Plans and Mussolini's "system." However, he said, American planning had to "start at the bottom," not only because it was democratic but also because it conformed to ideals of "science," collecting data and experimenting with projects that were left

flexible precisely because the force and reputation of the government was not behind them. Franklin D. Roosevelt, "Address at the University of Virginia on the Excessive Costs and Taxes in Local Government," Charlottesville, Va., 6 July 1931, in *Public Papers and Addresses of Franklin D. Roosevelt, 1928–32: The Genesis of the New Deal*, edited by Samuel Rosenman (New York: Russell and Russell, 1938), 1:299–301.

60. For examples of the difficulty presidents had in guiding state decisions, see Walter McDougall, . . . *the Heavens and the Earth: A Political History of the Space Age* (New York: Basic Books, 1985); Edmund Beard, *Developing the ICBM: A Study in Bureaucratic Politics* (New York: Columbia University Press, 1976); and Warner Schilling, "The H-Bomb Decision: How to Decide without Actually Choosing," *Political Science Quarterly* 76 (1961): 24–46.

61. Glenn H. Snyder, "The 'New Look' of 1953," in Schilling, Hammond, and Snyder, *Strategy, Politics, and Defense Budgets*, 379–524; Robert Divine, *Eisenhower and the Cold War* (New York: Oxford University Press, 1981); Burton J. Kaufman, *Trade and Aid: Eisenhower's Foreign Economic Policy* (Baltimore: Johns Hopkins University Press, 1982); Douglas Kinnard, *President Eisenhower and Strategy Management: A Study in Defense Politics* (Lexington: University Press of Kentucky, 1977); Charles C. Alexander, *Holding the Line: The Eisenhower Era, 1952–1961* (Bloomington: Indiana University Press, 1975); Robert Griffith, "Dwight

D. Eisenhower and the Corporate Commonwealth," *American Historical Review* 87 (1982): 87–122.

62. Alfred Grosser, *The Western Alliance: European-American Relations since 1945* (New York: Vintage, 1982), traces the experience with the development of the European Economic Community (EEC). For a contemporary view of implications, see George Ball, "The EEC," in *European Common Market: New Frontier for American Business*, edited by Elizabeth Marting (New York: American Management Association, 1958), 46–49.

63. Raymond J. Saulnier, *Constructive Years: The U.S. Economy under Eisenhower* (Lanham, Md.: University Press of America, 1991).

64. As Elaine May writes, this persona reflected Eisenhower's concern to reassert "traditional" gender, racial, and class roles that had been rendered unstable by the displacements of World War II. See "Cold War–Warm Hearth: Politics and the Family in Post-War America," in *The Rise and Fall of the New Deal Order, 1930–1980*, edited by Steve Fraser and Gary Gerstle (Princeton: Princeton University Press, 1989), 153–81.

65. Richard Melanson, *Revolutionary Eisenhower: American Foreign Policy in the 1950s* (Urbana: University of Illinois Press, 1987), and Richard Immerman, *The CIA in Guatemala: The Foreign Policy of Intervention* (Austin: University of Texas Press, 1982), portray Eisenhower's willingness to subvert liberal ideals for national security purposes.

66. This trait is treated positively in Fred I. Greenstein, *The Hidden-Hand Presidency: Eisenhower as Leader* (New York: Basic Books, 1982), and McDougall, . . . *the Heavens and the Earth*, and somewhat less appreciatively in James R. Killian, *Sputniks, Scientists, and Eisenhower: A Memoir of the First Special Assistant to the President for Science and Technology* (Cambridge: MIT Press, 1977).

67. Nelson Rockefeller, *The Future of Federalism* (Cambridge: Harvard University Press, 1962); John F. Kennedy, *A Strategy for Peace*, edited by Allan Nevins (New York: Harper, 1960).

68. Material on the Special Studies Project is located in the Rockefeller Brothers Fund, RG V4, Rockefeller Archives Center (RAC), Tarrytown, N.Y. Rockefeller also tapped veterans of Hoover and FDR-era planning battles, like William Yandell Elliott and Adolph Berle, but the bulk of the staff and advisers came from a new generation.

69. See, for example, Max Millikan and Walt Rostow, *A Proposal: Key to an Effective Foreign Policy* (New York: Harper, 1957). Henry Kissinger's career exemplifies this path: from Harvard's Department of Political Science to contract work for the NSC and Pentagon to staff directorship of Rockefeller's Special Studies Project, back to Harvard, more contract government work, and in 1969 to the NSC. There are more books on the funding institutions than on policy scientists as a social class, but see James A. Smith, *The Idea Brokers: Think Tanks and the Rise of the New Policy Elite* (New York: Free Press, 1991); Peter deLeon, *Advice and Consent: The Development*

of the Policy Sciences (New York: Russell Sage Foundation, 1988); Ellen Condliffe Lagemann, *The Politics of Knowledge: The Carnegie Corporation, Philanthropy, and Public Policy* (Middletown, Conn.: Wesleyan University Press, 1989); and Gene M. Lyons, *The Uneasy Partnership: Social Science and the Federal Government in the Twentieth Century* (New York: Russell Sage Foundation, 1969).

70. Victor Turner, *The Ritual Process: Structure and Anti-Structure* (Ithaca: Cornell University Press, 1969) and *Dramas, Fields, and Metaphors: Symbolic Action in Human Society* (Ithaca, N.Y.: Cornell University Press, 1974), 231–71; Turner, "Variations on a Theme of Liminality," in *Secular Ritual*, edited by Sally F. Moore and Barbara G. Meyerhoff (Amsterdam: Assen, 1977), 37; Turner, "Liminal to Liminoid in Play, Flow, and Ritual: An Essay in Comparative Symbology," *Rice University Studies* 60 (Summer 1974): 53–92. Turner coined the term *liminoid* to distinguish modern idea producers from elites in the traditional-society sense of the word, i.e., as people who both articulated the connections between traditions and current experiences and defended traditions against encroachment from outside. By contrast, liminoids assist in the transformation or discarding of traditions.

71. For example, see the argument in Stacy May, "Strategy in the International Field," 16 November 1956: "Growth enable(s) us to bring time on our side for [the real way to oppose Communism was to] get more buying power to other people in the world in a way that would maintain their self-respect and encourage self-initiative." Rockefeller Brothers Fund, Special Studies Project, RG V4C, folder 208, box 19, RAC.

72. There was muted but real dismay about the quality of the policy scientists' work, in particular, about what they did *not say* in their recommendations about how policies might work. See, for example, proposals that pushed a "fast track" economy but did not consider the political implications of a tax hike or persistent budget deficits to accomplish expanded defense and social programs. There is a dry note from Dean Rusk (then president of the Rockefeller Foundation) to Rockefeller that nudges him to reconsider supporting policies that required curtailing consumption and to promote sacrifice. "I am not sure, from a public opinion point of view," Rusk wrote, "that any institution . . . which bears the name Rockefeller can warn the country about consumption habits" (19 December 1957), RG V4A, folder 13, box 1, RAC.

73. Rostow, "Notes on the Role of Leadership," [n.d.], V4A, folder 17, box 2, RAC, pp. 3–5.

74. Ibid., pp. 6–9.

75. Ibid., p. 9.

76. Rostow subtly insulted Rockefeller in a memorandum on strategy to the Kennedy campaign (2 January 1960). Scholars and "responsible journalists," he asserted, had "wait[ed] eagerly for Rockefeller to get the mush out of his mouth . . . which he never did." Quoted from McDougall, . . . *the Heavens and the Earth*, 219.

77. Willy Brandt, *People and Poli-*

tics: *The Years 1960–1975*, translated by J. Maxwell Brownjohn (Boston: Little, Brown, 1978), 13–41; David Nunnerley, *President Kennedy and Britain* (New York: St. Martin's, 1972); Charles Bohlen, *Witness to History, 1929–1969* (New York: Norton, 1973); Michael Beschloss, *Crisis Years: Kennedy and Khrushchev, 1960–63* (New York: Edward Burlingame, 1991); Richard D. Mahoney, *JFK: Ordeal in Africa* (New York: Oxford University Press, 1983).

78. "Commencement Address at Yale University," 11 June 1962, in *Public Papers of the Presidents of the United States: John F. Kennedy, 1962* (Washington, D.C.: GPO, 1963), 470–75.

79. Ibid., 473–74.

80. See Joseph Kraft, *The Grand Design: From Common Market to Atlantic Partisanship* (New York: Harper, 1962), and Denise Artaud, "Le Grand Dessin de J. F. Kennedy: Proposition Mythique ou Occasion Manquée?," *Revue d'Histoire Moderne et Contemporaine* 29 (1982): 235–66; Frank Costigliola, "The Failed Design: Kennedy, de Gaulle, and the Struggle for Europe," *Diplomatic History* 8 (Summer 1984): 227–51; Raymond Aron and Alfred Grosser, "A European Perspective," in *Cuba and the U.S.*, edited by John Plank (Washington, D.C.: Brookings, 1967), 141–57; Grosser, *Western Alliance*, chaps. 7–8; Richard J. Barnet, *The Alliance—America, Europe, Japan: Makers of the Postwar World* (New York: Simon and Schuster, 1983); Andrew Schonfeld, ed., *International Economic Relations: The Western System in the 1960s and 1970s*

(Beverly Hills, Calif.: Sage, 1976); Thomas A. Wolf, *U.S. East-West Trade Policy: Economic Warfare versus Economic Welfare* (Lexington, Mass.: Lexington Books, 1973); Bruno Bandulet, *Adenauer zwischen West und Ost* (Munich: Weltforum, 1970); Catherine McArdle Kelleher, *Germany and the Politics of Nuclear Weapons* (New York: Columbia University Press, 1975); Harold van B. Cleveland, *The Atlantic Idea and Its European Rivals* (New York: McGraw-Hill, 1966); George Lichtheim, *Europe and America: The Future of the Atlantic Community* (London: Thames and Hudson, 1963).

81. Dean G. Acheson, "The Practice of Partnership," *Foreign Affairs* 41 (January 1963): 247–60 (quotation, p. 251).

82. Ibid., 249, 257.

83. Ibid., 252–53.

84. Notwithstanding the many fine monographs that trace the roots of the Vietnam War to the 1940s. See George Herring, *America's Longest War: The US and Vietnam, 1950–75*, 2d rev. ed. (Philadelphia: Temple University Press, 1986); Young, *The Vietnam Wars*; and Richard Immerman, "Prologue: Perceptions by the U.S. of Its Interests in Indochina," in *Dien Bien Phu and the Crisis of Franco-American Relations, 1954–1955*, edited by Lawrence S. Kaplan, Denise Artaud, and Mark R. Rubin (Wilmington, Del.: SR Books, 1990), 1–26.

85. Anthropologists who discuss the nature of elites include Elias, *The Court Society*, and Marshall Sahlins, *Islands of History* (Chicago: University of Chicago Press, 1985).

86. Melanie Billings-Yun, *Decision Against War: Eisenhower and Dien Bien Phu, 1954* (New York: Columbia University Press, 1988); George Herring and Richard Immerman, "Eisenhower, Dulles, and Dienbienphu: 'The Day We Didn't Go to War' Revisited," *Journal of American History* 71 (September 1984): 343–63.

87. For example, see George Ball, *The Past Has Another Pattern: Memoirs* (New York: Norton, 1982), and David L. DiLeo, *George Ball, Vietnam, and the Rethinking of Containment* (Chapel Hill: University of North Carolina Press, 1991).

88. David Halberstam, *The Best and the Brightest* (New York: Random House, 1969), 369. Norman Mailer had captured this quality precisely in his coverage of the 1960 Democratic convention. "For all his good, sound, conventional liberal record," Mailer sighed, "[Kennedy] has a patina of that other life, the second American life, the long electric night with the fires of neon leading down the highway to the murmur of jazz." Norman Mailer, *An American Dream* (New York: Dial, 1965), 7. See also Mailer, "Superman Goes to the Supermart," *Esquire*, November 1960, 119–27.

89. Deborah Shapley, *Promise and Power: The Life and Times of Robert McNamara* (Boston: Little, Brown, 1992); Leslie Gelb and Richard K. Betts, *The Irony of Vietnam: The System Worked* (Washington, D.C.: Brookings, 1979); Herbert Schandler, *The Unmaking of a President: Lyndon Johnson and Vietnam* (Princeton: Princeton University Press, 1977).

90. Burton I. Kaufman, "Foreign Aid and the Balance of Payments Problem: Vietnam and Johnson's Foreign Economic Policy," in *The Johnson Years: Volume Two*, edited by Robert Divine (Lawrence: University Press of Kansas, 1987), 2:79–109; Donald F. Kettl, "The Economic Education of Lyndon B. Johnson: Guns, Butter, and Taxes," in ibid., 2:54–78; James Hawley, "Interests, State Foreign Economic Policy, and the World System: The Case of US Capital Control Programs, 1961–74," in *Foreign Policy and the Modern World System*, edited by P. McGowan and C. Kegley (Sage Yearbook of Foreign Policy Studies; Beverly Hills, Calif.: Sage, 1983), 29–33.

91. This relative autonomy of the state in relation to economics leads to something quite different from corporate liberalism. See generally Ralph Miliband, *The State in Capitalist Society* (New York: Basic Books, 1969); Nicos Poulantzas, "The Problem of the Capitalist State," in *Ideology in Social Science*, edited by Robin Blackburn (New York: Vintage, 1973), 238–53; Fred Block, "The Ruling Class Does Not Rule: Notes on the Marxist Theory of the State, *Socialist Revolution* 33 (May–June 1977): 6–28; Theda Skocpol, "Political Response to Capitalist Crisis: Neo-Marxist Theories of the State and the Case of the New Deal," *Politics and Society* 10 (1980): 155–201; and Theda Skocpol, Peter B. Evans, and Dietrich Rueschemeyer, eds., *Bringing the State Back In* (Cambridge: Cambridge University Press, 1985).

92. By establishing themselves as humble translators, not creators, of

cultural identity, and by arguing that, with effective compromises, that identity did not have to change, they neither resisted nor completely accepted presidential authority. Instead, they engaged in the "challenge and riposte" process described by Bourdieu, in which social subgroups try to shape intrusive forms by recasting them into terms and conditions to suit themselves, thus giving themselves a measure of mastery over an unstable world. In this case, by asserting cultural continuity, members of the knowledge classes also asserted an identity for themselves, albeit not as a dominated fraction of the dominant class, the functionaries in someone else's system, but as in-house guardians and articulators of a national self. Pierre Bourdieu, *Outline of a Theory of Practice*, translated by Richard Nice (New York: Cambridge University Press, 1977), 12, and *Distinctions: A Social Critique of the Judgement of Taste*, translated by Richard Nice (Cambridge: Harvard University Press, 1984).

93. Sidney Blumenthal, "The Sorcerer's Apprentices," *New Yorker*, 19 July 1993, 29–31, neatly summarizes this in reference to the budget problem.

CHESTER J. PACH, JR.*

And That's the Way It Was

The Vietnam War on the Network Nightly News

"As I sat in my office last evening, waiting to speak," Lyndon B. Johnson told the National Association of Broadcasters on 1 April 1968, the day after he announced he would not seek another term as president, "I thought of the many times each week when television brings the [Vietnam] war into the American home." What Americans saw each night in their living room, Johnson believed, was a distorted picture of the war, one dominated by "dramatic" events, such as the spectacular but temporary enemy successes during the recent Tet Offensive. Johnson conceded that it was impossible to determine exactly how "those vivid scenes" had

*The author would like to thank David Farber, John Lewis Gaddis, Donald R. McCoy, Robert D. Schulzinger, Melvin Small, Sandra C. Taylor, and Patrick S. Washburn for comments on earlier versions of this article.

shaped popular attitudes. He also acknowledged that "historians must only guess at the effect that television would have had . . . during the Korean war, . . . when our forces were pushed back there to Pusan" or during World War II when the Germans counterattacked at the Battle of the Bulge. Still, Johnson suggested that it was no accident that previous administrations had weathered these military reverses, but his had suffered a debilitating loss of popular support during the Tet Offensive. The reason for the "very deep and very emotional divisions" in public opinion was that Vietnam was America's first televised war.[1]

Johnson was one of many who have criticized, albeit for different reasons, TV coverage of the Vietnam War. Like Johnson, some observers have faulted television for oversimplifying the complexities of Vietnam or for emphasizing spectacular, but horrifying scenes of combat that shocked viewers into opposing the war.[2] In contrast, other commentators have denounced TV journalists for all too easily accepting official pronouncements of progress, at least until Tet, or for making the war's brutality seem so stylized, trivialized, or routine that the result was acceptance or ennui rather than revulsion.[3] Many scholars have argued that television news came of age during Vietnam, although one influential critic has insisted that fundamental weaknesses in American journalism produced a distorted assessment of the Tet Offensive as an American failure.[4] The most extreme critics blame television for reporting so ignorant, biased, or deceptive that it turned the victory American soldiers had won on the battlefields of Vietnam into defeat by producing irresistible political pressures for withdrawal.[5]

Television, however, did better at covering the war than many of these critics allow. To be sure, television's view of the war was limited, usually to what the camera could illustrate with vivid images. Too many film reports on the network newscasts dealt with American military operations, and too often they concentrated on immediate events—a firefight or an airstrike—with little, if any, analysis of how those incidents fit into larger patterns of the war. Yet television also showed the war as it was—a confused, fragmented, and questionable endeavor. Brief reports, usually no more than three minutes long, of isolated, disconnected military engagements, broadcast night after night, week after week, magnified the confusing features of a war that, at best, was hard to fathom—one usually without fronts, clearly identifiable enemies, reliable progress toward victory, or solid connections to American security. Because of the nature of the medium rather than any conscious effort, television nightly news exposed the irrationalities of a war that lacked coherent strategy or clear purpose.

When Johnson decided in 1965 to send American combat troops to Vietnam, TV journalists faced a unique challenge. Vietnam was television's first war. The three major networks rapidly enlarged their operations in Vietnam and by 1967 were each spending over $1 million annually on covering the war. The expansion of the nightly newscasts on CBS and NBC from fifteen to thirty minutes in September 1963—ABC did not follow suit until January 1967—provided more time for Vietnam news. The state of broadcast technology, however, made for substantial delays in airing stories from Vietnam. Not until February 1967 was it possible to relay film by satellite from Tokyo to New York, but then only at a cost of as much as $5,000 for a five-minute transmission. Thus all but the most urgent stories continued to be flown from Saigon to New York for broadcasting. Television viewers usually learned about the most recent developments in Vietnam from the anchor's summary of wire service copy. They commonly had to wait another two days to see film reports of those events.[6]

Unlike those who covered World War II or Korea, Vietnam correspondents did not have military censors review their reports, but they did face informal restrictions and pressures. Johnson was obsessed with the news—"television and radio were his constant companions," wrote one biographer—and he was determined to get reporters to promote his version of the national interest. "I'm the only president you've got, and . . . I need your help," he told members of the White House press corps. But if they did not cooperate, Johnson warned them, "I know how to play it both ways, too." Like Johnson, public information officers for the U.S. command in Vietnam tried to use informal pressures to shape reporting on Vietnam. They rejected censorship because they doubted its effectiveness and feared that it would anger correspondents. Instead, they outlined a series of guidelines that restricted identification of specific units or disclosure of the exact number of casualties in individual battles. They relied on daily news briefings, derisively known as the "Five O'Clock Follies," to influence the coverage of military operations. And they hoped that a vast array of incentives—transportation on military aircraft, interviews with commanders, lodging at bases—would secure or maintain a good working relationship with correspondents and thus favorable coverage of the war effort.[7]

The war that these reporters covered had a superficial, but ultimately specious logic. In South Vietnam, U.S. ground forces tried to win the war with a strategy of attrition. Their primary mission was to search out and destroy the main units of the Vietcong and the North Vietnamese army. The U.S. commander, General William C. Westmoreland, insisted that wearing down these conventional forces had to take precedence over rooting out guerrillas from populated areas. "It was, after all, the enemy's big units—not the guerrillas—that eventually did the South Vietnamese in," he later explained. Although he would have preferred an invasion of North Vietnam—an option that Johnson refused to sanction—Westmoreland still believed that enormous advantages in mobility and firepower would enable American forces to win the big-unit war. Helicopters would allow American troops to bring the North Vietnamese or Vietcong to battle even in remote jungles or mountains, artillery and airpower would inflict enormous losses on enemy manpower and equipment, and seemingly inexhaustible stores of supplies would let American forces maintain the offensive. The combination of aggressive ground operations and the bombing of North Vietnam and the Ho Chi Minh Trail would push the enemy's main units beyond the crossover point, a level of casualties and equipment losses so great that they could not be replaced. This was war American-style—a high-tech, conventional way of fighting that accorded with U.S. army experience, training, and doctrine that the surest way to win was to pound the enemy into submission. Westmoreland's strategy of attrition, according to Earle Wheeler, the chairman of the Joint Chiefs of Staff, provided "the best assurance of military victory in South Vietnam."[8]

Despite Wheeler's assertion, the strategy of attrition utterly failed. The big battles that Westmoreland sought occurred only infrequently. Instead, by 1967 Vietnam had become a small-unit war in which 96 percent of the engagements involved an enemy force no larger than a company (150 soldiers). These battles usually took place only when the enemy chose to fight. By seizing the initiative, the North Vietnamese and the Vietcong were able to control their casualties and frustrate the strategy of attrition. Even though the body count always added up to an American victory, the more telling figures were in intelligence reports that showed that despite American bombing, Hanoi had increased the flow of reinforcements into South Vietnam and mobilized sufficient resources to carry on the war indefinitely.[9] Equally dismal were the results of the "other war," the effort to win the hearts and minds of the South Vietnamese. While American combat units engaged in search-and-destroy missions, the Vietcong stepped up guerrilla attacks on population centers. When U.S. forces mounted counterinsurgency operations, their heavy reliance on artillery, napalm, herbicides, and defoliants produced countless civilian casualties, hordes of refugees, environmental devastation, and untold resentment against the South Vietnamese government and its profligate patron.[10]

Attrition proved to be, at best, an incoherent strategy, at worst, no strategy at all. A study ordered by the army's chief of staff found that there was "no unified effective pattern" to U.S. military operations. Troops in the field reached the same conclusion through hard experience. The lack of front lines or territorial objectives made them frustrated and cynical. "Without a front, flanks, or rear, we fought a formless war against a formless enemy who evaporated like the morning jungle mists, only to materialize in some unexpected place," recalled Philip Caputo, a marine officer who saw action in 1965–66. "It was a haphazard, episodic sort of combat." Attrition produced a war of disconnected military operations, whose surest result was a relentless demand for more American soldiers and supplies. From 184,000 at the end of 1965, U.S. troop strength rose to 385,000 a year later and to 486,000 at the close of 1967. "Boiled down to its essence," as one official army historian has observed, "American 'strategy' was simply to put more U.S. troops into South Vietnam and see what happened."[11]

On television, the most important story about Vietnam was the fighting that involved U.S. forces. About half of the film reports on network newscasts concerned U.S. troops on foot or in helicopters searching out the enemy, exchanging fire with snipers, calling in air strikes on base camps and supply depots, or clearing guerrillas from hostile villages. This "bang, bang" coverage crowded out stories about pacification or the inefficiencies of the South Vietnamese government, reports that would have provided viewers a deeper understanding of the complexities of counterinsurgency warfare. Yet TV journalists thought that they were giving their audience the news it wanted. "There are approximately 500,000 American men there," one reporter explained. "When this is multiplied by parents, friends and other relatives, there is no doubt what is of most importance to Americans." TV journalists also believed that they were using their visual medium to best advantage. "The sensationalism in Vietnam is obviously in the combat," remarked one network reporter. "Editors want combat footage. They will give it good play." If forced to choose, declared ABC news executive Nick Archer, "a good fire fight is going to get on over a good pacification story." Indeed, the executive producer of the "CBS Evening News" considered "a really great piece of war film . . . irresistible."[12]

Such footage, however, was rare. Despite its potential to "describe in excruciating, harrowing detail what war is all about," the television camera only infrequently did so.[13] Obtaining combat film was difficult; the television crew had to get out to the field, be lucky enough to accompany a unit that made contact with the enemy, and make sure that its equipment worked properly. "Then, if the battle is fierce," noted NBC's John Paxton, "the cameraman does not get the film because he usually has his face in the dirt."[14]

If the camera operator did film the action, though, it might not be aired. In Saigon and Washington, military authorities cautioned television journalists that networks that showed objectionable scenes of American casualties might have their reporters barred from combat zones. Because of these warnings or their own scruples, editors hardly ever allowed ghastly pictures of the dead or dying into American homes during the dinner hour. Indeed, just 3 percent of news reports from Vietnam showed heavy fighting.[15] Those who remember graphic scenes of death and suffering simply recall a war that television did not show.

Instead, television provided only suggestive glimpses of the war. Typical was a report by Morley Safer on 17 November 1965 from the attack troop ship *Paul Revere*, which was carrying marines to beaches south of Danang to begin a search-and-destroy mission. Safer's film captured the anticipation of combat, but none of the fighting.[16] Network correspondents covered the Battle of the Ia Drang Valley, the first engagement between North Vietnamese regulars and U.S. soldiers in October–November 1965, mainly from rear areas. Viewers who watched ABC, for example, heard correspondent Ray Maloney describe the "very hard" fighting from the American base at Pleiku and listened to Lieutenant Colonel Hal Moore recount the action. But the only combat footage showed strikes against North Vietnamese positions by B-52s, which for the first time flew missions to support ground troops.[17] In a similar way, television provided only a flavor of other big American operations during 1966–67. During Operation Attleboro, a sweep through Tay Ninh province in November 1966 involving some 22,000 U.S. troops, ABC's Kenneth Gale and his crew filmed the defoliation of hedgerows with flamethrowers and the interrogation of a Vietcong prisoner. CBS reporter Ike Pappas opted for much lighter fare—the "seeming unreality" of performances by the First Infantry Division's band during pacification of a Vietcong village—while NBC's George Page took a familiar approach—an interview with General John Deane that summarized the accomplishments of the operation. When U.S. forces returned to the same area in February 1967 during Operation Junction City, some became the first Americans to make a combat jump in Vietnam, as Safer reported on the "CBS Evening News." His film showed

e soldiers parachuting from the plane, but not their landing, which, as
ifer mentioned, was "virtually unopposed." One of the great frustrations
[Vietnam for Americans in the field was the elusiveness of the enemy.
"Reporters," as Erik Barnouw has noted, "seldom saw 'the war' or 'the
enemy.'"[18]

Often television focused not on battles but on the Americans who
fought them. Human interest features reflected television's tendency to
entertain as well as inform. A personalized story, TV journalists believed,
appealed to their mass audience, perhaps because it often simplified—or
avoided—complex or controversial issues.[19] A staple of network newscasts
was the combat interview, either with a commander or a hero. NBC's
George Page, for example, reported in May 1967 from the Mekong Delta,
where he talked to soldiers in the Ninth Infantry Division whose bravery
had saved the lives of their comrades. Several days later, the "CBS Evening News" carried an interview that correspondent Mike Wallace had
conducted with Lieutenant Colonel Robert Schweitzer, who had been
wounded eight times and decorated on eleven occasions.[20] Roger Stau-
bach was no war hero, but he had been a college football star at Annapolis,
and so his routine duties at a naval supply depot merited a film report by
CBS's Ike Pappas in October 1966. Occasionally newsworthy were the
lives of ordinary soldiers away from battle, as when Safer interviewed a
group on rest and recreation traveling to Hong Kong to catch up, they
said, on sleeping, letter writing, and drinking "good homogenized milk."[21]
Stories about the air war frequently concentrated on the pilots rather than
the bombing, since correspondents could not fly on the B-52 missions
over North Vietnam. Typical was a report by CBS's Peter Kalischer in
November 1965 from Andersen Air Base on Guam, which showed the
preflight routines of the pilots and lauded each mission as a "minor mas-
terpiece" of planning and execution. Television viewers, then, often saw
the war from the perspective of the Americans in Vietnam who were
experiencing it.[22]

Interpreting the war news was difficult, and television reporters often
failed to provide analysis or commentary. The anchors of the nightly
newscasts—Walter Cronkite on CBS, Chet Huntley and David Brinkley on
NBC, and, successively, Peter Jennings, Bob Young, Frank Reynolds, and
Howard K. Smith on ABC—offered no interpretation in more than half of
the stories that they read. Their reticence was a result of their role in the
program, which was to read short news items or introduce correspondents' reports. Less than one-fifth of their stories exceeded seventy-five
words, which left little room for analytical comments. The canons of

objective journalism—accuracy, balance, fairness, impartiality—also encouraged anchors to limit interpretive remarks. So too did the importance of inspiring confidence and loyalty among viewers, who often chose which network newscast to watch on the basis of their reaction to the personal qualities of the anchor. Walter Cronkite did not earn his reputation as the most trusted man in America by making partisan, gratuitous, or controversial comments about the news, but by reporting it "the way it was."[23]

Network correspondents also did not supply much analysis in many of their stories about the war. Again, time limitations affected the content of their reports. With just twenty-two minutes each weekday night to present the news—commercials took up the rest of the half-hour program—television functioned as an electronic front page, covering little more than the day's most important occurrences, often in spare summaries. Correspondents' reports almost never ran more than three minutes and often considerably less. Television's preoccupation with the immediate—today's news—severely limited analytical reports intended to provide perspective. One of the infrequent attempts to do so, Morley Safer's wrap-up of the Battle of the Ia Drang Valley, failed to examine the effectiveness of search and destroy or the significance of new tactics of carrying troops to battle in helicopters. Instead, the only perspective came from the soldier in the field, as Safer interviewed members of a company of the Seventh Cavalry who had survived some of the deadliest combat with the North Vietnamese. Viewers of the nightly news, then, often got information about the Vietnam War without much analysis or interpretation.[24]

Yet television journalists did try to make sense of the war, frequently by comparing current military operations with previous ones. Measuring the size, scope, or cost of a military action was a convenient, albeit simplistic, way of assessing its importance. Network correspondents and anchors, for example, described the Battle of the Ia Drang Valley as the "biggest engagement yet," the "bloodiest, longest" battle since Korea, "classic infantry warfare," and "the biggest American victory yet in Vietnam."[25] Viewers learned that Operations Attleboro and Junction City were, successively, the largest of the war and that Operation Cedar Falls (January 1967) yielded the "biggest prize" so far, when U.S. troops captured the base camp of a Vietcong regiment.[26] Television journalists also imputed significance to military operations in Vietnam by comparing them with those in World War II. Reporting in November 1965 on marines preparing for an amphibious landing near Danang, Morley Safer thought that the scenes he witnessed resembled the Pacific war. CBS correspondent John Laurence suggested that the bloody, prolonged Battle of Hue in early

1968 looked like World War II action, a comparison endorsed by a marine battalion commander. On 4 July 1966 Dean Brelis closed his report from "the First Infantry Division, the Big Red 1 of North Africa, Omaha Beach, Normandy, Germany, and now the Cambodian border." Comparisons such as Brelis's, of course, associated intervention in Vietnam with a heroic and victorious tradition of American warfare.[27]

Television reporters also tried to understand current military events by speculating about their relationship with future developments in the war. Reasoning by extrapolation—projecting what happened today into next week or next month—was an easy, if risky, way of simplifying the complexities of Vietnam. Cronkite, for example, declared that the Battle of the Ia Drang Valley was a portent of "dramatic change" in the Vietnam War, while Dean Brelis considered it a harbinger of more big battles. Yet staggering losses encouraged the North Vietnamese to avoid major engagements after Ia Drang and utilize guerrilla tactics instead.[28] One year later, Cronkite predicted that a series of North Vietnamese and Vietcong military initiatives "could set the pattern of the war for months to come." But the anticipated major offensive did not occur. ABC's Bill Brannigan reported in February 1967 about the forced removal of villagers near Danang to a relocation center and speculated that such evacuations would become the preferred method of depriving the Vietcong of civilian support. Yet the American command began to modify its policy of mandatory relocation only two months later and abandoned it at the end of the year.[29] However logical or appealing to television journalists, extrapolation clearly was a dubious method of discerning the future in Vietnam.

Much of the information and many of the interpretive comments in television newscasts prior to the Tet Offensive suggested that the United States was winning the war. When TV journalists assessed the results of battles during 1965–67, they concluded that about two-thirds were American victories.[30] A key to this success, network correspondents frequently emphasized, was American firepower. In November 1965, for example, Ray Maloney informed viewers of the "ABC Evening News" that the Vietcong were defenseless against B-52 strikes and that airpower was "turning the tide in Vietnam." A year later, Bruce Morton covered the air attacks supporting Operation Attleboro and declared that firepower was a "principle" that had proved its worth. Reporting in January 1967 from the Iron Triangle northwest of Saigon during Operation Cedar Falls, NBC's George Page assured those who tuned into the "Huntley-Brinkley Report" that high-tech weaponry would destroy the region's elaborate tunnel system and so deprive the Vietcong of an important base area. The same night,

CBS's John Hart explained how airstrikes with napalm had silenced Vietcong snipers that had pinned down American troops. Another major advantage, according to television reporters, was the high quality of American troops. During the Ia Drang fighting, for example, Brelis interviewed Lieutenant Colonel Hal Moore, who asserted that "we have the best soldiers that the world has ever seen." From time to time military officials appeared in news reports to assure the public that American troops were achieving their goals, as when General John Deane told Page in November 1966 that the war was going "very well."[31]

Television journalists also frequently reported that the air war was producing favorable results. Interviews with pilots always generated assurances that the bombing of North Vietnam was effective. That was what CBS's Bruce Morton heard, for example, when he talked to fliers in February 1967. Despite their objections to political restrictions on targets, the pilots were still making sure that the air campaign achieved its goals, Morton concluded, largely because of their professionalism in carrying out their missions. During the first year of the air war, television newscasts carried several stories that lauded the sophistication or superiority of American aircraft. Typical was Chet Huntley's narration in September 1965 of a Defense Department film of the A-4 Skyhawk, a fighter that eventually made more bombing raids in Vietnam than any other navy plane. The A-4 had produced "spectacular" results, Huntley exclaimed, and "should have even better shooting in the days ahead" because of improving weather.[32]

John Hart's report on the "CBS Evening News" in February 1967 on a lesser-known part of the air war, aerial defoliation and crop destruction, was so one-sidedly favorable that it bordered on propaganda. Hart asserted that the herbicides that the air force sprayed on jungles and forests were no stronger than dandelion killer and caused no damage to the soil. Air Force Major Charlie Hubbs added that Operation Ranch Hand, as the defoliation campaign was known, was not a form of chemical warfare, but a "humane" way of fighting. Although the toxic effects of Agent Orange, the principal herbicide, on the environment and humans were not yet fully known, many scientists had urged the Johnson administration to halt this form of warfare, something Hart did not mention. He simply noted that Ranch Hand pilots were "sensitive to criticism that came regularly from conservationists in the United States" but even more concerned about hostile fire from enemy guns. Yet the air force had not altered its Ranch Hand operations at all because of the objections of civilian scientists. Defoliation operations actually reached a peak in 1967.[33]

The favorable treatment of the war effort reflected television's acceptance of the cold war outlook that was responsible for U.S. intervention in Vietnam. TV journalists did not challenge President Johnson's conviction that the national interest required the containment of communism or the president's decision to commit U.S. combat troops to Vietnam. Those policies had such strong, mainstream support in 1965 that the network newscasts did not present them as matters of legitimate controversy. Instead, TV journalists responded to Johnson's decision to go to war in Vietnam less as objective journalists than as patriotic citizens. They reported the war effort in language that revealed a lack of detachment. Commonly in 1965–66, they referred to "our" troops, planes, and losses in Vietnam. The North Vietnamese or Vietcong were usually the "enemy," frequently the "Communists," and occasionally the "Reds." On one occasion Huntley mocked the term *National Liberation Front* as "Hanoi's name for its own forces." Editorial comments on television newscasts about the North Vietnamese or the Vietcong were overwhelmingly negative. Indeed, in one remarkable instance, the name of the Vietnamese revolutionaries became a synonym for deception and mendacity, when NBC correspondent Garrick Utley dismissed a National Liberation Front film as "unadulterated Vietcong."[34]

There were several reasons why the network newscasts seemed "to express a massive political consensus" at the beginning of the Vietnam War. Dependent on advertising revenues, subject to federal regulation, and vulnerable to pressure from affiliates, television networks were wary of controversial programming or discordant opinions. When J. William Fulbright (D-Ark.), the chair of the Senate Foreign Relations Committee, held hearings in February 1966 that disputed the Johnson administration's Vietnam policies, CBS broke off its coverage in favor of reruns of "I Love Lucy," "The Real McCoys," and "The Andy Griffith Show." Network executives cited neither commercial nor ideological reasons for their decision, but—fantastically—the danger that extended telecasting of the hearings would "obfuscate" or "confuse" the issues about the war. Yet it is hard to believe that political considerations had no role in the network's action, since CBS president Frank Stanton considered a previous interview with Fulbright "a dirty trick . . . to play on the President of the United States."[35]

Such episodes have persuaded many observers that television in the mid-1960s was "the most timid" of the news media, the most willing to accept official statements at face value, the most reluctant to air dissenting opinions, the most likely to knuckle under to government pressure. Yet recent studies have cast doubt on the independence of newspaper reporting of the Vietnam War. One analysis of six newspapers of different sizes and political orientations revealed that reporters and editors relied heavily on government sources for information about military operations and tended not to doubt their credibility.[36] Another concluded that print journalists generally accepted "the assumptions and consensus of the foreign policy establishment" and hoped for the success of "foreign policies designed to meet the nation's problems," at least when those policies were first carried out.[37] Television newscasts may have expressed this consensual outlook in unique or distinctive ways—by focusing, for example, on "our boys" in Vietnam or stigmatizing the Vietcong as representatives of alien, evil ways. But the news media in general seems to have shared dominant core values that made it inclined in 1965–66 to support—or, at least, not to question—the fundamental reasons for American intervention in Vietnam.[38]

Television may have expressed those consensual values in unique or distinctive ways because network newscasts were not simply a source of information but also of entertainment. As media analyst Peter Braestrup has argued, the job of the network correspondent in Vietnam "was not to produce news in the sense of 'fact-finding'. . . , but to obtain and produce film vignettes" that were "presented as 'typical' or a 'microcosm'" of the entire war. The correspondents who submitted these film reports often had only the most rudimentary knowledge of Vietnamese politics and culture, since their overseas assignments usually lasted between six months and one year. Their expertise was not in Southeast Asian affairs or even in international relations, but in producing vivid, engaging, and dramatic stories. Even more than the correspondents, the editors and producers in New York who assembled the nightly newscasts were masters not of interpreting the news but of packaging it. Their concern was good television—reports from Vietnam that provided spectacular images that would attract large audiences and somehow encapsulate the entire war effort in one three-minute segment. This was neither adversarial nor even deeply analytical journalism. Instead, it was theatrical reporting, a reflection of the nature of the expertise of television journalists.[39]

Yet television journalists did question the implementation of American policy in Vietnam, and their stories occasionally caused controversy, as when CBS correspondent Morley Safer and his crew filmed a report in Cam Ne about a search-and-destroy operation. The mission was one of the first of its kind for U.S. marines, who had been previously concentrated on protecting air bases and other important military installations. On 3 August 1965 a marine company swept into Cam Ne, a village complex south-east of Danang that was supposed to be an enemy stronghold. "If there were Viet Cong in the hamlets," Safer asserted in his film report, "they were long gone" by the time the U.S. forces arrived.[40] The only certain Vietnamese casualties were a ten-year-old boy, who was killed, and four villagers, who were wounded, by the marine fire. The apparent lack of enemy resistance made all the more sensational the image of a marine using a cigarette lighter to set afire a thatched hut. The U.S. forces had orders to "level" Cam Ne, Safer explained just before the camera showed another marine incinerating a hut with a flamethrower. "There is little doubt that American fire power can win a military victory here. But to a Vietnamese peasant whose home means a lifetime of backbreaking labor, it will take more than presidential promises to convince him that we are on his side."[41]

Enraged military authorities immediately accused Safer of inaccuracy and distortion. U.S. forces, they said, had faced not just the "burst of gunfire" that Safer had reported, but snipers that had wounded four Americans and forced the marines to withdraw under the cover of an artillery barrage. Cam Ne was no ordinary village, but an "extensively entrenched and fortified hamlet" with hundreds of booby traps and an elaborate network of tunnels. Although the marines may have burned the huts of innocent civilians, they did so incidentally, according to the bat-talion commander, while trying "to neutralize bunkers, trenches, and firing positions actually in use by the VC." The hut ignited by the cigarette lighter appeared to be "a tactical installation rather than a peaceful dwell-ing," according to a military spokesperson in Saigon. The marines, an-other information officer added, had not wantonly or callously used force but, like all American troops in South Vietnam, followed Westmoreland's orders to exercise "the utmost discretion, judgment and restraint" in applying firepower.[42]

Safer stood by his story. In reply to the nervous inquiries of CBS news president Fred W. Friendly, he confirmed the accuracy of his film report before it aired on 5 August. Despite the barrage of official criticism, he also maintained that friendly fire, not Vietcong resistance, was responsible for the American casualties at Cam Ne.[43] In a follow-up story several days later, Safer provided additional evidence that the marines entered Cam Ne determined to "teach [the villagers] a lesson."[44] Was it necessary to burn "all the houses . . . to fulfill the mission?" he asked a marine who had seen action at Cam Ne. It was, the marine replied, in order "to show these people over a period of time that we're done playing with them." Another marine declared, "You can't have a feeling of remorse for these people. I mean, like I say, they are an enemy until proven innocent." A third disclosed that he entered villages such as Cam Ne, where marines had previously faced hostile fire or suffered casualties, with a desire for revenge. Such statements belied official assurances that U.S. policy was "to bend over backward" to avoid harming civilians or their property, "even at possible cost of U.S. lives."[45]

Even more vehement than the official criticism of Safer's reporting was the attack on his integrity. Leading the assault was Lyndon B. Johnson. "Are you trying to fuck me?" Johnson asked caustically in a telephone conversation with CBS president Frank Stanton. "Your boys shat on the American flag." The president was convinced that Safer was a communist, but an investigation proved only that he was a Canadian. "Well, I knew he wasn't an American," Johnson sneered. "Why do you have to use foreigners to cover that war?" inquired Bill Moyers, an aide to Johnson, of another CBS correspondent. Canadian birth was reason enough for Arthur Sylvester, the assistant secretary of defense for public affairs, to demand Safer's relief. "I think that an American reporter," Sylvester wrote Friendly, "would be more sensitive" to the need for "balance" in reporting U.S. actions in Vietnam. Friendly dismissed Sylvester's letter as "character assassination," but Stanton repeatedly expressed doubts about Safer. A friend of Johnson, Stanton did not like having CBS accused of undercutting the president's war policies, especially since the source of trouble was a reporter who had been working for the network only a year and whose background he considered "sketchy." CBS news executives, however, kept Safer from learning about Stanton's reservations and Johnson's accusations while he remained in Vietnam.[46]

Nevertheless, Safer was terribly aware of the hostility he faced in Vietnam, and that pressure may have affected his reporting. Safer feared for his life and began carrying a gun after hearing a rumor that he might become the victim of "an accident" and after watching a drunk marine officer fire his pistol in front of the press center while yelling "Communist Broadcasting System."[47] Despite these threats, Safer insisted that he did not temper his reporting. Yet although he continued to cover the war's nasty side, he began describing it as part of the timeless brutality of warfare. Thus he explained the casualties that resulted from a mistaken U.S. bombing strike on the South Vietnamese village of Bong Son in October 1965 as an "inevitable" error. He also portrayed the Vietnamese hustlers and prostitutes who swarmed around the American installations at Danang as an "age-old misfortune of war." And in a report that must have pleased the American high command, he concluded that the South Vietnamese army regular, if led well, fought as effectively "as any other soldier."[48]

The upshot of Safer's Cam Ne story, then, was an intense debate, not over the effectiveness of search-and-destroy tactics but the legitimacy of critical television reporting of the war. Morley Safer raised all the right issues—the difficulty of identifying the enemy, the adverse effects of heavy firepower, and the problem of innocent victims of military action in populated areas. Yet an official expression of regret about civilian casualties and assurances of restraint in future missions effectively ended any discussion of whether operations such as Cam Ne could help win the war. Instead, government officials thought more about whether reports such as Safer's might help lose it. Pentagon officials began recording the network newscasts in order to monitor more effectively television's coverage of the war. Once more military authorities studied the feasibility of censoring war stories, but these reconsiderations only confirmed previous conclusions that such severe restriction of the news would be ineffective and counterproductive. Still, the inflamed reaction to Safer's story revealed the narrow limits of acceptable war reporting on television.[49]

Despite the furor over Cam Ne, television newscasts did occasionally examine problems with the war effort in 1965–66. Some of the most perceptive stories came from NBC correspondent Ron Nessen. After the first engagements in the Ia Drang Valley, Nessen was the only TV journalist who recognized that the North Vietnamese were dictating the terms of battle. Their attack had come as a surprise, he explained, and they had succeeded with the same tactics that had worked against the French. Even though they had retreated in the face of American and South Vietnamese reinforcements, the fighting "could break out again," Nessen correctly predicted, whenever the North Vietnamese wanted to resume it.[50] One year later, Nessen probed the difficulties of "the other war," when he reported from Voila, a village that had been "pacified" four times. The real problem at Voila was the ineffectiveness of South Vietnamese government efforts to win the loyalty of the villagers. For example, the revolutionary development cadre that was supposed to provide security, improve public services, and rally support for the government once had all but two of its fifty-nine members desert. Each night, Nessen declared, the Vietcong proved that government forces could not protect the village. Pacification would succeed, he concluded, only when Voila was secure.[51]

Another problem that attracted the attention of television journalists in 1965–66 was the sordid conditions of life in South Vietnam. On the "CBS

Evening News" on 14 September 1965, Walter Cronkite introduced a film report about "one of the ugliest and saddest aspects of the Vietnam War." What followed was correspondent John Laurence narrating footage of South Vietnamese civilians who swarmed like "flies" and fought like "animals" in a U.S. marine garbage dump. Laurence explained that these "scavengers of war" risked crippling injury as well as infection, since the dump contained live ammunition. Seconds later, a grenade exploded, wounding a youth. The following month, Morley Safer described the degradation of the "once charming" city of Danang, the victim of con men and call girls who hustled for American dollars. A year later, he reported about an impending crackdown on the Saigon black market. Safer noted wryly, though, that business as usual would resume "next week at the latest."[52]

During 1967 network newscasts contained stronger and more frequent criticisms of American methods of warfare. New sources of information cast doubt on official evaluations of the war effort. At the end of 1966, Harrison Salisbury of the *New York Times* had become the first American correspondent to visit North Vietnam since the beginning of the air war. Salisbury said in interviews on the three networks in mid-January 1967 what he had written in articles for the *Times*—that the bombing had caused extensive civilian casualties but had not diminished the North's capacity to move war materiel to the South. By exposing the North Vietnamese to a common danger, Salisbury added, the bombing had actually raised civilian morale and united the country. One week later, Harry Ashmore, a Pulitzer Prize–winning former newspaper correspondent who had also traveled to Hanoi, endorsed Salisbury's conclusions in an interview with CBS's Charles Kuralt.[53]

Network correspondents made more interpretive comments in 1967 that cast doubt on the effectiveness of American military operations. Typical were David Burrington's stories in February about U.S. efforts to clear the Vietcong from their tunnel complexes. Experience showed, Burrington said, that the guerrillas would be back in a few days or weeks. During Operation Cedar Falls, NBC and ABC aired reports that pointed out the persistent problems in relocation camps and refugee resettlement programs. Adam Raphael informed CBS viewers in February about a failed search-and-destroy mission after which American troops took out their frustration on a suspected Vietcong prisoner. When the cameras were off, Raphael revealed, the suspect's treatment may not have been "exactly according to the Geneva Convention." Though common, such critical comments did not dominate the network newscasts in 1967. Indeed, favorable remarks about the American war effort were still far more numerous. But television journalists were more inclined to question American methods of warfare, perhaps because of their growing familiarity with the difficulties of achieving victory in Vietnam.[54]

There were far more profound doubts about American strategy in the White House and the Pentagon, and television newscasts revealed those reservations in sensational stories in May 1967. Several weeks earlier General Westmoreland had asked for an additional 200,000 troops, a request that added to the fears of Secretary of Defense Robert S. McNamara that the strategy of attrition would continue to produce a larger war, higher casualties, but no clear progress toward victory. "When we add divisions, can't the enemy add divisions? If so, where does it all end?" Johnson asked Westmoreland. With his own military advisers divided, Johnson denied Westmoreland the desired reinforcements. The administration's deliberations leaked out in a story on the "Huntley-Brinkley Report" on 8 May, and correspondent George Page concluded that Westmoreland's request showed that there was no limit to the number of troops that might be needed to protect South Vietnam. Two weeks later, ABC's Frank Reynolds reported on Johnson's Memorial Day proclamation, in which the president described the war as a "bloody impasse." This dramatic phrase, though, was misleading, since the president still clung to the hope that Westmoreland could make slow but steady progress toward victory without additional troops. Reynolds then added his own note of pessimism. The "isolated victories on the battlefield," he declared, "do not add up to any sort of overall victory against the North Vietnamese or Vietcong." Since enemy resolve had not lessened, the United States faced a "predicament from which there is no obvious escape."[55]

What kind of war, then, did a television viewer watch on the network nightly news during the American buildup in Vietnam from 1965 through 1967? He or she saw, as critic Michael Arlen has remarked, a "generally distanced overview of a disjointed conflict which was composed mainly of scenes of helicopters landing, tall grasses blowing in the helicopter wind, American soldiers fanning out across a hillside on foot, rifles at the ready, with now and then (on the soundtrack) a far-off ping or two, and now and then (as the visual grand finale) a column of dark, billowing smoke a half mile away, invariably described as a burning Vietcong ammo dump."[56] Night after night the American people peered at these scenes of battle from a war that had been domesticated by TV cameras. The war was always there on the screen, close enough to fascinate or repel but not so close as to spoil dinner. Most television battles ended in American victories, although increasingly they revealed problems that suggested that all might not be well. Rarely, though, could the viewer see beyond the battlefield. Television's war was a series of disconnected episodes of combat. Television reporters usually did not look for the connections, but when they did, they had trouble finding them. That was because the strategy of attrition had produced a war of isolated engagements. The fragmented war on television was precisely the war fought in Vietnam.

TV journalists reported the war this way not because of their perceptual acuity or analytical power, but because of the routines of their medium. Television consists of bits and pieces—segments, in the vocabulary of scholars who use semiotics to analyze communications. Each channel broadcasts a flow of programs, commercials, and announcements, and each program, in turn, consists of smaller segments. On a network newscast, those segments include reports, either by the anchor or correspondents, that together total only twenty-two minutes. Because of the shortness of time, these reports condense and simplify the news. And because of journalists' preoccupation with immediacy, the reports usually focus only on today's news, with little, if any, analysis of how recent events fit into larger patterns. Anchors may try to provide some context for the reports, but they usually must do so in a few sentences. Some studies have shown, however, that viewers often fail to make the intended connection between an anchor's introduction or conclusion and a correspondent's story. Brevity and segmentation thus made television likely to cover large events, such as the Vietnam War, through a series of largely self-contained reports. Television's fragmented reporting just happened to coincide with a disjointed war.[57]

Television suddenly had a different war to cover once the Tet Offensive began. On 30 January 1968 the North Vietnamese and Vietcong launched a coordinated series of attacks that seemed to turn almost all of South Vietnam into a battlefield. They struck with 100,000 troops in practically all major cities, most provincial and many district capitals, and quite a few hamlets—altogether more than 150 places. Vietcong sapper teams assaulted the most visible symbols of American and South Vietnamese authority—the embassy in Saigon and the presidential palace, respectively. At the last two locations, U.S. and South Vietnamese forces repelled the attacks within a few hours; almost everywhere else, they regained the advantage in a matter of days. Yet the breadth and fury of the Tet Offensive surprised American intelligence authorities and stunned public opinion. No one had imagined that the North Vietnamese and Vietcong were capable of such extraordinary action, especially since the Johnson administration had recently mounted a "progress campaign," a major public relations effort to show, as Westmoreland proclaimed, that the war had advanced into a new stage "when the end begins to come into view." Upon learning of the Tet attacks, Walter Cronkite expressed the bewilderment and betrayal felt by many Americans when he snapped, "What the hell is going on? I thought we were winning the war."[58]

Tet was high drama on television. No longer was the war in the background; instead, the fighting intruded into film reports in frightening and uncontrollable ways. Within a week, viewers saw two members of television crews suffer wounds while covering battle. During the fighting near the presidential palace, ABC's Piers Anderton and his camera operator recorded the anguish of an injured South Vietnamese soldier moaning in the street, while NBC's Douglas Kiker described the agony of Ban Me Thuot, as the film showed a city of rubble and refugees. "The nastiest kind of street fighting" occurred in Hue, CBS's Robert Schakne observed, and it exacted a heavy toll on U.S. marines, who had to clear out the enemy house by house, and on the city, which had ceased to function. From Danang, Saigon, Khe Sanh, and elsewhere correspondents reported that the fighting was hard and unpredictable. Not merely spectators at these engagements, yet not fully participants, they captured in words and images the surprise, horror, and confusion that engulfed South Vietnam during Tet.[59]

The most sensational story during Tet was the cold-blooded execution of a Vietcong officer in the streets of Saigon. The shooting followed a street battle between the Vietcong and South Vietnamese marines. An NBC crew recorded the fighting and the assassination in its entirety; an ABC camera operator stopped filming at the moment of death. Both reports aired on the nightly newscasts on 2 February; both contained commentary that was extraordinarily restrained. As the victim was led to his death, NBC's Howard Tuckner explained, "Government troops had captured the commander of the Viet Cong commando unit. He was roughed up badly but refused to talk. A South Vietnamese officer held the pistol taken from the enemy officer. The chief of South Vietnam's national police, Brigadier General Nguyen Ngoc Loan, was waiting for him." Neither Tuckner nor Roger Peterson, who narrated the ABC film, suggested that the shooting was an atrocity or a measure of the authoritarianism of the South Vietnamese regime. For Robert Northshield, the executive producer of the "Huntley-Brinkley Report," the film was newsworthy not because of its political implications but on account of its stunning images of death. Northshield, though, considered some of the scenes too "rough" for the television audience, and so he trimmed footage of blood spurting from the shattered skull of the victim. Perhaps as many as 20 million people watched the execution film on NBC; many more saw a photograph of the moment of death, published in almost every major newspaper.[60]

Although there is no way of knowing the impact on public opinion of this single story, the overall effect of the Tet Offensive in early 1968 was to deepen doubts about the war and destroy confidence in the Johnson administration's handling of it. Public support for the war did not suddenly vanish during Tet. Throughout 1967 more people had disliked Johnson's war policies than endorsed them, although the president won back some support during the "progress campaign" late in the year. The first public response to Tet was to rally behind the war effort, but that reaction lasted only briefly. By the time the enemy attacks had waned, 50 percent of the American people thought it had been a mistake to send troops to Vietnam, an increase of 5 percent over December 1967. Public support for the administration's management of the war plummeted from 39 percent in January 1968 to 26 percent by late March. Even more startling, those who thought that the United States was making progress in the war declined from half the population to less than one-third.[61]

The shift in attitudes toward the war, some observers maintain, occurred because the American people were misinformed about Tet. These critics blame the news media for reporting so sensational, inaccurate, or distorted that it prevented the public from realizing that the Tet Offensive was an American victory. The most influential of these critics is Peter Braestrup, a former war correspondent for the *New York Times* and *Washington Post*, who has argued that American journalists were so overwhelmed during Tet that they got the story wrong. "Essentially, the dominant themes of the words and film from Vietnam . . . added up to a portrait of defeat" for the United States and South Vietnam, Braestrup has written, when in fact Tet was "a severe military-political setback for Hanoi."[62]

Making sense of the welter of events during Tet was difficult, but television journalists were not overwhelmed. They dutifully reported official reactions in Washington and Saigon, which usually emphasized that enemy successes were transient and casualties enormous. Sometimes, though, they took issue with those interpretations, as when David Brinkley, in reaction to General Westmoreland's statement about heavy Vietcong losses, commented tersely, he "did not say it [the Tet Offensive] was not effective." Editorial comments, many of them openly skeptical of official pronouncements, were far more numerous in the nightly newscasts than before Tet. Often, journalists expressed the shock and disbelief so many people felt, as when ABC news analyst Joseph C. Harsch asserted that Tet was at odds with "what the government had led us to expect." CBS's Robert Schakne expressed the same idea more vividly when he exclaimed that Tet had turned the world upside down. Journalists occasionally tried to discern the long-term effects of Tet by projecting current developments into the future. Thus, Schakne declared that there could be another major offensive and warned that "our troubles in Vietnam may be just beginning." As the current wave of attacks waned, NBC's Douglas Kiker reported that U.S. intelligence authorities feared another Vietcong assault, this one even more effective. Yet these predictions were no more pessimistic than General Wheeler's private assessment of the situation for Johnson. "The enemy . . . has the will and capability to continue," Wheeler found after visiting in South Vietnam in late February. The Tet Offensive, the general concluded, was "a very near thing."[63]

Although pessimism was common, television journalists did not declare that Tet was a victory for the North Vietnamese and Vietcong. "First and simplest, the Vietcong suffered a military defeat," Walter Cronkite reported from Saigon on 14 February. Their suicidal attacks had produced staggering losses, and they had not succeeded in persuading large numbers of South Vietnamese to support their cause. Yet Cronkite also found that Tet had caused severe political problems by widening the Johnson administration's credibility gap and weakening the South Vietnamese government. "Pacification," he believed, "may have been set back by years, certainly months." Cronkite reiterated these conclusions two weeks later in a special evening program. "To say that we are closer to victory today is to believe, in the face of the evidence, the optimists who have been wrong in the past," he declared. "To suggest we are on the edge of defeat is to yield to unreasonable pessimism. To say that we are mired in stalemate seems the only realistic, yet unsatisfactory, conclusion." No other television journalist offered such a full evaluation of Tet. Yet the brief, fragmentary comments of other reporters and anchors did not fundamentally conflict with this assessment.[64]

The results of the Tet Offensive were by no means as clear as Braestrup has insisted. By the standards of conventional war—those that shaped the U.S. army's strategy of attrition—Tet was indeed a defeat for the North Vietnamese and the Vietcong. The attackers had absorbed huge losses and had failed to maintain control of the cities and towns they had seized. By the standards of revolutionary war, however, the North Vietnamese and Vietcong seem to have been victorious. The attack proved the vulnerability of practically every South Vietnamese city or hamlet. It set back pacification, and it dealt U.S. morale a withering blow. "At the time of the initial attacks, the reaction of our military leadership approached panic," reflected Clark Clifford, who took over as secretary of defense in March 1968. "There was, for a brief time, something approaching paralysis, and a sense of events spiraling out of the control of the nation's leaders." The Johnson administration was bitterly divided over how to react to the enemy initiative. Not until 31 March—two months after the Tet Offensive began—did Johnson make a major statement on Vietnam. Then he announced a partial bombing halt, a new peace initiative, and his own withdrawal from the presidential race. The administration sealed its own fate with misleading optimism, ineffective war making, and inaction. At the very least, then, Tet represented a major psychological triumph for the North Vietnamese and Vietcong.[65]

After Tet, TV reporting of the war in many ways followed earlier patterns. Most stories contained no editorial comments; again, television focused on Americans soldiers in the field. The portrayal of the war, though, was far less heroic than before. American troops began going home in 1969 under President Richard M. Nixon's strategy of Vietnamization. Really the mirror image of attrition, Vietnamization was no strategy at all; it consisted of pulling American troops out, hoping for peace, and seeing what happened. Those U.S. forces that remained frequently expressed their dissatisfaction with the war, and news stories reflected this disillusionment. CBS's Gary Shepard, for example, reported in October 1969 from Saigon about the use of marijuana in Vietnam, while on the same night NBC's Fred Briggs covered an antiwar protest in Fayetteville, North Carolina, by Vietnam veterans. Six months later, NBC's Kenley Jones did a story about soldiers in the Twenty-second Infantry who were "near revolt" over their orders to invade Cambodia. The troops complained that they did not understand what the United States was doing in Cambodia or, for that matter, Vietnam. "This is a different war," Jones concluded, and these soldiers wanted no part of it. Neither did a majority of the American people.[66]

Did it matter that the Vietnam War was covered on television? How did TV reporting affect public attitudes toward the war? These are important questions, but they cannot be answered as precisely as we might wish. Television did affect public understanding of the war, since by 1970 a majority of Americans got most of their news from television. Yet what they learned from nightly newscasts is by no means clear. Studies have revealed that most viewers have trouble remembering anything from news programs that they just finished watching. Perhaps that is because, as one scholar has observed, television "is designed to be watched intermittently, casually, and without full concentration. Only the commercials command and dazzle." Even if one does watch intently, the meaning one extracts from a news report is a product of individual values and attitudes. NBC's George Page recalled reporting on a battle in a way that he thought might create "a dovish attitude" among viewers. Then he got a letter from someone who had doubts about U.S. goals in Vietnam but who reacted to Page's story by saying, "Go, Marines. Go."[67]

Yet even if it cannot be precisely measured, television's influence during the Vietnam War was important. Images do have powerful effects, however much the reaction varies among individual viewers. It is no accident that Morley Safer's Cam Ne report created such a stir while similar stories in newspapers went almost unnoticed.[68] The reporting of the Tet Offensive on television undoubtedly shocked many people, especially after previous coverage of the war had been comparatively tame. Walter Cronkite's declaration that the war was a stalemate had a profound effect on at least one viewer, Lyndon Johnson, and, nearly a quarter century later, on George Bush. Certain that unrestricted reporting from Vietnam had undermined popular support of the war, Pentagon officials in the Bush administration restricted reporters' access to troops in the Persian Gulf and censored their reports.[69]

While the Bush administration vastly oversimplified the "lessons" of Vietnam, it does seem that nightly news coverage did contribute to popular dissatisfaction with the war. Television presented a war that was puzzling and incoherent—a series of disjointed military operations that were often individually successful but collectively disastrous. Night after night, television slowly exposed the illogic of attrition. If viewers grew weary or discontent or outraged, it was partly because television just happened to show them an important part of the Vietnam War "the way it was."

NOTES

1. *Public Papers of the Presidents of the United States: Lyndon B. Johnson, 1968–69*, 2 vols. (Washington, D.C.: GPO, 1970), 1:482–86.

2. William C. Westmoreland, *A Soldier Reports* (Garden City, N.Y.: Doubleday, 1976).

3. Michael Arlen, *Living-Room War* (New York: Penguin Books, 1982).

4. Peter Braestrup, *Big Story: How the American Press and Television Reported and Interpreted the Crisis of Tet 1968 in Vietnam and Washington*, 2 vols. (Boulder, Colo.: Westview Press, 1977).

5. Robert Elegant, "How to Lose a War," *Encounter* 57 (August 1981): 73–90.

6. Braestrup, *Big Story*, 1:36–40; Daniel C. Hallin, *The "Uncensored War": The Media and Vietnam* (New York: Oxford University Press, 1986), 105–6; Leonard Zeidenberg, "The 21-Inch View of Vietnam: Big Enough Picture?," *Television* 25 (January 1968): 28–32, 56–58; Edward Jay Epstein, *News From Nowhere: Television and the News* (New York: Random House, 1973), 33; George Bailey, "Television War: Trends in Network Coverage of Vietnam, 1965–1970," *Journal of Broadcasting* 20 (Spring 1976): 150.

7. Doris Kearns, *Lyndon Johnson and the American Dream* (New York: Harper and Row, 1976), 7 (first quotation); Kathleen J. Turner, *Lyndon Johnson's Dual War: Vietnam and the Press* (Chicago: University of Chicago Press, 1985), 44–45 (second quotation); David Culbert, "Johnson and the Media," in *Exploring the Johnson Years*, edited by Robert A. Divine (Austin: University of Texas Press, 1981), 214–48; William M. Hammond, *Public Affairs: The Military and the Media, 1962–1968*, U.S. Army in Vietnam (Washington, D.C.: Center of Military History, 1988), 133–48, 233; Peter Braestrup, *Battle Lines: Report of the Twentieth-Century Fund Task Force on the Military and the Media* (New York: Priority Press Publications, 1985), 64–65.

8. Westmoreland, *A Soldier Reports*, 148; Andrew F. Krepinevich, Jr., *The Army and Vietnam* (Baltimore: Johns Hopkins University Press, 1986), 164–68 (quotation, p. 166); George C. Herring, *America's Longest War: The United States and Vietnam, 1950–1975*, 2d ed. (New York: Knopf, 1986), 145, 150.

9. When U.S. marines began Operation Harvest Moon in December 1965, south of Danang, they learned that one of the units they would be fighting was the First Vietcong Regiment. "Jesus Christ, that's the outfit we wiped out at Chu Lai," said one platoon leader, referring to a battle that had occurred four months earlier. "Guess you forgot to wipe out their recruiting department," cracked another marine. Philip Caputo, *A Rumor of War* (New York: Ballantine Books, 1977), 243–44.

10. Krepinevich, *The Army and Vietnam*, 177–214; Enthoven to McNamara, memorandum, 4 May 1967, in *The Pentagon Papers: The Defense Department History of United States Decisionmaking on Vietnam*, Senator Gravel Edition, 4 vols. (Boston: Beacon Press, n.d.), 4:461–63; Herring, *America's Longest War*, 150–56; Bruce Palmer, Jr., *The 25-Year War: America's Military Role in Vietnam* (New York: Simon and Schuster, 1984), 42–43; Mark Clodfelter, *The Limits of Air Power: The American Bombing of North Vietnam* (New York: Free Press, 1989), 134–46; Guenter Lewy, *America in Vietnam* (New York: Oxford University Press, 1978), 66.

11. *The Pentagon Papers*, 2:576–80; Caputo, *A Rumor of War*, 89; George Donelson Moss, *Vietnam: An American Ordeal* (Englewood Cliffs, N.J.: 1990), 377; Krepinevich, *The Army*

and Vietnam, 165, 182–83; Harry G. Summers, Jr., *On Strategy: The Vietnam War in Context* (Carlisle Barracks, Pa.: U.S. Army War College, 1981), 56; Jeffrey J. Clarke, *Advice and Support: The Final Years, 1965–1973*, U.S. Army in Vietnam (Washington, D.C.: Center of Military History, 1988), 106.

12. Zeidenberg, "The 21-Inch View of Vietnam," 56 (quotations); Hallin, *The "Uncensored War,"* 111–12; Lawrence Lichty, "A Television War?," in *Vietnam Reconsidered: Lessons from a War*, edited by Harrison Salisbury (New York: Harper and Row, 1984), 86.

13. Morley Safer, quoted in Braestrup, *Battle Lines*, 67.

14. Arlen, *Living-Room War*, 97–98; Zeidenberg, "The 21-Inch View of Vietnam," 57.

15. Hammond, *Public Affairs*, 236–38; Braestrup, *Battle Lines*, 68–69.

16. Report by Safer, 17 November 1965, CBS, reel A15, Weekly News Summary, Assistant Secretary of Defense for Public Affairs, Record Group 330, National Archives, Washington, D.C. (hereafter cited as DOD Weekly News Summary).

17. Reports by Maloney, 17–19 November 1965, ABC, reels A15, A16, ibid.; George C. Herring, "The First Cavalry and the Ia Drang Valley, 18 October–24 November 1965," in *America's First Battles, 1776–1965*, edited by Charles E. Heller and William A. Stofft (Lawrence: University Press of Kansas, 1986), 300–326.

18. Reports by Pappas, 14 November 1966, CBS; Gale, 15 November 1966, ABC; Page, 16 November 1966, NBC, all on reel A68, DOD Weekly

News Summary; report by Safer, 23 February 1967, CBS, reel A83, ibid.; Erik Barnouw, *Tube of Plenty: The Evolution of American Television*, 2d rev. ed. (New York: Oxford University Press, 1990), 378.

19. Daniel C. Hallin, "We Keep America on Top of the World," in *Watching Television*, edited by Todd Gitlin (New York: Pantheon Books, 1986), 11–15; Arlen, *Living-Room War*, 111–13.

20. Reports by Page, 5 May 1967, NBC, and Wallace, 8 May 1967, CBS, both on reel A94, DOD Weekly News Summary.

21. Reports by Pappas, 28 October 1966, CBS, reel A65, and Safer, 21 November 1966, CBS, reel A68, ibid. See also report by John Dancy, 21 November 1966, NBC, reel A68, ibid.

22. Report by Kalischer, 19 November 1965, CBS, reel A16, ibid.; Hallin, *The "Uncensored War,"* 124–25, 135–38; Hal Himmelstein, *Television Myth and the American Mind* (New York: Praeger, 1984), 197–206.

23. Bailey, "Television War," 147–58; Bailey, "Interpretive Reporting of the Vietnam War by Anchormen," *Journalism Quarterly* 53 (Summer 1976): 319–24; Daniel C. Hallin, "The American News Media: A Critical Theory Perspective," in *Critical Theory and Public Life*, edited by John Forester (Cambridge: MIT Press, 1985), 121–31; Hallin, *The "Uncensored War,"* 63–68.

24. Report by Safer, 22 November 1965, CBS, reel A16, DOD Weekly News Summary; Lawrence W. Lichty, "Video Versus Print," *Wilson Quarterly* 5 (Special Issue 1982): 52–53;

Robert MacNeil, *The People Machine: The Influences of Television on American Politics* (New York: Harper and Row, 1968), 38–55.

25. Comments by anchors, 16 November 1965, NBC; 18 November 1965, CBS; report by Ray Maloney, 18 November 1965, ABC, all on reel A15, DOD Weekly News Summary; report by Dean Brelis, 22 November 1965, NBC, reel A16, ibid.

26. Comments by anchors, 11 November 1966, NBC, reel A68; 23 February 1967, NBC, reel A82; 12 January 1967, CBS, reel A77, all in ibid.

27. Reports by Safer, 17 November 1965, CBS, reel A15, and Laurence, 21 February 1968, CBS, reel A135, ibid.; Hallin, *The "Uncensored War,"* 142–43.

28. Comments by Cronkite, 16 November 1965, CBS, reel A15, and report by Brelis, 22 November 1965, NBC, reel A16, DOD Weekly News Summary; Herring, "The First Cavalry and the Ia Drang Valley," 322–23.

29. Report by Brannigan, 23 February 1967, ABC, reel A83, DOD Weekly News Summary; Krepinevich, *The Army and Vietnam,* 225–27; Hammond, *Public Affairs,* 304–5.

30. Based on his evaluation of a sample of network newscasts from August 1965 through January 1968, Daniel C. Hallin determined that when TV journalists assessed the outcome of battles, they found that 62 percent were American or South Vietnamese victories, 28 percent were losses, and 2 percent were inconclusive. There appears to be an error in Hallin's total of 92 percent, since he considered only those engagements that reporters or anchors assessed. Hallin, *The "Uncensored War,"* 146.

31. Reports by Maloney, 15 November 1965, ABC, reel A15; Morton, 21 November 1966, CBS, reel A68; Page, 17 January 1967, NBC, reel A78; Hart, 17 January 1967, CBS, reel A78; Brelis, 18 November 1965, NBC, reel A15; Page, 16 November 1966, NBC, reel A68, all in DOD Weekly News Summary.

32. Comments by Huntley, 10 September 1965, NBC, reel A6; report by Morton, 2 February 1967, CBS, reel A80, both in ibid. See also report by Nessen on the F-5, 19 November 1965, NBC, reel A16, ibid.

33. Report by Hart, 20 February 1967, CBS, reel A83, ibid.; William A. Buckingham, Jr., *Operation Ranch Hand: The Air Force and Herbicides in Southeast Asia, 1961–1971* (Washington, D.C.: Office of Air Force History, 1982), 129, 138–40.

34. Comments by Huntley, 23 November 1965, NBC, reel A16, and Utley, n.d. (ca. 23 October 1965), NBC, reel A12, DOD Weekly News Summary; James Aronson, *The Press and the Cold War* (New York: Monthly Review Press, 1970), 218–30; Nicholas O. Berry, *Foreign Policy and the Press: An Analysis of the New York Times' Coverage of U.S. Foreign Policy* (Westport, Conn.: Greenwood Press, 1990), 27–52, 139–50; Hallin, *The "Uncensored War,"* 114–26, 148; Bailey, "Interpretive Reporting of the Vietnam War," 322–23.

35. Barnouw, *Tube of Plenty,* 381–84 (quotations, pp. 381–82); Fred W. Friendly, *Due to Circumstances beyond Our Control . . .* (New York: Vintage

Books, 1968), 212–40; Gary Paul
Gates, *Air Time: The Inside Story of
CBS News* (New York: Harper and
Row, 1978), 123–24; Epstein, *News
From Nowhere*, 44–59.

36. Clarence R. Wyatt, "'At the Cannon's Mouth': The American Press
and the Vietnam War," *Journalism
History* 13 (Autumn–Winter 1986):
109–11.

37. Berry, *Foreign Policy and the
Press*, xii–xiii.

38. Michael Mandelbaum, "Vietnam: The Television War," *Daedalus*
111 (Fall 1982): 160–61; Todd Gitlin,
*The Whole World Is Watching: Mass
Media in the Making & Unmaking of
the New Left* (Berkeley: University of
California Press, 1980), 252–82.

39. Braestrup, *Big Story*, 1:36–43;
Hallin, "We Keep America on Top of
the World," 9–15, 23–26.

40. Jack Shulimson and Charles M.
Johnson, *U.S. Marines in Vietnam: The
Landing and the Buildup, 1965* (Washington, D.C.: History and Museums
Division, U.S. Marine Corps, 1978),
64.

41. Hammond, *Public Affairs*, 186–
88.

42. Ibid.; Shulimson and Johnson,
U.S. Marines in Vietnam, 63; *New York
Times*, 6 August 1965.

43. Safer later claimed that the real
reason for the operation in Cam Ne
was that the province chief wanted the
villagers punished for not paying their
taxes. He said that he got this information months afterward from Richard
Critchfield, a correspondent for the
Washington Star. Critchfield, however,
maintains that "Safer has his villages
(or mine) confused. After the CBS
telecast created such a stir, I went to
Cam Ne and concluded that it had
concealed a heavily fortified Viet Cong
military post. . . . All I can say . . . is
that Safer, in support of his own reporting of the burning of Cam Ne,
somehow got it wrong." See Morley
Safer, *Flashbacks: On Returning to
Vietnam* (New York: Random House,
1990), 92; Richard Critchfield, *Villages*
(Garden City, N.Y.: Anchor Press/
Doubleday, 1981), 350; and David
Halberstam, *The Powers That Be* (New
York: Laurel, 1979), 680.

44. Safer, *Flashbacks*, 89.

45. Hammond, *Public Affairs*, 188–
90 (Safer/marine Q&A); Gates, *Air
Time*, 160–62; *New York Times*, 4 August 1965.

46. Halberstam, *The Powers That
Be*, 683–85; Gates, *Air Time*, 122–23,
161–62; Hammond, *Public Affairs*,
190–91; Safer, *Flashbacks*, 93–97.

47. Safer, *Flashbacks*, 88–93; Gates,
Air Time, 162.

48. Reports by Safer, 23–24 October 1965, CBS, reel A12, and 30 October 1965, CBS, reel A13, DOD Weekly
News Summary.

49. *New York Times*, 5 August 1965;
Hammond, *Public Affairs*, 193–95.

50. Reports by Nessen, 28–29 October 1965, NBC, reels A12, A13, DOD
Weekly News Summary.

51. Report by Nessen, 9 November
1966, NBC, reel A66, ibid.; Clarke, *Advice and Support*, 171–81.

52. Reports by Laurence, 14 September 1965, CBS, reel A6, and Safer,
n.d. (ca. 23 October 1965 and 18
November 1966), CBS, reels A12, A68,
DOD Weekly News Summary; Hammond, *Public Affairs*, 200–201.

53. Interviews with Salisbury, 11–12 January 1967, ABC; 12 January 1967, CBS; 12 January 1967, NBC, all on reel A77, DOD Weekly News Summary.

54. Reports by Page, 16 January 1967, NBC; Gale, 17 January 1967, ABC; Raphael, 16 February 1967, CBS; Burrington, 17, 20 February 1967, NBC, all on reels A78, A82–A83, ibid.; Hallin, The "Uncensored War," 159–63.

55. Larry Berman, Lyndon Johnson's War: The Road to Stalemate in Vietnam (New York: Norton, 1989), 31–38 (LBJ quotation, p. 35); Public Papers of the Presidents of the United States: Lyndon B. Johnson, 1967, 2 vols. (Washington, D.C.: GPO, 1968), 1:554–55; Report by Page, 5 May 1967, NBC, reel A94, and comments by Reynolds, 22 May 1967, ABC, reel A98, DOD Weekly News Summary.

56. Michael J. Arlen, "The Air: The Falklands, Vietnam, and Our Collective Memory," New Yorker, 16 August 1982, 73.

57. Gitlin, The Whole World Is Watching, 265–66; John Fiske, Television Culture (London: Routledge, 1987), 99–105, and "Moments of Television: Neither the Text Nor the Audience," in Remote Control: Television, Audiences, and Cultural Power, edited by Ellen Seiter et al. (London: Routledge, 1989), 63–64; Robert C. Allen, Channels of Discourse: Television and Contemporary Criticism (Chapel Hill: University of North Carolina Press, 1987), esp. intro., chaps. 1–2; Jane Feuer, "The Concept of Live Television: Ontology as Ideology," in Regarding Television: Critical Ap-

proaches—An Anthology, edited by E. Ann Kaplan (Frederick, Md.: University Publications of America, 1983), 15.

58. Berman, Lyndon Johnson's War, 114–19 (Westmoreland quotation, p. 116); Don Oberdorfer, Tet! (New York: Da Capo, 1984), 21–33, 142, 158 (Cronkite quotation); Herring, America's Longest War, 189–80; Krepinevich, The Army and Vietnam, 239.

59. Reports by Ogonesof, 26 January 1968, CBS; Tuckner, 1 February 1968, NBC; Hall, 1 February 1968, NBC; Syvertsen, 1 February 1968, CBS; and Anderton, 1 February 1968, ABC, all on reel A132; report by Tuckner, 6 February 1968, reel A133; reports by Paul Cunningham, 14 February 1968, NBC; Fromson, 14 February 1968, CBS; and Schakne, 15 February 1968, CBS, all on reel A134; reports by Jaffe, 21 February 1968, ABC, and Laurence, 21 February 1968, CBS, reel A135, all in DOD Weekly News Summary; Braestrup, Big Story, 2:599–617.

60. Reports by Tuckner, NBC, and Peterson, ABC, 2 February 1968, reel A133, DOD Weekly News Summary; George A. Bailey, "Rough Justice on a Saigon Street: A Gatekeeper Study of NBC's Tet Execution Film," Journalism Quarterly 49 (Summer 1972): 221–29, 238; Braestrup, Big Story, 1:463–65.

61. Burns W. Roper, "What Public Opinion Polls Said," in Braestrup, Big Story, 1:674–704; John E. Mueller, War, Presidents, and Public Opinion (New York: Wiley, 1973), 54–58.

62. Braestrup, Big Story, 1:705.

63. Comments by Huntley, 31 January 1968, NBC, and Brinkley, 1 Febru-

ary 1968, NBC, and report by Harsch, 1 February 1968, ABC, reel A132; report by Schakne, 5 February 1968, CBS, and anchor comments, 6 February 1968, NBC, reel A133; report by Kiker, 21 February 1968, NBC, reel A135, all in DOD Weekly News Summary; *The Pentagon Papers*, 4:546–47.

64. Report by Cronkite, 14 February 1968, CBS, reel A134, DOD Weekly News Summary; Braestrup, *Big Story*, 2:180–89 (second quotation).

65. Krepinevich, *The Army and Vietnam*, 248–50; Clark Clifford with Richard Holbrooke, *Counsel to the President: A Memoir* (New York: Random House, 1991), 474, 476.

66. Reports by Shepard, CBS, and Briggs, NBC, 13 October 1969, reel A221; reports by Shepard, CBS, and Jones, NBC, 6 May 1970, reel A250, all in DOD Weekly News Summary; Hallin, *The "Uncensored War,"* 174–80.

67. Lichty, "Video Versus Print," 53–54; Hallin, *The "Uncensored War,"* 107; Feuer, "The Concept of Live Television," 15; Zeidenberg, "The 21-Inch View of Vietnam," 32.

68. Hallin, *The "Uncensored War,"* 108, 123

69. John R. MacArthur, *Second Front: Censorship and Propaganda in the Gulf War* (New York: Hill and Wang, 1992), 112–45.

D A V I D R . C O L B U R N &

G E O R G E E . P O Z Z E T T A

4......

Race, Ethnicity, and the Evolution of Political Legitimacy

"Integration is a subterfuge for the maintenance of white supremacy and reinforces, among both black and white, the idea that 'white' is automatically better and 'black' is by definition inferior," wrote Stokely Carmichael in September 1966, barely three months after leading black Mississippians in a call for "Black Power."[1] In less militant language but evoking a similar ethnic appeal, the Committee for the Defense of the Polish Name insisted that "What the Polish American community needs more than anything else is an effective process of conscious raising."[2] Over fifty thousand Italian Americans gathered for the Columbus Circle

Unity Day rally in 1970 amid shouts of "Italian Power"; the buttons pinned on their lapels asserted proudly, "KISS ME I'M ITALIAN."[3]

By the end of the sixties, despite nearly fifteen years of racial progress and legislative reform, American society seemed about to unravel into a maze of ethnic and racial self-interest groups. Social relations were often typified by confrontational tactics that stirred up old hatreds and fostered dissent rather than unity. As if to dramatize the irony and paradox of the age, Watts, one of the nation's largest black ghettos in Los Angeles, exploded in a wave of rioting and destruction at literally the same moment that civil rights proponents celebrated passage of the Voting Rights Act of 1965.

These developments stunned most observers of American society who had assumed that the civil rights reforms would resolve the nation's racial dilemma. They were equally perplexed by the resurgence of ethnicity after social analysts in the late 1950s and early 1960s noted the growing conformity and homogeneity of the American people. Policymakers and intellectual leaders of the 1950s believed that consensus rather than conflict served as the dominant motif of a society that was well on its way toward erasing social and ethnic distinctions and accommodating demands for social change within traditional liberal, democratic norms.[4]

Such a view blurred the reality of an America that still retained deep racial and ethnic fault lines and of social movements that sought much more than individual access. To be sure, European ethnics had benefited from the postwar economic expansion, and many had been able to enter the middle class. Moreover, the public dimensions of traditional ethnic life had begun to fade as old neighborhoods declined and new generations came of age, conveying the impression that ethnicity itself was fast disappearing as a force in American life. Although blacks still resided at the margins of society and struggled against racism and discrimination, some analysts believed that the early achievements of the civil rights movement held promise for their eventual inclusion in the great American mainstream.

The resurgence of black militancy and white ethnic identity in the latter half of the 1960s dramatically reversed the social and political trends of the postwar era. Had intellectuals and other observers of American society in this period been fooled by these developments, as some social historians have contended? Were the manifestations of black power and ethnic pride the result of more deeply rooted conditions and expectations in American society that reflected the nation's long struggle with such conflicting issues as individual versus group identity and assimilation ver-

David R. Colburn and George E. Pozzetta

sus diversity? Or were they merely superficial responses to the social, economic, and political turmoil of the late 1960s and, as a consequence, only passing trends that captured the national spotlight for a brief historical moment?[5]

The convergence of the civil rights movement and ethnic activism, in time and often in place, led many to assume that the white ethnic revival was merely a backlash against black demands for equality in the public and private sectors. Although others acknowledged that the ethnic revival drew much of its philosophy and tactics from civil rights campaigns, they argued that a greater array of factors motivated ethnic activism.[6] With the passage of time, it now seems clear that the two movements overlapped in important respects but that they also had their own dynamic qualities.

This chapter examines the crafting of an ethnic identity among different racial and ethnic groups and argues that the pursuit of group solidarity represented an effort by these groups not only to redefine themselves, but also to restructure America's public and political culture. Black power and ethnic activism sought more than just equal rights, employment opportunities, and political gains; they also wanted to change the rules that governed American political life, to move beyond issues of individual rights and equality in order to address larger group needs and concerns.[7] At their heart, these movements questioned the nature of political legitimacy in the American system.

Beyond the Civil Rights Movement

The roots of African American self-assertion and black nationalism resided deep within the struggle for freedom. The appeal of Marcus Garvey in the 1920s, A. Philip Randolph in the 1930s and 1940s, and Malcolm X in the 1960s, as well as many others, demonstrated that black Americans had long sought something more than just legal equality in American society.[8] Within the civil rights movement, members of the Student Nonviolent Coordinating Committee (SNCC) evinced open dissatisfaction with such concepts as assimilation and integration as early as 1962 during the civil rights campaign in Albany, Georgia. As the civil rights movement came closer to achieving its initial goal of legal equality, unity within the movement began to shatter. Various groups insisted that a fundamental political and economic restructuring were the real keys to achieving genuine equality and freedom for African Americans. The seeds for such division had always existed within the movement, and splits had periodically emerged, even within the Southern Christian Leadership Conference (SCLC), but SNCC activists were the first to break away fully from the liberal, integration/assimilationist model.[9]

In analyzing the civil rights campaign in Mississippi in 1964 and 1965, Herbert Haines has written that the experiences persuaded many SNCC activists "that the whole ideology of black civil rights required rethinking."[10] Living with poor black families in Mississippi and bearing witness to the trials of their daily existence as well as the violence and intimidation they encountered as they tried to register to vote persuaded SNCC to pursue a more radical agenda. In the words of Allan Matusow, the Mississippi experience led SNCC "to see the world from the bottom up, and as it did, it scornfully rejected middle-class aspirations. Gradually the radical conviction took hold that a nation which tolerated Mississippi's poverty and racism was fundamentally flawed."[11]

Events at the Democratic National Convention in 1964 reinforced the belief of SNCC members that traditional American politics remained immune to genuine reform. Led by Bob Moses, the spokesman for the Mississippi campaign, SNCC veterans made one last effort to work within the political mainstream when they launched an effort to unseat the regular Mississippi delegation to the Democratic convention with representatives of their Mississippi Freedom Democratic party (MFDP). Despite some initial encouragement from Vice-President Hubert H. Humphrey, the MFDP's efforts were rejected by President Lyndon B. Johnson, who opposed any effort to alter the regular proceedings of the convention and threaten the tenuous consensus between blacks and white southerners. A proposal by Johnson to seat two members of the MFDP with the Mississippi delegation was resoundingly and emotionally rejected by leaders of the movement. August Meier and Elliott Rudwick wrote that the action of the Democratic party "only served to confirm the loss of faith in the Democratic Party's leadership" and the basic corruption of the national political system. Bayard Rustin reflected the views of SNCC leaders when he emphasized in the wake of the Democratic convention that "the civil rights movement has now to face the fact that it has to go deeper into the economic and social questions."[12]

"Spurred by the defeat of the MFDP challenge," wrote Clayborne Carson, SNCC workers came to realize that integration was unlikely and "began to look beyond their own experiences for ideological insights." Frantz Fanon and Malcolm X proved particularly critical in the evolution of their thinking. The charismatic Malcolm X urged the "absolute separation of the black and white races" and called for the establishment of a distinct black culture and political ideology so that blacks could overcome

David R. Colburn and George E. Pozzetta

their dependency on whites and the sense of inferiority that slavery and Jim Crow had fastened on them. In 1966 SNCC echoed these views, urging "black Americans [to] begin building independent political, economic and cultural institutions" that would be used "as instruments of social change." Those who shared the ideology of SNCC and Malcolm X espoused it as part of a radical attack on traditional American values.[13] The call for establishing an independent and vibrant African American culture coincided with a recognition of the need for fundamental political and economic reform, and together they effectively widened the chasm between blacks and whites at a time when the nation appeared to be resolving its racial inequities.

By 1965 questions of group and national identity became increasingly prominent among civil rights activists as they reflected upon the place of African Americans in the nation and as they continued to encounter persistent racism, despite the implementation of the Civil Rights Act of 1964. Voting rights and housing reforms still topped the agenda for the vast majority of black Americans, but cultural issues were rapidly infusing the movement and influencing its interaction with the larger society. W. E. B. Du Bois, who had advocated the development of an African-based culture for years, had warned blacks in 1960 that the civil rights campaign would not rid the country of its racial problems if, by emphasizing assimilation, it got "rid of the Negro race" in the process. Du Bois understood that equality alone would not satisfy black Americans or ensure their freedom.[14]

The notion of "who we are" had been a troubling one for African Americans in the United States, and it was especially so during this era. The heritage of slavery and Jim Crow generally undermined the development of a positive group image. Several scholars contended in the early 1960s, for example, that blacks constituted the one fully Americanized group because their cultural roots had been erased by their experience in America. Writing during this period, sociologist L. Singer argued that blacks were not ethnics but comprised instead a loose collection of individuals "without the community of tradition, sentiment, and so forth that has marked and given rise to ethnic groups such as Italian immigrants."[15] James Baldwin indicated much the same when he wrote, in *Notes of a Native Son*, "the American Negro has arrived at his identity by virtue of the absoluteness of his estrangement from his past."[16]

A great deal more is now known about African American history and culture during slavery and segregation, and about the ways in which African Americans retained and redefined their heritage despite the oppression of slavery and segregation. But in the early 1960s, blacks expressed frustration with an identity that had allegedly been constructed in slavery and sought to fashion a new one for themselves.[17]

The movement toward cultural pluralism in black America enjoyed its greatest support among the young, and it united civil rights activists in the South with urban blacks in the North for the first time. Leaders of the black nationalist movement, who were philosophically and emotionally indebted to Malcolm X and the Muslims, became chief spokespersons for the black nationalist movement. They stood for what Allan P. Sindlar has described as "a rejection of the white view of the Negro as inferior, a positive affirmation of the Negro's history and his future, and a turning inward of the Negro group, accompanied by some repudiation of the white world."[18] Stokely Carmichael and Charles Hamilton further characterized this movement as a return to an African history that predated the forced introduction of blacks into the United States and in which black people were "energetic, determined, intelligent, beautiful and peace-loving." It was this positive depiction of Africa as a rich source of culture, combined with a call "for the cultural and political autonomy of black communities" by Stokely Carmichael, that many young blacks received enthusiastically.[19] For militants like Carmichael, Malcolm X, and Eldridge Cleaver, Africa also stood as an example of a place and a time when blacks resorted to violence to overthrow white suppression. Through these images, the black nationalist movement provided a positive self-image and a psychological release for African Americans that facilitated cultural creativity and political activism.[20] Moreover, it initiated a cultural debate that dominated discussion within the black community for much of the remainder of the decade.

One of the central aspects of the cultural debate concerned language and whether or not blacks should use ethnic or racial terms in defining themselves. Initially the discourse proposed *black* as a substitute for *Negro*, and Stokely Carmichael and SNCC boldly used this expression during the James Meredith march and in their fight against Jim Crow in Mississippi. Most young blacks joined with Carmichael in rejecting the term Negro, because they viewed it as an expression that whites had invented and not an identity that blacks had constructed for themselves. But, as the discussion continued in the black community in the sixties and beyond, a more ethnic reference emerged as black spokespersons initially proposed *Afro American* and then *African American*.[21]

The debate over language and terminology broadened discussions among African Americans about their heritage and about their place in

David R. Colburn and George E. Pozzetta

American society. As black leaders embraced terms like Afro American and African American, they did so with the understanding that they had begun to redefine themselves as more than just a racial group. This cultural movement spread rapidly through the black community and enjoyed a significant following within the black mainstream as early as the mid-1960s. In New York City in February 1965, for example, Dr. Robert Pritchard, an internationally respected musician, helped establish a guild society called the American Festival of Negro Art, which promoted Africa as the "fount and reservoir of our cultural strength." Pritchard did not see himself as a radical or a separatist but as an advocate of a cultural pluralism that encouraged blacks to reveal "respect for [their] own sources." In the same month, Morris College, a small liberal arts school in Sumter, South Carolina, sponsored a Negro History Week, which featured African arts and crafts, a special course on the Swahili language, and presentations on black history in the United States and black contributions to American culture through jazz and literature. These events constituted only two examples of numerous celebrations that occurred within black communities throughout this period, and they reflected a strong desire by blacks to establish their own independent identity and heritage.[22]

Such festive culture and the observance of ritualized celebrations had always been part of the black experience, but these activities became more pronounced in the sixties and, more important, began to shift away from programs that linked blacks to the social and political mainstream. The festive culture of the sixties reflected the efforts of blacks to redefine their place in American society by placing their heritage within the context of the history of black people in Africa and the Caribbean and by emphasizing their commitment to group as opposed to individualistic values of American society. Cultural innovation revealed itself during this era in language—"black is beautiful"—and in such visual symbols as the new "Afro" haircuts, the dashiki shirt, and African robes. West Coast nationalist Maulana Ron Karenga developed a black cultural catechism, which included a black holiday (Kwanzaa), the Swahili language, and cultural imagery of traditional Tanzanian society.[23] Together these elements were designed to celebrate the history of African Americans, their culture, and the values that shaped their heritage.

Through this cultural transformation, black militants sought to create a heightened sense of group identity that challenged the national adherence to traditional Puritan and free labor ideologies with their emphasis on individual advancement through self-help and hard work. Civil rights experiences from Mississippi in 1964 to Chicago in 1966 had made it clear that removal of segregation barriers alone did not resolve the fundamental needs existing in the black community. In the aftermath of the Voting Rights Act of 1965, these militants came to believe that racism was endemic to American corporate liberalism and that civil rights reform was insufficient to expunge its racist character. By the end of the decade, they insisted upon a restructuring of American political culture and proposed group solutions to improve the lot of African Americans and to remove centuries of inequity.[24]

Not all black leaders rushed to embrace the cultural revival, an African American ethnicity, and group entitlement. Led by the NAACP, most black moderates rejected ethnicity outright as socially and politically dangerous. Others saw value in the symbols and pageantry of the nationalist movement and perceived an African American ethnicity as an effective way to maintain a sense of group pride and unity in the movement's aftermath, but they did not support a political and economic restructuring of American society. Still others embraced this new ethnic identity as a way to revamp the U.S. political and economic process, which they regarded as being fundamentally at odds with the needs of the black community.[25]

The NAACP, which was generally supported by SCLC, led the attack against the efforts of groups like the Congress on Racial Equality (CORE), SNCC, and a variety of other more outspoken organizations because they saw them as a direct challenge to the struggle for integration. The confrontation became more than a struggle over tactics; integrationists saw cultural nationalism as an effort by militant organizations to assume leadership and direction of the black community and to redefine the terms of its relationship with white society. The NAACP and SCLC believed it was totally unrealistic and dangerous for a black minority to pursue a nonliberal, nonintegrationist agenda. Leaders of these organizations argued that such an approach would place blacks once again in a subservient position and subject them to the wrath of whites. They also opposed the concept of cultural nationalism because they felt that whites had long used ethnicity to separate themselves from blacks and to spotlight their own uniqueness and, by inference, superiority. In this context, black integrationists in the sixties feared that by raising the banner of ethnicity, blacks would facilitate the reconstruction of the color line and devastate the racial progress of the previous ten years.[26] They emphasized as well the connection between the black past and the United States and noted Alex Haley's book, *Roots*, as documentation for their argument that the black heritage was formed principally in the United States.[27]

The difficulty for the NAACP in this confrontation with the cultural nationalists was that the organization was trying to preserve a heritage with which many blacks were decidedly uncomfortable. It also was engaged in a battle for the status quo in an age of transition, not just for African Americans but for the larger society as well. Stokely Carmichael and his allies understood the dynamics of this age much better than Roy Wilkins and the NAACP.

Leaders of the ethnic movement and cultural revival took their campaign into the public schools and universities, where they sought to make African American history part of the curriculum and thus part of the permanent cultural heritage of black Americans and the nation. In an era that was often marked by paradox and irony, black leaders turned the traditional social function of public education upside down. Frequently used as a mechanism to facilitate social control and acceptance of mainstream cultural values in the late nineteenth and twentieth centuries, the public schools acted as an extension of society in keeping blacks (and indeed other ethnic minorities) in their place. In the late 1960s black leaders sought to change the educational environment so that it no longer denied their children access to their African American heritage and forced them to conform to Euro-centered norms. This effort encountered strong opposition from teachers' unions and other parent groups, especially in New York; however, the black leaders refused to compromise and gained strong allies among university faculties. Whereas public school and university educators had previously ignored black history, they gradually responded to the demands of militants and black families to recognize the richness and diversity of the black past.[28]

By the end of the decade, this cultural awakening had made enormous gains in the black community; even conservative black institutions like the *Pittsburgh Courier* recognized the importance of certain features of cultural pluralism. One editorial asked rhetorically, "How great can the American Negro become in self-esteem and personal dignity if his history and culture are lost, both to him and his white colleagues."[29] This development served as one of the cornerstones of the efforts of blacks to redefine their place in society on their own terms and to revolutionize their perceptions of American political and social values.

The debate over black identity and cultural nationalism within the black community provided the middle class with an opportunity to vent its exasperation with the extent and pace of racial reform in the United States, but it offered little or no solace for members of the lower class, few of whom could see beyond the drudgery of daily life. Despite the demise of Jim Crow, the urban ghettos in the North witnessed mounting unrest as lower-class residents failed to see any improvement in their own lives and watched silently as the middle class departed in increasing numbers to the suburbs. When congressional leaders joked about about a proposed rat eradication bill to address the health needs of the urban poor, spokespersons for the nation's ghettos angrily shouted: "We no longer want to belong to this country. We shall declare our independence." Repeated clashes between ghetto residents and police over incidents that were often marked by blatant racism kept discontent at a high level and ultimately fostered massive violence. The ghettos exploded in a wave of rioting that began in Harlem in 1964 and continued through 1969. During this five-year period, over 300 riots occurred, destroying more than a billion dollars in property and resulting in 250 deaths, with the worst occurring in Newark and Detroit in 1967.[30]

Sociologists, political scientists, and historians remain divided about the exact causes of the riots, but most note that, despite racial and economic progress, profound disillusionment prevailed in the urban ghettos. In 1967, for example, 62 to 65 percent of all blacks acknowledged that racial advancements had taken place, but more than one-third saw little or no change in their own lives. Significantly, young blacks and residents of the ghetto were much more likely to believe that conditions had either stayed the same or had actually worsened.[31] For these people, the political gains continued to elude them, and riots were their way of expressing their anger and of demanding fundamental change.

While the riots served as an outlet of expression for the poor and the young, they offered no long-term solutions for the needs of the black community and they troubled the middle class greatly. Increasingly the black mainstream looked to the voting rights provided by the 1965 law to transform the political process and to provide social and economic reform that would help ease the crisis in the ghetto. In city after city beginning in the second half of the 1960s, black voters threw out the old clientage politics in which white candidates and white-dominated political machines received their votes in exchange for limited political and economic favors to black leaders.[32]

Civil rights activism of the sixties mobilized blacks politically, and debates over issues of identity and culture heightened the emphasis on group concerns. The black power movement, in particular, "represented a recognition of the urgent need for black solidarity in politics" in order to achieve a fundamental restructuring of American society. In combination with a widespread belief that more was owed the black community for

David R. Colburn and George E. Pozzetta

nearly three centuries of slavery and segregation, these developments sparked a dramatic political trend in cities where blacks constituted a majority of the voters. For the first time since Reconstruction, blacks rejected traditional white political appeals and looked to their own community to address their political and economic concerns.[33]

Louis Martin, journalist and political adviser to Presidents John F. Kennedy and Lyndon Johnson, observed that the Voting Rights Act ushered in a new breed of minority urban politicians who understood that "political power is generated in the black precincts and does not come from the hand of the great white father." These black political leaders came overwhelmingly from the ranks of the middle class, and most had been involved in civil rights activism and in local politics prior to their campaigns for mayor.[34]

The election of black mayors in Cleveland, Ohio, and Gary, Indiana, in 1967 reflected the gradual transition of black activism from the street to the ballot box. Although these new urban politicians did not radically alter the political process, they did pursue a different agenda from their white predecessors. Carl Stokes of Cleveland and Richard Hatcher of Gary undertook new programs to enhance urban redevelopment in order to offset the loss of old industries; in the process, they also sought to broaden the base of participation by increasing benefits for the black community. Through "Cleveland Now" and "One Gary," Stokes and Hatcher succeeded in enhancing leadership and employment opportunities for blacks through political appointments and minority set-aside programs. Despite these achievements, communities like "Gary faced so many problems," as Charles Levine observed, "that local efforts could only improve conditions at the margin of daily life." Gary, Newark, and many other northern communities, for example, lost as many as half of the old industrial jobs in the 1960s and early 1970s.[35]

As the urban environment of the old Northeast and Midwest fell into decline because of the out-migration of companies and workers and because of the stagflation that resulted from Vietnam, black voters looked beyond the cities to the federal government for answers that would redress urban and racial inequities and provide group, rather than individual, solutions. In the House of Representatives, nine black congressional leaders, led by Representative Charles Diggs, Jr., organized themselves into an informal committee in 1969 to lobby Congress for civil rights and social welfare reforms to meet the demands of their black constituents. Two years later the Congressional Black Caucus emerged from this ad hoc committee to become a permanent part of the political structure in the

House and the Senate. In an age of rising conservatism, the caucus sought to protect the gains of the Kennedy-Johnson years and to secure new legislation that would provide social and economic advancement for black Americans. They also initiated proposals to obtain federal support for programs that highlighted the African American past and enhanced a sense of community. Congressman John Conyers from Detroit, for example, sponsored a resolution in 1968 that established 14 February, the date Frederick Douglass chose to celebrate his birthday, as the beginning of Afro American History Week.[36]

Black political efforts to secure substantive economic concessions from the federal government coincided with the efforts of women to redress widespread gender discrimination in the workplace. This powerful coalition came together in the late 1960s and lobbied federal officials for a program that would not just remove racial and gender barriers but that would also promote employment opportunities for both blacks and women. They settled on the concept of affirmative action, a plan that received broad-based support from a government bureaucracy that was committed to continued civil rights reform and from a federal court establishment that was willing to accept for the first time special programs to remedy past discrimination against racial minorities and women.[37]

Ethnic Activism

As black leaders asserted the need for additional social and economic reforms, whites generally and white ethnics particularly expressed resentment. Tensions quickly surfaced over urban renewal projects, affirmative action, and labor reforms. Many Polish and Italian Americans and Jews argued that they had worked their way out of poverty when government aid was nonexistent, mass public education was severely limited, and manpower development programs did not exist. These ethnics found it difficult to understand and accept black demands for "high income and high position now."[38] White ethnics did not oppose many of the fundamental reforms of the civil rights era, but they believed that changes in the areas of jobs, housing, and schools should be broad-based and not racially specific.

Affirmative action particularly frustrated white ethnics. Although the program was committed to erasing all distinctions of race, color, religion, or national origin, it mandated for the first time the keeping of meticulous records on precisely these attributes. Having struggled for decades to erase such distinctions, for they invariably imposed handicaps, European

: *David R. Colburn and George E. Pozzetta*

ethnics now were excluded from such designations at precisely the time when their ethnicity offered the prospect of economic and political rewards from the government.[39] The end result was to divide more formally the nation into racial and ethnic categories than ever before.[40]

Adding to the anger and alienation of white ethnics was the fact that American mass culture had long treated them with disdain, despite their integration into society. Polish Americans, for example, bore up under a host of negative stereotypes, perhaps best exemplified by the "Polish joke," that eroded their ability to form positive group and personal identities.[41] Similarly, Italian Americans were expected to accept demeaning references to the Mafia and organized crime without complaint. At a time when overt racism against blacks was prohibited by law and becoming socially unacceptable, the persistence of antiethnic biases rankled deeply. Middle-class bigotry directed against working-class ethnics, it seemed, was still legitimate, and images of "racist-bigot-redneck-ethnic-Irish-Italian-Pole-Hunkie-Yahoo" became etched in the public mind.[42]

Simultaneously, the national media began to focus on instances of black/ethnic conflict.[43] On television news and in newspaper headlines, ethnics appeared as the major stumbling blocks to black progress and the return of peace to America's increasingly troubled urban landscape. This was true in spite of research that showed that there was less bigotry among white ethnics than other segments of the population, and that lower-income whites typically were able to identify with the problems of blacks. One 1969 Gallup poll, for example, found that 48 percent of respondents surveyed nationally answered yes to the question, "Is integration moving too fast?," while only 42 percent of blue-collar Catholics responded positively. A Lou Harris poll one year later revealed that one-half of native whites, compared to only two-fifths of Irish, Italian, and Polish Americans, believed that the push for racial equality had been too fast.[44] Also, fewer ethnics than native whites opposed the Supreme Court's decision on desegregation. Steven N. Adubato, director of the Center for Urban Ethnic Affairs of New Jersey, perhaps phrased it most accurately: "We want no slowdown in the advancement of blacks or brown," he explained, "but we don't want their advancement at the expense of the white ethnics."[45]

By the mid-to-late 1960s white ethnics had become the "forgotten" Americans, those individuals who fit somewhere between the slums and the suburbs.[46] Not eligible for federally funded compensatory programs, white ethnics were carrying much of the tax load for social programs and bearing the painful costs of various government initiatives to restructure society.[47] One resident of Jersey City voiced his perception of the transformations overwhelming his neighborhood in the sixties: "We became guinea pigs for the experiments of the liberal intellectuals and politicians. They bused our kids, made radical, unwanted changes in the liturgy of the church. . . . We begged for law and order and the liberals sneered and called us racists. We wanted to save, and we got inflation. We've been used, manipulated, and scorned."[48] Activist Monsignor Geno Baroni put it more succinctly: "Ethnic whites are economically, culturally, socially, and politically alienated and disillusioned."[49]

Substantial numbers of Catholic and Jewish ethnics had resisted suburban flight and remained behind in their urban enclaves. As the decade progressed, the neighborhoods in which many ethnics lived were themselves under assault on a variety of fronts. Supermarket chains undercut the small groceries that sustained many family fortunes. Property values declined as insurance and real estate companies red-lined ethnic neighborhoods in the face of black residential movement.[50] School integration proposals involving forced busing as well as deteriorating city budgets, increasing crime rates, and residential displacement all sounded alarm bells in ethnic settlements. Cherished family homes, products of years of saving and hard work, not only eroded in dollar terms, but also often lost the familiar neighborhood settings that gave them such psychological worth.[51] One South Boston ethnic expressed his frustration this way: "My kids don't have a place to swim, my parks are full of glass, and I'm supposed to bleed for a bunch of people on relief?"[52] These patterns of community change and alienation underwrote the increasing levels of conflict and confrontation characterizing urban America.[53]

European ethnics were also painfully aware that, despite the appearance of upward mobility, many were only precariously situated in the lower middle class, while others remained poor. One survey of members of Polish American organizations located in Pittsburgh during the mid-1960s found that they typically earned between $5,000 and $6,000 a year, incomes that placed them at the poverty line. The median income in Irish South Boston during the same period was $5,000 a year.[54] Out of pride or cultural dictates, residents of these neighborhoods seldom used welfare subsidies for support. The thrust of government programs promising aid to blacks and supplying affirmative action guarantees in the marketplace were further proofs of how marginalized these people had become. As Eric Hoffer put it in 1969, "We are told we have to feel guilty. We've been poor all our lives and now we're being preached to by every son of a bitch who comes along. The ethnics are discovering that you can't trust the Mayflower boys."[55] The least mobile and economically secure members of ethnic groups were most often those left in the central cities, areas that had become in the sixties the contested terrain of social protest and black activism.

Ethnic responses to these conditions contained a hard bite. "Everybody wants a gun," proclaimed a Slavic community worker in Milwaukee. "They think they've heard from black power, wait till they hear from white power."[56] Such rhetoric led many to believe that the ethnic revival was motivated primarily by a racist backlash to the demands of black activists. As one observer remarked of ethnics, "They've always been anti-negro, but they've never been pressured to say it publicly before."[57] Paul Deac, head of the National Confederation of American Ethnic Groups, gave substance to these charges in 1969, when he proclaimed, "We spend millions and the Negroes get everything and we get nothing."[58]

But the revival consisted of more than aggrieved urban residents employing ethnicity to protect their self-interests and forge political advantage. A wider debate transcended particular locales and involved the images that ethnic groups possessed in the broader public. Generalizations are difficult to frame, as each group followed a course based upon its own cultural values and its unique historical experiences. Moreover, in the sixties no single voice spoke for any white ethnic group; such groups were too segmented by generation, class, residence, and ideology for that to happen. Hence, the discourse within groups over the proper symbols and images to use in contemporary American society often generated an intensity that matched that of the dialogue with the dominant society.

Like blacks, ethnic Americans responded to the social and economic transformations not only with political protest, but also with cultural creativity. To observe the larger national patterns at work, the experiences of two widely different white ethnic groups—Italian Americans and Scottish Americans—provide insight. Italian Americans were a relatively recent group that comprised a substantial population, possessed significant internal diversity, and had a distinctive image in the national mind. Scottish Americans, by contrast, represented a long-settled group that was considered fully within the mainstream.

As Rudolph J. Vecoli has noted, a striking aspect of Italian American activism during the late 1960s was the extraordinary expansion of organizational activity. Scores of groups sprang up, and dozens of older organizations underwent revitalization. Moreover, a spate of new publications representing a broad spectrum of viewpoints appeared in the marketplace.[59] These institutions helped to support and direct a broad-based interest in the history and culture of Italian Americans. They also provided the human and financial capital that underwrote the resurgence (and sometimes creation) of numerous festivals, celebrations, and rituals invoking the group's historical roots. Contained within this range of activities, and largely unseen by outsiders, was a spirited contest among Italian Americans for the right to speak for all and project a particular image of the group to the larger society.

Some successful Italian American professionals and upwardly mobile middle-class individuals expressed dissatisfaction with characterizations of Italian Americans as unskilled, uneducated boors. Certain organizations attempted to fashion a more positive view by focusing on the glories of Italian high culture (that is, a "Renaissance motif"). This strategy sought to connect Italian Americans with the accomplishments of Dante, da Vinci, and other renowned Italians.[60] Status-conscious Italian Americans also attempted to utilize favorable symbols drawn from contemporary Italy, as evidenced by the appeal of Italian high fashion and the prestige attached to labels such as Gucci, Pucci, and Ferrari.[61]

Concern over negative stereotypes that had lingered from the years of peasant immigration also led to renewed attempts to define the "contributions" of Italians to the development of America. This strategy proved equally selective in its use of symbols. Filiopietistic endeavors to highlight the exploits of Italian and Italian American "heroes" in the nation's past were evident in various campaigns to promote the issuance of a commemorative stamp to Fillipo Mazzei; bring recognition to the work of such individuals as Constantine Brumedi, Eusebio Kino, and John Cabot (or Juan Caboto); and build monuments to other overlooked notables. Perhaps the most vigorously fought—and ultimately successful—struggle was that to have Columbus Day declared a federal holiday.[62]

The attempt to rewrite American history selectively so as to recognize the contributions of Italians had implications beyond efforts to remake the group's image. The legitimization of the place of Italian Americans in contemporary society ("We are as American as anyone else!") prompted some organizations to demand increased representation for Italian Americans in government appointments and on private boards.[63] The intense lobbying in support of Judge Antonino Scalia for appointment to the Supreme Court was indicative of this trend.[64]

Ethnic expression among Italian Americans has not been restricted to these constituencies and issues. For working- and lower-middle-class Italian Americans residing in many urban enclaves, ethnicity helped mobilize residents to respond to deteriorating neighborhoods, black encroachment, and the larger problems of alienation, neglect, and feelings of pow-

David R. Colburn and George E. Pozzetta

erlessness. As Jonathan Rieder has pointed out, "Ethnic identity did not come only from the givens of biological nature or the passions of racism. It was equally a product of a tense opposition, a reaction to the attempts of rivals to name themselves and to identify their enemies."[65] Organizations such as the Italian American Civil Rights League and the Joint Civic Committee of Italian Americans attempted to use group solidarity based upon a "commonality of heritage" for assistance in preserving neighborhoods and resisting intrusive government programs (for example, forced busing).[66]

In Canarsie, South Boston, and other locations, where blue-collar Italian Americans felt themselves under direct threat, ethnicity played an important role in framing the debate. Faced with the unsettling implications of neighborhood change, these Italian Americans dipped into their cultural reservoir to select values that, for them, represented standards that they personally cherished and that they believed were compatible with the mores of American society. A favorite was the "bootstraps" interpretation of the past, a view that focused on the group's ability to succeed based on the immigrant work ethic, sacrifice, family, and loyalty. This effort to ennoble the ethnic past was not necessarily false; it was a selective refashioning that contrasted sharply with the demands for special treatment by African Americans.[67]

Italian Americans who were removed from the charged atmosphere of the embattled urban neighborhood also engaged in the crafting of an ethnic heritage. Settlements across the nation witnessed an array of ethnic celebrations, festivals, and parades. Whether they were feast days of saints or commemorations of special events in the local history of a particular "Little Italy," these events became part of a grass roots cultural movement that shared a number of common themes.[68] Typically, celebrations highlighted the benefits of close family networks, domesticity, intimate neighborhoods offering stability and security, smaller value structures and loyalties, and the nonmaterialist qualities of ethnic life-styles.[69]

Although the contrast was not always made overtly, the fact that these values offered a corrective to America's individualist materialism and the faceless anonymity that marked the nation's mass consumption society was evident. In the words of one Italian American, the old immigrant life-styles could supply an antidote to "the abandonment of values in modern society."[70] Even middle- and upper-middle class Italian Americans who perceived the peasant, immigrant past as too harsh to frame acceptable identities have often been able to choose usable elements from their ethnic traditions. As Donald Tricarico has observed, "Cultivated Italian-

Americans have discovered folk arts and crafts, like the marionette theater and the work of painters like Ralph Fasanella and writers like Pietro DiDonato" in their efforts to shape identities.[71]

A second broad pattern of activity consisted of a defensive, though quite aggressive, antidefamation effort to attack uncomplimentary stereotypes and present more favorable images before the broader society. One aspect of this Italian American "negotiation," for example, centered on prevailing conceptions of Italian criminality and the Mafia that enjoyed wide acceptance in the United States. Italian Americans had long complained about these characterizations, but by the late 1960s they began to do so in a different manner. Various Italian American groups brought direct pressure against the Federal Bureau of Investigation (FBI) and the media for their repeated references to the Cosa Nostra and the Mafia.[72] Similar motivations underlay various attempts to halt Italian jokes, commercials, and other media representations that depicted Italian Americans as coarse, uneducated ethnics. Protests forced the cancellation, for example, of a spaghetti sauce commercial that featured a poorly clad, swarthy man muttering, "That'sa some spicy meatball!"[73]

Throughout the revival, various Italian American organizations attempted to demonstrate the group's contribution to American society while simultaneously promoting internal solidarity. The line between the two was not always clear-cut, as Italian Americans debated internally what constituted their Americanness and their ethnic identity. Since they participated in the creation of American society and since they believed their heritage possessed values that offered correctives to the dominant culture, Italian Americans perceived themselves as American as any other group.[74]

Though prominent in the ethnic revival, Italian Americans represented only one aspect of the movement. Rowland Berthoff's examination "under the kilt" of contemporary Scottish American festivals argued that even groups thought to have assimilated totally were affected. In the 1960s and 1970s, Berthoff noted the extraordinary expansion of "Highland games" and Scottish family associations (clans) in America, during which "the new often professed to be more traditional than the old."[75] Yet virtually all of these ethnic manifestations had become so thoroughly intermixed with contemporary practices and symbols that they scarcely resembled "authentic" Scottish culture.

Why were Scottish Americans now attempting to revive an identity that had been largely forgotten for nearly two hundred years? As quintessential WASPs, they seemingly had no need to defend themselves against ethnic slurs or protect a working-class life-style. Berthoff's analysis identi-

David R. Colburn and George E. Pozzetta

fied a number of influences, but he argued principally that Scottish Americans were using ethnicity as a defense against a "society whose official commitment to equality of personal rights . . . has recently come to seem oddly oppressive."[76] Thus, the games and clans provided "an acceptable refuge from the courts and commissions that since 1954 have been ordering racial integration in other public and quasi-private places."[77]

Such responses could not fail to display elements of racism, yet Berthoff believed that Scottish American ethnicity involved far more than an aversion to blacks or an assertion of racial superiority. At root it was a reaction to the loss of "communal equality" in the modern world, a desire to have "a known place among people like oneself." It also provided an antidote to the social and economic instability of the sixties. The revived clans and games, for example, offered a sense of shared community to meet these needs. The outward forms of the resulting ethnicity were, in fact, invented. As Berthoff pointed out, "The kinship may be attenuated and even mistaken, the symbolism contrived, the legends mostly romance, and none of it quite what it is taken for," but ethnicity had real force for people who were by all the usual criteria thoroughly assimilated Americans.[78]

Although the Scots did not seek political reform, many ethnics—following the example of blacks—used politics to address the events that were transforming their lives. Political activists began at the grass roots level, aggressively defending the rights of neighborhoods and usually employing ethnic appeals to generate unity and support. Congresswoman Barbara Mikulski, of Maryland, who assumed office during the late 1960s, represented this type of ethnic politician. Mikulski spoke eloquently of the "urban villages" that had been created in America's cities by ethnic groups and passionately defended the communal spirit and quality of life that characterized them. Another advocate, Congressman Roman Pucinski of Illinois, phrased the message more succinctly by urging people to realize that "the Melting Pot has never worked quite so well in life as in nostalgic myth."[79]

In addition to seeking redress for economic, political, and social grievances, all ethnic groups attempted to forge new identities and social positions for themselves in American society. Cultural creativity, for example, marked the experiences of Chinese Americans who adopted many of the approaches of African Americans while pursuing their own political demands. The Red Guards of San Francisco and New York heightened ethnic consciousness among Chinese Americans by celebrating the legacies of the Chinese revolution and spawning a variety of community-based institutions.[80] Mexican Americans were not silent during these years as they too created a host of community-based protest organizations, such as the Brown Berets and the Mexican American Youth Organization. These institutions helped them to construct a new identity as Chicanos, an image built upon fresh conceptions of the role that Mexican Americans have played in the building of American society.[81] By refusing to accept fully the traditional assimilationist pathway, ethnic Americans were signaling that there were alternate ways of integrating into American society.[82]

Conclusion

The emergence and evolution of black and ethnic activism during the sixties suggests that issues of identity constituted more than just a reactionary force in American life. In this period of political, social, and economic instability, groups turned inward to rediscover values that gave their lives meaning and that assisted them in formulating strategies to address their needs and concerns.

Although the reinvention of culture was an important aspect of black and ethnic activism, it was by no means the only goal or even the most significant achievement. Implicit in these movements was an effort to change fundamentally the rules of political behavior in the United States. African Americans rejected the old liberal politics that welcomed them at the political table and invited them, in the aftermath of the Voting Rights Act, to participate in the bargaining process for individual benefits. Ethnics, too, in response to black activism, challenged the national emphasis on individualism and individual achievement in an effort to earn respect for themselves and their group.

During the decade, blacks and white ethnics became more politically assertive, more willing to organize collectively to seek group benefits, more prepared to use the courts and public forums to address their grievances than ever before. As part of this new approach to American politics, they also demonstrated a willingness to employ confrontational tactics, often directed against powerful governmental agencies such as the FBI, the Department of Justice, and the Census Bureau. Many organizations that came into being during these years provided group cohesion and political mobilization to underpin effective public protest.

But the black power movement and the ethnic revival were more than just new-styled manifestations of the old political game of interest group politics—the broker state model of pluralism in which activists pounded on the table in order to bring home political rewards for their group. Many politicians made the mistake of assuming that if enough minor

David R. Colburn and George E. Pozzetta

concessions were granted, disaffected groups could be quieted and nothing basic about what it meant to be an American and about how Americans related to government and other primary social institutions would change. Under this formula, the common codes of linguistic and civil behavior would remain unaffected. Although bargaining for political chips did take place, an important component of both movements sought much more. They aimed at a fundamental redefinition of group culture and, ultimately, American culture itself.

This pattern was very evident in the black power movement. A telling development occurred in the wake of the civil rights movement when blacks finally succeeded in winning a place at the bargaining table but many refused to sit. The new emphasis on black culture and identity, which spanned the ideological spectrum from civil rights activism to black nationalism and even separatism, generated an energy and a direction of its own that ultimately redefined expectations and goals.

Black activism and the ethnic revival succeeded in initiating a process by which ethnicity was repositioned in American society. They did so by providing ethnic identification with a positive status that few would have deemed possible a decade earlier. In Andrew Greeley's view, the civil rights and black nationalist movements were particularly critical in legitimizing cultural pluralism and ethnic expression.[83] In consort with the ethnic revival, they made it possible to "be American" in a greater variety of ways than had been previously accepted.[84] According to linguist Joshua Fishman, ethnicity came to occupy during this period much the same position as religion in American society.[85] For the major European ethnic groups, ethnicity extended beyond considerations of class, ideology, or connotations of being more or less American. In Fishman's words, ethnicity has become "part of the American experience [and is] seen as not only 'natural' but as being humanizing and strengthening in some general sense and those who display it situationally are not outside the mainstream."[86]

The elevated status of ethnicity also meant that the unquestioned acceptance of American individualist values was shaken by the efforts of the ethnic revival and black protest movements.[87] The vigorous assertion of the right, not only of groups but also of neighborhoods and communities, to have representation in the American political system challenged the nation's previously enshrined notions of individual freedom and free enterprise.[88] These new assumptions altered the political discourse in the nation and challenged notions of assimilation into American society.[89]

Black power and then ethnic power were also means of demonstrating political legitimacy in the classic sense of the term. They were ways of defining how government should be constructed and how the political system was supposed to provide an equitable process of governance. Black power was a continuation of the early civil rights movement's emphasis on group regeneration, not simply a political tactic to bring home more bacon. The ethnic revival, although in part an effort to defend jobs and neighborhoods, was also an attempt to express a relationship between the individual and the body politic. Both movements constituted a reformulation of from whom and to whom political legitimacy stems.

These two movements in large part flowed from the failure of the liberal model of political legitimacy to meet the needs of racial and ethnic minorities. With its emphasis on the centrality of individual self-interest, the liberal model offered limited opportunity to these groups. During the sixties many blacks and ethnics embraced group identity politics because they reflected, at their core, the inadequacies of the old rules of political legitimacy. They rejected the liberal model because it was calculated to keep the race for individual self-interest more or less fair, while ignoring or denigrating the group inequities that underpinned racial and ethnic alienation. Such a political configuration was no longer acceptable to them.

The two movements also had, however, important and fundamental differences. African American militants wanted much more than a repudiation of American individualism. They sought the reconfiguration of the role of group in the American liberal, capitalist state. Their belief in the inherent racism of a system that precluded genuine equal opportunity led them to demand a group entitlement program that would be underwritten by state power. Affirmative action programs were the most visible and controversial results of their efforts. This form of group recognition challenged the basic belief in the rationality of individuals and markets, which elites had long held to be the essence of the American capitalist system.

Ethnic Americans could not be persuaded to go this far. They sought national recognition of the group respectability that they believed they had earned through their social and economic achievements and through the strength of their family structures. The group values they defended most vigorously were those that sustained the individual members, both against the atomizing, mass consumer culture and a paternalistic, intrusive federal government. By the sixties they had done sufficiently well in the economic sector to resist vehemently any government efforts to overthrow the market-based system that allocated rewards to individuals.

Thus, in the end, after sharing a great deal along the way, the black power movement and the ethnic revival chose to follow separate paths. The result was a permanent shattering of the Democratic New Deal coalition that had dominated national politics for over thirty years.

NOTES

1. Allan Matusow, *The Unraveling of America: A History of Liberalism in the 1960s* (New York: Harper and Row, 1984), 355.

2. David R. Colburn and George E. Pozzetta, eds., *America and the New Ethnicity* (Port Washington, N.Y.: Kennikat Press, 1979), 152. This effort to change the ethnic identity of Polish Americans was to include, according to Helen Lopata, an attempt on the part of the intelligentsia "to create ideologies and select cultural items which could be used outside the community to project a new image." Helen Z. Lopata, *Polish Americans: Status Competition in an Ethnic Community* (Englewood Cliffs, N.J.: Prentice-Hall, 1976).

3. Nicolas Pileggi, "Risorgimento: The Red, White, and Greening of New York," in *New Ethnicity*, edited by Colburn and Pozzetta, 118–19; Perry L. Weed, *The White Ethnic Movement and Ethnic Politics* (New York: Praeger, 1973), 51, 58.

4. See Daniel Bell, *The End of Ideology* (New York: Free Press, 1960); William Whyte, *The Organization Man* (Garden City, N.Y.: Doubleday, 1957); Snell Putney, *The Adjusted American* (New York: Harper and Row, 1966); and David Reisman, *The Lonely Crowd* (Garden City, N.Y.: Doubleday, 1953).

5. For differing views of the civil rights movement and the sixties, see William Chafe, *The Unfinished Journey: America since World War II* (New York: Oxford University Press, 1968); Harvard Sitkoff, *The Struggle for Black Equality, 1954–1980* (New York: Hill and Wang, 1981); Steven F. Lawson, *Running for Freedom: Civil Rights and Black Politics in America since 1941* (Philadelphia: Temple University Press, 1990); William L. O'Neil, *Coming Apart: An Informal History of America in the 1960s* (New York: Quadrangle, 1971); and Jim Heath, *Decade of Disillusionment: The Kennedy-Johnson Years* (Bloomington: Indiana University Press, 1975). On ethnic revival, see Colburn and Pozzetta, *New Ethnicity*; Weed, *White Ethnic Movement*; Orlando Patterson, *Ethnic Chauvinism: The Reactionary Impulse* (New York: Stein and Day, 1977); Stephen Steinberg, *The Ethnic Myth: Race, Ethnicity, and Class in America* (Boston: Beacon Press, 1981); David R. Goldfield, *Black, White, and Southern: Race Relations and Southern Culture, 1940 to the Present* (Baton Rouge: Louisiana State University Press, 1990); William H. Chafe, *Civilities and Civil Rights: Greensboro, North Carolina, and the Black Struggle for Freedom* (New York: Oxford University Press, 1980); Michael Novak, *The Rise*

of the Unmeltable Ethnics: Politics and Culture in the 1970s (New York: Macmillan, 1971); Todd Gitlin, *The Sixties: Years of Hope, Days of Rage* (New York: Bantam, 1989); and Matusow, *Unraveling of America.*

6. In this essay the term *revival* refers to ethnic developments during the sixties, but it was only one of many that contemporary analysts employed. Other designations were *reawakening, reassertion, resurgence, revolt, revitalization, renaissance, rediscovery, backlash, new pluralism, new ethnicity, reactive ethnicity,* and *ethnic chauvinism.* Each of these terms carries a certain set of assumptions and judgments regarding the nature of ethnicity and assimilation in American society. Taken collectively, they point to the difficulty of easily defining such a complex phenomenon as ethnicity in modern society.

7. The concept of the invention of ethnicity derives from the pioneering work of Eric Hobsbawm and Terence Ranger, eds., *The Invention of Tradition* (Cambridge: Cambridge University Press, 1983), and Werner Sollors, ed., *The Invention of Ethnicity* (New York: Oxford University Press, 1985). For a recent reformulation, see Kathleen Conzen, David Gerber, Ewa Morawska, George Pozzetta, and Rudolph Vecoli, "The Invention of Ethnicity: A Perspective from the U.S.A.," *Altreitalie* 4 (Fall 1990): 37–61.

8. Wilson Jeremiah Moses, *The Golden Age of Black Nationalism, 1850–1925* (New York: Oxford University Press, 1978), 197–219. See also Judith Stein, "Defining the Race, 1980–1930," in *Invention of Ethnicity,* edited by Sollors, 82; Malcolm X, *The*

Autobiography of Malcolm X (New York: Grove Press, 1965), 211–65; Stokely Carmichael and Charles Hamilton, *Black Power: The Politics of Liberation in America* (New York: Random House, 1967); Judith Stein, *The World of Marcus Garvey: Race and Class in Modern Society* (Baton Rouge: Lousiana State University Press, 1986); Paula F. Pfeffer, *A. Philip Randolph: Pioneer of the Civil Rights Movement* (Baton Rouge: Louisiana State University Press, 1990), 45–168.

9. Doug McAdam, *Freedom Summer* (New York: Oxford University Press, 1988), 116–60; Clayborne Carson, *In Struggle: SNCC and the Black Awakening of the 1960's* (Cambridge: Harvard University Press, 1981), 71–74, 141–42.

10. Herbert H. Haines, *Black Radicals and the Civil Rights Mainstream, 1954–1970* (Knoxville: University of Tennessee Press, 1988), 41, 49. See also Julius Lester, "The Angry Children of Malcolm X," in *Black Protest Thought in the Twentieth Century*, 2d ed., edited by August Meier, Elliott Rudwick, and Francis L. Broderick (Indianapolis: Bobbs-Merrill, 1971), 470.

11. Haines, *Black Radicals,* 49; Chafe, *Unfinished Journey,* 303; Matusow, *Unraveling of America,* 346.

12. Chafe, *Unfinished Journey,* 313–14; Carson, *In Struggle,* 123–29; McAdam, *Freedom Summer,* 81–82, 118–20; August Meier and Elliott Rudwick, *CORE: A Study in the Civil Rights Movement, 1942–1968* (New York: Oxford University Press, 1973), 279–81; David J. Garrow, *Bearing the Cross: Martin Luther King, Jr. and the*

Southern Christian Leadership Conference (New York: Morrow, 1986), 288. This view may well have been purposefully exaggerated, but black activists had difficulty understanding why the president would support the white delegation from Mississippi inasmuch as many of its members had indicated that they would vote for Republican candidate Barry Goldwater.

13. Carson, *In Struggle*, 216; C. Eric Lincoln, *The Black Muslims in America* (Boston: Beacon Press, 1973), xxiii; Manning Marable, *Race, Reform, and Rebellion: The Second Reconstruction in Black America, 1945–1982* (Jackson: University Press of Mississippi, 1984), 109; Carmichael and Hamilton, *Black Power*, 37–39. Carson (*In Struggle*) describes Carmichael's identification with the cultural revolution and political autonomy.

14. *Pittsburgh Courier*, 23 April 1960.

15. L. Singer, "Ethnogenesis and Negro-Americans Today," *Social Research* 29 (Winter 1962): 429.

16. James Baldwin, *Notes of a Native Son* (Boston: Beacon Press, 1962), 174. For an elaboration of these points, see Allan P. Sindler, "Negroes, Ethnic Groups, and American Politics," *Current History* 55 (1968): 209–10.

17. Marable, *Race, Reform, and Rebellion*, 91–94; Carson, *In Struggle*, 216–19.

18. Sindler, "Negroes, Ethnic Groups," 211. See also Malcolm X, *Autobiography*, 211–65.

19. Carmichael and Hamilton, *Black Power*, 37–39; Carson, *In Struggle*, 209–10.

20. William Toll, *The Resurgence of Race: Black Social Theory from Reconstruction to the Pan-American Conference* (Philadelphia: Temple University Press, 1979), 168–73. See also Lincoln, *Black Muslims in America*, xxiii. According to the Muslim view, black Americans were descendants of the tribe of Shabazz, which first explored the planet. Although the campaign for redefining black identity and the African American heritage was most closely associated with militant groups of the late 1960s, this movement had been influential in black communities since the 1920s. Marcus Garvey, among others, had heightened a black and African consciousness by his condemnation of white racism in American society and by his efforts to assist black Americans in relocating to Africa.

21. Carson, *In Struggle*, 209–10; Moses, *Golden Age of Black Nationalism*, 214–17. Again, this debate over language and terminology was not new. In 1906 T. Thomas Fortune argued for "Afro-American" as the proper designation of people of African origin. The reemergence of this debate, however, occurred in a new context, and it reflected a pervasive view in the black community that language and terms of identity carried new meaning.

22. *Pittsburgh Courier*, 27, 13 February 1965.

23. Ibid., 27 February 1965; Marable, *Race, Reform, and Rebellion*, 118.

24. Carson, *In Struggle*, 215–19; McAdam, *Freedom Summer*, 127–32.

25. Carson, *In Struggle*, 219–20.

26. *Pittsburgh Courier*, 16, 22 July, 22 October 1966; Sidney Fine, *Vio-*

lence in the Model City: The Cavanagh Administration, Race Relations, and the Detroit Riot of 1967 (Ann Arbor: University of Michigan Press, 1989), 24.

27. New Pittsburgh Courier, 28 June 1965.

28. Ira Katznelson, City Trenches: Urban Politics and the Patterning of Class in the United States (Chicago: University of Chicago Press, 1981), 136–89; Lawson, Running for Freedom, 131–32; Robert G. Weisbord and Arthur Stein, Bittersweet Encounter: The Afro-American and the American Jew (Westport, Conn.: Negro University Presses, 1970), 164–75; Diane Ravitch, The Great School Wars, New York City, 1805–1973: A History of the Public Schools as a Battlefield of Social Change (New York: Basic Books, 1974); Chicago Daily Defender, 10–16 July 1971. An important part of this initiative involved the preservation and dissemination of black history. In 1968 a bill was introduced in the House of Representatives that led to the establishment of the National Afro American Museum in Wilberforce, Ohio. New Pittsburgh Courier, 27 January 1968.

29. New Pittsburgh Courier, 27 January 1968.

30. Garrow, Bearing the Cross, 498–529; Thomas B. Edsall and Mary D. Edsall, Chain Reaction: The Impact of Race, Rights, and Taxes on American Politics (New York: Norton, 1991), 65; Lawson, Running for Freedom, 127–28. See also James W. Button, Black Violence: Political Impact of the 1960s Riots (Princeton: Princeton University Press, 1978).

31. Chafe, Unfinished Journey, 337; Matusow, Unraveling of America, 362; Robert M. Fogelson, Violence as Protest: A Study of Riots and Ghettos (Garden City, N.J.: Doubleday, 1971), 90–94.

32. Martin Kilson, "Political Change in the Negro Ghetto, 1900–1940's," in Key Issues in the Afro-American Experience, edited by Nathan I. Huggins, Martin Kilson, and Daniel M. Fox (New York: Harcourt, Brace, Jovanovich, 1971), 171–74.

33. William E. Nelson, Jr., and Philip J. Meranto, Electing Black Mayors: Political Activism in the Black Community (Columbus: Ohio State University Press, 1977), 12–17.

34. Chicago Defender, 3–9 April 1971, 23 November 1970. See also Pittsburgh Courier, 4 February 1967, 16 November 1968.

35. Nelson and Meranto, Electing Black Mayors, 12–17; Charles Levine, Racial Conflict and the American Mayor: Power, Polarization, and Performance (Lexington, Mass.: Lexington Books, 1974) 77, 81 (quotation); William E. Nelson, Jr., "Cleveland: The Evolution of Black Political Power," in The New Black Politics: The Search for Political Power, edited by Michael B. Preston, Lenneal J. Henderson, Jr., and Paul L. Puryear (New York: Longman, 1982), 173, 178, 182; Edward Greer, Big Steel: Black Politics and Corporate Power in Gary, Indiana (New York: Monthly Review Press, 1979), 26, 36, 45, 47, 50; Peter K. Eisinger, "Black Mayors and the Politics of Racial Economic Advancement," in Readings in Urban Politics: Past, Present, and Future (New York: Longman, 1984), edited by

   David R. Colburn and George E. Pozzetta

Harlan Hahn and Charles Levine, 249–60. See also Carl B. Stokes, *Promises of Power: A Political Biography* (New York: Simon and Schuster, 1973).

36. *New Pittsburgh Courier*, 2 March 1965; Lawson, *Running for Freedom*, 140–41.

37. Hugh Davis Graham, *The Civil Rights Era: Origins and Development of National Policy, 1960–1972* (New York: Oxford University Press, 1990), 197–200, 205–32, 278–97. See also Susan M. Hartman, *American Women and Politics since 1960* (New York: Knopf, 1989).

38. Nathan Glazer and Daniel P. Moynihan, *Beyond the Melting Pot: The Negroes, Puerto Ricans, Jews, Italians and Irish of New York City* (Cambridge: MIT Press, 1963), 12; William Hamilton Harris, *The Harder We Run: Black Workers since the Civil War* (New York: Oxford University Press, 1982), 161.

39. John Lescott-Leszczynski, *The History of U.S. Ethnic Policy and Its Impact on European Ethnics* (Boulder, Colo.: Westview Press, 1984), 156.

40. Richard Krickus, *Pursuing the American Dream: White Ethnics and the New Populism* (Garden City, N.Y.: Anchor Press, 1976), 295–96.

41. John Bukowczyk, *And My Children Did Not Know Me: A History of the Polish Americans* (Bloomington: Indiana University Press, 1987), 112–14.

42. Rudolph J. Vecoli, "The Coming of Age of the Italian Americans," *Ethnicity* 5 (1978): 137–38; Peter Schrag, *Out of Place in America: Essays for the End of an Age* (New York: Random House, 1967), 14.

43. Schrag, *Out of Place*, 14.

44. Murray Friedman, ed., *Overcoming Middle-Class Rage* (Philadelphia: Westminster Press, 1971), 44–45.

45. *New York Times*, 4 May 1973.

46. Friedman, *Overcoming Middle-Class Rage*, 34–35.

47. Peter Rose, *They and We: Racial and Ethnic Relations in the United States*, 2d ed. (New York: Random House, 1974), 224; "A Rising Cry: Ethnic Power," *Newsweek*, 20 December 1970, 32.

48. *New York Times*, 29 September 1975, sec. A.

49. Ibid., 16 March 1972, sec. B.

50. John Bukowczyk, "The Decline and Fall of a Detroit Neighborhood: Poletown vs. G.M. and the City of Detroit," *Washington and Lee Law Review* 41 (Winter 1984): 49–76.

51. Pileggi, "Risorgimento," 118–19.

52. Peter Schrag, "Forgotten American," *Harper's*, August 1969, 27.

53. John F. Stack, "Ethnicity, Racism, and Busing in Boston: The Boston Irish and School Desegregation," *Ethnicity* 6 (1979): 21–28.

54. Schrag, "Forgotten American," 31.

55. "The Troubled American," *Newsweek*, 6 October 1969, 33.

56. Ibid., 32.

57. Ibid., 33.

58. Ibid., 31.

59. Vecoli, "Coming of Age," 137. The author makes the point that these publications were important for intragroup discourse. Included among the many were *Fra Noi*, a Catholic newspaper published in Chicago, *Italian Americana*, a scholarly journal printed in Buffalo, and *Attenzione*, a glossy,

upscale cultural magazine printed in New York for upper- and upper-middle-class Italian Americans.

60. Donald Tricarico, "The 'New' Italian American Ethnicity," *Journal of Ethnic Studies* 12 (Fall 1984): 75–93; Alfred Aversa, Jr., "Italian Neo-Ethnicity: The Search for Self-Identity," *Journal of Ethnic Studies* 6 (Summer 1978): 49–56.

61. Rudolph J. Vecoli, "The Search for an Italian American Identity: Continuity and Change," in *Italian Americans: New Perspectives in Italian Immigration and Ethnicity*, edited by Lydio F. Tomasi (New York: Center for Migration Studies, 1985), 106–7.

62. Ibid., 108.

63. The National Italian American Foundation has exemplified this approach. It now has a permanent staff in Washington, D.C., which serves as a watchdog for ethnic slurs directed against Italian Americans, as a political lobbying force for the group, and as a forum for celebrating group accomplishments.

64. Vecoli, "Coming of Age," 137. These initiatives have often clashed with the work of academics, many of whom were Italian Americans themselves. These individuals believed that the common experiences of millions of Italian peasants who immigrated represented the key element in the Italian American story. Of necessity, this effort has revealed the less pleasing aspects of the past (crime, poverty, social backwardness).

65. Jonathan Reider, *Canarsie: The Jews and Italians of Brooklyn against Liberalism* (Cambridge: Harvard University Press, 1985), 127; Colin Greer,

"The Ethnic Question," in *The Sixties without Apology*, edited by Sohnyn Sayres (Minneapolis: University of Minnesota Press, 1984), 126–27.

66. Vecoli, "Italian American Identity," 100.

67. Fred Barbaro, "Ethnic Affirmation, Affirmative Action, and the Italian American," *Italian Americana* 1 (Autumn 1974): 41–58; Rieder, *Canarsie*, 35, 102, 113.

68. In some cases these celebrations took on an almost panethnic quality as they attracted thousands of non–Italian American participants. The *Feste Italiana* in Milwaukee and the San Gennaro festival in New York City are examples.

69. At times residents created an idealized older world, the "magic days" in which the neighborhood manifested all the cherished old values. For a manifestation of this tendency, see Gary Mormino and George Pozzetta, *The Immigrant World of Ybor City: Italians and Their Latin Neighbors in Tampa, 1885–1985* (Champaign: University of Illinois Press, 1987), chap. 8.

70. Tricarico, "Italian American Ethnicity," 81.

71. Ibid., 82 (quotation); Donald Tricarico, *The Italians of Greenwich Village: The Social Structure and Transformation of an Ethnic Community* (New York: Center for Migration Studies, 1984). Some evidence of the effectiveness of this message is also revealed in the ability of people like Geraldine Ferraro, Mario Cuomo, and Lee Iacocca to emphasize family values in promoting their own careers. See Thomas J. Ferraro, "Blood in the

Marketplace: The Business of Family in the Godfather Narratives," in Sollors, *Invention of Ethnicity*, 176–208.

72. Rudolph J. Vecoli, "The Italian Americans," *The Center Magazine* 7 (July–August, 1974): 41. By the 1970s these efforts had gained results as newspapers, television stations, and government agencies generally agreed to stop using these terms and control their surveillance techniques. Yet such efforts continued. *L'Italo Americano*, 26 October 1989, reported the protests of the Sons of Italy on Attorney General Richard Thornberg's reference to the Mafia. For other incidents, see the publications of such organizations as the Italian American Civil Rights League, the Congress of Italian American Organizations (CIAO), the National Italian American Foundation, and Fra Noi.

73. *New York Times*, 17 October 1966, sec. D; Vecoli, "Italian Americans," 41. Mexican Americans were not immune to this sort of strategy, as they filed successful lawsuits against the Frito Lay Company to force removal of advertisements featuring the "Frito-Bandito."

74. W. Greenbaum, "America in Search of a New Identity: An Essay on the Rise of Pluralism," *Harvard Education Review* 44 (August 1974): 411–40. This is not to suggest that Italian Americans have not absorbed any American middle-class values.

75. Rowland Berthoff, "Under the Kilt: Variations on the Scottish-American Ground," *Journal of American Ethnic History* 1 (Spring 1982): 5–8, 15 (quotation).

76. Ibid., 18–25 (quotation, p. 25).

77. Ibid., 26.

78. Ibid., 26–27. Berthoff believes that ethnicity fills a void in American society created by the fact that America's commitment to equality of opportunity has not created equality of condition. Ethnicity thus can unite people on the basis of "equality of likeness, as shared community, as cultural likeness."

79. "Troubled American," 33; Barbara Mikulski, *The Ethnic American*, pamphlet published by the Polish Women's Alliance, 1969, 3.

80. Sanford Lyman, *Chinese Americans* (New York: Random House, 1974), 165; Shih-Shan Henry Tsai, *The Chinese Experience in America* (Bloomington: Indiana University Press, 1986), 167.

81. Rudolfo Acuna, *Occupied America: A History of Chicanos*, 2d ed. (New York: Harper and Row, 1981), 350–58.

82. Greenbaum, "America in Search," 415.

83. Rose, *They and We*, 229.

84. John Bukowczyk has pointed out that in many ways American mass consumerism has co-opted ethnicity, making it a commodity to be bought and sold on the open market. Yet even the process of co-optation implies a level of acceptance. Bukowczyk, *My Children Did Not Know Me*, 119.

85. Joshua A. Fishman, Michael H. Gerter, Esther G. Lowy, and William G. Milán, *The Rise and Fall of the Ethnic Revival* (New York: Mouton Publishers, 1985), 500–510.

86. Ibid., 269, 511 (quotation); Peter Schrag, *The Decline of the Wasp* (New York: Simon and Shuster, 1970), 242–47.

87. The classic statement of ethnic activism is Novak, *Rise of the Unmeltable Ethnics*, which pictures the dominant Anglo-American core as the real enemy of ethnics. For a discussion of the crises that challenged core American values, see Philip Gleason, "American Identity and Americanization," in *Harvard Encyclopedia of American Ethnic Groups* (Cambridge: Harvard University Press, 1980), 31–58.

88. Aversa, "Italian Neo-Ethnicity," 53; Fishman, *Rise and Fall*, 501.

89. John Bukowczyk has documented the efforts of Polish neighborhoods to resist plant closings, highway expansion projects, and other urban renewal agendas. Such initiatives have, in his view, called into question "the extreme individualism enshrined in American law." Bukowczyk, "Decline and Fall of a Detroit Neighborhood," 49–76. No enduring realignment of political structures or power relationships has yet ensued from these developments.

5......

Nothing Distant about It

Women's Liberation and Sixties Radicalism

On 7 September 1968 the sixties came to the Miss America Pageant when one hundred women's liberationists descended upon Atlantic City to protest the pageant's promotion of physical attractiveness and charm as the primary measures of women's worth. Carrying signs that declared, "Miss America Is a Big Falsie," "Miss America Sells It," and "Up Against the Wall, Miss America," they formed a picket line on the boardwalk, sang anti–Miss America songs in three-part harmony, and performed guerrilla theater. The activists crowned a live sheep Miss America and paraded it on the boardwalk to parody the way the contestants, and, by extension, all women, "are appraised and judged like animals at a county fair." They tried to convince women in the crowd that the tyranny of beauty was but one of the many ways that women's bodies were colonized. By announcing beforehand that they would not speak to male reporters (or to any man for that matter), they challenged the sexual division of labor that consigned women reporters to the "soft" stories and male reporters to the "hard" news stories. Newspaper editors who wanted to cover the protest were thus forced to pull their female reporters from the society pages to do so.[1]

The protesters set up a "Freedom Trash Can" and filled it with various "instruments of torture"—high-heeled shoes, bras, girdles, hair curlers, false eyelashes, typing books, and representative copies of *Cosmopolitan*, *Playboy*, and *Ladies' Home Journal*. They had wanted to burn the contents of the Freedom Trash Can but were prevented from doing so by a city ordinance that prohibited bonfires on the boardwalk. However, word had been leaked to the press that the protest would include a symbolic bra-burning, and, as a consequence, reporters were everywhere.[2] Although they burned no bras that day on the boardwalk, the image of the bra-burning, militant feminist remains part of our popular mythology about the women's liberation movement.

The activists also managed to make their presence felt inside the auditorium during that night's live broadcast of the pageant. Pageant officials must have known that they were in for a long night when early in the evening one protester sprayed Toni Home Permanent Spray (one of the pageant's sponsors) at the mayor's booth. She was charged with disorderly conduct and "emanating a noxious odor," an irony that women's liberationists understandably savored. The more spectacular action occurred later that night. As the outgoing Miss America read her farewell speech, four women unfurled a banner that read, "Women's Liberation," and all sixteen protesters shouted "Freedom for Women," and "No More Miss America" before security guards could eject them. The television audience heard the commotion and could see it register on Miss America's face as she stumbled through the remainder of her speech. But the program's producer prevented the cameramen from covering the cause of Miss America's consternation.[3] The TV audience did not remain in the dark for long, because Monday's newspapers described the protest in some detail. As the first major demonstration of the fledgling women's liberation movement, it had been designed to make a big splash, and after Monday morning no one could doubt that it had.

In its wit, passion, and irreverence, not to mention its expansive formulation of politics (to include the politics of beauty, no less!), the Miss America protest resembled other sixties demonstrations. Just as women's liberationists used a sheep to make a statement about conventional femininity, so had the Yippies a week earlier lampooned the political process by nominating a pig, Pegasus, for the presidency at the Democratic National Convention.[4] Although Atlantic City witnessed none of the violence that had occurred in Chicago, the protest generated plenty of hostility among the six hundred or so onlookers who gathered on the boardwalk. Judging from their response, this new thing, "women's liberation," was about as popular as the antiwar movement. The protesters were jeered, harassed, and called "commies" and "man-haters." One man suggested that it "would be a lot more useful" if the protesters threw themselves, and not their bras, girdles, and makeup, into the trash can.[5]

Nothing—not even the verbal abuse they encountered on the boardwalk—could diminish the euphoria women's liberationists felt as they started to mobilize around their own, rather than other people's, oppression. Ann Snitow speaks for many when she recalls that in contrast to her involvement in the larger, male-dominated protest Movement,[6] where she had felt sort of "blank and peripheral," women's liberation was like "an ecstasy of discussion." Precisely because it was about one's own life, "there was," she claims, "nothing distant about it."[7] Robin Morgan has contended that the Miss America protest "announced our existence to the world."[8] That is only a slight exaggeration, for as a consequence of the protest, women's liberation achieved the status of a movement both to its participants and to the media; as such, the Miss America demonstration represents an important moment in the history of the sixties.[9]

Although the women's liberation movement only began to take shape toward the end of the decade, it was a paradigmatically sixties movement. It is not just that many early women's liberation activists had prior involvements in other sixties movements, although that was certainly true, as has been ably documented by Sara Evans.[10] And it is not just that, of all the sixties movements, the women's liberation movement alone carried on and extended into the 1970s that decade's political radicalism and rethinking of fundamental social organization. Although that is true as well. Rather, it is also that the larger, male-dominated protest Movement, despite its considerable sexism, provided much of the intellectual foundation and cultural orientation for the women's liberation movement. Indeed, many of the broad themes of the women's liberation movement—especially its concern with revitalizing the democratic process and reformulating "politics" to include the personal—were refined and recast versions of ideas and approaches already present in the New Left and the black freedom movement.

Moreover, like other sixties radicals, women's liberationists were responding at least in part to particular features of the postwar landscape. For instance, both the New Left and the women's liberation movement can be understood as part of a gendered generational revolt against the ultradomesticity of that aberrant decade, the 1950s. The white radicals who participated in these movements were in flight from the nuclear family and the domesticated versions of masculinity and femininity that prevailed in postwar America. Sixties radicals, white and black, were also responding to the hegemonic position of liberalism and its promotion of government expansion both at home and abroad—the welfare/warfare state. Although sixties radicals came to define themselves in opposition to liberalism, their relation to liberalism was nonetheless complicated and ambivalent. They saw in big government not only a way of achieving greater economic and social justice, but also the possibility of an increasingly well-managed society and an ever more remote government.

In this chapter I will attempt to evaluate some of the more important features of sixties radicalism by focusing on the specific example of the women's liberation movement. I am motivated by the problematic ways in which "the sixties" has come to be scripted in our culture. If conservative "slash and burn" accounts of the period indict sixties radicals for everything from crime and drug use to single motherhood, they at least heap guilt fairly equally upon antiwar, black civil rights, and feminist activists alike. By contrast, progressive reconstructions, while considerably more positive in their assessments of the period, tend to present the sixties as if women were almost completely outside the world of radical politics. Although my accounting of the sixties is in some respects critical, I nonetheless believe that there was much in sixties radicalism that was original and hopeful, including its challenge to established authority and expertise, its commitment to refashioning democracy and "politics," and its interrogation of such naturalized categories as gender and race.

Women's discontent with their place in America in the sixties was, of course, produced by a broad range of causes. Crucial in reigniting feminist consciousness in the sixties was the unprecedented number of women (especially married white women) being drawn into the paid labor force, as the service sector of the economy expanded and rising consumer aspirations fueled the desire of many families for a second income.[11] As Alice Kessler-Harris has pointed out, "homes and cars, refrigerators and washing machines, telephones and multiple televisions required higher incomes." So did providing a college education for one's children. These new patterns of consumption were made possible in large part through the emergence of the two-income family as wives increasingly "sought to aid their husbands in the quest for the good life." By 1960, 30.5 percent of all wives worked for wages.[12] Women's growing participation in the labor force also reflected larger structural shifts in the U.S. economy. Sara Evans has argued that the "reestablishment of labor force segregation following World War II ironically reserved for women a large proportion of the new jobs created in the fifties due to the fact that the fastest growing sector of the economy was no longer industry but services."[13] Women's increasing labor force participation was facilitated as well by the growing number of women graduating from college and by the introduction of the birth control pill in 1960.

Despite the fact that women's "place" was increasingly in the paid work force (or perhaps because of it), ideas about women's proper role in American society were quite conventional throughout the 1950s and the early 1960s, held there by a resurgent ideology of domesticity—what Betty Friedan coined the "feminine mystique." But, as Jane De Hart-Mathews has observed, "the bad fit was there: the unfairness of unequal pay for the same work, the low value placed on jobs women performed, the double burden of housework and wage work."[14] By the mid-1960s at least some American women felt that the contradiction between the realities of paid work and higher education on the one hand and the still pervasive ideology of domesticity on the other had become irreconcilable.

Without the presence of other oppositional movements, however, the women's liberation movement may not have developed at all as an organized force for social change. It certainly would have developed along vastly different lines. The climate of protest encouraged women, even those not directly involved in the black movement and the New Left, to question conventional gender arrangements. Moreover, many of the women who helped form the women's liberation movement had been involved as well in the male-dominated Movement. If the larger Movement was typically indifferent, or worse, hostile, to women's liberation, it was nonetheless through their experiences in that Movement that the young and predominantly white and middle-class women who initially formed the women's liberation movement became politicized. The relationship between women's liberation and the larger Movement was at its core paradoxical. If the Movement was a site of sexism it also provided white women a space in which they could develop political skills and self-confidence, a space in which they could violate the injunction against female self-assertion.[15] Most important, it gave them no small part of the intellectual ammunition—the language and the ideas—with which to fight their own oppression.

Sixties radicals struggled to reformulate politics and power. Their struggle confounded many who lived through the sixties as well as those trying to make sense of the period some thirty years later. One of the most striking characteristics of sixties radicals was their ever-expanding opposition to liberalism. Radicals' theoretical disavowal of liberalism developed gradually and in large part in response to liberals' specific defaults—their failure to repudiate the segregationists at the 1964 Democratic National Convention, their lack of vigor in pressing for greater federal intervention in support of civil rights workers, and their readiness (with few exceptions) to support President Lyndon B. Johnson's escalation of the Vietnam War. But initially some radicals had argued that the Movement should acknowledge that liberalism was not monolithic but contained two discernible strands—"corporate" and "humanist" liberalism. For instance, in 1965 Carl Oglesby, an early leader of the Students for a Democratic Society (SDS), contrasted *corporate liberals*, whose identification with the system made them "illiberal liberals," with *humanist liberals*, who he hoped might yet see that "it is this movement with which their own best hopes are most in tune."[16]

By 1967 radicals were no longer making the distinction between humanist and corporate liberals that they once had. This represented an important political shift for early new leftists in particular who once had felt an affinity of sorts with liberalism.[17] Black radicals were the first to decisively reject liberalism, and their move had an enormous impact on white radicals. With the ascendancy of black power many black militants maintained that liberalism was intrinsically paternalistic, and that black liberation required that the struggle be free of white involvement. This was elaborated by white radicals, who soon developed the argument that authentic radicalism involved organizing around one's own oppression rather than becoming involved, as a "liberal" would, in someone else's struggle for freedom. For instance, in 1967 Gregory Calvert, another SDS leader, argued that the "student movement has to develop an image of its own revolution . . . instead of believing that you're a revolutionary because you're related to Fidel's struggle, Stokely's struggle, always someone else's struggle."[18] Black radicals were also the first to conclude that nothing short of revolution—certainly not Johnson's Great Society programs and a few pieces of civil rights legislation—could undo racism. As leftist journalist Andrew Kopkind remembered it, the rhetoric of revolution proved impossible for white new leftists to resist. "With black revolution raging in America and world revolution directed against America, it was hardly possible for white radicals to think themselves anything less than revolutionaries."[19]

Radicals' repudiation of liberalism also grew out of their fear that liberalism could "co-opt" and thereby contain dissent. Thus, in 1965 when President Johnson concluded a nationally televised speech on civil rights by proclaiming, "And we *shall* overcome," radicals saw in this nothing more than a calculated move to appropriate Movement rhetoric in order to blunt protest. By contrast, more established civil rights leaders reportedly cheered the president on, believing that his declaration constituted a significant "affirmation of the movement."[20] Liberalism, then, was seen as both compromised and compromising. In this, young radicals were influenced by Herbert Marcuse, who emphasized the system's ability to reproduce itself through its recuperation of dissent.[21]

Just as radicals' critique of materialism developed in the context of relative economic abundance, so did their critique of liberalism develop at a time of liberalism's greatest political strength. The idea that conservativism might supplant liberalism at some point in the near future was simply unimaginable to them. (To be fair, this view was not entirely unreasonable given Johnson's trouncing of Barry Goldwater in the 1964 presidential election.)

This was just one of many things that distinguished new leftists from old leftists, who, having lived through McCarthyism, were far more concerned about the possibility of a conservative resurgence. For if sixties radicals grew worlds apart from liberals, they often found themselves in conflict with old leftists as well. In general, new leftists rejected the economism and virulent anticommunism of the noncommunist Old Left. In contrast to old leftists, whose target was "class-based economic oppression," new leftists (at least before 1969, when some new leftists did embrace dogmatic versions of Marxism) focused on "how late capitalist society creates mechanisms of psychological and cultural domination over *everyone*."[22] For young radicals the problem went beyond capitalism and included not only the alienation engendered by mass society, but also other systems of hierarchy based on race, gender, and age. Indeed, they were often more influenced by existentialists like Camus or social critics like C. Wright Mills and Herbert Marcuse, both of whom doubted the working class's potential for radical action, than by Marx or Lenin. For instance, SDS president Paul Potter contended that it would be "through the experience of the middle class and the anesthetic of bureaucracy and mass society that the vision and program of participatory democracy will come."[23] This rejection of what Mills dubbed the "labor metaphysic" had everything to do with the different circumstances radicals confronted in the sixties. As Arthur Miller observed, "The radical of the thirties came out of a system that had stopped and the important job was to organize new production relations which would start it up again. The sixties radical opened his eyes to a system pouring its junk over everybody, or nearly everybody, and the problem was to stop just that, to escape being overwhelmed by a mindless, goalless flood which marooned each individual on his little island of commodities."[24]

If sixties radicals initially rejected orthodox and economistic versions of Marxism, many did (especially over time) appropriate, expand, and recast Marxist categories in an effort to understand the experiences of oppressed and marginalized groups. Thus exponents of what was termed "new working-class theory" claimed that people with technical, clerical, and professional jobs should be seen as constituting a new sector of the working class, better educated than the traditional working class, but working class nonetheless. According to this view, students were not members of the privileged middle class, but rather "trainees" for the new working class. And many women's liberationists (even radical feminists who rejected Marxist theorizing about women's condition) often tried to use Marxist methodology to understand women's oppression. For example, Shulamith Firestone argued that just as the elimination of "economic classes" would require the revolt of the proletariat and their seizure of the means of production, so would the elimination of "sexual classes" require women's revolt and their "seizure of control of reproduction."[25]

If young radicals often assumed an arrogant stance toward those remnants of the Old Left that survived the 1950s, they were by the late 1960s unambiguously contemptuous of liberals. Women's liberationists shared new leftists' and black radicals' rejection of liberalism, and, as a consequence, they often went to great lengths to distinguish themselves from the liberal feminists of the National Organization for Women (NOW). (In fact, their disillusionment with liberalism was more thorough during the early stages of their movement building than had been the case for either new leftists or civil rights activists because they had lived through the earlier betrayals around the Vietnam War and civil rights. Moreover, male radicals' frequent denunciations of women's liberation as "bourgeois" encouraged women's liberationists to distance themselves from NOW.) NOW had been formed in 1966 to push the federal government to enforce the provisions of the 1964 Civil Rights Act outlawing sex discrimination — a paradigmatic liberal agenda focused on public access and the prohibition of employment discrimination. To women's liberation activists, NOW's integrationist, access-oriented approach ignored the racial and class inequities that were the very foundation of the "mainstream" that

NOW was dedicated to integrating. In the introduction to the 1970 best-seller, *Sisterhood Is Powerful,* Robin Morgan declared that "NOW is essentially an organization that wants reforms [in the] second-class citizenship of women—and this is where it differs drastically from the rest of the Women's Liberation Movement."[26] In *The Dialectic of Sex,* Shulamith Firestone described NOW's political stance as "untenable even in terms of immediate political gains" and deemed it "more a leftover of the old feminism rather than a model of the new."[27] Radical feminist Ti-Grace Atkinson went even further, characterizing many in NOW as only wanting "women to have the same opportunity to be oppressors, too."[28]

Women's liberationists also took issue with liberal feminists' formulation of women's problem as their exclusion from the public sphere. Younger activists argued instead that women's exclusion from public life was inextricable from their subordination in the family and would persist until this larger issue was addressed. For instance, Firestone claimed that the solution to women's oppression was not inclusion in the mainstream, but rather the eradication of the biological family, which was the "tapeworm of exploitation."[29]

Of course, younger activists' alienation from NOW was often more than matched by NOW members' disaffection from them. Many liberal feminists' were appalled (at least initially) by women's liberationists' politicization of personal life. NOW founder Betty Friedan frequently railed against women's liberationists for waging a "bedroom war" that diverted women from the real struggle of integrating the public sphere.[30]

Women's liberationists believed that they had embarked upon a much more ambitious project—the virtual remaking of the world—and that theirs was the real struggle.[31] Nothing short of radically transforming society was sufficient to deal with what they were discovering: that gender inequality was embedded in everyday life. In 1970 Shulamith Firestone observed that "sex-class is so deep as to be invisible."[32] The pervasiveness of gender inequality and gender's status as a naturalized category demonstrated to women's liberationists the inadequacy of NOW's legislative and judicial remedies and the necessity of thoroughgoing social transformation. Thus, whereas liberal feminists talked of ending sex discrimination, women's liberationists called for nothing less than the destruction of capitalism and patriarchy. As defined by feminists, patriarchy, in contrast to sex discrimination, defied reform. For example, Adrienne Rich contended: "Patriarchy is the power of the fathers: a familial-social, ideological, political system in which men—by force, direct pressure, or through ritual, tradition, law and language, customs, etiquette, education, and the division of labor, determine what part women shall or shall not play, and in which the female is subsumed under the male."[33]

Women's liberationists typically indicted capitalism as well. Ellen Willis, for instance, maintained that "the American system consists of two interdependent but distinct parts—the capitalist state, and the patriarchal family." Willis argued that capitalism succeeded in exploiting women as cheap labor and consumers "primarily by taking advantage of women's subordinate position in the family and our historical domination by man."[34]

Central to the revisionary project of the women's liberation movement was the desire to render gender meaningless, to explode it as a significant category. In the movement's view, both masculinity and femininity represented not timeless essences, but rather "patriarchal" constructs. (Of course, even as the movement sought to deconstruct gender, it was, paradoxically, as many have noted, trying to mobilize women precisely on the basis of their gender.)[35] This explains in part the significance abortion rights held for women's liberationists, who believed that until abortion was decriminalized, biology would remain women's destiny, thus foreclosing the possibility of women's self-determination.[36]

Indeed, the women's liberation movement made women's bodies the site of political contestation. The "colonized" status of women's bodies became the focus of much movement activism. (The discourse of colonization originated in Third World national liberation movements but, in an act of First World appropriation, was taken up by black radicals who claimed that African Americans constituted an "internal colony" in the United States. Radical women trying to persuade the larger Movement of the legitimacy of their cause soon followed suit by deploying the discourse to expose women's subordinate position in relation to men. This appropriation represented an important move and one characteristic of radicalism in the *late* 1960s, that is, the borrowing of conceptual frameworks and discourses from other movements to comprehend the situation of oppressed groups in the United States—with mixed results at best. In fact, women's liberationists challenged not only tyrannical beauty standards, but also violence against women, women's sexual alienation, the compulsory character of heterosexuality and its organization around male pleasure (inscribed in the privileging of the vaginal over clitoral orgasm), the health hazards associated with the birth control pill, the definition of contraception as women's responsibility, and, of course, women's lack of reproductive control. They also challenged the sexual division of labor in the home, employment discrimination, and the absence of quality child-care facilities. Finally, women's liberationists recognized the power of language to shape culture.

The totalism of their vision would have been difficult to translate into a concrete reform package, even had they been interested in doing so. But electoral politics and the legislative and judicial reforms that engaged the energies of liberal feminists did little to animate most women's liberationists. Like other sixties radicals, they were instead taken with the idea of developing forms that would prefigure the utopian community of the imagined future.[37] Anxious to avoid the "manipulated consent" that they believed characterized American politics, sixties radicals struggled to develop alternatives to hierarchy and centralized decision making.[38] They spoke often of creating "participatory democracy" in an effort to maximize individual participation and equalize power. Their attempts to build a "democracy of individual participation" often confounded outsiders, who found Movement meetings exhausting and tedious affairs.[39] But to those radicals who craved political engagement, "freedom" was, as one radical group enthused, "an endless meeting."[40] According to Gregory Calvert, participatory democracy appealed to the "deep anti-authoritarianism of the new generation in addition to offering them the immediate concretization of the values of openness, honesty, and community in human relationships."[41] Women's liberationists, still smarting from their first-hand discovery that the larger Movement's much-stated commitment to egalitarianism did not apply equally to all, often took extraordinary measures to try to ensure egalitarianism. They employed a variety of measures in an effort to equalize power, including consensus decision making, rotating chairs, and the sharing of both creative and routine movement work.

Fundamental to this "prefigurative politics," as sociologist Wini Breines terms it, was the commitment to develop counterinstitutions that would anticipate the desired society of the future.[42] Staughton Lynd, director of the Mississippi Freedom Schools and a prominent new leftist, likened sixties radicals to the Wobblies (labor radicals of the early twentieth century) in their commitment to building "the new society within the shell of the old."[43] According to two early SDSers, "What we are working for is far more than changes in the structure of society and its institutions or the people who are now making the decisions. . . . The stress should rather be on wrenching people out of the system both physically and spiritually."[44]

Radicals believed that alternative institutions would not only satisfy needs unmet by the present system, but also, perhaps, by dramatizing the failures of the system, radicalize those not served by it but currently outside the Movement. Tom Hayden proposed that radicals "build our own free institutions—community organizations, newspapers, coffeehouses—at points of strain within the system where human needs are denied. These institutions become centers of identity, points of contact, building blocks of a new society from which we confront the system more intensely."[45]

Among the earliest and best known of such efforts were the Mississippi Freedom Democratic party and the accompanying Freedom Schools formed during Freedom Summer of 1964. In the aftermath of that summer's Democratic National Convention, Bob Moses [Parris] of the Student Nonviolent Coordinating Committee (SNCC) even suggested that the Movement abandon its efforts to integrate the Democratic party and try instead to establish its own state government in Mississippi. And as early as 1966 SNCC's Atlanta Project called on blacks to "form our own institutions, credit unions, co-ops, political parties."[46] This came to be the preferred strategy as the sixties progressed and disillusionment with traditional politics grew. Rather than working from within the system, new leftists and black radicals instead formed alternative political parties, media, schools, universities, and assemblies of oppressed and unrepresented people.

Women's liberationists elaborated on this idea, creating an amazing panoply of counterinstitutions. In the years before the 1973 Supreme Court decision decriminalizing abortion, feminists established abortion referral services in most cities of any size. Women's liberationists in Chicago even operated an underground abortion clinic, "Jane," where they performed about one hundred abortions each week.[47] By the mid-1970s most big cities had a low-cost feminist health clinic, a rape crisis center, and a feminist bookstore. In Detroit, after "a long struggle to translate feminism into federalese," two women succeeded in convincing the National Credit Union Administration that feminism was a legitimate "field" from which to draw credit union members. Within three years of its founding in 1973, the Detroit credit union could claim assets of almost one million dollars. Feminists in other cities soon followed suit. Women's liberation activists in Washington, D.C., formed Olivia Records, the first women's record company, which by 1978 was supporting a paid staff of fourteen and producing four records a year.[48] By the mid-1970s there existed in most cities of any size a politicized feminist counterculture, or a "women's community."

The popularity of alternative institutions was that at least in part they seemed to hold out the promise of political effectiveness without co-optation. Writing in 1969, Amiri Baraka (formerly LeRoi Jones), a black nationalist and accomplished poet, maintained, "But you must have the cultural revolution. . . . We cannot fight a war, an actual physical war with the forces of evil just because we are angry. We can begin to build. We must build black institutions . . . all based on a value system that is beneficial to black people."[49]

Jennifer Woodul, one of the founders of Olivia Records, argued that ventures like Olivia represented a move toward gaining "economic power" for women. "We feel it's useless to advocate more and more 'political action' if some of it doesn't result in the permanent material improvement of the lives of women."[50] Robin Morgan termed feminist counterinstitutions "concrete moves toward self-determination and power."[51] The situation, it turned out, was much more complicated. Women involved in nonprofit feminist institutions such as rape crisis centers and shelters for battered women found that their need for state or private funding sometimes militated against adherence to feminist principles.

Feminist businesses, by contrast, discovered that while they were rarely the objects of co-optation, the problem of recuperation remained. In many cases the founders of these institutions became the victims of their own success, as mainstream presses, recording companies, credit unions, and banks encroached upon a market they had originally discovered and tapped.[52] For instance, by the end of the 1970s Olivia was forced to reduce its staff almost by half and to scuttle its collective structure.[53] Today k. d. lang, Tracy Chapman, Michelle Shocked, and Sinead O'Connor are among those androgynous women singers enjoying great commercial success, but on major labels. Although Olivia helped to lay the groundwork for their achievements, it finds its records, as Arlene Stein has observed, "languishing in the 'women's music' section in the rear [of the record store] if they're there at all."[54]

The move toward building counterinstitutions was part of a larger strategy to develop new societies "within the shell of the old," but this shift sometimes had unintended consequences. While feminist counterinstitutions were originally conceived as part of a culture of resistance, over time they often became more absorbed in sustaining themselves than in confronting male supremacy, especially as their services were duplicated by mainstream businesses. In the early years of the women's liberation movement this alternative feminist culture did provide the sort of "free space" women needed to confront sexism. But as it was further elaborated in the mid-1970s, it ironically often came to promote insularity instead—becoming, as Adrienne Rich has observed, "a place of emigration, an end in itself," where patriarchy was evaded rather than confronted.[55] In practice, feminist communities were small, self-contained subcultures that proved hard to penetrate, especially to newcomers unaccustomed to their norms and conventions. The shift in favor of alternative communities may have sometimes impeded efforts at outreach for the women's liberationists, new leftists, and black radicals who attempted it.

On a related issue, the larger protest Movement's great pessimism about reform—the tendency to interpret every success a defeat resulting in the Movement's further recuperation (what Robin Morgan called "futilitarianism")—may have encouraged a too-global rejection of reform among sixties radicals. For instance, some women's liberation groups actually opposed the Equal Rights Amendment (ERA) when NOW revived it. In September 1970 a New York–based group, The Feminists, denounced the ERA and advised feminists against "squandering invaluable time and energy on it."[56] A delegation of Washington, D.C., women's liberationists invited to appear before the senate subcommittee considering the ERA, testified: "We are aware that the system will try to appease us with their [sic] paper offerings. We will not be appeased. Our demands can only be met by a total transformation of society which you cannot legislate, you cannot co-opt, you cannot *control*."[57] In *The Dialectic of Sex*, Firestone went so far as to dismiss child-care centers as attempts to "buy women off" because they "ease the immediate pressure without asking why the pressure is on *women*."[58]

Similarly, many SDS leaders opposed the National Conference for New Politics (NCNP), an abortive attempt to form a national progressive organization oriented around electoral politics and to launch an antiwar presidential ticket headed by Martin Luther King, Jr., and Benjamin Spock. Immediately following NCNP's first and only convention, in 1967, the SDS paper *New Left Notes* published two front-page articles criticizing NCNP organizers. One writer contended that "people who recognize the political process as perverted will not seek change through the institutions that process has created."[59] The failure of sixties radicals to distinguish between reform and reformism meant that while they defined the issues, they often did little to develop policy initiatives around those issues.[60] Moreover, the preoccupation of women's liberationists with questions of internal democracy (fueled in part by their desire to succeed where the men had failed) sometimes had the effect of focusing attention away from the larger struggle in an effort to create the perfect movement. As feminist activist Frances Chapman points out, women's liberation was "like a generator that got things going, cut out and left it to the larger reform engine which made a lot of mistakes."[61] In eschewing traditional politics rather than entering them skeptically, women's liberationists, like other sixties radicals, may have lost an opportunity to foster critical debate in the larger arena.

If young radicals eschewed the world of conventional politics they nonetheless had a profound impact upon it, especially by redefining what is understood as "political." Although the women's liberation movement popularized the slogan "the personal is political," the idea that there is a political dimension to personal life was first embraced by early SDSers who had encountered it in the writings of C. Wright Mills.[62] Rebelling against a social order whose public and private spheres were highly differentiated, new leftists called for a reintegration of the personal with the political. They reconceptualized apparently personal problems—specifically their alienation from a campus cultural milieu characterized by sororities and fraternities, husband and wife hunting, sports, and careerism, and the powerlessness they felt as college students without a voice in campus governance or curriculum—as political problems. Thus SDS's founding Port Huron Statement of 1962 suggested that for an American New Left to succeed, it would have to "give form to . . . feelings of helplessness and indifference, so that people may see the political, social, and economic sources of their private troubles and organize to change society."[63] Theirs was a far more expansive formulation of politics than what prevailed in the Old Left, even among the more renegade remnants that had survived into the early sixties.[64] Power was conceptualized as relational and by no means reducible to electoral politics.

By expanding political discourse to include personal relations, new leftists unintentionally paved the way for women's liberationists to develop critiques of the family, marriage, and the construction of sexuality. (Of course, nonfeminist critiques of the family and sexual repressiveness were hardly in short supply in the 1950s and 1960s, as evidenced by *Rebel without a Cause, Catcher in the Rye,* and Paul Goodman's *Growing Up Absurd,* to mention but a few.) Women's liberationists developed an understanding of power's capillarylike nature, which in some respects anticipated those being formulated by Michel Foucault and other poststructuralists.[65] Power was conceptualized as occupying multiple sites and as lodging everywhere, even in those private places assumed to be the most removed from or impervious to politics—the home and, more particularly, the bedroom.

The belief of sixties radicals that the personal is political also suggested to them its converse—that the political is personal. Young radicals typically felt it was not enough to sign leaflets or participate in a march if one returned to the safety and comfort of a middle-class existence. Politics was supposed to unsettle life and its routines, even more, to transform life. For radicals the challenge was to discover, underneath all the layers of social conditioning, the "real" self unburdened by social expectations and conventions. Thus, SNCC leader Stokely Carmichael advanced the slogan, "Every Negro is a potential black man."[66] Shulamith Firestone and Anne Koedt argued that among the "most exciting things to come out of the women's movement so far is a new daring . . . to tear down old structures and assumptions and let real thought and feeling flow."[67] Life would not be comfortable, but who wanted comfort in the midst of so much deadening complacency? For a great many radicals, the individual became a site of political activism in the sixties. In the black freedom movement the task was very much to discover the black inside the Negro, and in the women's liberation movement it was to unlearn niceness, to challenge the taboo against female self-assertion.[68]

Sixties radicalism proved compelling to many precisely because it promised to transform life. Politics was not about the subordination of self to some larger political cause; instead, it was the path to self-fulfillment. This ultimately was the power of sixties radicalism. As Stanley Aronowitz notes, sixties radicalism was in large measure about "infus[ing] life with a secular spiritual and moral content" and "fill[ing] the quotidian with personal meaning and purpose."[69] But "the personal is political" was one of those ideas whose rhetorical power seemed to sometimes work against or undermine its explication. It could encourage a solipsistic preoccupation with self-transformation. As new leftist Richard Flacks presciently observed in 1965, this kind of politics could lead to "a search for personally satisfying modes of life while abandoning the possibility of helping others to change theirs."[70] Thus the idea that "politics is how you live your life, not who you vote for," as Yippie leader Jerry Rubin put it, could and did lead to a subordination of politics to life-style.[71] If the idea led some to confuse personal liberation with political struggle, it led others to embrace an asceticism that sacrificed personal needs and desires to political imperatives. Some women's liberation activists followed this course, interpreting the idea that the personal is political to mean that one's personal life should conform to some abstract standard of political correctness. At first this tendency was mitigated by the founders' insistence that there were no personal solutions, only collective solutions, to women's oppression. Over time, however, one's self-presentation, marital status, and sexual preference frequently came to determine one's standing or ranking in the movement. The most notorious example of this involved the New York radical group, The Feminists, who established a quota to limit the number of married women in the group.[72] Policies such as these prompted Barbara Ehrenreich to question "a feminism which talks about universal sisterhood, but is horrified by women who wear spiked heels or call their friends 'girls.' "[73] At the same time, what was personally satisfying was sometimes upheld as politically correct. In the end, both the women's liberation movement and the larger protest Movement suffered, as the idea that the personal is political was often interpreted in such a way as to make questions of life-style absolutely central.

The social movements of the sixties signaled the beginning of what has come to be known as "identity politics," the idea that politics is rooted in identity.[74] Although some New Left groups by the late 1960s did come to endorse an orthodox Marxism whereby class was privileged, class was not the pivotal category for these new social movements.[75] (Even those New Left groups that reverted to the "labor metaphysic" lacked meaningful working-class participation.) Rather, race, ethnicity, gender, sexual preference, and youth were the salient categories for most sixties activists. In the women's liberation movement, what was termed "consciousness-raising" was the tool used to develop women's group identity.

As women's liberationists started to organize a movement, they confronted American women who identified unambiguously as women, but who typically had little of what Nancy Cott would call "we-ness," or "some level of identification with 'the group called women.' "[76] Moreover, both the pervasiveness of gender inequality and the cultural understanding of gender as a natural rather than a social construct made it difficult to cultivate a critical consciousness about gender even among women. To engender this sense of sisterhood or "we-ness," women's liberationists developed consciousness-raising, a practice involving "the political reinterpretation of personal life."[77] According to its principal architects, its purpose was to "awaken the latent consciousness that . . . all women have about our oppression." In talking about their personal experiences, it was argued, women would come to understand that what they had believed were personal problems were, in fact, "social problems that must become social issues and fought together rather than with personal solutions."[78]

Reportedly, New York women's liberationist Kathie Sarachild was the person who coined the term *consciousness-raising*." However, the technique originated in other social movements. As Sarachild wrote in 1973, those who promoted consciousness-raising "were applying to women and to ourselves as women's liberation organizers the practice a number of us had learned in the civil rights movement in the South in the early 1960's."[79] There they had seen that the sharing of personal problems, grievances, and aspirations—"telling it like it is"—could be a radicalizing experience. Moreover, for some women's liberationists consciousness-raising was a way to avoid the tendency of some members of the movement to try to fit women within existing (and often Marxist) theoretical paradigms. By circumventing the "experts" on women and going to women themselves, they would be able to not only construct a theory of women's oppression but formulate strategy as well. Thus women's liberationists struggled to find the commonalities in women's experiences in order to generate generalizations about women's oppression.

Consciousness-raising was enormously successful in exposing the insidiousness of sexism and in engendering a sense of identity and solidarity among the largely white, middle-class women who participated in "c-r" groups. By the early 1970s even NOW, whose founder Betty Friedan had initially derided consciousness-raising as so much "navel-gazing," began sponsoring c-r groups.[80] But the effort to transcend the particular was both the strength and the weakness of consciousness-raising. If it encouraged women to locate the common denominators in their lives, it inhibited discussion of women's considerable differences. Despite the particularities of white, middle-class women's experiences, theirs became the basis for feminist theorizing about women's oppression. In a more general sense the identity politics informing consciousness-raising tended to privilege experience in certain problematic ways. It was too often assumed that there existed a kind of core experience, initially articulated as "women's experience." Black and white radicals (the latter in relation to youth) made a similar move as well. When Stokely Carmichael called on blacks to develop an "ideology which speaks to our blackness," he, like other black nationalists, suggested that there was somehow an essential and authentic "blackness."

With the assertion of difference within the women's movement in the 1980s, the notion that women constitute a unitary category has been problematized. As a consequence, women's experiences have become ever more discretely defined, as in "the black female experience," "the Jewish female experience," or "the Chicana lesbian experience." But, as Audre Lorde has argued, there remains a way in which, even with greater and greater specificity, the particular is never fully captured.[81] Instead, despite the pluralization of the subject within feminism, identities are often still imagined as monolithic. Finally, the very premise of identity politics—that identity is the basis of politics—has sometimes shut down possibilities for communication, as identities are seen as necessarily either conferring or foreclosing critical consciousness. Kobena Mercer, a British film critic, has criticized the rhetorical strategies of "authenticity and authentication" that tend to characterize identity politics. He has observed: "if I preface a point by saying something like, 'as a black gay man, I feel marginalized by your discourse,' it makes a valid point but in such a way that preempts critical dialogue because such a response could be inferred as a criticism not of what I say but of what or who I am. The problem is replicated in the familiar cop-out clause, " 'as a middle-class, white, heterosexual male, what can I say?' "[82]

The problem is that the mere assertion of identity becomes in a very real sense irrefutable. Identity is presented as not only stable and fixed, but as also insurmountable. While identity politics gives the oppressed the moral authority to speak (perhaps a dubious ground from which to speak), it can, ironically, absolve those belonging to dominant groups from having to engage in a critical dialogue. In some sense, then, identity politics can unintentionally reinforce Other-ness. Finally, as the antifeminist backlash and the emergence of the New Right should demonstrate, there is nothing inherently progressive about identity. It can be, and has been, mobilized for reactionary as well as for radical purposes.[83] For example, the participation of so many women in the antiabortion movement reveals just how problematic the reduction of politics to identity can be.

Accounts of sixties radicalism usually cite its role in bringing about the dismantling of Jim Crow and disfranchisement, the withdrawal of U.S. troops from Vietnam, and greater gender equality. However, equally important, if less frequently noted, was its challenge to politics as usual. Sixties radicals succeeded both in reformulating politics, even mainstream politics, to include personal life, and in challenging the notion that elites alone have the wisdom and expertise to control the political process. For a moment, people who by virtue of their color, age, and gender were far from the sites of formal power became politically engaged, became agents of change.

Given the internal contradictions and shortcomings of sixties radicalism, the repressiveness of the federal government in the late 1960s and early 1970s, and changing economic conditions in the United States, it is not surprising that the movements built by radicals in the sixties either no longer exist or do so only in attenuated form. Activists in the women's liberation movement, however, helped to bring about a fundamental realignment of gender roles in this country through outrageous protests, tough-minded polemics, and an "ecstasy of discussion." Indeed, those of us who came of age in the days before the resurgence of feminism know that the world today, while hardly a feminist utopia, is nonetheless a far different, and in many respects a far fairer, world than what we confronted in 1967.

NOTES

1. See Carol Hanisch, "A Critique of the Miss America Protest," in *Notes from the Second Year: Women's Liberation*, edited by Shulamith Firestone and Anne Koedt (New York: Radical Feminism, 1970), 87, and Judith Duffet, "Atlantic City Is a Town with Class—They Raise Your Morals While They Judge Your Ass," *The Voice of the Women's Liberation Movement* 1, no. 3 (October 1968). The protesters also criticized the pageant's narrow formulation of beauty, especially its racist equation of beauty with whiteness. They emphasized that in its forty-seven-year history, the pageant had never crowned a black woman Miss America. That weekend the first Black Miss America Pageant was held in Atlantic City.

2. See Lindsy Van Gelder, "Bra Burners Plan Protest," *New York Post*, 4 September 1968, which appeared three days before the protest. The *New York Times* article by Charlotte Curtis quoted Robin Morgan as having said about the mayor of Atlantic City: "He was worried about our burning things. He said the boardwalk had already been burned out once this year. We told him we wouldn't do anything dangerous—just a symbolic bra-burning." Curtis, "Miss America Pageant Is Picketed by 100 Women," *New York Times*, 8 September 1968.

3. See Jack Gould's column in the *New York Times*, 9 September 1968.

4. The Yippies were a small group of leftists who, in contrast to most of the Left, had enthusiastically embraced the growing counterculture. For a fascinating account of the 1968 convention, see David Farber, *Chicago '68* (Chicago: University of Chicago Press, 1988).

5. Curtis, "Miss America Pageant."

6. For the sake of convenience, I will use the term *Movement* to describe the overlapping protest movements of the sixties—the black freedom movement, the student movement, the antiwar movement, and the more self-consciously political New Left. I will refer to the women's liberation movement as the *movement*; here I use the lower case simply to avoid confusion.

7. Snitow, interview with author, New York City, 14 June 1984. Here one can get a sense of the disjuncture in experiences between white and black women; presumably, black women had not felt the same sense of distance about their civil rights activism.

8. Robin Morgan, *Going Too Far: The Personal Chronicle of a Feminist* (New York: Random House, 1978), 62.

9. Yet virtually all of the recently published books on the sixties either slight or ignore the protest. This omis-

sion is emblematic of a larger problem, the failure of authors to integrate women's liberation into their reconstruction of that period. Indeed, most of these books have replicated the position of women in the larger, male-dominated protest Movement—that is, the women's liberation movement is relegated to the margins of the narrative. Such marginalization has been exacerbated as well by the many feminist recollections of the sixties that demonize the Movement and present women's liberation as its antithesis. Sixties books that textually subordinate the women's liberation movement include James Miller, *Democracy Is in the Streets: From Port Huron to the Siege of Chicago* (New York: Simon and Schuster, 1987), Tom Hayden, *Reunion: A Memoir* (New York: Random House, 1988), Todd Gitlin, *The Sixties: Years of Hope, Days of Rage* (New York: Bantam, 1987), and Nancy Zaroulis and Gerald Sullivan, *Who Spoke Up?: American Protest against the War in Vietnam.* A notable exception is Stewart Burns, *Social Movements of the 1960's: Searching for Democracy* (Boston: Twayne, 1990).

10. Sara Evans, *Personal Politics: The Roots of Women's Liberation in the Civil Rights Movement and the New Left* (New York: Vintage Books, 1979).

11. Sara Evans has argued that in their attempt to combine work inside and outside the family, educated, middle-class, married white women of the 1950s were following the path pioneered by black women. See Evans, *Born for Liberty: A History of Women in America* (New York: Free Press, 1989), 253–54. As Jaqueline Jones and others have demonstrated, black women have a "long history of combining paid labor with domestic obligations." According to Jones, in 1950 one-third of all married black women were in the labor force, compared to one-quarter of all married women in the general population. One study cited by Jones "concluded that black mothers of school-aged children were more likely to work than their white counterparts, though part-time positions in the declining field of domestic service inhibited growth in their rates of labor force participation." Jones, *Labor of Love, Labor of Sorrow: Black Women, Work, and the Family, from Slavery to the Present* (New York: Vintage Books, 1986), 269.

12. Alice Kessler-Harris, *Out to Work: A History of Wage-Earning Women in the United States* (New York: Oxford University Press, 1982), 302.

13. Evans, *Born for Liberty*, 252.

14. Jane De Hart-Mathews, "The New Feminism and the Dynamics of Social Change," in *Women's America: Refocusing the Past*, 2d ed., edited by Linda Kerber and Jane De Hart-Mathews (New York: Oxford University Press, 1987), 445.

15. I think that this was an experience specific to white women. The problem of diffidence seems to have been, if not unique to white women, then, especially acute for them. This is not to say that issues of gender were unimportant to black women activists in the sixties, but that gender seemed less primary and pressing an issue than race. However, much more research is needed in this area. It could

be that the black women's noninvolvement in women's liberation had as much, if not more, to do with the movement's racism than any prioritizing of race.

16. Carl Oglesby, "Trapped in a System," reprinted as "Liberalism and the Corporate State," in *The New Radicals: A Report with Documents*, edited by Paul Jacobs and Saul Landau (New York: Vintage Books, 1966), 266. For a useful discussion of the New Left's relationship to liberalism, see Gitlin, *The Sixties*, 127–92.

17. See Howard Brick, "Inventing Post-Industrial Society: Liberal and Radical Social Theory in the 1960's" (paper delivered at the 1990 American Studies Association Conference). In September 1963 the electoral politics faction of SDS had even succeeded in getting the group to adopt the slogan, "Part of the Way with LBJ." Johnson's official campaign slogan was, "All the Way with LBJ." See Gitlin, *The Sixties*, 180.

18. Gregory Calvert, interview in *The Movement* 3, no. 2 (1967): 6.

19. Andrew Kopkind, "Looking Backward: The Sixties and the Movement," *Ramparts* 11, no. 8 (February 1973): 32.

20. That evening 7 million people watched Johnson's speech to Congress announcing voting rights legislation. According to C. T. Vivian, "a tear ran down" Martin Luther King's cheek as Johnson finished his speech. Juan Williams, *Eyes on the Prize: America's Civil Rights Years, 1954–65* (New York: Penguin, 1988), 278.

21. Elinor Langer discusses the ways in which Marcuse's notion of repressive tolerance was used by the Movement. See her wonderful essay, "Notes for Next Time," *Working Papers for a New Society* 1, no. 3 (Fall 1973): 48–83.

22. Ellen Kay Trimberger, "Women in the Old and New Left: The Evolution of a Politics of Personal Life," *Feminist Studies* 5, no. 3 (Fall 1979): 442.

23. Potter quoted from Miller, *Democracy Is in the Streets*, 196.

24. Miller quoted from Gitlin, *The Sixties*, 9. Although the broad outlines of Miller's argument are correct, some recent scholarship on 1930s radicalism suggests that it was considerably more varied and less narrowly economistic than has been previously acknowledged. For example, recent books by Paula Rabinowitz and Robin Kelley demonstrate that some radicals in this period understood the salience of such categories as gender and race. See Paula Rabinowitz, *Labor and Desire: Women's Revolutionary Fiction in Depression America* (Chapel Hill: University of North Carolina Press, 1991); Robin Kelley, *Hammer and Hoe: Alabama Communists during the Great Depression* (Chapel Hill: University of North Carolina Press, 1990).

25. Shulamith Firestone, *The Dialectic of Sex: The Case for Feminist Revolution*, rev. ed. (New York: Bantam Books, 1971), 10–11.

26. Robin Morgan, in Morgan, ed., *Sisterhood Is Powerful* (New York: Vintage Books, 1970), xxii.

27. Firestone, *The Dialectic of Sex*, 33. For a very useful history of women's rights activism (as opposed to women's liberation) in the postwar

years, see Cynthia Harrison, *On Account of Sex: The Politics of Women's Issues, 1945–68* (Berkeley: University of California Press, 1988).

28. T. Grace Atkinson, *Amazon Odyssey* (New York: Link Books, 1974), 10. In contrast to other founders of early radical feminist groups, Atkinson came to radicalism through her involvement in the New York City chapter of NOW, admittedly the most radical of all NOW chapters. Atkinson made this remark in October 1968 after having failed badly in her attempt to radically democratize the New York chapter of NOW. Upon losing the vote she immediately resigned her position as the chapter's president and went on to establish The Feminists, a radical feminist group.

29. Firestone, *The Dialectic of Sex*, 12.

30. Betty Friedan, *It Changed My Life: Writings on the Women's Movement* (New York: Random House, 1976), 153. Friedan was antagonistic to radical feminism from the beginning and rarely missed an opportunity to denounce the man-hating and sex warfare that she claimed it advocated. Her declamations against "sexual politics" began at least as early as January 1969.

31. Due to limitations of space and the focus of this chapter, I do not discuss the many differences among womn's liberationists, most crucially, the conflicts between "radical feminists" and "politicos" over the relationship between the women's liberation movement and the larger Movement and the role of capitalism in maintaining women's oppression. This is taken up at length in Alice Echols, *Daring to Be Bad: Radical Feminism in America, 1967–75* (Minneapolis: University of Minnesota Press, 1989).

32. Firestone, *The Dialectic of Sex*, 1. It is the opening line of her book.

33. Adrienne Rich quoted from Hester Eisenstein, *Contemporary Feminist Thought* (Boston: G. K. Hall, 1983), 5.

34. Ellen Willis, "Sequel: Letter to a Critic," in *Notes from the Second Year*, edited by Firestone and Koedt, 57.

35. See Ann Snitow, "Gender Diary," *Dissent* (Spring 1989): 205–24; Carole Vance, "Social Construction Theory: Problems in the History of Sexuality," in *Homosexuality, Which Homosexuality?*, edited by Anja van Kooten Niekark and Theo van der Maer (Amsterdam: An Dekken/Schorer, 1989).

36. Ellen Willis discusses the centrality of abortion to the women's liberation movement in the foreword to *Daring to Be Bad*. For the young, mostly white middle-class women who were attracted to women's liberation, the issue was forced reproduction. But for women of color, the issue was as often forced sterilization, and women's liberationists would tackle that issue as well.

37. Stanley Aronowitz, "When the New Left Was New," in *The Sixties without Apology*, edited by Sohnya Sayres, Anders Stephanson, Stanley Aronowitz, and Fredric Jameson (Minneapolis: University of Minnesota Press, 1984), 32.

38. C. Wright Mills, quoted from Miller, *Democracy Is in the Streets*, 86.

39. The phrase is from SDS's founding statement, "The Port Huron State-

ment," which is reprinted in full as an appendix to Miller's book, *Democracy Is in the Streets*, 333. For instance, Irving Howe, an influential member of the Old Left who attended a couple of SDS meetings, called them "interminable and structureless sessions." Howe, "The Decade That Failed," *New York Times Magazine*, 19 September 1982, 78.

40. The statement appeared in a pamphlet produced by the Economic Research and Action Project of SDS. Miller quotes it in *Democracy Is in the Streets*, 215.

41. Gregory Calvert, "Participatory Democracy, Collective Leadership, and Political Responsibility," *New Left Notes* 2, no. 45 (18 December 1967): 1.

42. See Breines's summary of prefigurative politics in *Community and Organization in the New Left, 1962–68* (New York: Praeger, 1982), 1–8.

43. Staughton Lynd, "The Movement: A New Beginning," *Liberation* 14, no. 2 (May 1969).

44. Pat Hansen and Ken McEldowney, "A Statement of Values," *New Left Notes* 1, no. 42 (November 1966): 5.

45. Tom Hayden, "Democracy Is . . . in the Streets," *Rat* 1, no. 15 (23 August–5 September 1968): 5.

46. The Atlanta Project's position paper has been reprinted as "SNCC Speaks for Itself," in *The Sixties Papers: Documents of a Rebellious Decade*, edited by Judith Clavir Albert and Stewart Albert (New York: Praeger, 1984), 122. However, the title assigned it by the Alberts is misleading because at the time it was written in the spring of 1966, it did not reflect majority opinion in SNCC.

47. Rosalind Petchesky, *Abortion and Woman's Choice: The State, Sexuality, and Reproductive Freedom* (New York: Longman Press, 1984), 128.

48. Michelle Kort, "Sisterhood Is Profitable," *Mother Jones*, July 1983, 44.

49. Amiri Imanu Baraka, "A Black Value System," *The Black Scholar*, November 1969.

50. Jennifer Woodul, "What's This about Feminist Businesses?" *off our backs* 6, no. 4 (June 1976): 24–26.

51. Robin Morgan, "Rights of Passage," *Ms.*, September 1975, 99.

52. For a fascinating case study of this as it relates to women's music, see Arlene Stein, "Androgyny Goes Pop," *Out/Look* 3, no. 3 (Spring 1991): 26–33.

53. Kort, "Sisterhood Is Profitable," 44.

54. Stein, "Androgyny Goes Pop," 30.

55. Adrienne Rich, "Living the Revolution," *The Women's Review of Books* 3, no. 12 (September 1986): 1, 3–4.

56. Quoted from Jane Mansbridge, *Why We Lost the Era* (Chicago: University of Chicago Press, 1986), 266.

57. "Women's Liberation Testimony," *oob* 1, no. 5 (May 1970): 7.

58. Firestone, *The Dialectic of Sex*, 206.

59. Steve Halliwell, "Personal Liberation and Social Change," in *New Left Notes* (quotation); Rennie Davis and Staughton Lynd, "On NCNP," *New Left Notes* 2, no. 30 (September 4, 1967): 1.

60. See Charlotte Bunch, "The Re-

form Tool Kit," *Quest* 1, no. 1 (Summer 1974).

61. Frances Chapman, interview with author, New York City, 30 May 1984. Here Chapman was speaking of the radical feminist wing of the women's liberation movement, but it applies as well to women's liberation activists.

62. For more on the prefigurative, personal politics of the sixties, see Breines, *Community and Organization in the New Left*; Miller, *Democracy Is in the Streets*; and Aronowitz, "When the New Left Was New."

63. Quoted from Miller, *Democracy Is in the Streets*, 374.

64. Although individual social critics such as C. Wright Mills influenced the thinking of new leftists, the noncommunist Left of the 1950s and early 1960s remained economistic and anticommunist. Indeed, the fact that the board of the League for Industrial Democracy—the parent organization of SDS in SDS's early years—ignored the values section of the Port Huron Statement suggests the disjuncture between old and new leftists. For another view stressing the continuities between the Old and the New Left, see Maurice Isserman, *If I Had a Hammer . . . The Death of the Old Left and the Birth of the New Left* (New York: Basic Books, 1987).

65. See Judith Newton, "Historicisms New and Old: 'Charles Dickens' Meets Marxism, Feminism, and West Coast Foucault," *Feminist Studies* 16, no. 3 (Fall 1990): 464. In their assumption that power has a source and that it emanates from patriarchy, women's liberationists part company with

Foucauldian approaches that reject large-scale paradigms of domination.

66. Carmichael quoted from Clayborne Carson, *In Struggle: SNCC and the Black Awakening of the 1960's* (Cambridge: Harvard University Press, 1981), 282.

67. Firestone and Koedt, "Editorial," in *Notes from the Second Year*, edited by Firestone and Koedt.

68. However, the reclamation of blackness was often articulated in a sexist fashion, as in Stokely Carmichael's 1968 declaration, "Every Negro is a potential black man." See Carmichael, "A Declaration of War," in *The New Left: A Documentary History*, edited by Teodori Massimo (Indianapolis: Bobbs-Merrill, 1969), 277.

69. Aronowitz, "When the New Left Was New," 18.

70. Richard Flacks, "Some Problems, Issues, Proposals," in *The New Radicals*, edited by Jacobs and Landau, 168. This was a working paper intended for the June 1965 convention of SDS.

71. Excerpts from Jerry Rubin's book, *Do It*, appeared in *Rat* 2, no. 26 (26 January–9 February 1970).

72. "The Feminists: A Political Organization to Annihilate Sex Roles," in *Notes from the Second Year*, edited by Firestone and Koedt, 117.

73. Ehrenreich quoted from Carol Ann Douglas, "Second Sex 30 Years Later," *off our backs* 9, no. 11 (December 1979): 26.

74. The term *identity politics* was, I think, first used by black and Chicana feminists. See Diana Fuss, *Essentially Speaking: Feminism, Nature, and Difference* (New York: Routledge, 1989), 99.

75. Jeffrey Weeks locates the origins of identity politics in the post-1968 political flux. He argues that "identity politics can be seen as part of the unfinished business of the 1960's, challenging traditionalist hierarchies of power and the old, all-encompassing social and political identities associated, for example, with class and occupation." Perhaps Weeks situates this in the post-1968 period, because class held greater significance for many British new leftists than it did for their American counterparts. Weeks, "Sexuality and (Post) Modernity" (unpublished paper).

76. Nancy Cott, *The Grounding of Modern Feminism* (New Haven: Yale University Press, 1987), 5.

77. Amy Kesselman, interview with author, New York City, 2 May 1984.

78. "The New York Consciousness Awakening Women's Liberation Group" (a handout from the Lake Villa Conference of November 1968).

79. Kathie Sarachild, "Consciousness-Raising: A Radical Weapon," in *Feminist Revolution*, edited by Redstockings (New Paltz, N.Y.: Redstockings, 1975), 132.

80. Betty Friedan, *It Changed My Life* (New York: Norton, 1985), 101.

81. Audre Lorde, *Zami: A New Spelling of My Name* (Freedom, Calif.: Crossing Press, 1982), 226.

82. Lorraine Kenney, "Traveling Theory: The Cultural Politics of Race and Representation: An Interview with Kobena Mercer," *Afterimage*, September 1990, 9.

83. Mercer makes this point as well in Kenney, "Traveling Theory," 9.

6......

The New American Revolution

The Movement and Business

In 1970 the editors of *Forbes*, in an article it published on changes advocated by environmental and consumer activists, warned the business community that the "companies that understand these changes and move with them are the companies that will rank high in the *Forbes* Directory Issues in the years to come." *Business Week* agreed: "No longer can a company officer live a cloistered life behind the walls of private enterprise, concerning himself solely with turning out a product and a profit. These days, tenacious demonstrators and persistent consumers are insisting that he do something about the worldly issues of minority rights and the environment." By the next year *Saturday Review* was alarmed about the "new values" promoted by activists: "That business *must* respond is no longer a matter for debate.... The new American revolution has begun."[1]

A decade of social activism, often called the "movement," had a significant impact on American business. Company presidents lectured their executives on the merits of "social responsibility," business professors gave seminars on "public interest," while journalists published an increasing number of articles. In 1965 *A Reader's Guide to Periodicals* listed only six articles on the social aspects of business, but from 1970 to 1973 over a hundred appeared, not counting new categories concerning business and race problems and the environmental movement.

From 1960 to the early 1970s, the sixties era, activists attacked and in some respects changed America's way of "doing business," a topic neglected by historians.[2] This chapter will examine the rise of protests against various businesses, including issues, aims, and tactics. It also will explore the duel impact that the activists had on business—the rise of their own enterprises, often called "hippie capitalism," and the expansion of corporate social responsibility.

Movement is a slippery term, one used throughout the sixties to describe activists who marched and protested for a myriad of causes, the most prominent being civil rights, student power, peace in Vietnam, and women's liberation. Some also protested against products, pollution, and discriminatory or unfair practices of corporations. There is no one definition of movement; in their underground writings, activists defined and redefined the term usually by introducing issues and declaring objectives. A flier of an antiwar mobilization committee stated that the group was "for peace in Vietnam, for human rights, and for economic justice." The term *movement* was "self-descriptive," one activist has written. "There was no way to join; you simply announced or felt yourself to be part of the movement—usually through some act like joining a protest march. Almost a mystical term, 'the movement' implied an experience, a sense of community and common purpose."[3]

Unlike most scholarship on the movement, this essay will not define the term by examining one organization or a few "leaders," for the movement was a coalition of hundreds of groups that had been formed by thousands of organizers. There was no premier organization that set the agenda, and in a traditional sense the movement was leaderless. Nor will this essay define social activism toward business as a clash between capitalism and the New Left ideology expressed by a few radicals. While most activists naturally held common beliefs during the decade, leftist rhetoric did not motivate them to picket segregated businesses, defense contractors, or polluters. Unlike Great Depression activists, who framed many issues in terms of capitalism versus socialism, most sixties activists, organizing during affluence, aimed not to destroy capitalism, but to reform it.

The activists of the sixties were descendants of previous social reformers. Throughout American history citizens had posed questions about the fairness, responsibility, and power of business, as well as its role in the community. Populists had attempted to fight the system, the establishment, and to increase control over their own economic lives and over their own communities; Progressives had advocated increasing government regulation of business; and New Dealers had fought poverty and employed economic and social planning in an attempt to achieve a better society and nation.

The movement also grew out of the prosperity of the 1950s, a time when corporations seemed so successful, when company presidents appeared so influential, that Secretary of Defense Charles Wilson could declare that the "business of America is business." A few social thinkers disagreed. They criticized the expanding power of corporations and multinationals, and they influenced some students in the younger generation who pondered the ideas expressed in Sloan Wilson's best-selling novel, *The Man in the Gray Flannel Suit*, or in John Kenneth Galbraith's *The Affluent Society*, C. Wright Mill's *The Power Elite*, Paul Goodman's *Growing Up Absurd*, or William H. Whyte, Jr.'s *The Organization Man*.

Sixties activists, then, reexamined many traditional issues in American business history and raised the venerable questions: How powerful should business be? What is more important, personal and community or private and corporate rights? The activists again asked: What is legitimate corporate behavior? These activists also had some new issues for business, issues that they had developed on the picket line. They felt that the national promise, "All Men Are Created Equal," was not a reality for a majority of Americans—minorities and females. "The whole country was trapped in a lie," civil rights worker Casey Hayden said, "We were told about equality but we discovered it didn't exist."[4] Activists eventually demanded that corporations behave equitably without regard to race or gender. Who will companies hire and promote, white males or all citizens? Who will be paid equally, white males or all employees? Furthermore, activists responded to what they considered other national ills of the decade—a war in Vietnam and mounting pollution—and they tried to influence and change certain businesses that they felt practiced or profited from those evils.

Finally, social activism during the sixties paralleled government activism of the two Democratic administrations. Congress passed the Equal Pay Act of 1963, the Civil Rights Act of 1964, and then scores of consumer and environmental legislation while President Johnson established stronger affirmative action regulations. The movement played a significant role in the passage of most of these acts, and all of the subsequent laws and regulations had an impact on changing American business. But the issue here is not the movement and government, for the activists had a direct impact on business itself.

Civil rights advocates began the era by picketing businesses that engaged in discriminatory hiring, firing, sales, and service practices, and they scored the movement's first victories. The original tactic—the boycott—was as old as the American Revolution; it had been used in the 1950s to integrate buses in Baton Rouge and Montgomery. In February 1960 young black activists started a new phase of the struggle in Greensboro, North Carolina, by employing a novel tactic, the sit-in. Intended to end the practice of segregated lunch counters, the strategy was simple and direct. Franklin McCain, one of the Greensboro 4, later stated that if the business "did not serve blacks, it was certainly going to be hit. . . . You just can't continue to have people come in and sit around. The cash registers have to ring."[5] During the next year activists integrated lunch counters in two hundred cities in thirteen states.

The successful use of boycotts and sit-ins against segregated businesses had an impact on later activists. Blacks would continue to employ these tactics, and whites would adopt them as the movement expanded in the early 1960s. During the southern sit-ins sympathetic white students at Yale, Berkeley, and Michigan boycotted and picketed national chain stores that discriminated in the South. After a few dozen activists formed Students for a Democratic Society (SDS), one of their first acts of civil disobedience was to sit in at the New York headquarters of Chase Manhattan Bank to protest U.S. bank loans to companies in South Africa. In Berkeley, white and black activists employed "shop-ins" against Lucky supermarkets; after filling grocery carts with food, they would go through the checkout line and then say, "Sorry, I forgot my money. If you would hire some Negroes I would remember it next time." By 1965 activists with the Congress of Racial Equality (CORE) passed out fliers proclaiming, "Selma, Alabama and Bogalousa, Louisiana. . . . Here in Oakland?" Charging that prominent east bay restaurants only hired blacks as cooks, busboys, and dishwashers, CORE urged citizens and students to join the boycott against the establishments.[6]

By 1967 radical organizer Saul Alinsky developed a new tactic—proxy power. Charging that Eastman Kodak was not hiring enough blacks and that the only thing that the corporation had done for the race problem was to "introduce color film," he and a local black ghetto organization called FIGHT bought a few shares of Kodak stock, which gave them the right to attend the annual stockholders' meetings. They also approached several churches holding stock in the corporation and asked them to pressure the company by voting against the board's proposals. Eventually, Alinsky's coalition controlled the votes of several thousand shares; though the stock represented a tiny percentage of the 160 million shares outstanding, management realized the dire possibilities and increased minority recruitment.[7]

The rise of black power led to more vehement demands and more aggressive tactics. Black unionists at Ford and Dodge plants in the Detroit area formed "revolutionary unions," FRUM and DRUM, demanding an end to racism, the hiring of black foremen and superintendents, and equal pay for white and black workers in the South African plants of General Motors (GM); moreover, they insisted that black workers not be required to pay union dues and that the dues paid by whites be given to the local black community to "aid in self determination for black people." By the early 1970s the League of Revolutionary Black Workers advocated breaking with the United Automobile Workers and forming a black separatist union because UAW was "totally incapable and unwilling to stamp out racism" at Chrysler, a corporation of "slave drivers" that did not give "a good goddam about Black Workers."[8]

Brown power advocates launched a more subtle attack on racism. Alternative Media Action, a movement watchdog group, published an "Advertiser's Racism Chart" naming companies whose ads unfavorably portrayed Hispanic Americans. The group also sent out fliers claiming that Frito-Lay's use of Frito Bandito to sell corn chips conveyed the message that "Mexicans = sneaky, thieves" and that Arid's ad with a Mexican bandit spraying his underarms while the announcer was saying, "If it works for him, it will work for you," really meant "Mexican = stink the most."[9]

Most corporate executives who lived outside of the South supported the civil rights movement and even many of the policies of President Lyndon B. Johnson's War on Poverty and Great Society. The economy in the mid-1960s was booming, political liberalism was in vogue, and many agreed with a *Fortune* article stating that business needed "creative federalism" to guide the nation and continue prosperity. One expert wrote in 1966 that the "modern company officer accepts government (much like he accepts the labor union) and works actively with it."[10]

Consequently, it was relatively easy for sixties activists to win civil rights concessions from national corporations, but that was not usually the case concerning defense contractors during the Vietnam War. Reminiscent of the 1930s ideas of the "merchant of death" and the "devil theory of war," activists attacked defense corporations. Oil companies like Standard, Tenneco, Texaco, and Gulf, aircraft corporations like Boeing, Lockheed, McDonald-Douglas, and United Aircraft, and other defense-related businesses such as General Electric (GE), Texas Instruments, American Telephone and Telegraph (AT&T), and General Motors were just a few of the companies picketed during the era.

Yet none received as much attention as Dow Chemical and Honeywell. Dow was a natural target because it manufactured napalm, a mixture of gasoline, naphthenic acid, and palm oil, which stuck to whatever it contacted, burning or suffocating a victim. U.S. forces used massive quantities in Vietnam. Dow won a government contract in 1965 and became the largest producer of napalm, but over a dozen other companies also manufactured the weapon. After a few small demonstrations against those companies that year, the first large protest targeted Witco Chemical in April 1966. Denzil Longton, a Brooklyn housewife, organized her neighbors and local antiwar groups and held a demonstration at the nearby company. The size of the crowd was surprisingly large, so good that Longton and others formed the Citizens' Campaign against Napalm and billed 28 May as the first "anti-napalm day." Activists demonstrated at Dow's napalm manufacturing plant in Torrance, California, and at its sales office in New York City.[11] Furthermore, they launched a boycott of Saran Wrap, a Dow product, began a letter campaign, and gave away buttons that said "NO MORE NAPALM."

Dow's president, Herbert Dow Doan, was perplexed. To the World War II generation, producing weapons that helped U.S. soldiers was patriotic— it constituted legitimate corporate behavior. But apparently many young people disagreed. They were demanding a new standard: that companies should not profit from an immoral war. Doan met the activists and gave the usual business response; Dow was manufacturing napalm "because we feel that our company should produce those items which our fighting men need in time of war." For Dow to inquire into the use of its products in Vietnam "would in itself be in a sense immoral," and it was unfair to blame industry for taking government contracts.[12]

By 1967 Dow was the only company producing napalm, and to activists it became the symbol of a corporate "war profiteer." Actually, that was unfair. Dow made eight hundred products, from measles vaccine to antifreeze, and all government contracts combined counted for less than 5 percent of the multinational's annual profit. Dow sales to the Defense Department ranked seventy-fifth in 1968, and napalm contracts were only

Terry H. Anderson

about $5 million a year, meaning that they represented only one-fourth of 1 percent of Dow's sales.[13]

Such facts, however, were not important to antiwar activists; napalm had become a symbol of the war, and by autumn 1966 the campaign against Dow had reached the university campus. Student activists held small demonstrations at Princeton, Berkeley, Brown, and Wayne State in Detroit. They employed a novel tactic—obstructing company recruiters from holding job interviews on campus. The maneuver was perfected the next year by students at the University of Wisconsin. In October, hundreds of activists held a noisy sit-in and obstructed interviews, chanting "Down with Dow." Talks between officials and activists failed, and the university called in police to disperse the crowd. After a brutal confrontation, university administrators suspended the company's interviews for the remainder of the semester. In the meantime, students at Harvard, Illinois, Indiana, Minnesota, and Pennsylvania held Dow recruiters prisoner, while activists at other colleges waved signs declaring "Making Money Burning Babies" and handed out fliers inscribed "Dow Shalt Not Kill."[14]

As frustration mounted over the seemingly endless war, a few activists adopted more radical tactics. In March 1969 six Catholic priests and three supporters staged an early morning raid on Dow's offices in Washington, D.C. They threw files out the window, hung pictures of Vietnamese peasants and children burned during a napalm attack, and poured blood on furniture and equipment. They left a statement declaring outrage at Dow: You "exploit, deprive, dehumanize and kill in search of profit. . . . Your product is death." Because of this, it continued, "Your offices have lost their right to exist. It is a blow for justice that we strike today."[15]

Although the priests were arrested, stood trial, and were found guilty, the verdict gave little solace to company officials: The protest movement had an impact on Dow. From 1966 to 1970 there were 221 major anti-Dow demonstrations on campuses. Although sales of the company's household products did not decline, the harassment was not worth the negative publicity or the small profits gained from napalm. Dow chairman Carl Gerstacker admitted: "We've been hurt by these demonstrations. . . . The only question is how badly we've been hurt. . . . I wish we'd never heard of napalm." The multinational quietly allowed its napalm contract to expire in 1969 and another producer, American Electric, of La Mirada, California, won the contract. When *Newsweek* reporters called for an interview, spokesmen for American Electric stated that they would answer only written questions but refused to give their address.[16]

The movement had much less impact on Honeywell. Although the company is known for manufacturing thermostats, by 1970 it received almost $400 million in defense contracts, about 40 percent of its profits from producing a variety of weapons: people sniffers detected human urine in free fire zones, spider mines fired thousands of steel needles, gravel mines fired fiberglass pellets, and the silent button bomblet was a sensor device made of brown plastic to look like animal droppings. If moved a thirty-second of an inch, the sensor relayed a message to a computer that signaled for artillery fire. As one reporter for an underground paper wrote, "shit turns informer."[17]

Rockeye II missiles delivered the most prominent Honeywell weapon, the antipersonnel fragmentation bomb, sometimes called a CBU (cluster bomb unit). First used in Laos in 1966, each CBU was filled with 640 baseball-size secondary bomblets that were released half a mile above ground and dispersed over 1,000 yards. When the bomblets exploded, about 250 steel pellets burst out in all directions for 300 yards. The bomb, which had little value against reinforced military targets such as tanks, was used against human targets, for it was especially effective in tearing through flesh.

CBUs again raised the issue of what constituted legitimate corporate behavior. In December 1968 twenty-five clerics, students, and draft resisters in Minneapolis organized the Honeywell Project, a "serious group concerned with how the corporation uses its vast resources." They demanded an end to CBU production and more worker and community control of the company. Honeywell chairman James Binger would not submit to such demands and so the project became more aggressive, picketing outside plant facilities and even meeting with members of Binger's church after he attended services. Since Honeywell's directors were involved in local cultural events and sat on the board of the Guthrie Theater, project leaders sponsored a counterculture event in which actors from the theater performed antiwar guerrilla theater at Honeywell headquarters. In 1970 students and faculty at the University of Minnesota combined their resources and sponsored the "Honeywell Stock Buy-In." At $150 each, they purchased thirty-nine shares, which they claimed were "tickets of entry" to the upcoming stockholders meeting. Three thousand activists assembled at the meeting. A few holding proxies were admitted while demonstrators in the parking lot chanted and held a "people's stockholders meeting." Inside, Binger called the meeting to order over protests of dissidents, hastily dispensed with all official business, and adjourned in ten minutes.[18]

By the early 1970s, after five years of protest, it seemed that the Honeywell Project had only a minor impact. Clergy and Laymen Concerned about Vietnam and other antiwar organizations publicized the cause, and activists thorughout the country disrupted campus interviews. Chairman Binger, fearing that his corporation might become the "Dow of the seventies," stated his opposition to the war. Yet Honeywell's position, unlike Dow's, was similar to that of other major defense contractors, whose 1970 income from defense contracts was 40 percent of their overall profits—too high to abandon production. Although faced with almost daily demonstrations at their headquarters, they continued to manufacture weapons; their position remained consistent throughout the war: they were simply fulfilling a contract. To them, this was legitimate corporate behavior, as their defense production was "entirely appropriate . . . as a matter of good citizenship."[19]

Good citizenship, of course, meant something else to the movement. Activists felt that business should be responsive to their, "the people's," demands. By the end of the decade those demands expanded from civil rights and the war to new issues concerning women's liberation and ecology. Earlier activists had begun the attack, publicized the issues, and developed the tactics; their assault had an impact on many businesses. Many feminists and ecologists had participated in earlier demonstrations, and they enlarged the movement to include their own concerns, sexism in the workplace and corporate pollution.

Women played a major role in the movement.[20] While marching for black equal rights, they were irritated by male chauvinism: while attempting to end racism, they were appalled by sexism. Furthermore, they suffered from educational, legal, and economic discrimination. Indeed, this last issue provoked activism against business since male employees did not give female employees equal opportunities or salaries.

While some sisters began proclaiming liberation at the end of the sixties, others described their problems in the work force. The Women's Strike for Equality in August 1970 publicized discrimination. Activists urged workers to cover their typewriters, unplug switchboards, and put down mops until male bosses guaranteed that all jobs in the firm were open to female employees—with equal pay. During the next year the National Organization for Women and the Women's Equity Action League initiated a barrage of lawsuits against 1,300 corporations receiving federal funds or grants and demanded that those companies conform to the Equal Pay Act of 1963. While those businesses were reviewing their policies, a half-million telephone operators and other workers struck the nation's single largest employer of women, American Telegraph and Telephone. The corporation had no women in the top fifty management positions and almost none in craft jobs, whereas women comprised 99.9 percent of low-paying operators. "Maybe it's about time for a little more women's lib in the union," said one operator. Feminists in Madison printed fliers urging all activists to support the strikers, claiming that at Wisconsin Bell the "weight of institutional male supremacy is brought to bear full force on the working woman. . . . Women are relegated to the dullest jobs, paid sub-standard wages, and are treated like both small children and slaves." Bluntly, these activists charged: "Ma Bell Is a Cheap Mother!"[21]

Feminists attacked not only establishment businesses for sexism, but also enterprises that were part of the protest movement. When a coopera-tive food store, Erewhon Trading Company, ran ads that seemed sexist, a feminist wrote to the local underground that a boycott should commence until the offensive practice ended. It was one of many such episodes dem-onstrating that activists demanded the same behavior from their stores as from major corporations.[22]

Feminists, antiwar protesters, and others joined with ecologists to attack polluters as the environment became a national issue by the end of the sixties. This was not just a movement issue, for in 1970 the Johnson administration promoted various clean air acts, and popular opinion polls showed that more Americans were concerned about the environment than any other domestic problem. In fact, the largest "demonstration" of the era occurred that April, when 20 million participated in Earth Day. Activists focused on this issue because they perceived war production, racism and sexism on the job, and pollution as symptoms of a sick business establishment: Businessmen were greedy so they profited from bombs and kept wages for women and minorities low; they were irresponsible so they poured their refuse into streams.

It was a natural alliance, and activists initiated a frontal assault. *Liber-ated News Service* condemned General Motors as a producer of fighter planes and M-16 rifles and as the company that has "put more smog, dirt, and poison into the air than any other industry or corporation in the country." Another Mother For Peace charged that Standard Oil sup-ported the war so that after victory it could turn Southeast Asia into "another South Louisiana–Texas type producing area." *The Common Woman* claimed that the corporation coveted a "big chunk of off shore oil in Indochina" while spilling petroleum in the Pacific and pumping out "smog at a killing level in California." Such behavior, a feminist charged, meant that Standard Oil was guilty of "Slick Imperialism."[23]

Power companies often were targets. The Chicago Department of Environmental Control listed Commonwealth Edison as the worst air polluter in the city, prompting a Catholic priest, the Reverend Leonard Dubi, to lead seventy proxy-holding protesters to the stockholders meeting demanding a cut of sulfur emissions and opposing construction of a nuclear plant.[24]

Not only air pollution but also aesthetic pollution became an issue. Adjacent to the Minneapolis campus of the University of Minnesota is a village with older brick buildings known for years as Dinkytown. In 1970 a fast-food hamburger franchise, Red Barn, Inc., purchased a building and announced that it intended to demolish it and erect one of its drive-ins, which resembled a large red plastic barn. Students, residents, and community leaders formed the Committee to Save Dinkytown in an attempt to "go all out to preserve the environment of the community." They met with company executives, collected petitions, demonstrated at the proposed site, and eventually occupied the building so it could not be demolished. The company responded by having police eject demonstrators before dawn, and then workers quickly tore down the building. Although the company had the law on it side, the maneuver so enraged the community that the activists won in the long run. "Red Barn Officials seem to think they can rape Dinkytown and still run a business," the *Minnesota Daily* proclaimed. They "have opened a sore this morning that will . . . contaminate our community with continual provocation for confrontation."[25] Shortly afterward activists reoccupied the site and proclaimed it a "people's park." Realizing the potential for long-term adverse publicity, the corporation decided to abandon its plans; it never built the Dinkytown Red Barn.

As consumerism became a national issue, the protest movement joined the fray and attacked large corporations and small local businesses. When hippies appeared in Seattle in the mid-1960s, some businesses refused them service; one was a popular campus hangout named Aggie's Restaurant. After longhairs sat at a table the waitress said, "we don't need or want your business," and called the police. An officer arrived immediately and declared, "If they were niggers, they could get away with it!"—but not hippies, who were taken to the police station for no reason. As a result, students boycotted the restaurant.[26] When Rennebohms, a variety store in Madison, Wisconsin, held a one-cent sale in 1970, activists compared before- and after-sale prices, then handed out leaflets proclaiming, "Rennebohms 1¢ Sale Screws You, the Consumer." In Berkeley, California, activists distributed fliers listing local companies that allegedly overcharged customers, collaborated with police, and prohibited panhandling (asking for "spare change"). These businesses were labeled "Pig Sties" and the "people" were asked to "take your own appropriate action." Supposedly, the most notorious "pig collaborator and pig business" was Earl Cunha Pontiac. "Earl and his showroom should be a prime target during the next people-pig confrontation," declared one flier, which also charged that the local U-Save convenience store "rips off as many as five hungry brothers a day. *DON'T SHOPLIFT THERE!!!*" Sooner or later, the flier claimed, "this store will be totally liberated and, or, leveled."[27]

The protest movement also extended to labor. In general, unions such as the AFL-CIO supported administration policies in Vietnam and were part of the establishment. Workers often felt that students were privileged and that they were attending college to avoid monotonous futures on assembly lines. In 1967 some Progressive Labor party and SDS activists attempted to forge a student-worker alliance, but without success.[28] Only on campus was the student-worker relationship close, and that was because both workers and students often were part-time; even there the alliance was temporary, lasting only for the duration of the food service worker or teaching assistant strike. Nevertheless, as more young workers joined the rank and file by the end of the decade, as inflation cut into pay checks and actual worker income declined, and as the number of strikes soared, activists attempted to capitalize on labor dissatisfaction by mobilizing the traditional adversary of management.

In December 1969 almost 150,000 workers went on strike at the nation's fourth largest corporation, General Electric, when a coalition of thirteen unions demanded higher wages. Although this was a typical issue for a walkout, two charges made by the strikers demonstrated the impact of the protest movement on business-labor relations. First, the strike fliers—written by union members and activists who formed a support group for workers, the Philadelphia Resistance—proclaimed that GE, the nation's second largest defense contractor, "missed no chance at the huge profits available in the Vietnam war. With the help of their contacts in the Pentagon (two former Secretaries of Defense and one former Secretary of the Army are on the board of directors) they were able to make deals worth seven billion dollars in war contracts between 1961–67." Second, strike fliers charged that "General Electric is part of the worldwide US system of imperialism." With branches and subsidiaries in twenty-five nations and plants in Thailand, Colombia, India, and South Africa, the corporation was condemned for having "investments throughout the world which soak billions off the backs and blood of oppressed peoples."[29]

In 1970 there was more cooperation between the movement and labor. When postal workers struck during the spring, some underground papers ran articles entitled "Workers vs. Masters," while others proclaimed, "you don't have to be a mailman to know which way the shit flows." The *Long Beach Free Press* wrote above its masthead: "This Issue Free to All Postal Workers."[30] In Los Angeles, Teamsters struck in May, a time when students were protesting the invasion of Cambodia. It became the largest trucking strike in the area since the 1940s, and union leaders called on local students to help serve on the picket lines. One hundred and fifty students left campus and blocked the main gate of Western Car Loading, the focus of the strike. Workers cheered: "the students have been a shot in the arm to every worker," one driver proclaimed, while another stated that "since the students joined us, the newspapers have begun to cover the strike." In return, Teamsters spoke at antiwar rallies held at UCLA, Southern California, and local California State campuses. At the same time in the Bay area, unions took out a full-page ad in the *San Francisco Chronicle* demanding: "We want a cease-fire—Now! We want out of Cambodia—Now! We want out of Vietnam—Now! We've had it!" By 1972 almost a thousand delegates representing over thirty national and international unions formed Labor for Peace, an organization dedicated to ending the Vietnam War.[31]

Indeed, by the early 1970s the attack reached a crescendo. While activists scrutinized all American institutions, the percentage of citizens expressing "a great deal of confidence in the leaders of major companies" and agreeing that "business tries to strike a fair balance between profits and the interest of the public" plummeted 50 percent from the late 1960s to 1971. David Rockefeller of Chase Manhattan Bank told an audience of businessmen: "It is scarcely an exaggeration to say that right now American business is facing its most severe public disfavor since the 1930s. We are assailed for demeaning the worker, deceiving the consumer, destroying the environment and disillusioning the younger generation."[32]

By the end of the 1960s, then, the business of America was no longer just business. Some corporations were under attack, but the assault was not against all forms of capitalism, for activists and hippies often established their own private ventures and they seldom became a target. Many activists, of course, held similar, vague ideas about the business establishment: capitalism equaled greed, big business was too powerful, and multinationals were imperialistic. Reformers had expressed similar themes during the populist-progressive era and the 1930s, and Tom Hayden and his colleagues did so in the Port Huron Statement. Written in 1962 as a declaration of the ideals of the new Students for a Democratic Society, the statement condemned the "remote control economy" that excluded the common person from "basic decisions affecting the nature and organization of work, rewards, and opportunities," and it called for "a more reformed, more human capitalism."[33] In fact, that was one of the intellectual threads of the sixties—an attempt by activists to pressure government, universities, and corporations to adopt a more humane, egalitarian behavior toward *all* Americans, whether it be on the streets, in class, or at work.

A handful of vocal radicals, of course, attacked capitalism. Groups such as the Socialist Workers party, Progressive Labor party, Black Panthers, and eventually SDS screamed for some sort of revolutionary alternative. These activists received considerable attention from the media, especially the business press. Editors at the *Wall Street Journal, Fortune,* and *Business Week* were so alarmed by such rhetoric that they basically declared war on the radicals. After a few hundred students "liberated" some buildings at Columbia University in 1968, *Barron's* declared: "The scene might have been the University of Havana or Peking. It wasn't. It took place just a few express stops from Wall Street.... The siege tactics which disrupted Columbia and brought its normal activities to a halt represent the latest assault by a revolutionary movement which aims to seize first the universities and then the industries of America."[34]

The press usually failed to mention that the self-proclaimed revolutionaries always were a tiny minority in a broad social movement, and that their provocative ideas were not attractive to labor or even to most students. Workers rarely joined New Left organizations, and although no accurate figures exist on SDS campus membership, the organization drew only a small number of outspoken students. A 1969 survey found that only 3 percent of noncollege youth and only 13 percent of college students identified with the New Left. Most campus activists were ambivalent about capitalism, yet the overwhelming majority—85 percent in one survey—felt throughout the early 1970s that business was entitled to make a profit, a clear indication that the movement was not aiming to dismantle free enterprise. As an activist later wrote, "We wanted to remake America, not destroy it."[35]

To the vast majority of activists, the issue was not abolishing capitalism. After all, a sizable portion of the young Americans who protested certain business practices eventually accepted jobs in private enterprise. Did they abandoned their values, their soul? Were they all hypocrites? This was hardly the case. Many accepted positions with corporations that did not contradict their values. *Forbes* noted in 1970 that businesses were hiring college graduates, "Rebels in Grey Flannel Suits," who were interested not just in profits but in social responsibility and the "quality of life." *Fortune* observed the next year that new trainees "reflect the passionate concerns of youth" such as "individuality, openness, humanism, concern, and change."[36] Moreover, thousands of businesses never witnessed one demonstration, because activists viewed them as fair, responsible, and assets to the community, organizations that provided jobs—even to activists and hippies.

The issue was how to change those businesses that did not conform to their views, that did not adhere to their definition of legitimate corporate behavior. To do that, activists used traditional as well as novel tactics. They employed boycotts, sit-ins, pickets, and other forms of economic pressure spiced with sixties rhetoric. To stop alleged unfair worker treatment or compensation, boycotts were initiated against numerous companies— Gallo Wine, Polaroid, Levi Strauss, Farah, AT&T, and Coors; in 1970 students at Skidmore College and Brandeis University led a national boycott of Coca-Cola and Philip Morris. In New York City, the Black Panther party handed out fliers listing addresses of defense contractors, so-called Neighborhood Imperialists. The National Boycott for Peace printed a "guide for conscientious consumers" on wallet cards naming a hundred companies and their products, declaring, "The Boycott will end when the war ends." To pressure corporations that profited from the youth market, organizers demanded that these corporations speak out against the war. Concerning savings institutions, protest fliers often stated that those in the movement should take the war to the banks by withdrawing their funds, and activists initiated a boycott of Bank of America. Some workers even used economic pressure against their own companies, and by 1973 the Oil, Chemical, and Atomic Workers Union struck against Shell Oil. During "America's First Environmental Strike," as it was billed, the workers asked citizens to boycott Shell products until the company eliminated pollution in the workplace.[37]

Economic strategy had more than new rhetoric; activists also devised some new tactics. Saul Alinsky formed Proxies for People, which attempted to sell proxies to activists, foundations, mutual funds, churches, and universities in an attempt to compel corporations to pursue social goals. A similar approach was devised by Philip W. Moore, who established the Project on Corporate Responsibility and, with the aid of consumer advocate Ralph Nader, Campaign GM. Moore and his associates bought General Motors stock and then demanded that the corporation give him the names of the other one million stockholders so he could solicit their help in forcing the corporation to place three "public directors" on the board who would support social and antipollution policies.[38] By the early 1970s "proxy power" groups were demonstrating at the annual stockholder meetings of numerous corporations such as General Electric, Union Carbide, AT&T, and the Columbia Broadcasting System; by 1972 activists in New York City were publishing the monthly *Corporate Examiner,* which analyzed the policies of the Fortune 500 businesses concerning military contracts, foreign investments, pollution, labor and minority practices, and corporate responsibility. Antiwar students saw possibilities in this tactic and demanded that their universities divest themselves of their holdings in firms that were defense contractors, that were polluting the environment, or that were doing business in South Africa.

Activists also applied economic pressure against the federal government. They urged Americans not to buy U.S. Savings Bonds, and the Committee to Unsell the War urged citizens not to pay their taxes. Fliers proclaimed that "war spending eats away at social programs" and that "this is a war to make Asia safe for American profits." Students at the University of California, Santa Cruz, hoarded nickels. Since those coins were common currency for vending machines, each activist attempted to stash twenty dollars worth, creating a shortage that would hurt local businesses and sent a message to Washington. Folk singer and antiwar activist Joan Baez refused to pay her taxes, informing the Internal Revenue Service that "I am not going to volunteer the 60% of my year's income tax that goes to armaments" so the Defense Department could build "one horrible kill machine upon another."[39]

Social activists formed a number of new organizations that became known as corporate responsibility action groups. Clergy and Laymen Concerned about Vietnam, founded in 1965 to "help unsell the war," later began introducing shareholder proposals to defense contractors that called for the establishment of worker-management committees to explore alternatives to war production. Ecologists, who organized in the late 1960s, publicized corporate pollution through the Environmental Defense Fund, Friends of the Earth, the National Resources Defense Council, and Environmental Action, Inc. Others, in groups such as Businessmen for the Public Interest, the Citizen's Action Program, the Council on Economic Priorities, the Project on Corporate Responsibility, and Ralph Nader's Corporate Accountability Research Group, acted as watchdogs and analyzed business behavior.[40]

As activists graduated from law school they used the legal system. In

1966 radical attorneys organized the Center for Constitutional Rights, "dedicated to the creative use of law as a positive progressive force and the training of young lawyers," and Nader formed his law firm, the Public Interest Research Group, which had over a hundred young lawyers, or "raiders," by the end of the decade. Charles Pillsbury, grandson of the founder of the Minneapolis milling company, bought 101 shares of Honeywell stock and filed suit against the company in an attempt to win the right to inspect the list of the company's other shareholders so he could solicit proxies and elect at least one director who would vote to stop production of CBUs; a similar suit was filed against Dow Chemical.[41] In response to Red Barn's plan to build a franchise, forty Minneapolis residents filed a class action suit, a tactic feminists used throughout the 1970s. Underground papers often ran articles or series such as "legal raps" to inform readers of their constitutional rights.

To mount public pressure against certain companies, activists employed ridicule and shame. Demonstrators wore buttons declaring, for example, that "Honeywell Kills People." Fliers mocked company slogans: "At GE, Profits is their most Important Product." Artists made slide shows and home movies, and the Strike Film Co-op produced a "documentary" depicting the Red Barn controversy. Satirists such as R. Cobb drew scathing cartoons for underground papers. The San Francisco Women for Peace handed out leaflets picturing a child using a toy bazooka ("War Toys for Christmas?" it asked) and naming local stores who had adopted policies not to advertise or display toys of violence.[42]

Company employees even ridiculed their bosses. As more younger workers joined the rank and file they occasionally formed "corporate underground" groups. The black power Polaroid Workers' Revolutionary Movement demanded that the company stop doing business in South Africa and handed out leaflets claiming that "Polaroid imprisons blacks in 60 seconds." Radicals embarrassed top executives and derided corporate policies by printing underground papers such as the *AT&T Express* and the *Met Lifer* at the Metropolitan Life Insurance Company, the latter inspiring the *Stranded Oiler* at Standard Oil of California. Edited by "Scarlet Punpernickle," the *Stranded Oiler* often was "written on company time, using a company IBM typewriter, while the writer was listening to KSAN at high volume." It aimed to raise the "consciousness of the modern day galley slaves," mock management, and ridicule corporate hypocrisy: Standard's statements about its concern for the environment while it vigorously opposed California's clean coastline acts were answered by headlines such as "power to the polluters."[43]

rise of "employee power" was supported by Ralph Nader, who in ︶nsored a Whistle-Blowers' Conference. He encouraged workers ︶e "on-the-job conscientious objectors" by refusing to carry out ︶ey considered illegal or immoral and by leaking corrupt or unethi- cal practices of their corporate bosses, what consumer activists called "crime in the suites."[44]

As the protest movement aged, and as frustration levels increased, tac- tics became more radical, desperate, even violent. Take Over, a group in Madison, Wisconsin, with a staff calling itself the "bang gang," printed fliers describing the "procedure" for making long-distance credit card calls and billing large corporations such as Magnavox, Standard Oil, and Dow and even the White House. Some activists occupied corporate head- quarters and destroyed offices. The radical feminist organization, WITCH, dressed in black costumes and invaded offices, where they put a hex on sexist bosses and dumped buckets of refuse.[45] After the invasion of Cam- bodia and the subsequent shooting of students at Kent State, marchers in Madison, Wisconsin, shattered storefront windows; Black Panthers in Oakland, California, distributed leaflets with instructions for making Mo- lotov cocktails; and an angry mob in Santa Barbara burned down the Isle Vista office of Bank of America. In 1970 and 1971 that bank reported twenty-four fires or bombings of their branches in California.[46]

One way to attack business was much more subtle—if the corporate establishment did not adhere to the values of the movement, or if estab- lishment businesses did not produce products for the youth revolt, many activists simply boycotted those stores and established their own enter- prises. Consequently, one of the most significant impacts of the movement on business was the development of hippie capitalism.

Critics mocked the movement for attacking capitalism while establish- ing profitable businesses such as Celestial Seasonings or *Rolling Stone Magazine*. This seemed like an inconsistency but, on closer inspection, it was not. The movement was a large social phenomenon, not an organiza- tion, party, or club espousing a common anticapitalist ideology. Further- more, activists were selective, favoring capitalist ventures that did not discriminate, that supplied meaningful employment, or that contributed to society. While they would picket a firm like Safeway for buying grapes or vegetables from corporate farms that paid migrant workers piecemeal, they would make their purchases at local family-owned stores, farmer markets, or cooperatives. If the marketplace did not offer companies that conformed to their views, then it was natural that these children of busi- nessmen would establish their own ventures—underground record and book stores, clothing or leather businesses, food cooperatives, head shops, and listener-sponsored FM stereo radio stations. Hip capitalists were the merchants of novelty.

Information in a democracy is an obsession, and that was particularly true in the sixties, when the protest movement often thought that it could not trust the establishment media; consequently, one of its most successful business ventures was the "underground media." *Rolling Stone* became the most profitable, with a circulation of over a quarter million in 1970 and lucrative advertising contracts with national record companies. Other publications such as the *Berkeley Barb, Fifth Estate, Great Speckled Bird, L.A. Free Press,* and *The Rag* also had large circulations; the *Las Vegas Free Press* boasted that with 25,000 readers it was the largest weekly newspaper in Nevada. Undergrounds were filled with information for the counterculture, and they often printed ads or business news. "Avoid Safeway, Colonial and Super Giant, be wary of A&P," while "Seigel's highly recommended for produce" and "Food Fair has excellent selection of fresh and frozen fish." Movement news became so popular that news services were established such as the Y.I.P. News Service, W.I.N.D. News Service, Underground Press Syndicate, and Liberation News Service, which by 1968 had three hundred undergrounds subscribing. To help these undergrounds the Communication Company of Columbus, Ohio, offered "free training to persons for Movement and social change/social service groups," and media activists in California established the Media Workshop.[47]

The movement also established its own FM stereo stations. This generation was raised on rock and roll, and it tired of commercial AM stations that usually played the top twenty hits along with twenty ads. By 1968 one of the most popular "hip stations" was KSAN-FM in San Francisco, and the next year activists in Madison, Wisconsin, established "listener-sponsored FM." A late-night weekend program, "radio free," was aired on station Up against the Wall–FM; it was followed by a full-time station, WORT. During the early 1970s listener-sponsored stations went on the air in Berkeley, Fresno, Los Angeles, Houston, New York City, and Washington D.C.

Small movement businesses proliferated during this era of "the media is the message." Young entrepreneurs sold their beliefs on T-shirts, buttons, and posters. A hippie could make a purchase in person at the Love Poster shop in New Orleans or by mail order from The Dirty Linen, which sold "Fuck the Draft" posters and offered this promotion: "Here's a little something for Mother's Day. . . . Send for five posters ($5) and we'll send a sixth one free to the mother of your choice," which included Madame Ngo Dinh Nhu, Lady Bird Johnson, or General William Westmoreland. A group calling itself the Jesus Freaks sold day-glo buttons inscribed "Truckin with Jesus" and "No 'jive' Jesus is Alive." In Philadelphia the Edward Horn Company advertised a thousand buttons for $70; an activist could design his or her own slogan or pick from standards like "Peace Now," the timely "Majority For A Silent Agnew," and "Hi. I'm an Effete, Impudent Intellectual Snob."[48]

Food and clothing co-ops were established. The *Plain Dealer* wrote about the "Great Food Conspiracy:" "Dig—we don't have to eat all that shit they've fed us into believing is food." The Philadelphia underground claimed that "Madison Avenue—Pen Fruit—Kelloggs Korn Flakes" really were "chemical coated plastics in fancy boxes."[49] The alternative was to buy at movement food stores such as Germantown People's Food in that Maryland city, the Ecology Food Co-op in Madison, Wisconsin, the Liberated Area in Richmond, Virginia, and Ma Revolution's Natural Food Collective or the Hillegass Food Conspiracy in Berkeley, California. Student free markets were opened on many campuses, as were clothing co-ops in many cities that sold second-hand merchandise. Stores traditionally involved with this business, the Salvation Army and Goodwill Industries, witnessed scores of hippies in their checkout lines.

Drugs, naturally, were a movement business. While undergrounds— from *The Mystic* in Fargo-Moorhead, North Dakota, to *Monolith* in Huntsville, Texas—ran articles on the availability of the best local marijuana, paraphernalia or head shops proliferated. The Entrepreneur in Chicago, the Family Dog in San Francisco, The Third Eye in Los Angeles, and The Trance in Columbia, Missouri, all sold pipes and cigarette papers made from rice, maize, licorice, even hemp; the brand name was Acapulco Gold. In San Francisco, Jerry McGregor and Warren Ziebarth manufactured plastic marijuana plants that were registered under the name Cannabis Sativa, and Yippie Abbie Hoffman informed the masses how to deal dope in his underground best-seller, *Steal This Book*.

The generation prided itself on sexual liberation, and many youthful entrepreneurs profited. Head shops might sell erotic lotions or sexual gadgets, and in Berkeley, a company called Namous sold Zap condoms using the motto "Zap the Clap." Undergrounds often published "personal" columns in which men would advertise for "groovy chicks who like to smoke weed and ball." In New York City, Underground Enterprises established a dating service called FUK, "For Turned-on people only.

Heads Do the Matching." Guys could apply by sending five dollars, "girls apply free."[50]

Some entrepreneurs profited from sarcasm and humor. Gilbert Shelton published comics about "Wonder Wart-Hog," "Little Orphan Amphetamine," and his most famous characters, "The Fabulous Furry Freak Brothers." R. Crumb, the "people's cartoonist," produced Motor City comics featuring "Lenore Goldberg and Her Girl Commandos" in addition to LSD-inspired characters in his Zap Comix and a symbol for the age, the "Keep on Truckin" slogan. Gonzo journalist Hunter S. Thompson published books on the Hell's Angels and later on his fear and loathing at a policemens' convention in Las Vegas. Calipso Joe of Los Angeles established Handicap Pictures since "everyone of our pictures is a 'Handicap.'" Produced in "True Bloody Color," these short films included titles such as "President Johnson the Defoliate President" and "Damn the Constitution–Undeclared Wars–Full Speed Ahead," with the theme song "Your Lyin, Cheatin Heart." Joe also was the press secretary for satirist General Hershey Bar, who spoke at rallies to "give war no quarter" because it "ain't worth a dime."[51]

By the end of the decade many had tired of activism and dropped out of the "plastic" society of industrial America to create their own hip culture. Steward Brand created their bible: *The Whole Earth Catalog*. The front page declared that the establishment had failed, and that the catalog supplied tools that would help an individual "conduct his own education, find his own inspiration, shape his own environment, and share his adventure with whoever is interested." During the early 1970s authors associated with the movement published manuals concerning female nutrition and hygiene, such as *Our Bodies, Ourselves*, or books about home carpentry, water supply systems, organic gardening, rural industry, solar power, or simply, as Alicia Bay Laurel entitled her book, *Living on the Earth*.[52]

While most movement businesses just survived financially, a few made healthy profits. Various editions of *The Whole Earth Catalog* sold a million copies. The Family Dog gross sales in 1967 were $380,000, and Celestial Seasonings, founded in 1971 by hippies "looking for something to do one summer," sold $16 million worth of natural teas and herbs annually by the end of the decade; one of their founders was a millionaire at age twenty-six. Hip capitalists profited entertaining the movement. Ticket sales at Bill Graham's Fillmore and Winterland auditoriums in San Francisco ranged between $10,000 and $35,000 a week in 1967 and the Middle Earth Light

& Power Co. grossed about $25,000 a month staging light shows at the Electric Circus in New York.[53]

In fact, the counterculture could be sold at a nice profit—and that became an issue in the movement. A few days after it opened in 1966, the Psychedelic Shop in San Francisco received this note: "You're selling out the revolution. . . . You're putting it on the market." To many underground writers, rock festivals "symbolized the struggle between two cultures, the tenuous attempt to balance commercialism with hip culture." The problem was that the promoters saw "profits first, and human needs afterward." They had turned "festivals of love" into "festivals for profit." After the Woodstock festival in 1969, underground writers became more cynical. A writer in *Seed* carped about all the concerts slated for summer 1970: "A whole swarm of sideburned entrepreneurs is preparing to capitalize on the hip culture's twin addictions: rock music and tribal gatherings." It was becoming clear that "freaks are getting more and more uptight with the rampant shucksterism involved in most of the festivals." To a writer in *Rat*, hip promoters were simply "part of the system."[54]

Activists, therefore, attacked movement enterprises as well as establishment businesses for making excessive profits. When promoters charged six dollars for a Led Zepplin concert, the *Las Vegas Free Press* urged a boycott. The fourteen-dollar admission price for a festival at Carbondale, Illinois, was condemned by an underground reporter who realized that musicians needed "bread" but questioned Sly and the Family Stone and The Band demanding $25,000 "in small bills, in advance" for a forty-five-minute set: "Holy shit, who was that that first said rock is getting a little commercial? How about 'mercenary'?" Indeed, as one hippie capitalist lamented in 1970, "Being a promoter these days is a bummer deal. You take it from the straights on one side and the crazies on the other."[55]

Profit, then, was debated in the movement. Some critics jeered that hippie entrepreneurs were no different than other capitalists, and for some that was true as they cashed in on the youth market. That was to be expected; many young merchants had been raised in the homes of successful business executives, and just because activists marched against some corporate practices did not mean that they rejected all forms of capitalism, a system that had benefited their parents and even themselves in childhood.

Some activists argued that people in the movement should make no profit. By the early 1970s many volunteers had established numerous free services. San Francisco listed thirty, ranging from crash pads, to a foot clinic, to a drug hot line, to the Animal Switchboard. Many others sold at cost or gave away their underground papers. *Nola Express* was "35¢ or barter," *Contempt*'s price was "from each, to each," *Leviathan* was "free to political prisoners," and the *Little Free Press* was "totally free. . . . If we want freedom, let's quit using money because the rich control the money; so they control us." The golden rule to them was "Those who have the gold make the rules."[56]

Most members of the counterculture realized the dilemma concerning profit. Some laughed off the issue. "Make all the money you want. Make billions!," suggested one writer in the underground *Planet*. Money equaled energy, and "if WE don't get that energy, someone else will." Yet others were more concerned about money and movement values. As another writer reflected in *Rat*, "We rap a lot about our groovy 'alternate' subculture; but its energy continues to be dampened by contradictions involved in the development of a truly human, revolutionary lifestyle within the confines of an exploitative commercial system."[57]

How could protesters carp about being "ripped off by big business" and then make a profit at their own head shops; how could they buy records from RCA? On a practical level, many entrepreneurs in the movement tried to keep profits reasonable, and many young buyers made their purchases from local crafts people, co-ops, and alternative businesses, thus purchasing from stores that conformed to their ideals. On a theoretical level, however, they never could resolve the problem. Yet the question itself became increasingly irrelevant by the turn of the decade, for by then young people realized that there was not going to be any "revolution" in a nation where the movement always represented a minority of citizens and where the counterculture always represented a minority within a minority.

Yet this vocal minority of activists did have an impact on the business establishment. While realizing that by the end of the sixties a majority of citizens had become disillusioned with business and all institutions, and that government passed significant regulatory legislation, the movement did contribute to business reform. What was significant about the legacy of what the *Saturday Review* called "the new American revolution?"

By the 1970s many businesses had developed new products to accommodate people in the sixties generation who had been influenced by the counterculture. Styles and advertisements became hip, but more important was the rise of a new industry that basically resulted from the hippie cooperative movement and its back-to-nature ideals—health foods. In 1970 Tom Chappell established Tom's of Maine and began selling hygiene products free of preservatives and other additives; later others formed

Nature's Gate. By the mid-1980s Tom's sales had reached $8 million annually, and food conglomerates like General Mills and Nabisco had modified recipes to delete additives and to add whole grains and other healthy ingredients. Since the 1970s, labels such as "no preservatives" and "organic" have been common and "natural" has become a mania in America.

As the movement blossomed with consumer and environmental activists, business became more sensitive to their demands. The number of consumer protection agencies soared, and public interest organizations doubled between 1968 and 1977. Moreover, activists founded five new environmental organizations between 1967 and 1971, and during the 1970s the membership of older groups like the Sierra Club increased by a third while 100,000 citizens joined Ralph Nader's Public Citizen and over twice that many joined Common Cause. These activists worked with local government and pressured corporations. With lawsuits on the dockets and pickets at factory gates, businesses replaced the old slogan "let the buyer beware" with a new saying, "let the seller beware." Corporations attempted to convince citizens that they were good neighbors. In Minneapolis, for example, the Northern States Power Company published an advertisement admitting that its "Riverside Power Plant causes air pollution. *We know it and we are in the process of correcting it.*" By 1974 business journalists concluded that, considering the environment, "Yesterday's standards are indeed yesterday's."[58]

The business community also responded to the movement by creating new investment opportunities. Pressured by activists, universities, and liberal foundations, some investment companies in the 1970s developed social awareness mutual funds such as the Dreyfus Third Century, First Spectrum, Pax World, Social Dimensions, and Working Assets. The Dreyfus Third Century Fund, for example, would consider investing only in companies that protected and improved the environment, and it practiced consumer protection and equal employment opportunity.[59]

The movement also redefined what was considered legitimate corporate behavior, an issue usually discussed under the rubric of social responsibility. This was, of course, not a new debate in the sixties, for the traditional philosophy of business—that decisions should be made to maximize profits, which will automatically result in the optimum benefits for society—had been questioned during the Great Depression.[60] Yet during and after World War II social responsibility had taken a back seat to other topics such as the expansion of government regulations, rise of multinationals, development of the military-industrial complex, and prosperity of the

1950s. The movement's attack rejuvenated the issue, and business responded by examining its behavior and adjusting to the times. "Whether business likes it or not," ORC chairman Hugh C. Hoffman said, "the public is redefining corporate responsibilities in general and telling the companies what their social responsibilities must be." Charles F. Luce, chairman of Consolidated Edison, agreed, declaring that now managers must become concerned with "whether Negroes and Puerto Ricans have decent jobs and housing and education." Gulf Oil president B. R. Dorsey went further, stating that the "*first* responsibility of business is to operate for the *well-being* of society." By the end of the 1970s most business leaders would agree with one authority, who wrote that the "effective modern chief executive is concerned less and less with internal issues" of his company "and more and more with the problems of the outside world."[61]

By 1970 articles examining "business and youth," "business and responsibility to a changing society," and the "executive as social activist" flooded papers and magazines. During that decade the number of books on social responsibility soared.[62] Corporations increased their visibility and advertisements in an attempt to convince the public that they were good citizens. General Motors announced the establishment of a "public policy committee" to advise the giant corporation on business matters that affected the local community. Bank of America appointed an executive vice-president of social policy, and corporations such as RCA, Control Data, Boise Cascade, and Owens-Corning increased their participation and funding in local education and community projects. This interest also had an impact on education, as business colleges established professorships of corporate responsibility.

This enlightened corporate ethic was a form of awareness that also appeared in hiring and management practices—perhaps the most profound impact of the sixties protest movement on business is that it increased employment opportunities for minorities and women. In the late 1960s Henry Ford II stated that the nation was in the "worst domestic crisis since the Civil War" and that businesses must respond by making "changes in our employment practices—in whom we hire, how we hire, and what we do with people and for people after they are hired." Soon afterward Ford opened two employment centers in the Detroit ghetto, and more than 60 percent of the new workers were minorities. Bank of America, under attack by CORE and other activists, tripled its number and doubled its percentage of minority workers from 1965 to 1973. Its competitors, First National City Bank of New York and Chase Manhattan, also named blacks to their boards of directors.[63] Sixteen companies had black directors by 1971, and the number increased to over eighty by the end of the decade. The appointment of women to managerial, officer, and board seats followed blacks but progressed more rapidly. Bank of America had hundreds of female workers in 1970 but not one officer; by the mid-1980s half of its officers were women. This trend appeared in boardrooms nationwide: women occupied only a few seats in 1970 but over 400 by 1980. Equal opportunity was a fundamental change in business practices, affecting all occupations. According to one business journal, the new positions for minorities and women were "clearly a response to social protest."[64]

Perhaps some companies returned to "business as usual" with the demise of social activism in the late 1970s and the rise of the conservative 1980s. Yet even during and after the Reagan years no corporate president would announce that the "business of America is business." Indeed, during the 1980s the nation did not return to the corporate values of the 1950s. Popular approval for environmental and consumer protection remained high, and so legitimate corporate behavior excluded discriminating in the work place or polluting the community. Since the movement of the sixties, a more appropriate maxim would be: the business of America is responsible business.

The movement naturally did not affect all companies, and the amount of change depended on whether activists' demands were supported by a broad sector of the population and whether a corporation had the means to make the necessary financial sacrifice. Consequently, businesses more readily accepted changes that had public support but hesitated on more controversial issues concerning war production. Defense contractors continued to produce weapons throughout the Vietnam War regardless of massive demonstrations; it was too profitable for the company and for the worker. The Honeywell Project's efforts to halt production of CBUs failed, as did its attempts to mobilize employees. Workers either avoided thinking about the issue, agreed with their company's views, or were more concerned about receiving their monthly pay. "Most people of Honeywell," wrote one worker, "are unwilling to take a firm stand on the Vietnam war for fear of jeopardizing their jobs—and in turn jeopardizing their families' well-being."[65] Dow Chemical lost interest in the napalm contract because the social cost of being a symbol of the war, and the actual cost of protecting its college recruiters, exceeded the tiny profit.

The amount of change also depended on individual business executives: What ideals did directors hold, and what company image did they want to project? Some corporate leaders, such as those at U.S. Steel, AT&T, or Standard Oil of California, often rejected activists' demands, stonewalled change, and considered it a victory as the turbulent 1960s became the complacent 1980s. Others, such as those at Levi Strauss, Xerox, Ford, Cummins Engine, Control Data, and eventually Dow Chemical, analyzed the demands, accepted change, and became progressive forces in the community.[66] In the final analysis, then, capitalism's "invisible hand" was attached to an executive, and when that person changed company procedure by hiring a black, promoting a woman, cleaning up a waste dump, or volunteering service in a community, then corporate leadership itself played a role in the new American revolution.

NOTES*

1. *Forbes*, 15 May 1970, 60; *Business Week*, 7 March 1970, 106; *Saturday Review*, 24 July 1971, 32.

2. Even business history textbooks do not examine what the business community then called a revolution. There are no articles on the topic, and the only books that address it are Charles Perrow's *The Radical Attack on Business* (New York: Harcourt, Brace, Jovanovich, 1972), which offers a selection of readings with commentary, and David Vogel's *Fluctuating Fortunes: The Political Power of Business in America* (New York: Basic Books, 1989), chaps. 2–5.

3. November 8 Mobilization Committee flier, 1966, Social Action Vertical File, box 37, State Historical Society of Wisconsin, Madison (hereafter cited as SAVF). See also *Rat*, 12–26 August 1969, 5: Bell & Howell Underground Newspaper Microfilm Collection (hereafter cited as BH); and Sara

Evans, *Personal Politics: The Roots of Women's Liberation in the Civil Rights Movement and the New Left* (New York: Viking, 1980 ed.), 102.

4. Casey Hayden quoted from Mary King, *Freedom Song: A Personal Story of the 1960s Civil Rights Movement* (New York: Morrow, 1987), 8.

5. McCain interview in Howell Raines, *My Soul Is Rested: Movement Days in the Deep South Remembered* (New York: Penguin Books, 1983 ed.), 75–82.

6. Kirkpatrick Sale, *SDS* (New York: Random House, 1973), 182; CORE flier, 7 October 1965, Social Protest Project, box 37b, Bancroft Library, University of California, Berkeley (hereafter cited as SPP).

7. Saul D. Alinsky, *Rules For Radicals: A Practical Primer for Realistic Radicals* (New York: Vintage Books, 1972 ed.), 137, 170–83; *New Republic*, 25 April 1970, 13.

*A note on "movement" sources: Books and articles on social activism during the sixties usually rely on the establishment press and rarely use manuscripts written by activists such as fliers, posters, or underground newspapers. This essay relies on both. Citing movement documents is complicated because the amateur journalists involved often forgot issue numbers, dates, or pages.

8. *Drum* 1, no. 9 (1968): 1, and *Forum*, 22 September 1971, 2–3, Underground Newspaper Collection, Bentley Historical Library, University of Michigan, Ann Arbor (hereafter cited as Bentley).

9. *Alternative Media Action*, [December 1971], 6, box 36a, SPP; Thomas Martinez, "Advertising and Racism: The Case of the Mexican-American," *El Grito* 2 (Summer 1969): 3–13.

10. Max Ways, "Creative Federalism and the Great Society," *Fortune*, January 1966, 122; Richard Barber, "The New Partnership," *New Republic*, 13 August 1966, 22—on this issue see Vogel, *Fluctuating Fortunes*, chap. 2.

11. E. N. Brandt (Dow Company historian) to author, 24 May 1988; Citizens' Campaign against Napalm fliers, n.d.: 1965–66, box 9, SAVF. See also Nancy Zaroulis and Gerald Sullivan, *Who Spoke Up?: American Protest against the War in Vietnam, 1963–1975* (Garden City, N.Y.: Doubleday, 1984), 104–6.

12. *The Dow Diamond*, no. 4, 1967, in Dow Company Archives, Midland, Mich.

13. *Forbes*, 15 March 1969, 37; E. N. Brandt, "The Public Relations of Protest," *Monitor*, July–August 1968, 9–10.

14. *Daily Cardinal*, 19 October 1967, 1; *Wisconsin Alumnus*, November 1967, 4–9; Dow Action Committee fliers, [1967], box 17, SAVF.

15. *Catholic Radical*, May–June 1969, 4.

16. Speech by C. A. Gerstacker, 3 June 1970, Dow Company Archives, Midland, Mich.; Brandt, "The Public

Relations of Protest," 24; *Newsweek*, 1 December 1969, 78. See also *Forbes*, 15 March 1969, 37.

17. *Hundred Flowers*, 22 July 1971, 3, BH.

18. Honeywell Project Papers, in unnumbered boxes, Robert Ross Papers, University Archives, Walter Library, University of Minnesota, Minneapolis (hereafter cited as Ross Papers). See also Clergy and Laymen Concerned about Vietnam folder, box 11, SAVF; *Minnesota Daily*, 8, 10 December 1969, 19 February, 28 April 1970.

19. *Minnesota Daily*, 10 December 1969; Mitchell K. Hall, *Because of Their Faith: CALCAV and Religious Opposition to the Vietnam War* (New York: Columbia University Press, 1990), 134–35, 142–44.

20. See Evans, *Personal Politics*; Jo Freeman, *The Politics of Women's Liberation* (New York: Longman, 1975); Alice Echols, *Daring to Be Bad: Radical Feminism in America, 1967–1975* (Minneapolis: University of Minnesota Press, 1989); and Winifred D. Wandersee, *On The Move: American Women in the 1970s* (Boston: Twayne, 1988).

21. *New York Times*, 15 July 1971; New American Movement flier, "The Case against AT&T," [1971], Ross Papers.

22. *Mole*, April 1971, 2, box 18b, SPP.

23. *Liberated News Service*, 19 November 1970, BH; *The Common Woman*, 18 March 1971, box 19a, SPP.

24. *Time*, 11 May 1970, 95.

25. *Minnesota Daily*, 4 March, 6 May 1970.

26. Untitled flier, 28 April 1967, box

labeled "People's Protest 1964–1967," Pacific Northwest Collection, Suzzallo Library, University of Washington, Seattle.

27. Untitled flier, 8 April 1970, folder labeled "U.W. Activities: chronological file," box 52, SAVF; Untitled flier from Berkeley, 21 April 1970, box 15a, SPP.

28. Sale, *SDS*, 333–34, 471.

29. *The Resister*, February 1970, 5, and untitled strike flier, 9 December 1969, box 15a, SPP.

30. *Seed*, 13 March 1970, 2, BH; *Long Beach Free Press*, 2–6 April 1970, box 18a, SPP.

31. *Liberation News Service*, 23 May 1970, 10, BH; *San Francisco Chronicle*, 18 May 1970.

32. Vogel, *Fluctuating Fortunes*, 54–58; *Los Angeles Times*, 3 January 1971.

33. For the Port Huron Statement, see James Miller, *"Democracy Is in the Streets: From Port Huron to the Siege of Chicago* (New York: Simon and Schuster, 1987), app.

34. *Barron's*, 20 May 1968. See also *New York Times*, 25 April 1968.

35. Daniel Yankelovich, *The New Morality: A Profile of American Youth in the '70s* (New York: McGraw-Hill, 1974), 68, 128; Mickey Kaus, "Confessions of an Ex-Radical," *Newsweek*, 5 September 1988, 24, 28.

36. *Forbes*, 15 September 1970, 46; *Fortune*, March 1971, 100–104. See also *Time*, 20 July 1970, 62; *Business Week*, 7 March 1970, 106–8, 14 October 1972, 94; Archie B. Carroll, ed., *Managing Corporate Social Responsibility* (Boston: Little, Brown, 1977), 13–15.

37. Black Panther flier, n.d. (box 6), National Boycott for Peace flier, n.d. (box 31), Committee to Support the Shell Strike flier, June 1973 (box 13), SAVF.

38. *Business Week*, 2 May 1970, 12, 12 February 1972, 21.

39. Committee to Unsell the War fliers, folder 1, box 1, Brian Peterson Papers, State Historical Society of Wisconsin, Madison; Chester Dunning, interview with author, College Station, Tex., 23 April 1991; Joan Baez, *And a Voice to Sing With: A Memoir* (New York: Summit Books, 1987), 120.

40. *Business and Society Review/ Innovation* 4 (Winter 1972–73): 81–86.

41. "CCR: The First Ten Years" (Center for Constitutional Rights pamphlet), box 8, SAVF; *Time*, 26 January 1970, 69; *Wall Street Journal*, 11 January 1972, 4.

42. San Francisco Women For Peace flier, n.d., box 20, Staughton Lynd Papers, State Historical Society of Wisconsin, Madison.

43. *Stranded Oiler*, September, October 1971, file drawers and box 9, SPP.

44. *Nation*, 13 September 1971, 206–12. See also Ralph Nader, Peter J. Petkas, and Kate Blackwell, eds., *Whistle Blowing: The Report of the Conference on Professional Responsibility* (New York: Bantam Books, 1972), and Ralph Nader, ed., *The Consumer and Corporate Accountability* (New York: Harcourt, Brace, Jovanovich, 1973).

45. Take Over flier, n.d.: 1972, box 50, SAVF; Robin Morgan, ed., *Sisterhood Is Powerful* (New York: Vintage Books, 1970 ed.), 538–53.

46. Bank officials stated: "Funda-

mentally, the Isle Vista uprising was part of a national uprising of young people against Vietnam, against the war in Indochina." Bank of America video tape, "Evolution of Responsibility," 1976, Bank of America Headquarters, San Francisco.

47. *Richmond Chronicle*, 15–31 August 1969, BH; The Communication Company flier, n.d., "misc." folder, box 29, SAVF.

48. Dirty Linen Corp. flier, n.d., "anti-war" folder, box 5, SAVF; *Truth*, October 1972, box 16, SPP; Edward Horn Company flier, n.d., "anti-war" folder, box 5, SAVF.

49. *Plain Dealer*, 17–30 September 1970, BH.

50. Namous flier, 1972, box 36a, SPP; FUK flier, n.d., "anti-war activities New York City" folder, box 5, SAVF.

51. Handicap Pictures flier, n.d., Chicago Committee to End the War in Vietnam papers, "songs" folder, box 1, and General Hershey Bar flier, n.d., "Liberation News Service" folder, box 25, SAVF.

52. See Sonya Rudikoff, "O Pioneers!: Reflections on the Whole Earth People," *Commentary*, July 1972, 62–65.

53. *Business Week*, 27 January 1968, 84.

54. Jay Stevens, *Storming Heaven: LSD and the American Dream* (New York: Harper and Row, 1988 ed.), 302; *Seed*, 13 March 1970, 5–6; *Rat*, 12–26 August 1969, BH.

55. *Las Vegas Free Press*, 16–22 April 1970, 1; *Seed*, 13 March 1970, 5–6, BH; *Goose Lake Gags*, August 1970, Bentley.

56. *The Little Free Press*, November 1971, box 25, SAVF.

57. *Planet*, 15 June 1969, box 15a, SPP; *Rat*, 12–16 August 1969, 21, BH.

58. Jeffrey M. Berry, *Lobbying for the People: The Political Behavior of Public Interest Groups* (Princeton: Princeton University Press, 1977), 13; *Minnesota Daily*, 22 April 1970; *Business and Society Review* 12 (Winter 1974–75): 26–29.

59. John J. Corson and George A. Steiner, *Measuring Business's Social Performance: The Corporate Social Audit* (New York: Committee for Economic Development, 1974), 6–9.

60. Adolph A. Berle and Gardiner Means, *The Modern Corporation and Private Enterprise* (New York: Macmillan, 1932). For the debate in the late 1960s and 1970s, see Archie B. Carroll, ed., *Managing Corporate Social Responsibility* (Boston: Little, Brown, 1977).

61. *Business Week*, 17 June 1972, 103 (Hoffman); *Time*, 20 July 1970, 62 (Luce and Dorsey); David Clutterbuck, *How to Be a Good Corporate Citizen: A Manager's Guide to Making Social Responsibility Work—And Pay* (New York: McGraw-Hill, 1981), 4.

62. For example, see *Esquire*, October 1969, 6; *Harvard Business Review* 47 (July 1969): 154–56; *New Republic*, 25 April 1970, 13–14; *Time*, 20 July 1970, 62–68; and *Vital Speeches* 35 (15 July 1969): 595–98. See "How Social Responsibility Became Institutionalized," *Business Week*, 30 June 1973, 74–82, and David R. Farber, *Corporate Philanthropy: An Annotated Bibliography* (Chicago: Donors' Forum of Chicago, 1982). Books on

the subject include Jules Cohn, *The Conscience of the Corporations: Business and Urban Affairs, 1967–1970* (Baltimore: Johns Hopkins Press, 1971), Richard N. Farmer and W. Dickerson Hogue, *Corporate Social Responsibility* (Chicago: Social Research Associates, 1973), Lloyd L. Byars and Michael H. Mescon, *The Other Side of Profit* (Philadelphia: Saunders, 1975), Ralph Estes, *Corporate Social Accounting* (New York: Wiley, 1976), and Frank Koch, *The New Corporate Philanthropy: How Society and Business Can Profit* (New York: Plenum Press, 1979).

63. "The Executive as Social Activist," *Time*, 20 July 1970, 62–68 (Ford); Milton Moskowitz, "The Greening of the Bank of America," *Saturday Re-view of the Society*, 17 March 1973, 55–57; "The Bank of America's Rocky Road to Responsibility," *Business and Society Review* 22 (Summer 1977): 61–64.

64. Duncan Knowles (Bank of America), interview with author, 23 June 1988, Texas A&M University Oral History Collection; *Business and Society Review* 16 (Winter 1975–76): 5–10, and see 37 (Spring 1981): 25, and 43 (Fall 1982): 51.

65. *American Report*, 23 October 1972, 14.

66. See the "corporate responsibility awards" that were given from 1969 to 1973 by *Business Week* and after that by *Business and Society Review*.

7......

Who'll Stop the Rain?

Youth Culture, Rock 'n' Roll, and Social Crises

To many observers at the time, the most important change in American society during the sixties seemed to be the emergence of youth as a distinct political and cultural force.[1] Political activism by college students on and off campus, the popularity of youth-generated styles of dress, grooming, speech, and music, and perceptions of a "generation gap" denoting a difference in values between people born after World War II and those born before it all contributed to the idea that age might become as important an indicator of social identity as race, class, or gender.[2]

In retrospect, these claims seem excessive and overblown. Youthful activists did play an important role in the political struggles of the decade, but they represented specific interest groups and constituencies among youth, not youth as a whole. Young people who came of age in the sixties did have an enormous impact on popular culture, but their influence came more from their sheer numbers and purchasing power than from

206

any particular values or tastes. A generation gap might have been felt painfully in individual cases, but a series of sociological studies revealed that youth in the sixties had values that were remarkably consonant with those of their parents in most important matters.[3] ☆ *not too different*

Yet the social upheavals of the sixties greatly influenced what it meant to be young. If we broaden our definition of youth beyond the campus and the counterculture, we encounter individuals entering adulthood in a variety of contexts—on active duty in a shooting war thousands of miles away from home, living in inner-city neighborhoods set ablaze by the domestic insurrections that expressed the rage and frustration of people seeking jobs and justice in a segregated society, and entering the work force at a time when the future seemed to offer no guarantees. The emerging availability of contraceptive devices and the trend toward longer periods of schooling allowed men and women to redefine the relationships between sexual pleasure and procreation or family formation. New developments in technology and commerce encouraged the establishment of new venues for communication and recreation, while government social welfare programs and local activist organizations created new social spaces conducive to experiments in social relations.

It is not easy to reconstruct retrospectively the experiences of youth in the sixties. Conventional historical methods that privilege the public records of political, economic, or military institutions are indispensable to historical understanding, but they tend to slight the experiences of ordinary people and the ways in which they make meaning for themselves. They are particularly deficient in understanding young people because public records most often reflect the concerns of those in power and only rarely contain evidence of the thoughts, action, or aspirations of teenagers and young adults unless those groups are seen as some kind of threat to people with power.

In this chapter, I examine some of the popular music of the sixties to see what clues it contains about the experiences of young people and the problem of "youth culture" in that decade. Although grounded in empirical facts about the production and reception of music, my argument necessarily relies on reasoned speculation about this evidence in order to offer one interpretation of the experiences of youth in the sixties. Studies of youth crime, comic books, or teen fashion magazines might lead to very different conclusions. Even in respect to music, my study emphasizes the artists and songs most associated with alternative youth countercultures and slights the music of other youth subcultures—surfers, dancers, car customizers. *music a more effective way of understanding youth than public records*

Yet the power of popular music in shaping and reflecting cultural changes makes it an important site for social and historical analysis. While indices of commercial popularity cannot measure the depth of attachment or engagement with any particular song, the broad-based nature of musical production and reception gives us significant clues to trends and tendencies across the broad population of consumers. Taken in conjunction with other evidence, it can help us assess some of the short-term and long-term consequences of sixties youth culture.

That music was central to the experience and consciousness of many young people in the sixties seems undeniable. In his history of the United States since World War II, William Chafe identifies music as "the most important 'sacrament' for the young" in the sixties, as the center of a lifestyle and a counterculture that "testified powerfully to the fragmentation taking place within the society."[4] Indeed, perhaps no area of American culture better epitomizes the complicated realities of the sixties than popular music. During that decade, rock and roll emerged as the core practice of an exuberant youth counterculture, growing from a youth-oriented genre to the dominant form of American popular music. The music industry expanded its reach and scope through the cultivation of an entire generation of avid consumers, yet music also emerged as an important site for cultural conflict and dialogue about prevailing values. The tumultuous decade defined by the civil rights movement and the Vietnam War, by destructive riots and demoralizing assassinations, also gave birth to the popularity of the Beatles and the Rolling Stones, of Janis Joplin and Jimi Hendrix, and of Bob Dylan and Aretha Franklin. Yet in music, no less than in politics, there was no one distinct sixties experience. Instead, music making in the sixties emerged from a plurality of experiences, all riddled with contradictions.

Any retrospective account of the sixties inevitably runs up against our collective societal capacities for remembering and forgetting. In politics, we may recall the sixties as a time of radical change, forgetting that Dr. Martin Luther King, Jr., *lost* most of the battles he fought (the 1965 Voting Rights Act was his only clear-cut victory, while defeats included the campaigns in Atlanta in 1960, in Albany, Georgia, in 1962, in Chicago and the Meredith march in Mississippi in 1966, and in Memphis and elsewhere with the Poor People's campaign in 1968, as well as the antiwar protests of 1967 and 1968). We may forget that most Americans supported the war in Vietnam throughout the sixties, and that they opposed most of the specific objectives of both the civil rights and black power movements.[5] Similarly, in music, we may remember the sixties as the decade of Janis Joplin and

George Lipsitz

Jimi Hendrix but forget that Elvis Presley, Brenda Lee, and Connie Francis joined the Beatles and Ray Charles as the five best-selling artists of the decade.[6] We may recall the emergence of folk-rock and the popularity of psychedelic acid rock, while forgetting that the best-selling song of the sixties was Percy Faith's saccharine instrumental ballad "Theme from a Summer Place." If the motion picture *Woodstock* (1970) leaves indelible impressions of the searing social commentary encoded in Hendrix's satirical "Star Spangled Banner" or Country Joe and the Fish's "Feel Like I'm Fixin' to Die Rag," it may allow us to forget the appearance on the best-seller charts of Sergeant Barry Sadler's "The Ballad of the Green Berets" (1966), or of countersubversive prowar classics like Pat Boone's "Wish You Were Here Buddy" (1966), Victor Lundberg's "An Open Letter to My Teenage Son" (1967), or Merle Haggard's "Okie From Muskogee" (1969).

Although American society and culture did not change as much during the sixties as contemporary popular memory indicates, it is nonetheless indisputable that important changes were made during those years. The disruption and turmoil of the decade left a deep impression on Americans, offering an often unspoken social subtext to all of the cultural creations and practices produced in its wake. More than mere nostalgia drives us back to the texts of sixties popular culture. In them we encounter reserves of collective memory that unite cultural texts with their historical contexts, that encapsulate powerful dynamics of imagination and desire, and that enable us to gauge the successes and failures of yesterday's hopes and dreams. Above all, we encounter some of the radical transformations engendered within American popular culture because of the social movements of the sixties. Even when they failed to achieve their immediate political goals, those social movements often created both physical and figurative spaces for cultural transformations.

Looking for the Sixties

Decades are always artificial constructs, but in discussions of the sixties artifice has been accompanied by mythology as well. It has seemed appropriate to many observers to note that the decade that began in hope with the nonviolent civil rights protest by four teenagers at the Woolworth's lunch counter in Greensboro, North Carolina, in February 1960 ended in hopelessness and resignation at a rock music festival in Altamont, California, in December 1969, when Hell's Angels beat to death a black spectator while the Rolling Stones performed on stage.[7] This periodization gives the decade an organic trajectory, one that roughly corresponds to the hopes of civil rights workers and student activists who could envision their cause as ascendant in the early years of the decade, but doomed by its finish. Yet many other schema could be applied to the same calendar of events. An optimist might start the decade with the election of President John F. Kennedy in November 1960 and conclude it with the landing of Americans on the moon in July 1969. A critic of American foreign policy might point to the Bay of Pigs invasion of Cuba in 1961 and the My Lai massacre of Vietnamese civilians in 1969 as the relevant boundary points for understanding the sixties. But events take place in response to forces that rarely conform to the contours of the calendar, and in a country as deeply divided over politics, economics, and culture as the United States was in the sixties, it is dangerous to assign a single narrative trajectory to events.

Similarly, monumental changes within sixties popular culture followed no single linear path of development. Yet the enormous differences between the 1970s and the 1950s raise important questions about exactly what took place in the intervening decade. In 1961 Johnny Burnette had a minor hit with "For God, Country, and My Baby"—a patriotic affirmation of a soldier's willingness to serve during the Berlin crisis of that year. Ten years later, country singer Arlene Harden reached the best-seller charts with "Congratulations," a bitter indictment of the war in Vietnam from the perspective of an army wife who "congratulates" the army for "making a man" out of her husband by turning him into a tormented and embittered person "whose eyes tell of where he has been." The distance between "For God, Country, and My Baby" and "Congratulations" provides an important clue to the cultural distance between 1971 and 1961 for some Americans. Similarly, Bobby Darin began his career as a ducktailed teen idol in pegged pants in 1958, when his juvenile party song "Splish Splash" reached the best-seller charts, but by 1969 he had long hair and wore a leather jacket with buckskin fringe as he recorded songs like Tim Hardin's antiestablishment "Simple Song of Freedom." Dion Di Mucci was twenty-one years old when he recorded his first hit record, "Lonely Teenager," in 1960, and his next eighteen hit songs all concerned themselves with teenage love affairs. But in 1968, he reached the best-seller charts with "Abraham, Martin, and John," a song about the assassinations of John and Robert Kennedy and Martin Luther King, Jr.[8] For young women, popular music in the first half of the decade might have meant listening to "girl groups" like the Crystals, Angels, and Shangri-las singing hymns to their boyfriends. In the second half of the decade, however, Aretha Franklin and Janis Joplin soared to popularity with strong and self-assertive songs telling stories from a female point of view.[9]

The commercial nature of the music industry makes it an imperfect mirror of social relations. Direct and indirect censorship coupled with fears of alienating distributors and consumers render overt political statements within popular culture relatively rare. Yet by the late 1950s, several artists were already attempting to insert political concerns into their songs. Songwriters Jerry Leiber and Mike Stoller tried to make a veiled attack on white supremacy in their 1959 song parodying western movies, "Along Came Jones." But their record company persuaded them to make the lyrics inoffensive in order to guarantee airplay on commercial radio stations.[10] Barry Mann and Cynthia Weil had a similar experience trying to write about race relations in their 1964 song, "Only in America." In its original form, the song included lyrics stating that "Only in America, land of opportunity, can they save a seat in the back of the bus just for me" and "Only in America, where they preach the Golden Rule, will they start to march when my kids want to go to school." But again, nervous record company executives persuaded the songwriters to change their lyrics to secure commercial acceptance. In its hit version sung by Jay and the Americans, the song became simply about romance and upward mobility, celebrating America as "a land of opportunity" where "a classy girl like you can fall for a poor boy like me."[11] Yet by 1969, Sly and the Family Stone's "Stand," Jefferson Airplane's "Volunteers," and Creedence Clearwater Revival's "Fortunate Son" all made the best-seller charts with lyrics that explicitly attacked racism, government repression, and militarism.

Were these changes reflective of a genuine shift in cultural values and political ideals in America, or did they merely manifest efforts by marketers to cash in on changing trends? Was popular music in the sixties the product of young people struggling to establish their own artistic visions, or was it the creation of marketing executives eager to cash in on demographic trends by tailoring mass media commodities to the interests of the nation's largest age cohort?

Taking Care of Business

From a business point of view, the dynamic interaction between young people and popular music in the sixties began in 1964, when the Beatles made their first tour of the United States. Marketers had developed a growing appreciation of teenagers as consumers by 1959. In that year the average teen spent $555 a year on goods and services not provided directly by parents.[12] But after a spectacular leap in sales between 1955 and 1959, music industry revenues remained static until 1964.[13] By the late 1960s, popular music had become big business, bringing a much higher rate of return on investment than most other areas of the entertainment industry. The Beatles alone had sold $154 million in records by 1968, and by 1970 the music industry's total sales of records and tapes exceeded $2 billion, surpassing the total sales generated by motion pictures ($1.6 billion) and by all sports events ($600 million).[14] Rock music accounted for almost all of the increased sales; by the early 1970s rock and roll accounted for nearly 80 percent of recorded music.[15]

Demographics played an important role in shaping the music industry. In 1964 seventeen-year-olds became the largest age cohort in the United States, and their purchases of records by the Beatles and other rock groups demonstrated their potential as an economic and cultural force. In succeeding years, the taste preferences of this group displayed considerable power to reshape the economy. In 1965 a decision by the Federal Communications Commission (FCC) requiring stations in large markets to broadcast separate programs on their AM and FM bands created an immediate need for "product" among FM programmers. FM technology made it possible to make broadcasts in stereo, making the emerging medium more conducive to music programming than AM radio had been.[16] The narrow playlists of the AM stations restricted the range of music available to radio listeners (many "top forty" stations played as few as fifteen different songs per week), leaving an emerging consumer demand unfilled. The relatively low capital requirements for entry into business in FM radio, coupled with the FCC's ruling, made FM radio a prime site for the development of the new rock and roll. In order to fill the available airtime and to take advantage of stereo technology, many of these stations played albums instead of single records. By 1969 albums accounted for 80 percent of popular music sales, and recording groups could be commercially successful without a hit single played on "top forty" AM stations.[17]

The popularity of FM stations and the emergence of album-oriented rock music shook up the music industry. As Joe Smith, then president of Warner Brothers Records, remembers, "We found we couldn't sell the Grateful Dead's records in a traditional manner. You couldn't take your ad in *Billboard* and sell a record that way. We found that they had to be seen. They had to play concerts. We had to advertise on FM stations which were just emerging about that time. The packaging was important. The cult was important. Free concerts where you handed out fruits and nuts were important."[18]

Along with FM radio, an "underground press" emerged in the sixties as an important adjunct to the music business. Following the lead of the eminently successful *Berkeley Barb* and the *Los Angeles Free Press*, guerrilla journalists all across the country started their own weekly newspapers. Mixing New Left politics with commentary on alternative "hippie" countercultures, these papers became an important source of information and inspiration for the young. At a time when few daily newspapers printed articles critical of the government or stories about rock music, the underground press became a vital resource for countercultural communities. But they served as well to identify the contours of an emerging youth market, advertising the wares of clothing stores, head shops selling drug paraphernalia, and, most important, record companies. Record companies discovered that favorable reviews in underground papers could "break" new acts successfully, while negative notices could produce serious sales problems even for established artists. Music industry executives began to funnel advertising dollars into the underground press, in some cases providing the bulk of their revenues.[19]

Record companies, FM radio stations, underground newspapers, and clothing, record, and head shops formed the infrastructure of the "youth culture" economy. Yet for all of the capital expended directly and indirectly to bring this market into being, the youth culture was not simply a creation of marketers. Rather, it coexisted and overlapped with a youth counterculture that emerged from the political and social transformations of the sixties.

Dancing in the Street

During the sixties, large numbers of middle-class white youths raised in suburban subdivisions surrounded by superhighways rediscovered the energy and intimacy of the urban street. From Dinkytown in Minneapolis to Houston's Montrose District, from Golden Gate Park in San Francisco to Tompkins Square Park in New York's East Village, young people poured into inexpensive dwellings on rundown streets, trying to find themselves by finding each other. Ellen Sander underscores the importance of the street in her remembrance of the emerging counterculture of that decade:

> Whatever it was that was making us so unhappy pulled us toward the street. It was the only way out and it was completely open. The street was the place to meet kindred souls of every physical description, the place to score dope, the place to hang out and find out what was happening. It was dotted with shops and coffeehouses where you could

find anything from a chess game to every conceivable assortment of sexual partner or partners. It was where we lived, learned, worked, played, taught, and survived; it was where you oriented yourself among it all. Naturally, it was the best place that anyone who wanted to could find and play and make and go to hear music.[20]

The movement of young people into the streets emerged in part as a reaction against the corporate culture of conformity that had shaped much of suburban life since World War II, but it also responded to the ways in which political struggle transformed the nature of urban space. In his moving reminiscence about participating in sixties antiwar and civil rights demonstrations, Marshall Berman recalls a "transforming experience" that enabled people to feel the kind of physical warmth and trust from strangers that they might have known previously only with one person in intimate privacy. The experience "gave many of us an ease and confidence in public spaces that we had never had before, and never expected to have at all," Berman observes.[21]

The reconstitution of public space by political movements had important ramifications for popular music. The popularity of folk music as an organizing tool within the civil rights and antiwar movements made musical expression an organic part of political protest. The popularity of folk-rock as a commercial genre and the identification of the mass rally as a site for music evolved organically out of the prominence of music making within oppositional movements. For years Bob Dylan had a relationship with a woman active in civil rights work with the Congress of Racial Equality. In the early 1960s he appeared in Mississippi to sing protest songs as part of the civil rights organizing in that state, and he also attended a national council meeting of the most important white student protest group, the Students for a Democratic Society.[22] Political movements established the legitimacy of singing in public, they demonstrated the ways in which music might make serious commentaries on political issues, and they brought diverse groups together in a way that set the stage for the subsequent appreciation of difference and diversity within public music performances and audiences.

In addition, as political "sit-ins" evolved into cultural "be-ins" and "love-ins," the ritualized sharing of public space with like-minded "brothers and sisters" remained at the core of the experience. William Chafe describes the countercultural sensibility that emerged from these spaces as one that held that " 'being' was more important than 'becoming,' living *now* more valuable than the drive to get ahead."[23] The music festival and large concert hall emerged as privileged sites for the making of music, and the ability of musicians like Jimi Hendrix, Janis Joplin, and Otis Redding to transform audiences through live performances provided an important basis for their prestige. Yet it was not just large numbers that made these gatherings important; on the contrary, it was the cultural unity that they affirmed. Presumptions of a common community with a mutuality of values pervaded festival rock concerts no less than they did political mass demonstrations.

In myriad ways, rock music in the sixties translated the energy and imagination of street politics into art. From "Dancing in the Street" (1964) by Martha and the Vandellas to Thee Midnighters's "Whittier Boulevard" (1966) to Wilson Pickett's "Funky Broadway" (1967), songs about the street conveyed hidden messages about riots, car cruising, and black power to knowing (or perhaps merely imaginative) listeners. In some cases, heavily politicized countercultural communities produced their own musical acts. In Detroit, the political activist and "white panther" John Sinclair managed the rock band MC5. Sinclair's white panthers specialized in street theater and agit-prop interventions, like the time they applied to the Detroit City government for permission to blow up the General Motors Building and, when refused, vowed that the experience taught them the futility of trying to work through the system. Despite limited radio airplay, unenthusiastic record company support, and outright censorship, the MC5's "Kick Out the Jams" reached the Billboard "Hot 100" charts in 1969, and their album *Back in the USA* reached the top thirty.[24] When John Sinclair was arrested for selling a small amount of marijuana to an undercover police officer, musicians rallied to his defense. A benefit to "free John Sinclair" in Ann Arbor, Michigan, in 1971 featured performances by John Lennon and Yoko Ono, Archie Shepp, Bob Seger, and Stevie Wonder.[25]

West Coast promoter Bill Graham discovered rock and roll music through a series of benefits that he produced for the radical theater ensemble that he managed, the San Francisco Mime Troupe. Graham produced the famous Merry Pranksters' Tripps Festival at San Francisco's Longshoreman's Hall in 1966 featuring the music of Mother McCree's Uptown Jug Champions, who would soon change their name to the Grateful Dead. Ten thousand people showed up for the three-day festival, and Graham soon began producing concerts for his own benefit at the rented Fillmore Auditorium. He would go on to become one of the most successful entrepreneurs of rock and roll, producing live music on both coasts and playing a major role in Woodstock and other rock festivals.

Even when musical groups had no direct links to community organizations, their art often reflected the values privileged in the streets. Aesthetics of amateurism and multiculturalism permeated sixties rock and roll. Audiences knew that Janis Joplin had been a secretary and that Jim Morrison had been a film studies major in college who only started singing when the prevailing aesthetic of amateurism invited their participation in the alternative music scene. The participatory democracy of the New Left that encouraged people to take control of the decisions that affected their lives found a cultural concomitant in a musical subculture that asserted that everyone could be a star. As one participant in the early San Francisco hippie subculture recalls while discussing the centrality of music (and drugs) to that community:

> We were held together by our own good vibrations and with the rise of the Sound, we were drawn together into a family. The Fillmore and Avalon [ballrooms] of 1966 radically changed our language, our interests, and our lives; from a goal-directed, school-directed way of living, we'd moved to a life-style directed way by our music and acid. Acid and the bands became the loci of our lives. Saturday night became the center around which the rest of the week was left to move; reminiscing about the last, planning for the next. All day Saturday spent in preparation, collecting flowers, buying new costumes, buying and selling dope, getting super stoned and listening to music.[26]

Multiculturalism also played an important role in the aesthetics of sixties rock music. The "Age of Aquarius" may have become an instant cliché when the Broadway musical *Hair* presented it as the supposed anthem of the counterculture, but a distinctly "Aquarian" desire for transcending differences did provide one of the driving mechanisms of sixties music. Just as folk-rock's connections to the civil rights and antiwar movements brought to the surface long-suppressed folk traditions in American music, the civil rights and black power movements placed a new emphasis on African American music through their emphasis on black pride. Within black communities songs like Aretha Franklin's "Respect" (1967), the Impressions's "We're a Winner" (1968), and James Brown's "Say It Loud— I'm Black and I'm Proud" (1968) served as important emblems of self-affirmation, but their popularity with white audiences also reflected an important, if limited, transformation in American race relations. The black-owned Motown label grossed over $30 million in 1967, with an estimated 70 percent of its sales to white audiences.[27] White artists and entrepreneurs in the sixties still received a disproportionate share of the rewards from a popular music that was undeniably African American in origin, while black innovators including Ray Charles, Sam Cooke, Jackie Wilson, Aretha Franklin, James Brown, and B. B. King never gained the critical or commercial respect due them for their achievements. White groups including the Beatles, the Rolling Stones, and the Young Rascals openly acknowledged their debt to the black musical tradition, yet all reaped benefits far beyond those available to black artists. Nonetheless, in comparison to previous and (perhaps) subsequent decades, the white popular music audience of the sixties did demonstrate an exceptional receptivity to multicultural dialogue.[28]

In Janis Joplin, a white woman steeped in black blues, and in Jimi Hendrix, a black man mastering the possibilities of psychedelic rock, the counterculture found "outsiders" able to transcend their personal histories and build new identities in an openly multiracial musical environment. Sly Stewart, of the group Sly and the Family Stone, enjoyed success with his gospel- and soul-oriented dance music played by a "family" mixed by gender and race.[29] The great James Brown revolutionized popular music by having all the instruments play rhythm and by breaking up bass lines into choppy two- or three-note patterns in the style of Puerto Rican and Afro-Cuban music.[30] At the same time, New York Puerto Ricans garnered extraordinary sales of records with blues chord progressions, English lyrics, and Latin rhythms including Joe Cuba's "Bang Bang" (1966) and Hector Rivera's "At the Party" (1967).[31]

Southern studio musicians and producers played a crucial role in fashioning the Muscle Shoals Sound popularized on records by black artists Aretha Franklin, Wilson Pickett, and Otis Redding.[32] Chicano rockers Cannibal and the Headhunters and Thee Midnighters reached the best-seller charts in 1965 with cover versions of "Land of a Thousand Dances" by the African American rhythm and blues singer Chris Kenner.[33] Mexican-born Carlos Santana enjoyed great success at the Fillmore West in San Francisco and at the Woodstock Festival in Bethel, New York, in 1969 with his blend of rock and roll, Afro-Cuban jazz, and blues. A white Texan named James Smith, recording under the name P. J. Proby, had a hit in 1967 with "Niki Hokey," a "swamp pop" song that sounded like black rhythm and blues from Louisiana, although it was written by Lolly and Pat Vegas who were American Indians from Los Angeles.[34] Counterculture bands including the Byrds, the Grateful Dead, and The Band rediscovered and popularized traditions from country music, while the country singer Johnny Cash recorded with Bob Dylan. Jazz great Miles Davis recorded a best-selling rock-jazz fusion album, headlined concerts with Laura Nyro and the

Grateful Dead, and regularly played private jam sessions with Jimi Hendrix.[35] Even the Englishman Eric Burdon got into the act with his tribute to Haight-Ashbury, "San Franciscan Nights," which talked about an "American Dream" that "includes Indians too." To many listeners to popular music, the social barriers dividing groups in American society seemed to be eroding, and the market categories that had segregated the music business suddenly seemed obsolete. For a brief time, Bob Dylan's audience was also James Brown's and Grateful Dead listeners could also be Beatles fans.

The youth subculture that developed around rock and roll music in the sixties owed enormous debts to black culture: from the musicians who provided the core vocabulary of rock music to the activists and intellectuals whose compelling moral vision and devastating social critiques alerted young whites to the shortcomings of their society. Yet white youths could not or would not embrace black culture and politics directly; for the most part they preferred to fashion alternative cultures and communities that spoke more to the alienations of middle-class life than they did to the racial and class inequities of American society. The music of the counterculture employed traditional blues techniques and devices, but its emphasis on electronic distortion (through feedback, reverb, and wa-wa pedals on electric guitars), the focus of its lyrics on alienation and drug use, and the extended length of individual songs and concerts all reflected the concerns and interests of an emerging (mostly) white subculture.

In retrospect, it may seem difficult to imagine how such an inner-directed subculture could see itself or be seen by others as "revolutionary" in a political sense. But the value placed on altered consciousness in the counterculture reflected a belief that social change had to start with self-knowledge. It was difficult to imagine how society could change unless people changed, but it was equally difficult to see how people could become different unless societal structures allowed them space for reflection and growth. For many young people, the policeman on the corner was less a barrier to social change than the policeman inside their heads. They wanted a movement that would be both subversive and therapeutic. One participant in San Francisco's counterculture remembers the inspiration he drew from the popular Peter Weiss play *Marat/Sade* to understand his own situation, "The protest politics of the early sixties had come to a dead end. The problem was described in Weiss's *Marat/Sade*: we'd left the politically revolutionary, albeit objective Marat to come to a position much closer to that of de Sade. 'Before I decide what is wrong and what is right, first we must find out what we are. . . . The only truths are the ever-changing truths of our own experience.' "[36]

For some musicians and some political activists, the youth counter-culture represented America's best hope for substantive change. John Sinclair, the manager of MC5 and self-described "white panther," proclaimed in his 1972 book *Guitar Army*: "The duty of the revolutionary is to make the revolution. The duty of the musician is to make the music. But there is an equation that must not be missed: MUSIC IS REVOLUTION. Rock and roll music is one of the most vital revolutionary forces in the West—it blows people all the way back to their senses and makes them feel good, like they're *alive* again in the middle of this monstrous funeral parlor of Western civilization."[37]

Within the counterculture itself, few would make such claims. Music might intersect with important social practices, at times it might even talk about social change. But it was also part of an industry organized to sell commercialized leisure, a functioning part of life in a capitalist country, and a reflection of all the ideological contradictions of the world surrounding it. Yet to its enemies, the claims of revolutionary significance sometimes seemed plausible. After the 1969 arrest of the Doors's Jim Morrison for alleged lewd behavior and indecent exposure at a Miami concert, a "rally for decency" in that city featuring Anita Bryant and the Lettermen drew a congratulatory telegram from President Richard M. Nixon.[38] Early in 1970 the chief government prosecutor in the Chicago Seven conspiracy trial justified the trial to the Loyola Academy Booster Club by explaining its cultural stakes: "We've lost our kids to the freaking fag revolution and we've got to reach out to them. . . . Our kids don't understand that we don't mean anything by it when we call people niggers. They look at us like we're dinosaurs when we talk like that."[39]

Of course, rock and roll did not initiate revolutionary change in America. But neither was it debased or immoral. Rather, it emerged as part of a complex cultural response to concrete historical conditions, and it is in the context of its dialogue with those conditions that it must be evaluated.

Trouble Coming Every Day

The cultural and political contestations of the sixties emerged from an extraordinary social and economic crisis, from the breakdown of a seemingly stable system. The affluence of the 1950s had been built within a highly stratified work force that manifested severe gaps between the wages paid to skilled and unskilled workers. When President Lyndon B. Johnson refused to raise taxes to pay for the Vietnam War, he started an inflationary cycle that undermined many of the gains of even relatively affluent workers. Civic insurrections contributed to the economic climate that already deterred investment in either urban infrastructure, affordable housing, or industry, setting the stage for the severe urban crises of the 1970s and 1980s.

Neither singularly malicious nor exceptionally heroic, most of the rebels of the sixties sought to make sense out of the same circumstances that confronted their political and cultural adversaries—instability and social change within a society suffering from a bloody war overseas and from racial conflagration at home. This context of social chaos frames all of the artifacts of popular culture from the sixties, and it adds an indispensable element to their interpretation.

During the 1965 Watts riots, 14,000 national guardsmen and 1,500 law enforcement officers occupied south-central Los Angeles for a week, in an effort to control an insurrection that destroyed $30 million worth of property. Six days of rioting left 34 people dead and more than 900 injured, as police officers arrested some 4,000 "suspects." The insurrection in Newark, New Jersey, in 1967 did $10 million worth of damage; it left 20 dead and more than 1,200 people wounded. In Detroit that same summer, police and national guard troops killed 43 people and wounded more than 1,000 in an attempt to control rioting that destroyed $250 million worth of property. In the summer of 1967 alone, there were 90 killed, 4,000 wounded, and 70,000 arrested in America's inner cities. At the same time, the number of those killed in Vietnam rose steadily. In his book about the decade, Todd Gitlin captures some of the tenor (and terror) of the late 1960s when he asks:

How can I convey the texture of this gone time so that you and I, reader, will be able to grasp, remember, believe that astonishing things actually happened, and make sense to the many who made them happen and were overtaken by them? Statistics are "background," we do not feel them tearing into our flesh. The years 1967, 1968, 1969, and 1970 were a cyclone in a wind tunnel. Little justice has been done to them in realistic fiction; perhaps one reason is that fiction requires, as Norman Mailer once said, a sense of the real. When history comes off the leash, when reality appears illusory and illusions take on lives of their own, the novelist loses the platform on which imagination builds its plausible appearances.[40]

Many of the song lyrics and the countercultural practices of the sixties were created to arbitrate these historically specific crises of the moment. They expressed the rage, frustration, and despair of people who felt that they had no future while at the same time projecting utopian fantasies about community, cooperation, and pleasure within a deeply divided society that routinely resorted to violence to advance its objectives.

The youth culture that emerged in and around rock 'n' roll music in the sixties represented both a rejection of the dominant culture in America and a peculiar reaffirmation of it at the same time. In the midst of an extraordinary social crisis where war, official misconduct, social disorder, and a growing recognition of inequality grievously undermined popular faith in the competence and the moral legitimacy of political leaders, rock 'n' roll music became a site of alternative, and sometimes oppositional, practices. Writers today often refer to the unrealistic utopianism of the sixties counterculture with its "All You Need Is Love" ethic, portraying its adherents as either naive or arrogant in their expectations of how rapidly change might be accomplished. Yet these accounts obscure the sixties counterculture's even more powerful apocalyptic strain. From Barry McGuire's angry "Eve of Destruction" (1965) to The Buffalo Springfield's resigned "For What It's Worth" (1967), to the Band's tragic "The Night They Drove Old Dixie Down" (1969), to the Doors's "The End" (1967), popular songs routinely projected fatalism and dread about political crises. Even in personal matters, despair and cynicism reigned, as evidenced by the Jefferson Airplane's 1967 "Somebody to Love," which began, "When the truth is found to be lies, and all the joy within you dies." The Byrds recorded Bob Dylan's disillusioned "Nothing Was Delivered," and the Doors sang about "the end of our elaborate plans, the end of everything that stands, the end." Jimi Hendrix covered Bob Dylan's "All Along the Watchtower" with its haunting last lines, "outside in the distance a wildcat did growl, two riders were approaching, the wind began to howl." Bob Dylan's insistence that "When you ain't got nothing, you got nothing to lose" in "Like a Rolling Stone" articulated the resignation and fatalism of a generation that saw itself caught between warring factions at home and abroad. Its strongest impulse was neither to defend nor to attack the American empire, but to get out of the way of the confrontation.[41]

For these reasons it is not surprising that a sizable part of the counterculture felt itself drawn to the appeal of Eastern religions with their emphasis on avoiding authority, to the lure of the rural commune severed from the modern world, and to the seductiveness of hallucinogenic drugs that could block out the ugliness of ghettos aflame and peasants' bodies scorched by napalm. Timothy Leary's injunction to young people to "turn on, tune in, and drop out" reflected more of an attempt to escape from society than to reform it. The reckless hedonism of a Janis Joplin or a Jim Morrison, the distorting and transforming combination of sight and sound in the psychedelic light show and rock concert, and the gallows humor of Country Joe MacDonald's "Ain't no need to wonder why, whoopee we're all gonna die" spoke to these alternative rather than oppositional impulses.

The 1967 album *Freak Out* by Frank Zappa and the Mothers of Invention served as an important icon of the counterculture, connecting alternative life-styles to a generalized condemnation of middle-class culture. Yet its political stance came less from revulsion against war, racism, and poverty than from a desire to avoid the consequences of those products of the system. Like Zappa's subsequent "We're Only in It for the Money" (a parody of the Beatles's "Sgt. Pepper's Lonely Hearts Club Band"), this record offered listeners the pleasures of cynicism, privileging a standpoint of bemused detachment rather than of engaged activism.[42] In this respect, the emblematic song on *Freak Out* was "There's No Way to Delay That Trouble Coming Every Day," which positioned listeners as passive and paralyzed media consumers. Contrasting the banalities of news reporting and advertising with the grim stories of destruction and death that form its content, Zappa evokes images of the urban insurrections then raging in America's ghettos, musing in apocalyptic dread that "there's no way to delay that trouble coming every day."

In its song lyrics, its musical structures, and even in its cover design, *Freak Out* seemed to make a decisive break with the culture of commercialism dominating the music industry and the rest of American culture as well. Yet its stance was more alternative than oppositional. In 1964 Malcolm X had warned Americans that they were sitting on a racial powderkeg about to go off, but his warning included a plea for social actions capable of remedying the conditions that caused such racial tensions in the first place. Listeners to *Freak Out* heard no such message, and the countercultural emphasis on avoiding authority—on "dropping out"— made it difficult for them to hear voices championing the cause of social reform. This is not to minimize the massive rejection of middle-class values signified by the emergence of the counterculture, but it is to call attention to the irrelevance of that middle-class strategy toward the real problems facing other aggrieved populations. The influx of hippies into slum neighborhoods like New York's East Village or San Francisco's Haight-Ashbury only led to increased rents and weakened community institutions for their existing inhabitants. "Liberated" zones in urban ghettos or rural communes might provide escape from the suffocating sterility and moral bankruptcy of middle-class suburban families, but they did little to help the already victimized inhabitants of those places who found that the presence of the counterculture brought them only higher rents and more oppressive police surveillance.

Countercultural communities built on sharing surplus wealth provided important alternatives for young people stifled by the unnecessary materialism of middle-class life, but they did little to generate more material resources for desperately poor populations of inner cities and rural slums. The trusting openness and undercurrent of pacifism permeating countercultural communities represented a significant alternative to the masculinist aggression of a society at war, but by itself the gentleness of the counterculture could not stop the systematic and unremitting use of violence in the sixties by America's police and military forces. Similarly, much of the preoccupation with sexual liberation within the sixties counterculture contained too little critique of dominant notions of sexuality, making it all too easy for the ideals of sexual freedom to become translated into practices that pressured women to be available sexually for men without a larger vision of an intersubjective, egalitarian, or emancipatory definition of sexual pleasure itself.

Within the countercultural community, escapist tendencies led "hippies" to fashion a better picture of what they were running from than of what they were running to. Individuals who originally prided themselves on their distance from dominant ideology found it hard to resist the attention of the media in cultural spheres and the temptations of violence in politics. Thus a romance with the television camera and the gun often led activists to confuse provoking one's enemies with helping one's friends. In its search to balance the ideals of an individualism without selfishness and a sense of community without totalitarian conformity, the counterculture could be both narcissistic and totalitarian. Finally, for all its oppositional intentions, the counterculture did too little to interrogate the axes of power in society—the systematic racism, class domination, sexism, and homophobia that constrained individual choices. It might be one thing for white middle-class youths to discover the benefits of Timothy Leary's advice to take drugs and expand consciousness, but many of their potential allies in the rest of society were too precariously placed in it to drop out, and too busy with all-encompassing problems to tune in to anything else. Listeners to George Harrison's "Within You Without You" (on the Beatles's 1967 *Sgt. Pepper's Lonely Hearts Club Band* album) might have gained real insight from hearing that "it's all within yourself, no one else can make a change," but for the victims of institutionalized racism and sexism such advice might be quite unacceptable and even dangerous.

Elites and those they rule often share a common culture. Cut from the same cloth, their practices often mirror one another. Societies often get both the leaders and the rebels they deserve. In the case of the sixties counterculture, its problem was not its radicalism, not the ways in which it differed so markedly from the culture it challenged, but rather the ways in which it so closely mirrored the system it claimed to be overturning. At key moments, alternative sixties cultural institutions faced the possibility of becoming oppositional, but in each case, they replicated rather than resisted the ruling cultural and ideological norms of American society. Relatively unstructured "free days" and "be-ins" that celebrated the diversity of participants' imaginations and desires eventually became ritualized "love-ins" with almost obligatory nudity and drug use. Cultural practices designed to bypass existing institutions like the "free" concerts staged by community groups worked so well that they became the model for "hippie-capitalist" promoters who found that antimaterialism sold very well to the right audiences. The Tripps Festival organized by Ken Kesey's Merry Pranksters in San Francisco in January 1966 combined music, strobe lights, and a festival setting to celebrate the creativity embodied in the emerging counterculture. But the festival also provided a model for Bill Graham and for other rock capitalists interested in marketing the new culture to semicomprehending audiences as just another novelty.[43] Even sober community organizing efforts designed to help empower working-class people like the Economic Research and Action Project of the Students for a Democratic Society dissolved when they failed to produce immediate results, bringing in their wake an escalation of revolutionary rhetoric, an idealization of anticolonial struggles in the Third World, and a romance with the television camera that equated appearances on the evening news with victories in the struggle for social change.

The eclipse of the Diggers by the Yippies encapsulates much of the trajectory of the counterculture's politics in the sixties. As Todd Gitlin relates in his excellent account, the Diggers emerged in San Francisco in the mid-1960s proclaiming "the death of money and the birth of the free."[44] Taking their name from the seventeenth-century rebels in Britain who despised private property and depicted the earth as a common treasury for all, the Diggers launched a series of programs designed to help people live outside the money economy. They collected surplus clothes for their Haight-Ashbury area "free store." They distributed free food every day for a year at a stand in the Panhandle of Golden Gate Park, and they promoted free concerts in the park as well. Although often expressing scorn for the world of work, the Diggers labored diligently at their many projects, trying desperately to prove to people that they could free themselves from the materialism of American society and bring about significant social changes through seemingly apolitical "service towards a new society in the making."[45]

Diggers wanted people to trust their own instincts, to live outside the cash economy, and to make culture for themselves rather than merely consuming what was placed before them by the culture industry. They disrupted New Left meetings as enthusiastically as they defaced advertising billboards, seeing themselves as the enemy of all manipulative discourse. Craving anonymity, they used each other's names on television appearances to confuse interviewers, and they attempted to confuse rather than illumine reporters who showed up at their creative disruptions and happenings.

Abbie Hoffman and Jerry Rubin, among others, tried to employ the spontaneity and creative anarchism of the Diggers for more directly political ends by proclaiming "Yippies" (the nonexistent Youth International party) as the politicized successors to the hippies. In part, Hoffman hoped to channel the "pre-political" rebelliousness of the counterculture toward an activism on behalf of social change. But whereas the Diggers tried to motivate people to rely on their own instincts, Hoffman and Rubin attempted to organize people by entertaining them. Rather than confounding the media, the Yippies tried to use it to become publicized media stars. They burned money at the New York Stock Exchange and attracted enormous media coverage with their efforts to turn antiwar demonstrations like the 1967 march on the Pentagon and the 1968 protests at the Democratic National Convention in Chicago into provocative street theater. Instead of "free" concerts, the Yippies tried to attach themselves to the stars of the culture industry, appearing on stage at Woodstock to appeal for funds for their defense at the Chicago conspiracy trial. In a much publicized emblematic incident demonstrating the schism between rock stars and cultural radicals, Peter Townshend of the British rock group, The Who, hit Hoffman over the head with his guitar to get the activist offstage so that the band could begin its set.

Yet the failure of the counterculture of the sixties to realize its own best hopes should not lead us to conclude that nothing of importance happened within the popular culture of that decade. The youth counterculture in and around rock 'n' roll music sometimes did raise profound challenges to the dominant culture. In their affirmations of sexual pleasure, their desire to cross racial barriers, their attempts to neutralize gender as fixed source of identity, their construction of voluntary affective relationships outside the realm of the biological family, their celebration of peace and love in a society being consumed by war and hatred, and their revolt against materialism and hierarchy, the counterculture made significant breaks with dominant cultural values in America. In addition, the rise of folk-rock, of Motown Records and the more rural "soul" sounds on Atlantic and Stax Volt, the emergence of Aretha Franklin and Janis Joplin as distinctively female yet powerful entertainers, the blending of races and cultures exemplified in the popularity of Jimi Hendrix, and the emergence of regionally and racially inflected music into the best-seller charts all represented important changes in American popular culture.

Darkness on the Edge of Town: Remembering the Sixties

The popular music of the sixties endures in the present as one of our few direct affective links to that decade. Political realignments, deindustrialization, and demographic shifts have led to the rapid senescence of much of sixties politics and culture, but in the realm of popular music, remakes and rereleases preserve fragments of that decade's "materials memory" within the everyday life experience of Americans in the 1990s.[46]

Frank Zappa claims that those like Robert Frost who debate whether the world will end "in fire or in ice" have seriously underestimated paperwork and nostalgia. A full discussion of paperwork will have to await another opportunity, but nostalgia provides an indispensable frame for understanding the popular culture of the sixties and its legacy for the present. In the 1990s, remakes and rereleases of sixties songs pervade the pop charts and provide a recurrent motif for television commercials. The lyrics in a series of popular songs ranging from Bruce Hornsby's "The Way It Is" (1986) to the Grateful Dead's "Touch of Gray" (1988) to Billy Joel's "We Didn't Start the Fire" (1990) reframe the sixties from the perspective of subsequent changes in society. Music videos, including Artists Against Apartheid's "Sun City" (1985), Jackson Browne's "For America" (1986), and Queen Latifah's "Ladies First" (1990), dramatize their messages with still photos and newsreel footage from sixties social protests. Perhaps most significant are the ways in which recombinant practices of 1990s popular culture ranging from performance art to popular fashions, from rap and hip-hop iconography to rock music lyrics, all employ strategic redeployments of remnants and remembrances of sixties culture.

Within the culture industry, memories of the sixties serve diverse ends. A popular song like the 1990 "This Old Heart of Mine" by Rod Stewart and Ron Isley can seem completely new to young listeners, while at the same time evoking memories of earlier versions of the same song by the Isley Brothers in 1966 and by Rod Stewart in 1976. Commercial music producers, radio programmers, and music store shelvers prefer releases by established names with proven track records because they minimize risks in an otherwise unpredictable business. Television advertisers employ sixties songs like the Beatles's 1968 "Revolution," Percy Sledge's 1966 "When a Man Loves a Woman," or Doris Troy's 1963 "Just One Look" because they tap the affective memories of the largest cohort of consumers in a way that connects material goods from today with pleasant sensory experiences from the past. Television programs that present a dialogue between the present and the past like "Family Ties" and "The Wonder Years" prove extremely efficient for network advertising sales personnel because they draw both youth and adult audiences.

Yet commercial considerations do not totally explain the deployment of sixties memories within contemporary popular culture. For rap artists like Public Enemy's Chuck D or Queen Latifah, visual images and spoken references to Malcolm X and Angela Davis connect the conditions confronting young African Americans in the 1990s with the uncompleted agenda of the sixties civil rights and black power movements. References to sixties music in John Cougar Mellencamp's 1986 "R.O.C.K. in the U.S.A." or to sixties social conditions in Bruce Springsteen's 1985 "My Hometown" problematize the present through poignant remembrances of the past. Even in films like *The Big Chill* and *Running on Empty* that completely obscure any semblance of the specific political and cultural struggles of the sixties, a deep sense of regret for lost idealism informs the nostalgia and undermines the smugness of the contemporary tendency to understand the present as inevitable and the past as exactly like the present.

There is *a* truth about the sixties and about its popular music that emerges from these contemporary sounds, images, and accounts, but it is hardly the whole truth. Because the entire decade of the sixties has become associated with the idea of tumultuous social change, collective popular memory often fails to recall how little actually changed and how persistently conservative American culture and political life remained during those years. Contemporary neoconservatives, including Allan

Bloom and William Bennett, have identified the legacy of sixties rock music as the product of a "destructive" and "nihilistic" counterculture organized around drug use, antiwar activity, and sexual experimentation. They have traced contemporary social problems dramatized by drugs, sexually transmitted diseases, and poor classroom performance to the "glamorization" of antisocial behavior by sixties rock stars like Janis Joplin, Jimi Hendrix, and Jim Morrison. Conversely, some leftist writers, including David Pichaske and Robert Pielke, have recalled the sixties as an era of authenticity and experimentation, as a time when barriers separating artists from audiences and dividing art from life temporarily broke down.[47] On the other hand, yet another school of leftist thought has indicted the rock music of the sixties because it was not radical enough, because it remained too much within the ideological consensus of mainstream American life and too much within the commercial apparatuses of the music industry.[48] These writers, including Todd Gitlin, David James, and John Street, have emphasized the paucity of social criticism within sixties song lyrics, the escapist and elitist aspects of countercultural practices, and the importance of popular music as a profitable element within a larger communications apparatus determined in large measure by the profit-making imperatives of large conglomerates.

In many respects, cultural politics in the 1990s has become a kind of referendum on the cultural politics of the 1960s. Some of the most significant redeployments of sixties memories occur within the discourse and ideology of those at the center of power in the American system. For them, the sixties serve a vital function, as the "revolution" that justifies a counterrevolution, and as a shorthand way of scapegoating all of the ills of the present upon the "mistakes" of the past. For example, in one of the stranger moments of the 1988 presidential election campaign, George Bush boasted that one of the proudest accomplishments of the Reagan years had been to change America from a nation that enjoyed films like *Easy Rider* to one that favored films like *Dirty Harry*.[49] One might well wonder how the nation has become better off by replacing a fantasy about countercultural hedonism with one about vigilante revenge, or how the country is better served by replacing an escape from responsibility with an escape into sadism. But even more curious, neither of these films were products of the Reagan era. *Easy Rider* and *Dirty Harry* were made and released only two years apart, during the early years of the Nixon administration (1969 and 1971); they represent the cinematic concerns of the late sixties, not the cultural changes engendered in the 1980s.[50] Yet while patently false as historical description, Bush's remarks reveal important truths about the ways in which competing imagery from the 1960s continues to inform and shape political discourse in the 1980s and 1990s.

Bush's identification of competing cinematic images about pleasure and authority as one of the stakes of political contestation speaks eloquently about the relationship between the politics of the 1980s and 1990s to the cultural legacy of the 1960s. His inscription of consumer preferences as a definitive index of proper citizenship typifies the merging of politics and popular culture embodied in the popularity of Ronald Reagan. Furthermore, Bush's opposition between the libertarian fantasies of *Easy Rider* and the authoritarian violence of *Dirty Harry* exposes many of the psychological and sexual undercurrents influencing the framing of political issues.

The sixties that emerges from these neoconservative accounts appears as a kind of organized lunacy that produced (rather than responded to) racism, changes in gender roles, and divisive debates about foreign policy. In this scenario, the activities of those in power before, during, and after the sixties largely escape critical scrutiny, while an infinitesimally small number of oppositional events and practices (like flag burning) receive blame for nearly all of society's current problems with drug use, sexually transmitted diseases, worker productivity, educational achievement, and crises within families.

In response to the neoconservative scapegoating of the sixties, liberals and leftists have launched a politics of recuperative countermemory. As exemplified in the title of the anthology by Sohnya Sayres, Anders Stephanson, Stanley Aronowitz, and Fredric Jameson, *The Sixties without Apology*, leftist intellectuals and activists have fashioned a picture of the sixties that, for all its problems, emerges as a moment of heroic citizen mobilization against racism and against an unjust war, and as a time of cultural resistance to oppressive regimes of authoritarian sexual codes, educational policies, and workplace discipline.[51] Yet contrary to conservative expectations, almost no liberal-leftist accounts of the sixties celebrate the decade uncritically. While lauding efforts at social and cultural change, these accounts remember a decade when assassins' bullets killed Malcolm X and Martin Luther King, when candidates elected because of their promises to bring peace escalated the Vietnam War, and where government agencies ignored wrenching problems in order to devote their energies to persecuting dissident critics. They remember how the expenditures on the war in Vietnam doomed the War on Poverty, how ghetto rebellions at home and nationalist insurgencies overseas revealed the antagonistic contradictions embedded in the American economy, and how efforts by women to secure full participation in political and economic life met with reactionary resistance and ridicule from male and female opponents across the political spectrum.

By the early 1970s, the counterculture knew that it had lost the battle, and the rhetoric of rock and roll changed accordingly. As John Street explains, the 1970s tended to substitute glitter for rhetoric, sequins for beads, decadence for politics, and open plagiarism for originality. Whereas the counterculture of the 1960s tried to defuse sexual tensions by having men and women take off their clothes, the "glam" and "glitter" rock of the 1970s encouraged men and women to wear each others' clothes. Fashion replaced pharmacology, and the ruling slogan of the day became "paint your face" rather than "feed your head."[52] In part, 1970s music emerged as a critique of what had been left out of the sixties (working-class anger, desires for androgyny), and new musical forms reflecting new social realities emerged. Yet while punk rock, disco, reggae, and revived rock music like Bruce Springsteen's departed in some ways from sixties aesthetics, they nonetheless carried on many of the projects and sensibilities of the previous decade.

In the seventies, economic stagnation and deindustrialization undermined the reigning assumptions of the sixties counterculture that had always presumed to be operating in an economy of abundance. Declining economic opportunities brought fundamental changes in work, gender roles, family relations, education, and welfare policies, as automation and capital flight overseas promoted deindustrialization at home. Increases in male unemployment and the necessity for more women to work transformed family relations, while tax breaks for property owners worked to curtail the growth in education and welfare spending that had characterized the sixties. For neoconservatives, these changes drew retrospective justification from the perceived excesses of the sixties, while for leftists the changes interrupted the nascent progress of the previous decade. Yet both arguments underestimated the radical transformations in society wrought by capital and the state in the 1970s. Consequently, the myth of the sixties has served as more of an impediment than an aid toward understanding contemporary cultural politics. This is not to belittle the changes brought about during the sixties, nor to underestimate the extraordinary creative cultural accomplishments of the decade. But idealizing or demonizing the historically specific practices of one decade in order to justify serious social decisions in another serves only as a form of reactionary nostalgia. One can understand the appeal of such accounts—to demonize or deify the sixties provides an easily recognizable image capable of mobilizing selected constituencies. But it does little to address the problems of our own day where the deadly serious oppressions of race, class, and gender still guarantee "no way to delay that trouble coming every day."

Youth culture of the sixties emerged in the context of social contradictions, and it reflected a full range of aesthetic and social stances, careening between idealism and cynicism, collectivity and individualism, hedonism and selflessness. Grass roots efforts to create "free spaces" succeeded in revitalizing urban spaces and building rural communes, but they also alerted capitalists to the potential of untapped market desires that could easily co-opt emancipatory impulses for mercenary ends. Political activists secured media coverage of their demonstrations and campaigns yet failed to see the harm done to their movement by overreliance on spectacle mediated through a communications apparatus that they did not control. The hippie counterculture articulated powerful defiance of the corporate culture of confidence and consensus that dominated life in post–World War II America, but it failed to find sustainable ways of living outside the system or establishing permanent alternative networks that might provide the basis for future change. Within popular music, young people created important new forms of performance and composition appropriate to the messages they sought to convey, but they never figured out a way to reconstruct society to make it look like the visions they conjured up in culture.

The counterculture rebels of the sixties were not as revolutionary as their spokespersons proclaimed nor as successful as their opponents alleged. Attempting to negotiate the contradictions of their time, they created a culture that was both a critique of their society and a symptom of its worst failings. But in their anarchistic impulses and erotic self-affirmation, in their egalitarian intentions and their spiritual strivings, they articulated an agenda that continues to be fought over today.

NOTES

1. Charles Reich, *The Greening of America* (New York: Bantam, 1971); Theodore Roszak, *The Making of a Counter Culture: Reflections on the Technocratic Society and Its Youthful Opposition* (Garden City, N.Y.: Doubleday, 1969).

2. Todd Gitlin, *The Sixties: Years of Hope, Days of Rage* (New York: Bantam, 1989), 19–20; William H. Chafe, *The Unfinished Journey: America since World War II* (New York: Oxford University Press, 1986), 326–27.

3. Jack Whalen and Richard Flacks, *Beyond the Barricades: The Sixties Generation Grows Up* (Philadelphia:

Temple University Press, 1989). Historically, perceptions about the degree of youth rebellion have often been exaggerated. See, for example, Paula Fass, *The Damned and the Beautiful: American Youth in the 1920s* (New York; Oxford University Press, 1987).

4. Chafe, *Unfinished Journey*, 326.

5. The Montgomery boycott of 1955–56 was successful because of judicial intervention, and the Birmingham campaign of 1963 won some, although not all, of its demands. But the 1963 March on Washington's call for "jobs and justice" brought *no* immediate results, and even the Civil Rights Act of 1964 (passed as a tribute to the martyred John F. Kennedy) was watered down into an important, but nonetheless limited bill that meant little in the way of combating housing or hiring discrimination. Although most Americans opposed those measures that kept blacks from voting, I think it would be a distortion of Dr. King's political program to reduce it merely to voting rights. Similarly, while a majority of Americans favored ending the Vietnam War by 1970, many of those felt that it should be ended because the United States was not winning, not because it was politically or morally wrong.

6. For sales of single records, not albums. Joel Whitburn, *Joel Whitburn's Top Pop Singles, 1955–1986* (Menomonee Falls, Wis.: Record Research, 1987), 724.

7. For an effective and convincing critique of this story, see Michael Frisch, "Woodstock and Altamont," in *True Stories from the American Past*, edited by William Graebner (New York: McGraw-Hill, 1993), 217–39.

8. Joe Ferrandino, "Rock Culture and the Development of Social Consciousness," in *Side Saddle on the Golden Calf: Social Structure and Popular Culture in America*, edited by George Lewis (Pacific Palisades, Calif.: Goodyear Publishing, 1972), 287–88; Whitburn, *Top Pop Singles*, 130, 146, 677.

9. Of course, in both their music and their personal lives, Franklin and Joplin still suffered from sexism and presented images of victimization along with their affirmative assertions of self. In addition, there were strong female voices in the early 1960s, especially black singers including Irma Thomas, Jan Bradley, and Betty Harris, but even the quintessential suburban white teenager Leslie Gore made a protofeminist transition from 1963s whining "It's My Party" to 1964s assertive "You Don't Own Me."

10. Bob Shannon and John Javna, *Behind the Hits: Inside Stories of Classic Pop and Rock and Roll* (New York: Warner Books, 1986), 121.

11. Ibid., 104.

12. Barbara Ehrenreich, Elizabeth Hess, and Gloria Jacobs, *Remaking Love: The Feminization of Sex* (Garden City, N.Y.: Doubleday/Anchor, 1986), 28.

13. Steve Chapple and Reebee Garofalo, *Rock 'n' Roll Is Here to Pay* (Chicago: Nelson-Hall, 1977), 69.

14. Ibid., 171.

15. Ibid., 172.

16. Ibid., 107.

17. Ibid., 76.

18. Ibid., 75.

19. Ibid.

20. Ellen Sander, *Trips: Rock Life in*

the Sixties (New York: Scribner, 1973), 9–10.

21. Marshall Berman, "Eternal City," Voice Literary Supplement, Village Voice, [November] 1989, 12.

22. Gitlin, The Sixties, 198.

23. Chafe, Unfinished Journey, 327.

24. Ed Ward, Geoffrey Stokes, and Ken Tucker, Rock of Ages: The Rolling Stone History of Rock and Roll (New York: Rolling Stone Press/Summit Books, 1986), 400.

25. Jon Wiener, Come Together: John Lennon in His Time (New York: Random House, 1984), 190–91.

26. Stewart Kessler, "Dancing in the Streets," in Rock and Roll Will Stand, edited by Greil Marcus (Boston: Beacon Press, 1969), 64.

27. Chapple and Garofalo, Rock and Roll Is Here to Pay, 88.

28. For an excellent discussion of how black artists received inadequate recognition and reward, see Nelson George, The Death of Rhythm and Blues (New York: Pantheon, 1988), 70–111.

29. Ibid., 108; Ward, Stokes, and Tucker, Rock of Ages, 376–78.

30. Ward, Stokes, and Tucker, Rock of Ages, 301.

31. John Storm Roberts, The Latin Tinge (New York: Oxford University Press, 1979), 167.

32. Peter Guralnick, Sweet Soul Music: Rhythm and Blues and the Southern Dream of Freedom (New York: Harper and Row, 1986), 376–80.

33. George Lipsitz, Time Passages: Collective Memory and American Popular Culture (Minneapolis: University of Minnesota Press, 1990), 145–46.

34. Whitburn, Top Pop Singles, 404, 413.

35. Miles Davis with Quincy Troupe, Miles: The Autobiography (New York: Simon and Schuster, 1989), 292–93.

36. Kessler, "Dancing in the Streets," 64.

37. Quoted from Herbert I. London, Closing the Circle: A Cultural History of the Rock Revolution (Chicago: Nelson-Hall, 1984), 102–3.

38. Ward, Stokes, and Tucker, Rock of Ages, 429.

39. Chicago Sun-Times, 27 February 1970.

40. Gitlin, The Sixties, 242–43.

41. The 1960 film Flaming Star, directed by Don Siegel and starring Elvis Presley, anticipated this consciousness that would become so powerful among youth later in the decade. See George Lipsitz, "Flaming Star and the Aquarian Ideal," Southwest Media Review 1 (1981): 19–23.

42. See Gary Burns, "Of Our Elaborate Plans, the End," Popular Music and Society 11 (Winter 1987): 47.

43. William O'Neill, Coming Apart: An Informal History of America in the 1960s (New York: Times Books, 1971), 243.

44. Gitlin, The Sixties, 222.

45. Ibid.

46. The idea of cultural forms containing a "materials memory" is explored by M. M. Bakhtin in The Dialogic Imagination (Austin: University of Texas Press, 1981).

47. See, for example, William Bennett's remarks on the anniversary of Woodstock and Allan Bloom's comments on rock and roll in Closing of the American Mind (New York: Simon

and Schuster, 1987. For writers celebrating the impulses and achievements of sixties rock and roll, see David Pichaske's still wonderful *A Generation in Motion* (New York: Schirmer Books, 1979) and London, *Closing the Circle.*

48. See David James, "The Viet Nam War and American Music," *Social Text,* no. 23 (Fall–Winter 1989): 122–43.

49. Maureen Dowd, "Bush Boasts of Turnaround from 'Easy Rider' Society," *New York Times,* 7 October 1988. See also Jeremy Larner, "From Easy Rider to Dirty Harry," *Dissent* 36 (Winter 1989): 109–13.

50. As a matter of fact, Hollywood's turn to the right took place most emphatically during the Carter administration. See Douglas Kellner and Michael Ryan, *Camera Politica: The Politics and Ideology of Contemporary Hollywood Film* (Bloomington: Indiana University Press, 1988).

51. Sohnya Sayres, Anders Stephanson, Stanley Aronowitz, and Fredric Jameson, eds., *The Sixties without Apology* (Minneapolis: University of Minnesota Press, 1984). See also Gitlin, *The Sixties.* For the most balanced and useful discussion of the decade's politics, see David Farber, *Chicago '68* (Chicago: University of Chicago Press, 1988).

52. John Street, *Rebel Rock: The Politics of Popular Music* (Blackwell: London, 1986), 172–74.

8.......

Sexual Revolution(s)

In 1957 America's favorite TV couple, the safely married Ricky and Lucy Ricardo, slept in twin beds. Having beds at all was probably progressive—as late as 1962 June and Ward Cleaver did not even have a bedroom. Elvis's pelvis was censored in each of his three appearances on the "Ed Sullivan Show" in 1956, leaving his oddly disembodied upper torso and head thrashing about on the TV screen. But the sensuality in his eyes, his lips, his lyrics was unmistakable, and his genitals were all the more important in their absence.[1] There was, likewise, no mistaking Mick Jagger's meaning when he grimaced ostentatiously and sang "Let's spend some *time* together" on "Ed Sullivan" in 1967. Much of the audience knew that the line was really "Let's spend the night together," and the rest quickly got the idea. The viewing public could see absence and hear silence—and therein lay the seeds of the sexual revolution.

What we call the sexual revolution grew from these tensions between public and private—not only from tensions manifest in public culture, but also from tensions between private behaviors and the public rules and ideologies that were meant to govern behavior. By the 1950s the gulf between private acts and public norms was often quite wide—and the distance was crucial. People had sex outside of marriage, but very, very few acknowledged that publicly. A woman who married the only man with whom she had had premarital sex still worried years later: "I was afraid someone might have learned that we had intercourse before marriage and I'd be disgraced."[2] The consequences, however, were not just psychological. Young women (and sometimes men) discovered to be having premarital sex were routinely expelled from school or college; gay men risked jail for engaging in consensual sex. There were real penalties for sexual misconduct, and while many deviated from the sexual orthodoxy of the day, all but a few did so furtively, careful not to get "caught."[3]

Few episodes demonstrate the tensions between the public and private dimensions of sexuality in midcentury America better than the furor that surrounded the publication of the studies of sexual behavior collectively referred to as the "Kinsey Reports."[4] Though a dry, social scientific report, *Sexual Behavior in the Human Male* (1948) had sold over a quarter of a million copies by 1953, when the companion volume on the human female came out. The male volume was controversial, but the female volume was, in *Look* magazine's characterization, "stronger stuff."[5] Kinsey made it clear that he understood the social implications of his study, introducing a section on "the pre-marital coital behavior of the female sample which has been available for this study" with the following qualification: "Because of this public condemnation of pre-marital coitus, one might believe that such contacts would be rare among American females and males. But this is only the overt culture, the things that people openly profess to believe and do. Our previous report (1948) on the male has indicated how far publicly expressed attitudes may depart from the realities of behavior—the covert culture, what males actually do."[6]

Kinsey, a biologist who had begun his career with much less controversial studies of the gall wasp, drew fire from many quarters, but throughout the criticism is evident concern about his uncomfortable juxtaposition of public and private. "What price biological science . . . to reveal intimacies of one's private sex life and to draw conclusions from inscriptions on the walls of public toilets?" asked one American in a letter to the editor of *Look* magazine.[7]

Much of the reaction to Kinsey did hinge on the distance between the "overt" and the "covert." People were shocked to learn how many men and women were doing what they were not supposed to be doing. Kinsey found that 50 percent of the women in his sample had had premarital sex (even though between 80 percent and 89 percent of his sample disapproved of premarital sex on "moral grounds"), that 61 percent of college-educated men and 84 percent of men who had completed only high school had had premarital sex, that over one-third of the married women in the sample had "engaged in petting" with more than ten different men, that approximately half of the married couples had engaged in "oral stimulation" of both male and female genitalia, and that at least 37 percent of American men had had "some homosexual experience" during their lifetimes.[8]

By pulling the sheets back, so to speak, Kinsey had publicized the private. Many people must have been reassured by the knowledge that they were not alone, that their sexual behaviors were not individual deviant acts but part of widespread social trends.[9] But others saw danger in what Kinsey had done. By demonstrating the distance between the overt and the covert cultures, Kinsey had further undermined what was manifestly a beleaguered set of rules. *Time* magazine warned its readers against the attitude that "there is morality in numbers," the *Chicago Tribune* called Kinsey a "menace to society," and the *Ladies' Home Journal* ran an article with the disclaimer: "The facts of behavior as reported . . . are not to be interpreted as moral or social justification for individual acts."[10]

Looking back to the century's midpoint, it is clear that the coherence of (to use Kinsey's terms) covert and overt sexual cultures was strained beyond repair. The sexual revolution of the 1960s emerged from these tensions, and to that extent it was not revolutionary, but evolutionary. As much as anything else, we see the overt coming to terms with the covert. But the revision of revolution to evolution would miss a crucial point. It is not historians who have labeled these changes "the sexual revolution"—it was people at the time, those who participated and those who watched. And they called it that before much of what we would see as revolutionary really emerged—before gay liberation and the women's movement and Alex Comfort's *The Joy of Sex* (1972) and "promiscuity" and singles' bars. The term was in general use by 1963—earlier than one might expect.[11]

To make any sense of the sexual revolution, we have to pay attention to the label people gave it. Revolutions, for good or ill, are moments of danger. It matters that a metaphor of revolution gave structure to the myriad of changes taking place in American society. The changes in sexual mores and behaviors could as easily have been cast as evolutionary—but they were not.

Looking back, the question of whether or not the sexual revolution was revolutionary is not easy to answer; it partly depends on one's political (defined broadly) position. Part of the trouble, though, is that the sexual revolution was not one movement. It was instead a set of movements, movements that were closely linked, even intertwined, but which often made uneasy bedfellows. Here I hope to do some untangling, laying out three of the most important strands of the sexual revolution and showing their historical origins, continuities, and disruptions.

The first strand, which transcended youth, might be cast as both evolutionary and revolutionary. Throughout the twentieth century, picking up speed in the 1920s, the 1940s, and the 1960s, we have seen a sexualization of America's culture. Sexual images have become more and more a part of public life, and sex—or more accurately, the representation of sex—is used to great effect in a marketplace that offers Americans fulfillment through consumption. Although the blatancy of today's sexual images would be shocking to someone transported from an earlier era, such representations developed gradually and generally did not challenge more "traditional" understandings of sex and of men's and women's respective roles in sex or in society.

The second strand was the most modest in aspect but perhaps the most revolutionary in implication. In the 1960s and early 1970s an increasing number of young people began to live together "without benefit of matrimony," as the phrase went at the time. While sex was usually a part of the relationship (and probably a more important part than most people acknowledged), few called on concepts of "free love" or "pleasure" but instead used words like "honesty," "commitment," and "family." Many of the young people who lived together could have passed for young marrieds and in that sense were pursuing fairly traditional arrangements. At the same time, self-consciously or not, they challenged the tattered remnants of a Victorian epistemological and ideological system that still, in the early 1960s, fundamentally structured the public sexual mores of the American middle class.

The third strand was more self-consciously revolutionary, as sex was actively claimed by young people and used not only for pleasure but also for power in a new form of cultural politics that shook the nation. As those who threw themselves into the "youth revolution" (a label that did not stick) knew so well, the struggle for America's future would take place not in the structure of electoral politics, but on the battlefield of cultural meaning. Sex was an incendiary tool of a revolution that was more than political. But not even the cultural revolutionaries agreed on goals, or on the role and meaning of sex in the revolution.

These last two strands had to do primarily with young people, and that is significant. The changes that took place in America's sexual mores and behaviors in the sixties were *experienced* and *defined* as revolutionary in large part because they were so closely tied to youth. The nation's young, according to common wisdom and the mass media, were in revolt. Of course, the sexual revolution was not limited to youth, and sex was only one part of the revolutionary claims of youth. Still, it was the intersection of sex and youth that signaled danger. And the fact that these were often middle-class youths, the ones reared in a culture of respectability (told that a single sexual misstep could jeopardize their bright futures), made their frontal challenges to sexual mores all the more inexplicable and alarming.

Each of these strands is complex, and I make no pretense to be exhaustive. Thus, rather than attempting to provide a complete picture of changes in behaviors or ideologies, I will examine several manifestations of seemingly larger trends. The sexualization of culture (the first strand) is illustrated by the emergence of *Playboy* and *Cosmo* magazines. For the "modest revolutionaries" (the second strand), I look to the national scandal over a Barnard College junior's "arrangement" in 1968 and the efforts of University of Kansas students to establish a coed dormitory. Finally, the cultural radicals (the third strand) are represented by the writings of a few counterculture figures.

By focusing on the 1960s, we lose much of the "sexual revolution." In many ways, the most important decade of that revolution was the 1970s, when the "strands" of the 1960s joined with gay liberation, the women's movement, and powerful assertions of the importance of cultural differences in America. Yet, by concentrating on the early years of the sexual revolution, we see its tangled roots—the sexual ideologies and behaviors that gave it birth. We can also understand how little had been resolved—even begun—by the end of the 1960s.[12]

Before the Revolution: Youth and Sex

Like many of the protest movements that challenged American tranquility in the sixties, the sexual revolution developed within the protected space and intensified atmosphere of the college campus. An American historian recalls returning to Harvard University in 1966 after a year of postgraduate study in England. Off balance from culture shock and travel fatigue, he entered Harvard Yard and knew with absolute certainty that he had "missed the sexual revolution." One can imagine a single symbolic act of copulation signaling the beginning of the revolution (it has a nicely ironic echo of "the shot heard round the world"). The single act and the revolution complete in 1966 are fanciful constructions; not everything began or ended at Harvard even in those glory years. But events there and at other elite colleges and universities, if only because of the national attention they received, provide a way into the public intersections of sex, youth, and cultural politics.

Harvard had set a precedent in student freedom in 1952, when girls (the contemporary term) were allowed to visit in Harvard men's rooms. The freedom offered was not supposed to be sexual—or at least not flagrantly so. But by 1963 Dean John Monro complained that he was "badly shaken up by some severe violations," for a once "pleasant privilege" had come to be "considered a license to use the college rooms for wild parties or sexual intercourse."[13] The controversy went public with the aid of *Time* magazine, which fanned the flames by quoting a senior's statement that "morality is a relative concept projecting certain mythologies associated with magico-religious beliefs." The Parietals Committee of the Harvard Council for Undergraduate Affairs, according to the *Boston Herald*, concluded that "if these deep emotional commitments and ties occasionally lead to sexual intercourse, surely even that is more healthy than the situation a generation ago when 'nice girls' were dated under largely artificial circumstances and sexual needs were gratified at a brothel."[14] Both justifications seemed fundamentally troubling in different ways, but at least the controversy focused on men. The sexual double standard was strong. When the spotlight turned on women, the stakes seemed even higher.

The media had a field day when the president of Vassar College, Sarah Blanding, said unequivocally that if a student wished to engage in premarital sex, she must withdraw from the college. The oft-quoted student reply to her dictum chilled the hearts of middle-class parents throughout the country: "If Vassar is to become the Poughkeepsie Victorian Seminary for young Virgins, then the change of policy had better be made explicit in admissions catalogs."[15]

Such challenges to authority and to conventional morality were reported to eager audiences around the nation. None of this, of course, was new. National audiences had been scandalized by the panty raid epidemic of the early 1950s; the antics and petting parties of college youth had provided sensational fodder for hungry journalists in the 1920s. The parents—and grandparents—of these young people had chipped away at the system of sexual controls themselves. But they had not directly and publicly denied the very foundations of sexual morality. With few exceptions, they had evaded the controls and circumvented the rules, climbing into dorm rooms through open windows, signing out to the library and going to motels, carefully maintaining virginity in the technical sense while engaging in every caress known to married couples. The evasions often succeeded, but that does not mean that the controls had no effect. On the contrary, they had a great impact on the ways people experienced sex.

There were, in fact, two major systems of sexual control, one structural and one ideological.[16] These systems worked to reinforce one another, but they affected the lives of those they touched differently.

The structural system was the more practical of the two but probably the less successful. It worked by limiting opportunities for the unmarried to have intercourse. Parents of teenagers set curfews and promoted double dating, hoping that by preventing privacy they would limit sexual exploration. Colleges, acting in loco parentis, used several tactics: visitation hours, parietals, security patrols, and restrictions on students' use of cars. When Oberlin students mounted a protest against the college's policy on cars in 1963, one male student observed that the issue was not transportation but privacy: "We wouldn't care if the cars had no wheels, just so long as they had doors."[17]

The rules governing hours applied only to women and, to some extent, were meant to guarantee women's safety by keeping track of their comings and goings. But the larger rationale clearly had to do with sexual conduct. Men were not allowed in women's rooms but were received in lounges or "date rooms," where privacy was never assured. By setting curfew hours and requiring women to sign out from their dormitories, indicating who they were with and where they were going, college authorities meant to limit possibilities for privacy. Rules for men were not deemed necessary—because of a sexual double standard, because men's safety and well-being seemed less threatened in general, and because the colleges and universities were primarily concerned with controlling their own populations. If women were supervised or chaperoned and in by 11:00 P.M., the men would not have partners—at least, not partners drawn from the population that mattered.

Throughout the 1950s, the structural controls became increasingly complex; by the early 1960s they were so elaborate as to be ludicrous. At the University of Michigan in 1962, the student handbook devoted nine of its fifteen pages to rules for women. Curfews varied by the night of the week, by the student's year in college, and even, in some places, by her grade point average. Students could claim Automatic Late Permissions (ALPs) but only under certain conditions. Penalties at Michigan (an institutional version of "grounding") began when a student had eleven "late minutes"—but the late minutes could be acquired one at a time throughout the semester. At the University of Kansas in the late 1950s, one sorority asked the new dean of women to discipline two women who had flagrantly disregarded curfew. The dean, investigating, discovered that the women in question had been between one and three minutes late signing in on three occasions.[18]

The myriad of rules, as anyone who lived through this period well knows, did not prevent sexual relations between students so much as they structured the times and places and ways that students could have sexual contact. Students said extended good-nights on the porches of houses, they petted in dormitory lounges while struggling to keep three feet on the floor and clothing in some semblance of order, and they had intercourse in cars, keeping an eye out for police patrols. What could be done after eleven could be done before eleven, and sex need not occur behind a closed door and in a bed—but this set of rules had a profound impact on the *ways* college students and many young people living in their parents homes *experienced* sex.

The overelaboration of rules, in itself, offers evidence that the controls were beleaguered. Nonetheless, the rules were rarely challenged frontally and thus they offered some illusion of control. This system of rules, in all its inconsistency, arbitrariness, and blindness, helped to preserve the distinction between public and private, the coexistence of overt and covert, that defines midcentury American sexuality.

The ideological system of controls was more pervasive than the structured system and probably more effective. This system centered on ideas of difference: men and women were fundamentally different creatures, with different roles and interests in sex. Whether one adopted a psychoanalytic or an essentialist approach, whether one looked to scholarly or popular analysis, the final conclusion pointed to *difference*. In sex (as in life), women were the limit setters and men the aggressors.

The proper limits naturally depended on one's marital status, but even within marriage sex was to be structured along lines of difference rather than of commonality. Marital advice books since the 1920s had stressed the importance of female orgasm, insisting that men must satisfy their wives, but even these calls for orgasm equality posited male and female pleasure as competing interests. The language of difference in postwar America, which was often quite extreme, can be seen as a defensive reaction to changing gender roles in American society.

One influential psychoanalytic study, provocatively titled *Modern*

Woman: The Lost Sex, condemned women who tried to be men and argued the natural difference between men and women by comparing their roles in sexual intercourse. The woman's role is "passive," the authors asserted. "[Sex] is not as easy as rolling off a log for her. It is easier. It is as easy as being the log itself. She cannot fail to deliver a masterly performance, by doing nothing whatever except being duly appreciative and allowing nature to take its course." For the man, in contrast, sexuality is "overt, apparent and urgent, outward and ever-present," fostered by psychological and physiological pressures toward orgasm. Men might experiment sexually with few or no consequences and no diminution of pleasure. Women, on the other hand, could not: "The strong desire for children or lack of it in a woman has a crucial bearing on how much enjoyment she derives from the sexual act. . . . Women cannot make . . . pleasure an end in itself without inducing a decline in the pleasure."[19]

These experts argued from a psychoanalytic framework, but much less theoretical work also insisted on the fundamental difference between men and women, and on their fundamentally different interests in sex. Texts used in marriage courses in American high schools and college typically included chapters on the differences between men and women—and these differences were not limited to their reproductive systems.

Women did in fact have a different and more imperative interest in controlling sex than men, for women could become pregnant. Few doctors would fit an unmarried woman with a diaphragm, though one might get by in the anonymity of a city with a cheap "gold" ring from a drugstore or by pretending to be preparing for an impending honeymoon. Relying on the ubiquitous condom in the wallet was risky and douching (Coca-Cola had a short-lived popularity) even more so. Abortion was illegal, and though many abortions took place, they were dangerous, expensive, and usually frightening and degrading experiences. Dependable and *available* birth control might have made a difference (many would later attribute "the sexual revolution" to "the pill"),[20] but sexual behaviors and sexual mores were not based simply on the threat of illegitimate pregnancy. Kinsey found that only 44 percent of the women in his sample said that they "restricted their pre-marital coitus" because of fear of pregnancy, whereas 80 percent cited "moral reasons." Interestingly, 44 percent of the sample also noted their "fear of public opinion."[21]

Women who were too "free" with sexual favors could lose value and even threaten their marriageability. In this society, a woman's future socioeconomic status depended primarily on her husband's occupation and earning power. While a girl was expected to "pet to be popular," girls and women who went "too far" risked their futures. Advice books and columns from the 1940s and 1950s linked girls' and womens' "value" to their "virtue," arguing in explicitly economic terms that "free" kisses destroyed a woman's value in the dating system: "The boys find her easy to afford. She doesn't put a high value on herself." The exchange was even clearer in the marriage market. In chilling language, a teen adviser asked: "Who wants second hand goods?"[22]

It was not only the advisers and experts who equated virtue and value. Fifty percent of the male respondents in Kinsey's study wanted to marry a virgin.[23] Even though a relatively high percentage of women had intercourse before marriage, and a greater number engaged in "petting," most of these women at least *expected* to marry the man, and many did. Still, there might be consequences. Elaine Tyler May, who analyzed responses to a large, ongoing psychological study of married couples in the postwar era, found that many couples struggled with the psychological burdens of premarital intimacy for much of their married lives. In the context of a social/cultural system that insisted that "nice girls don't," many reported a legacy of guilt or mistrust. One woman wrote of her husband: "I think he felt that because we had been intimate before marriage that I could be as easily interested in any man that came along."[24]

Of course, sexual mores and behaviors were highly conditioned by the sexual double standard. Lip service was paid to the ideal of male premarital chastity, but that ideal was usually obviated by the notion, strong in peer culture and implicitly acknowledged in the larger culture, that sexual intercourse was a male rite of passage. Middle-class boys pushed at the limits set by middle-class girls, but they generally looked elsewhere for "experience." A man who went to high school in the early 1960s (and did not lose his virginity until his first year of college) recalls the system with a kind of horror: "You slept with one kind of woman, and dated another kind, and the women you slept with, you didn't have much respect for, generally."[25]

The distinction was often based on class—middle-class boys and men had sex with girls and women of the lower classes, or even with prostitutes. They did not really expect to have intercourse with a woman of their own class unless they were to be married. Samuel Hynes, in his memoir of coming of age as a navy flier during World War II, describes that certain knowledge: "There were nice girls in our lives, too. Being middle-class is more than a social station, it's a kind of destiny. A middle-class boy from Minneapolis will seek out nice middle-class girls, in Memphis or anywhere else, will take them out on middle-class dates and try to put his hand inside their middle-class underpants. And he will fail. It was all a story that had already been written."[26]

Dating, for middle-class youth, was a process of sexual negotiation. "Good girls" had to keep their virginity yet still contend with their own sexual desires or with boys who expected at least some petting as a "return" on the cost of the date. Petting was virtually universal in the world of heterosexual dating. A 1959 *Atlantic* article, "Sex and the College Girl," described the ideal as having "done every possible kind of petting without actually having intercourse."[27]

For most middle-class youth in the postwar era, sex involved a series of skirmishes that centered around lines and boundaries: kissing, necking, petting above the waist, petting below the waist, petting through clothes, petting under clothes, mild petting, heavy petting. The progression of sexual intimacy had emerged as a highly ordered system. Each act constituted a stage, ordered in a strict hierarchy (first base, second base, and so forth), with vaginal penetration as the ultimate step. But in their attempts to preserve technical virginity, many young people engaged in sexual behaviors that, in the sexual hierarchy of the larger culture, should have been more forbidden than vaginal intercourse. One woman remembers: "We went pretty far, very far; everything but intercourse. But it was very frustrating. . . . Sex was out of the question. I had it in my mind that I was going to be a virgin. So I came up with oral sex. . . . I thought I invented it."[28]

Many young men and women acted in defiance of the rules, but that does not make the rules irrelevant. The same physical act can have very different meanings depending on its emotional and social/cultural contexts. For America's large middle class and for all those who aspired to "respectability" in the prerevolutionary twentieth century, sex was overwhelmingly secret or furtive. Sex was a set of acts with high stakes and possibly serious consequences, acts that emphasized and reinforced the different roles of men and women in American society. We do not know how each person felt about his or her private acts, but we do know that few were willing or able to publicly reject the system of sexual controls.

The members of the generation that would be labeled "the sixties" were revolutionary in that they called fundamental principles of sexual morality and control into question. The system of controls they had inherited and lived within was based on a set of presumptions rooted in the previous century. In an evolving set of arguments and actions (which never became thoroughly coherent or unified), they rejected a system of sexual controls organized around concepts of difference and hierarchy.

Both systems of control—the structural and the ideological—were firmly rooted in a Victorian epistemology that had, in most areas of life, broken down by the early twentieth century. This system was based on a belief in absolute truth and a passion for order and control. Victorian thought, as Joseph Singal has argued persuasively, insisted on "preserving absolute standards based on a radical dichotomy between that which was deemed 'human' and that regarded as 'animal.'" On the "human" side were all forces of civilization; on the "animal," all instincts, passions, and desires that threatened order and self-control. Sex clearly fell into the latter category. But the Victorian romance was not restricted to human versus animal, civilized versus savage. The moral dichotomy "fostered a tendency to see the world in polar terms." Thus we find rigid dichotomous pairs not only of good and evil, but of men and women, body and soul, home and world, public and private.[29]

Victorian epistemology, with its remarkably comfortable and comforting certainties and its stifling absolutes, was shaken by the rise of a new science that looked to "dynamic process" and "relativism" instead of the rigid dichotomies of Victorian thought. It was challenged from within by those children of Victorianism who "yearned to smash the glass and breathe freely," as Jackson Lears argued in his study of antimodernism.[30] And most fundamentally, it was undermined by the realities of an urban industrial society. American Victorian culture was, as much as anything, a strategy of the emerging middle classes. Overwhelmed by the chaos of the social order that had produced them and that they sought to manage, the middling classes had attempted to separate themselves from disorder and corruption. This separation, finally, was untenable.

The Victorian order was overthrown and replaced by a self-consciously "modern culture." One place we point to demonstrate the decline of Victorianism is the change in sexual "manners and mores" in the early twentieth century. Nonetheless, sex may be the place that Victorian thought least relinquished its hold. This is not to say that prudishness reigned—the continuity is more subtle and more fundamental. Skirts rose above the knee, couples dated and petted, sexologists and psychologists acknowledged that women were not naturally "passionless," and the good judge Ben Lindsey called for the "companionate marriage." But the systems of control that regulated and structured sex were Victorian at their core, with science replacing religion to authorize absolute truth, and with inflexible bipolar constructions somewhat reformulated but intact. The system of public controls over premarital sex was based on rigid dichotomous pairings: men and women, public and private. This distinction would be rejected—or at least recast—in the cultural and sexual struggles of the sixties.

Revolutionaries

All those who rejected the sexual mores of the postwar era did not reject the fundamental premises that gave them shape. _Playboy_ magazine played an enormously important (if symbolic) role in the sexual revolution, or at least in preparing the ground for the sexual revolution. _Playboy_ was a men's magazine in the tradition of _Esquire_ (for which its founder had worked briefly) but laid claim to a revolutionary stance partly by replacing _Esquire_'s airbrushed drawings with airbrushed flesh.

Begun by Hugh Hefner in 1953 with an initial print run of 70,000, _Playboy_ passed the one million circulation mark in three years. By the mid-1960s Hefner had amassed a fortune of $100 million, including a lasciviously appointed forty-eight-room mansion staffed by thirty Playboy "bunnies" ("fuck like bunnies" is a phrase we have largely left behind, but most people at the time caught the allusion). Playboy clubs, also staffed by large-breasted and long-legged women in bunny ears and cottontails, flourished throughout the country. Though _Playboy_ offered quality writing and advice for those aspiring to sophistication, the greatest selling point of the magazine was undoubtedly its illustrations.[31]

Playboy, however, offered more than masturbatory opportunities. Between the pages of coyly arranged female bodies—more, inscribed in the coyly arranged female bodies—flourished a strong and relatively coherent ideology. Hefner called it a philosophy and wrote quite a few articles expounding it (a philosophy professor in North Carolina took it seriously enough to describe his course as "philosophy from Socrates to Hefner").[32]

Hefner saw his naked women as "a symbol of disobedience, a triumph of sexuality, an end of Puritanism." He saw his magazine as an attack on "our ferocious anti-sexuality, our dark antieroticism." But his thrust toward pleasure and light was not to be undertaken in partnership. The Playboy philosophy, according to Hefner, had less to do with sex and more to do with sex roles. American society increasingly "blurred distinctions between the sexes . . . not only in business, but in such diverse realms as household chores, leisure activities, smoking and drinking habits, clothing styles, upswinging homosexuality and the sex-obliterating aspects of togetherness," concluded the "Playboy Panel" in June 1962.[33] In Part 19 of his extended essay on the Playboy philosophy, Hefner wrote: "PLAY-BOY stresses a strongly heterosexual concept of society—in which the separate roles of men and women are clearly defined and compatible."[34]

Read without context, Hefner's call does not necessarily preclude sex as a common interest between men and women. He is certainly advocating heterosexual sex. But the models of sex offered are not partnerships. Ever innovative in marketing and design, *Playboy* offered in one issue a special "coloring book" section. A page featuring three excessively voluptuous women was captioned: "Make one of the girls a blonde. Make one of the girls a brunette. Make one of the girls a redhead. It does not matter which is which. The girls' haircolors are interchangeable. So are the girls."[35]

Sex, in the Playboy mode, was a contest—not of wills, in the model of the male seducer and the virtuous female, but of exploitative intent, as in the playboy and the would-be wife. In *Playboy*'s world, women were out to ensnare men, to entangle them in a web of responsibility and obligation (not the least of which was financial). Barbara Ehrenreich has convincingly argued that *Playboy* was an integral part of a male-initiated revolution in sex roles, for it advocated that men reject burdensome responsibility (mainly in the shape of wives) for lives of pleasure through consumption.[36] Sex, of course, was part of this pleasurable universe. In *Playboy*, sex was located in the realm of consumption, and women were interchangeable objects, mute, making no demands, each airbrushed beauty supplanted by the next month's model.

It was not only to men that sexual freedom was sold through exploitative visions. When Helen Gurley Brown revitalized the traditional women's magazine that was *Cosmopolitan* in 1965, she compared her magazine to *Playboy*—and *Cosmo* did celebrate the pleasures of single womanhood and "sexual and material consumerism." But before Brown ran *Cosmo*, she had made her contribution to the sexual revolution with *Sex and the Single Girl*, published in May 1962. By April 1963, 150,000 hard-cover copies had been sold, garnering Brown much media attention and a syndicated newspaper column, "Woman Alone."[37]

The claim of *Sex and the Single Girl* was, quite simply, "nice, single girls *do*." Brown's radical message to a society in which twenty-three-year-olds were called old maids was that singleness is good. Marriage, she insisted, should not be an immediate goal. The Single Girl sounds like the Playboy's dream, but she was more likely a nightmare revisited. Marriage, Brown advised, is "insurance for the worst years of your life. During the best years you don't need a husband." But she quickly amended that statement: "You do need a man every step of the way, and they are often cheaper emotionally and more fun by the dozen."[38]

That fun explicitly included sex, and on the woman's terms. But Brown's celebration of the joys of single life still posed men and women as adversaries. "She need never be bored with one man per lifetime," she enthused. "Her choice of partners is endless and they seek *her*. . . . Her married friends refer to her pursuers as wolves, but actually many of them turn out to be lambs—to be shorn and worn by her."[39]

Brown's celebration of the single "girl" actually began with a success story—her own. "I married for the first time at thirty-seven. I got the man I wanted," begins *Sex and the Single Girl*. Brown's description of that union is instructive: "David is a motion picture producer, forty-four, brainy, charming and sexy. He was sought after by many a Hollywood starlet as well as some less flamboyant but more deadly types. And *I* got him! We have two Mercedes-Benzes, one hundred acres of virgin forest near San Francisco, a Mediterranean house overlooking the Pacific, a full-time maid and a good life."[40]

While Brown believes "her body wants to" is a sufficient reason for a woman to have an "affair," she is not positing identical interests of men and women in sex. Instead, she asserts the validity of women's interests—interests that include Mercedes-Benzes, full-time maids, lunch ("Anyone can take you to lunch. How bored can you be for an hour?"), vacations, and vicuna coats.[41] But by offering a female version of the Playboy ethic, she greatly strengthened its message.

Unlike the youths who called for honesty, who sought to blur the boundaries between male and female, *Playboy* and *Cosmo* offered a vision of sexual freedom based on difference and deceit, but within a shared universe of an intensely competitive market economy. They were revolutionary in their claiming of sex as a legitimate pleasure and in the directness they brought to portraying sex as an arena for struggle and exploitation that could be enjoined by men and women alike (though in different ways and to different ends). Without this strand, the sexual revolution would have looked very different. In many ways *Playboy* was a necessary condition for "revolution," for it linked sex to the emerging culture of consumption and the rites of the marketplace. As it fed into the sexual reconfigurations of the sixties, *Playboy* helped make sex more—or less—than a rite of youth.

In the revolutionary spring of 1968, *Life* magazine looked from the student protests at Columbia across the street to Barnard College: "A sexual anthropologist of some future century, analyzing the pill, the drive-in, the works of Harold Robbins, the Tween-Bra and all the other artifacts of the American Sexual Revolution, may consider the case of Linda LeClair and her boyfriend, Peter Behr, as a moment in which the morality of an era changed."[42]

The LeClair affair, as it was heralded in newspaper headlines and syndicated columns around the country, was indeed such a moment. Linda LeClair and Peter Behr were accidental revolutionaries, but as *Life* not so kindly noted, "history will often have its little joke. And so it was this spring when it found as its symbol of this revolution a champion as staunch, as bold and as unalluring as Linda LeClair."[43] The significance of the moment is not to be found in the actions of LeClair and Behr, who certainly lacked revolutionary glamour despite all the headlines about "Free Love," but in the contest over the meaning of those actions.[44]

The facts of the case were simple. On 4 March 1968 the *New York Times* ran an article called "An Arrangement: Living Together for Convenience, Security, Sex." (The piece ran full-page width; below it appeared articles on "How to Duck the Hemline Issue" and "A Cook's Guide to the Shallot.") An "arrangement," the author informs us, was one of the current euphemisms for what was otherwise known as "shacking up" or, more innocuously, "living together." The article, which offers a fairly sympathetic portrait of several unmarried student couples who lived together in New York City, features an interview with a Barnard sophomore, "Susan," who lived with her boyfriend "Peter" in an off-campus apartment. Though Barnard had strict housing regulations and parietals (the curfew was midnight on weekends and ten o'clock on weeknights, and students were meant to live either at home or in Barnard housing), Susan had received permission to live off campus by accepting a job listed through Barnard's employment office as a "live-in maid." The job had, in fact, been listed by a young married woman who was a good friend of "Susan's."[45]

Not surprisingly, the feature article caught the attention of Barnard administrators, who had little trouble identifying "Susan" as Linda LeClair. LeClair was brought before the Judiciary Council—not for her sexual conduct, but for lying to Barnard about her housing arrangements. Her choice of roommate was certainly an issue; if she had been found to be living alone or, as one Barnard student confessed to the *Times*, with a female cat, she would not have been headline-worthy.[46]

Linda, however, was versed in campus politics, and she and Peter owned a mimeograph machine. She played it both ways, appearing for her hearings in a demure, knee-length pastel dress and churning out pamphlets on what she and Peter called "A Victorian Drama." She and Peter distributed a survey on campus, garnering three hundred replies, most of which admitted to some violation of Barnard's parietals or housing regulations. Sixty women were willing to go public and signed forms that read: "I am a student of Barnard College and I have violated the Barnard Housing Regulations. . . . In the interest of fairness I request that an investigation be made of my disobedience."[47]

Two hundred and fifty students and faculty members attended LeClair's hearing, which was closed to all but members of the college community. Her defense was a civil rights argument: colleges had no right to regulate nonacademic behavior of adult students, and housing rules discriminated on the basis of sex (Columbia men had no such regulations). After deliberating for five hours, the faculty-student judiciary committee found LeClair guilty of defying college regulations; but it also called for reform of the existing housing policy. The punishment they recommended for LeClair was a sort of black humor to anyone who had been to college: they barred her from the Barnard cafeteria.[48]

Linda LeClair had not done anything especially unusual, as several letters from alumnae to Barnard's president, Martha Peterson, testified. But her case was a symbol of change, and it tells us much about how people understood the incident. The president's office received over two hundred telephone calls (most demanding LeClair's expulsion) and over one hundred letters; editorials ran in newspapers, large and small, throughout the country. Some of the letters were vehement in their condemnation of LeClair and of the college. Francis Beamen of Needham, Massachusetts, suggested that Barnard should be renamed "BARNYARD"; Charles Orsinger wrote (on good quality letterhead), "If you let Linda stay in college, I can finally prove to my wife with a front page news story about that bunch of glorified whores going to eastern colleges." An unsigned letter began: "SUBJECT: Barnard College—and the kow-tow to female 'students' who practice prostitution, PUBLICLY!"[49]

Though the term "alley cat" cropped up more than once, a majority of the letters were thoughtful attempts to come to terms with the changing morality of America's youth. Many were from parents who understood the symbolic import of the case. Overwhelmingly, those who did not simply rant about "whoredom" structured their comments around concepts of public and private. The word *flaunt* appeared over and over in the letters to President Peterson. Linda was "flaunting her sneering attitude"; Linda and Peter were "openly flaunting their disregard of moral codes"; they were "openly flaunting rules of civilized society."[50] Mrs. Bruce Bromley,

Jr., wrote her first such letter on a public issue to recommend, "Do not let Miss LeClair attend Barnard as long as she flaunts immorality in your face."[51] David Abrahamson, M.D., identifying himself as a former Columbia faculty member, offered "any help in this difficult case." He advised President Peterson, "Undoubtedly the girl's behavior must be regarded as exhibitionism, as her tendency is to be in the limelight which clearly indicates some emotional disturbance or upset."[52]

The public-private question *was* the issue in this case—the letter writers were correct. Most were willing to acknowledge that "mistakes" can happen; many were willing to allow for some "discreet" sex among the unmarried young. But Linda LeClair *claimed* the right to determine her own "private" life; she rejected the private-public dichotomy *as it was framed around sex*, casting her case as an issue of individual rights versus institutional authority.[53]

But public response to the case is interesting in another way. When a woman wrote President Peterson that "it is time for these young people to put sex back in its proper place, instead of something to be flaunted" and William F. Buckley condemned the "delinquency of this pathetic little girl, so gluttonous for sex and publicity," they were not listening.[54] Sex was not what Linda and Peter talked about. Sex was not mentioned. Security was, and "family." "Peter is my family," said Linda. "It's a very united married type of relationship—it's the most important one in each of our lives. And our lives are very much intertwined."[55]

Of course they had sex. They were young and in love, and their peer culture accepted sex within such relationships. But what they claimed was partnership—a partnership that obviated the larger culture's insistence on the difference between men and women. The letters suggesting that young women would "welcome a strong rule against living with men to protect them against doing that" made no sense in LeClair's universe.[56] When she claimed that Barnard's rules were discriminatory because Columbia men had no such rules, that "Barnard College was founded on the principle of equality between women and men," and asked, "If women are able, intelligent people, why must we be supervised and curfewed?" she was denying that men and women had different interests and needs.[57] Just as the private-public dichotomy was a cornerstone of sexual control in the postwar era, the much-touted differences between men and women were a crucial part of the system.

Many people in the 1960s and 1970s struggled with questions of equality and difference in sophisticated and hard-thought ways. Neither Peter Behr nor Linda LeClair was especially gifted in that respect. What they argued was commonplace to them—a natural language and set of assumptions that nonetheless had revolutionary implications. It is when a set of assumptions becomes natural and unself-conscious, when a language appears in the private comments of a wide variety of people that it is worth taking seriously. The unity of interests that Behr and LeClair called upon as they obviated the male-female dichotomy was not restricted to students in the progressive institutions on either coast.

In 1969 the administration at the University of Kansas (KU), a state institution dependent on a conservative, though populist, legislature for its funding, attempted to establish a coed dormitory for some of its scholarship students. KU had tried coed living as an experiment in the 1964 summer session and found students well satisfied, though some complained that it was awkward to go downstairs to the candy machines with one's hair in curlers.[58] Curlers were out of fashion by 1969, and the administration moved forward with caution.

A survey on attitudes toward coed housing was given to those who lived in the scholarship halls, and the answers of the men survive. The results of the survey go against conventional wisdom about the provinces. Only one man (of the 124 responses recorded) said his parents objected to the arrangement ("Pending further discussion," he noted). But what is most striking is the language in which the men supported and opposed the plan. "As a stereotypical answer," one man wrote, "I already am able to do all the roleplaying socially I need, and see communication now as an ultimate goal." A sophomore who listed his classification as both "soph." and "4-F I Hope" responded: "I believe that the segregation of the sexes is unnatural. I would like to associate with women on a basis other than dating roles. This tradition of segregation is discriminatory and promotes inequality of mankind." One man thought coed living would make the hall "more homey." Another said it would be "more humane." Many used the word "natural." The most eloquent of the sophomores wrote: "[It would] allow them to meet and interact with one another in a situation relatively free of sexual overtones; that is, the participating individuals would be free to encounter one another as human beings, rather than having to play the traditional stereotyped male and female roles. I feel that coed living is the only feasible way to allow people to escape this stereotypical role behavior."[59]

The student-generated proposal that went forward in December 1970 stressed these (as they defined them) "philosophical" justifications. The system "would NOT be an arrangement for increased "boy-meets-girl" contact or for convenience in finding dates," the committee insisted. Instead, coed living would "contribute to the development of each resident as a full human being." Through "interpersonal relationships based on friendship and cooperative efforts rather than on the male/female roles we usually play in dating situations" students would try to develop "a human concern that transcends membership in one or the other sex."[60]

While the students disavowed " 'boy-meets-girl' contact" as motivation, no one seriously believed that sex was going to disappear. The most cogently stated argument against the plan came from a young man who insisted: "[You] can't ignore the sexual overtones involved in coed living; after all, sex is the basic motivation for your plan. (I didn't say lust, I said sex)."[61] Yet the language in which they framed their proposal was significant: they called for relationships (including sexual) based on a common humanity.

Like Peter Behr and Linda LeClair, these students at the University of Kansas were attempting to redefine both sex and sex roles. Sex should not be negotiated through the dichotomous pairings of male and female, public and private. Instead, they attempted to formulate and articulate a new standard that looked to a model of "togetherness" undreamed of and likely undesired by their parents. The *Life* magazine issue with which this essay began characterized the "sexual revolution" as "dull." "Love still makes the world go square," the author concluded, for the revolutionaries he interviewed subscribed to a philosophy "less indebted to Playboy than Peanuts, in which sex is not so much a pleasure as a warm puppy." To his amusement, one "California girl" told him: "Besides being my lover, Bob is my best friend in all the world," and a young man insisted, "We are not sleeping together, we are living together."[62]

For those to whom Playboy promised revolution, this attitude was undoubtedly tame. And in the context of the cultural revolution taking place among America's youth, and documented in titillating detail by magazines such as *Life*, these were modest revolutionaries indeed, seeming almost already out of step with their generation. But the issue, to these "dull" revolutionaries, as to their more flamboyant brothers and sisters, was larger than sex. They understood that the line between public and private had utility; that the personal was political.

1967, The Summer of Love. It was a "holy pilgrimage," according to the Council for a Summer of Love. In the streets of Haight-Ashbury, thousands and thousands of "pilgrims" acted out a street theater of costumed fantasy, drugs and music and sex that was unimaginable in the neat suburban streets of their earlier youth. Visionaries and revolutionaries had preceded the deluge; few of them drowned. Others did. But the tide flowed in with vague countercultural yearnings, drawn by the pop hit "San Francisco (Be Sure to Wear Flowers in Your Hair)" and its promise of a "love-in," by the pictures in *Life* magazine or in *Look* magazine or in *Time* magazine, by the proclamations of the underground press that San Francisco would be "the love-guerilla training school for drop-outs from mainstream America . . . where the new world, a human world of the 21st century is being constructed."[63] Here sexual freedom would be explored; not cohabitation, not "arrangements," not "living together" in ways that looked a lot like marriage except for the lack of a piece of paper that symbolized the sanction of the state. Sex in the Haight was revolutionary.

In neat suburban houses on neat suburban streets, people came to imagine this new world, helped by television and by the color pictures in glossy-paper magazines (a joke in the Haight told of "bead-wearing *Look* reporters interviewing bead-wearing *Life* reporters").[64] Everyone knew that these pilgrims represented a tiny fraction of America's young, but the images reverberated. America felt itself in revolution.

Todd Gitlin, in his soul-searching memoir of the sixties, argues the cultural significance of the few:

> Youth culture seemed a counterculture. There were many more week-end dope-smokers than hard-core "heads"; many more readers of the *Oracle* than writers for it; many more co-habitors than orgiasts; many more turners-on than droppers-out. Thanks to the sheer number and concentration of youth, the torrent of drugs, the sexual revolution, the traumatic war, the general stampede away from authority, and the trend-spotting media, it was easy to assume that all the styles of revolt and disaffection were spilling together tributaries into a common torrent of youth and euphoria, life against death, joy over sacrifice, now over later, remaking the whole bleeding world.[65]

Youth culture and counterculture, as Gitlin argues so well, were not synonymous, and for many the culture itself was more a matter of lifestyle than revolutionary intent. But the strands flowed together in the chaos of the age, and the few and the marginal provided archetypes that were read into the youth culture by an American public that did not see the lines of division. "Hippies, yippies, flippies," said Mayor Richard Daley of Chicago.[66] "Free Love," screamed the headlines about Barnard's Linda LeClair.

But even the truly revolutionary youths were not unified, no more on the subject of sex than on anything else. Members of the New Left, revolutionary but rarely countercultural, had sex but did not talk about it all the time. They consigned sex to a relatively "private" sphere. Denizens of Haight-Ashbury lived a Dionysian sexuality, most looking nowhere but to immediate pleasure. Some political-cultural revolutionaries, however, claimed sex and used it for the revolution. They capitalized on the sexual chaos and fears of the nation, attempting to use sex to politicize youth and to challenge "Amerika."

In March 1968 the *Sun*, a Detroit people's paper put out by a "community of artists and lovers" (most notably John Sinclair of the rock group MC5), declared a "Total Assault on the Culture." Sinclair, in his "editorial statement," disavowed any prescriptive intent but informed his readers: "We *have* found that there are three essential human activities of the greatest importance to all persons, and that people are well and healthy in proportion to their involvement in these activities: rock and roll, dope, and fucking in the streets. . . . We suggest the three in combination, all the time."[67]

He meant it. He meant it partly because it was outrageous, but there was more to it. "Fucking" helps you "escape the hangups that are drilled into us in this weirdo country"—it negates "private lives," "feels good," and so destroys an economy of pain and scarcity. Lapsing into inappropriately programmatic language, Sinclair argued:

> Our position is that all people must be free to fuck freely, whenever and wherever they want to, or not to fuck if they don't wanna—in bed, on the floor, in the chair, on the streets, in the parks and fields, "back seat boogie for the high school kids" sing the Fugs who brought it all out in the open on stage and on records, fuck whoever wants to fuck you and everybody else do the same. America's silly sexual "mores" are the end-product of thousands of years of deprivation and sickness, of marriage and companionship based on the ridiculous misconception that one person can "belong" to another person, that "love" is something that has to do with being "hurt," sacrificing, holding out, "teardrops on your pillow," and all that shit.[68]

Sinclair was not alone in his paean to copulation. Other countercultural seekers believed that they had to remake love and reclaim sex to create community. These few struggled, with varying degrees of honesty and sincerity, over the significance of sex in the beloved community.

For others, sex was less a philosophy than a weapon. In the spring of 1968, the revolutionary potential of sex also suffused the claims of the Yippies as they struggled to stage a "Festival of Life" to counter the "Death

Convention" in Chicago. "How can you separate politics and sex?" Jerry Rubin asked with indignation after the fact. Yippies lived by that creed. Sex was a double-edged sword, to be played two ways. Sex was a lure to youth; it was part of their attempt to tap the youth market, to "sell a revolutionary consciousness."[69] It was also a challenge, "flaunted in the face" (as it were) of America.

The first Yippie manifesto, released in January 1968, summoned the tribes to Chicago. It played well in the underground press, with its promise of "50,000 of us dancing in the streets, throbbing with amplifiers and harmony . . . making love in the parks."[70] Sex was a politics of pleasure, a politics of abundance that made sense to young middle-class whites who had been raised in the world without limits that was postwar America.

Sex was also incendiary, and the Yippies knew that well. It guaranteed attention. Thus the "top secret" plans for the convention that Abbie Hoffman mimeographed and distributed to the press promised a barbecue and lovemaking by the lake, followed by "Pin the Tail on the Donkey," "Pin the Rubber on the Pope," and "other normal and healthy games."[71] Grandstanding before a crowd of Chicago reporters, the Yippies presented a city official with an official document wrapped in a *Playboy* centerfold inscribed, "To Dick with love, the Yippies."[72] The *Playboy* centerfold in the Yippies' hands was an awkward nexus between the old and the new sexuality. As a symbolic act, it did not proffer freedom so much as challenge authority. It was a sign of disrespect—to Mayor Richard Daley and to straight America.

While America was full of young people sporting long hair and beads, the committed revolutionaries (of cultural stripe) were few in number and marginal at best. It is telling that the LeClair affair could still be a scandal in a nation that had weathered the Summer of Love. But the lines were blurred in sixties America. One might ask with Todd Gitlin, "What was marginal anymore, where was the mainstream anyway?" when the Beatles were singing, "Why Don't We Do It in the Road?"

Conclusion

The battles of the sexual revolution were hard fought, its victories ambiguous, its outcome still unclear. What we call the sexual revolution was an amalgam of movements that flowed together in an unsettled era. They were often at odds with one another, rarely well thought out, and usually without a clear agenda.

The sexual revolution was built on equal measures of hypocrisy and honesty, equality and exploitation. Indeed, the individual strands contain mixed motivations and ideological charges. Even the most heartfelt or best intentions did not always work out for the good when put into practice by mere humans with physical and psychological frailties. As we struggle over the meaning of the "revolution" and ask ourselves who, in fact, *won*, it helps to untangle the threads and reject the conflation of radically different impulses into a singular revolution.

NOTES

1. In early 1956 Ed Sullivan had announced that he would never allow Elvis Presley's "smutty performance" on his show. Within three months he had offered $50,000 for the three performances but maintained control of camera angle. Douglas T. Miller and Marion Nowak, *The Fifties* (Garden City, N.Y.: Doubleday, 1977), 300–306, 410.

2. The quotation is from a subject in the Kelly Longitudinal Study of three hundred married couples conducted over two decades by a psychologist at the University of Michigan. Elaine May has analyzed these materials in *Homeward Bound: American Families in the Cold War Era* (New York: Basic Books, 1988), where she makes a strong case that the rules governing sexual behavior were not without weight, for breaking with the code often had emotional or psychological consequences. The quotation appears on pp. 122–23.

3. I have analyzed sexual misconduct and disciplinary procedures at the University of Kansas in the postwar era in "Sexual Containment," a paper presented at the "Ike's America" conference, Lawrence, Kansas, October 1990.

4. For a perceptive analysis of Kinsey, see Regina Markell Morantz, "The Scientist as Sex Crusader: Alfred C. Kinsey and American Culture," *American Quarterly* 29 (Winter 1979): 563–89.

5. Alfred Kinsey, Wardell B. Pomeroy, and Clyde E. Martin, *Sexual Behavior in the Human Male* (Philadelphia: Saunders, 948); "For Women Only . . . What Every Woman Should Know about Kinsey," *Look*, 8 September 1953, 78.

6. Alfred Kinsey, *Sexual Behavior in the Human Female* (Philadelphia: Saunders, 1953), 285.

7. "Letters to the Editor," *Look*, 20 October 1953, 12.

8. Kinsey, *Female*, 287 (premarital sex), 315 (moral grounds), 239 (petting), 399 (oral stimulation); *Male*, 623 (homosexual), 347–48 (premarital sex). On male homosexuality, Kinsey notes: "These figures are, of course, considerably higher than any which have previously been estimated; . . . We ourselves were totally unprepared to find such incidence data" (p. 625).

9. For example, Martin B. Duberman discusses the impact on Kinsey in his life in his autobiographical *Cures* (New York: Dutton, 1991).

10. Quotations from "5,940 Women," *Time*, 24 August 1953, 58; Barbara Benson, "What Women Want to Know about the Kinsey Book," *Ladies' Home Journal*, September 1953, 52–53; Editorial, *Chicago Tribune*, 20 August 1953, quoted in "The Scientist as Sex Crusader: Alfred Kinsey and American Culture," *American Quarterly* (Winter 1977): 563–89.

11. Most notably in a television show, David Susskind's "Open End," which featured a panel discussion on "The Sexual Revolution in America," scheduled for Fall 1963. New York's Channel 5 canceled it and withheld it from distribution; it was later aired on New York's Channel 11 and distributed nationally. For one account of the controversy, see "David Susskind," *Mademoiselle*, October 1963, 112.

12. One can, for example, date the symbolic beginning of the gay liberation movement to the police raid at the Stonewall Inn in Greenwich Village in late June 1969 and the subsequent rioting. One can also trace decades of struggle by gay men and lesbians before this galvanizing event. Yet I believe that gay liberation—as a national, public struggle—falls within the next generation of the larger movement.

13. *New York Times*, 1 November 1963, sec. A.

14. "Little Sex without Love," *Time*, 9 April 1965, 46; "Harvard Students Ask Longer Visits," *Boston Herald*, 10 December 1965, in Student Life file HUD965, 1965, Harvard University Archives.

15. "Vassar and Virginity," *Newsweek*, 21 May 1962, 86.

16. For an extended discussion, see "Sex Control," in *From Front Porch to Back Seat: Courtship in Twentieth-Century America*, by Beth Bailey (Baltimore: Johns Hopkins University Press, 1988).

17. Grace Hechinger and Fred M. Hechinger, "College Morals Mirror Our Society," *New York Times Magazine*, 14 April 1963.

18. Emily Taylor (former dean of women, University of Kansas), interview with author, Lawrence, Kans., June 1990. For other penalties, see Bailey, *Front Porch*, 84–85, 164.

19. Ferdinand Lundberg and Marynia F. Farnham, M.D., *Modern Woman: The Lost Sex* (New York: Harper, 1947), 275–76, 271.

20. One could make the argument that changing contraceptive technology is another important strand in the sexual revolution. Certainly people at the time linked the two closely. But oral contraceptives had to be prescribed by doctors. The ways in which birth control pills changed American sexual practices are important, but those depended on cultural changes that made it possible for unmarried women to *get* a prescription for oral contraceptives.

21. Kinsey, *Female*, 315.

22. Elizabeth Woodward, "Sub-deb: Bargain Buys," *Ladies' Home Journal*, May 1942, 8; Gay Head, "Boy Dates Girl," *Senior Scholastic*, 1945, 28.

23. Kinsey, *Male*, 364. The respondents ranged from adolescents to twenty-five-year-olds who had completed 13+ years of schooling. The comparable figure for those with no college is 40.8 percent.

24. May, *Homeward Bound*, 124.

25. Oral history conducted by Ben Grant for "History of Sexuality in America" course, Barnard College, Spring 1991.

26. Samuel Hynes, *Flights of Passage: Reflections of a World War II Aviator* (Annapolis, Md.: Naval Institute Press, 1990), 57.

27. Nora Johnson, "Sex and the College Girl," *Atlantic*, November 1959, 57–58; also quoted in May, *Homeward Bound*.

28. Oral history conducted by Jennifer Kriz for "History of Sexuality in America" course, Barnard College, Spring 1991.

29. Daniel Joseph Singal, "Towards a Definition of American Modernism," *American Quarterly* 39 (Spring 1987): 9.

30. T. J. Jackson Lears, *No Place of Grace: Antimodernism and the Transformation of American Culture, 1880–1920* (New York: Pantheon, 1981), 5.

31. For an interesting discussion of *Playboy*, see Barbara Ehrenreich, *The Hearts of Men: American Dreams and the Flight from Commitment* (New York: Anchor Press, 1983).

32. Vance Packard, *The Sexual Wilderness* (New York: McKay, 1968), 28.

33. "Playboy Panel," *Playboy*, June 1962, 43–44.

34. Hugh Hefner, "Playboy Philosophy, Part 19," *Playboy*, December 1964. For similar comments, see the article on David Susskind's show on the sexual revolution in *Mademoiselle*, October 1963, 113. Hefner was a member of the panel.

35. Marie Torre, "A Woman Looks at the Girly-Girly Magazines," *Cosmopolitan*, May 1963, 46.

36. Ehrenreich, *Hearts of Men*, 45.

37. Ibid.; Helen Gurley Brown, "New Directions for *Cosmopolitan*," *The Writer*, July 1965, 20; "Playboy Interview," *Playboy*, April 1963, 53.

38. Helen Gurley Brown, *Sex and the Single Girl* (New York: Pocket Books ed., 1963; first published by Bernard Geis, May 1962), 2.

39. Ibid., 4–5.

40. Ibid., 1.

41. Ibid., 101, 219.

42. William A. McWhirter, " 'The Arrangement' at College," *Life*, 31 May 1968, 56. This article is part of a large, special section on student sexuality.

43. Ibid., 58.

44. The 1960 census discovered 17,000 unrelated adults of the opposite sex sharing living quarters; the 1970 census reported 143,000 cohabiting.

45. Judy Klemesrud, "An Arrangement: Living Together for Convenience, Security, Sex," *New York Times*, 4 March 1968.

46. "60 More Barnard Girls Insist They've Been Naughty, Too," *New York Post*, 12 April 1968, in Linda LeClair clipping files, Barnard College Archives, New York (hereafter cited as LeClair files, Barnard Archives).

47. Ibid.; Frank Mazza, "Free-Love Portia Makes a Point," *New York Daily News*, 12 April 1968, LeClair files, Barnard Archives.

48. This account is pieced together from the many clippings in the LeClair files, Barnard Archives. The major New York newspapers, including the *Times*, covered the story extensively. I am indebted to Amy Ceccarelli for telling me of the existence of the

LeClair files. Ceccarelli's senior thesis, for which she received honors in American Studies, contains a nicely structured narrative on the LeClair affair. See Amy Ceccarelli, "Women, the New Left, and Women's Liberation: A Case Study of Barnard College, 1968–70" (Senior Thesis, Barnard College American Studies Program, 1991). My account is drawn primarily from "Linda the Light Housekeeper," *Time*, 26 April 1968, 51; Jean Crofton, "Barnard's Linda Has No Regrets," *New York Post*, 17 April 1968; Jean Crofton, "Will Barnard Terminate Linda's Lease?," *New York Post*, 17 April 1968; Jean Crofton, "A Campus Rah-Rah for Linda's Love-in Verdict," *New York Post*, 18 April 1968; Frank Mazza, "Free-Love Portia"; "60 More Barnard Girls . . ."; "Barnard Girl Defends Live-in with Beau," *Chicago Sun-Times*, 17 April 1968; Lee Stone, "Insistent Co-ed Caused a Crisis," *Salina Journal* (Kansas), 24 May 1968; and Frank Mazza, "Dad Cuts Off Linda's Allowance" (20 April 1968) and "Linda and Love Quit School" (19 April 1968), *New York Daily News*. All newspaper articles are in the LeClair files, Barnard Archives.

49. Frances Beamen to President Peterson, 18 April 1968; Charles Gunther Orsinger to President Peterson, 19 April 1968; Unsigned letter to "Mr. President," received 29 April 1968—all in LeClair files, Barnard Archives.

50. For "flaunt," see letters to President Peterson from Mrs. C. S. Parsons, Champaign, Ill., 19 April 1968; Catherine McGolly, no address, 20 April 1968; George W. Nilsson, Los Angeles, 22 April 1968 (Nilsson's enclosed quotations about Rome's fall from Will Durant, *The Story of Civilization*); Mary W. (Mrs. John D.) Gray, New York, 22 April 1968; Mrs. John McCarthy, Tallahassee, Fla., no date; E. Wendt, New York, no date; Mrs. Clara McShadey (handwriting illegible), Vancouver, Wash., 18 April 1968; and Mrs. John Ternell, Corona del Mar, Calif., 17 April 1968. Frank Hosiac of Cleveland, Ohio, wrote that LeClair's "boastful attitude" indicated "advanced depravity"; Mrs. M. J. Payne, Jr., of Bellingham, Wash., condemned LeClair's attempt to "live in open, sinful, immoral living-together." These letters, and many more, are in the LeClair files, Barnard Archives. Letters were written in support of LeClair and Behr, but they were a minority, and many came from recent Barnard graduates. Sometimes the writers used "flaunt" when they meant "flout."

51. Sally (Mrs. Bruce) Bromley to President Peterson, 19 April 1968, LeClair files, Barnard Archives.

52. David Abrahamson, M.D., to President Peterson, New York, 24 April 1968, ibid.

53. Obviously she did not reject any notion of privacy, for her argument hinged on claims to a realm of privacy beyond institutional control. Still, she assumed a different set of boundaries, in which the over/covert, public/private distinctions did not operate.

54. Mrs. C. S. Parsons to President Peterson, 19 April 1968, LeClair files, Barnard Archives. Buckley's column was syndicated nationally. It appeared as "The Linda LeClair Case; Is the Moral Code Dead?" in the Los Angeles

Times and as "Barnard Frowns—Linda Fibbed! in the *Boston Globe*, 27 April 1968.

55. Jean Crofton, "Barnard's Linda Has No Regrets," *New York Post*, 17 April 1968, in LeClair files, Barnard Archives.

56. Mary W. Gray to President Peterson, 22 April 1968, ibid.

57. Linda LeClair, "Letter to the Editor," *Barnard Bulletin*, 13 March 1968, ibid.

58. "Co-ed Dorms Get Hearty Approval," *University Daily Kansan*, 23 October 1964. The article began: "Peaceful co-existence came to KU this past summer, although university residence halls, not a summit conference, were the site of an experiment in human relations."

59. Quotations are from responses to "Coed Survey" of Stephenson Hall, 1969–70, in "Housing: Scholarship Halls" box, KU Archives, Lawrence.

60. Co-educational Living System," University of Kansas Scholarship Hall System, Preliminary Proposal, December 1970, in ibid. Several drafts survive; this is the latest and most complete.

61. "Coed Survey" for Battenfield Hall, ibid.

62. McWhirter, " 'The Arrangement,' " and Albert Rosenfeld, "The Scientists' Findings," in "Student Sexuality" section, *Life*, 31 May 1968.

63. Quotations from Abe Peck, *Uncovering the Sixties: The Life and Times of the Underground Press* (New York: Pantheon, 1985), 46. For more on Haight-Ashbury, see Charles Perry, *The Haight-Ashbury: A History* (New York: Vintage, 1984).

64. Peck, *Uncovering the Sixties*, 45.

65. Todd Gitlin, *The Sixties: Years of Hope, Days of Rage* (New York: Bantam, 1987), 214.

66. *Chicago Tribune*, 17 August 1968, cited in David Farber, *Chicago '68* (Chicago: University of Chicago Press, 1988), 160.

67. John Sinclair, *Guitar Army: Street Writings/Prison Writings* (New York: Douglas, 1972), 67–68.

68. Ibid., 69.

69. Farber, *Chicago '68*, 218.

70. Ibid., 17.

71. Ibid., 53.

72. Ibid., 37.

9

The Politics of Civility

As the 1960s opened, civility was, quite literally, the law of the land. In 1942 the U.S. Supreme Court had declared that certain words were not protected by the First Amendment. Not only fighting words, but also the "lewd," "obscene," and "profane" were all excluded from protection. A statute declaring that "no person shall address any offensive, derisive or annoying word to any other person who is lawfully in any street" was upheld by the Court as perfectly legal.[1] This decision, although modified in later years, was still law in 1960, and statutes like the one mentioned above continued to be on the books and enforced.[2] They implied that free speech was possible only in what eighteenth-century writers had called "civil society." Civility, in other words, had to precede civil rights.

One part of the contentious politics of the sixties, however, was a fight over this notion. From a number of perspectives, prevailing attitudes toward social etiquette were attacked. African Americans argued that civil society as constructed by whites helped structure racial inequality. Counterculturalists insisted that civil politeness suppressed more authentic social relations. Some student radicals infused the strategic disruption of civility with political meaning. And finally, there was a moderate loosening of civil control at the center of society. Under this onslaught, the nation's courts struggled to redefine the relationship between law and civil behavior.

No regime is without an approach to social order, which means that none is without an attitude toward decorum. Many governments impose order from the top. Others allow huge pockets of disorder, passion, and even violence provided it all does not threaten the regime.[3] A state ideologically committed to equal rights for all is especially hard-pressed to establish a standard of decorum, for any norm seems to undermine its deepest principles. Still, for nations with a professed belief in something resembling our First Amendment, there is more than one way to negotiate the contradiction between political principle and civil order. This essay charts the shift within the United States from one sense of order to another. In reaction to various social changes and pressures, federal courts, most importantly the Supreme Court, altered the law of decorum. From the belief that civility took precedence over civil rights, the Supreme Court decided that in public forums, incivility was protected by the First Amendment. But this major change was qualified. No incivility, the Court argued, could disrupt the normal workings of a school, workplace, or courtroom. Institutions had to function, the justices reasoned. Decorum there was mandatory.

Bourgeois Festivals of Misrule

The civil rights movement's nonviolent efforts to alter the social order marked the first powerful sortie into the politics of civility during the 1960s. As the sixties opened, nonviolent direct action was the tactic of choice for organizations like the Congress of Racial Equality (CORE), the Southern Christian Leadership Conference (SCLC), and the Student Nonviolent Coordinating Committee (SNCC). To be sure, this tactic did not rise and fall with the sixties. It went back to the 1940s when CORE was founded, and it was under attack as early as 1961. Still, it played an important role in the first half of the decade and never entirely died out. Practitioners of direct action used an assertively polite decorum to upset social assumptions and topple the system of segregation.

Nonviolent resistance asked demonstrators to peaceably and lovingly call attention to the inequities of the social system. For those believing in direct nonviolent action, the path of protest was a complicated and patient one, moving through four distinct stages—the investigation of a problem, efforts to negotiate a solution, public protest, and then further negotiation. One never proceeded to the next stage without warrant. Henry David Thoreau's "Civil Disobedience" was often cited as a precursor to direct action. Another important source was Mahatma Gandhi. Indeed, Gandhi's 1906 campaign in South Africa was seen as the first example of a mass direct nonviolent action.

But while Gandhi and Thoreau were sources, for both black and white activists committed to direct nonviolent action there was something far more important—the Gospel's injunction to love one's enemies. All the early leaders of CORE, SCLC, and SNCC were deeply influence by the Christian message of hope and redemption. SNCC's statement of purpose on its founding in May 1960 called attention to those "Judaic-Christian traditions" that seek "a social order permeated by love." Martin Luther King, Jr., who post facto described the Montgomery boycott in terms of a Gandhian four-stage protest, was in fact only gradually becoming aware of Gandhi in the mid-1950s. As King put it to one reporter, he "went to Gandhi through Jesus."[4]

These civil rights leaders placed great emphasis on orderly demonstrations. CORE's "Rules for Action" told members to "never use malicious slogans," to "make a sincere effort to avoid malice and hatred," and to "meet the anger of any individual or group in the spirit of good will and creative reconciliation." Similarly, Martin Luther King wanted activists to "protest courageously, and yet with dignity and Christian love." This was the "task of combining the militant and the moderate."[5]

Civil rights protest took a number of characteristic forms—the boycott, the sit-in, the freedom ride, and the mass march. At all, efforts were made to keep the protest civil. In 1960, when four neatly dressed black college students sat down at a white-only lunch counter in a downtown Woolworth's in Greensboro, North Carolina, one began the protest by turning to a waitress and saying, "I'd like a cup of coffee, please." Although the students were not served, they continued to be well mannered, sitting "politely" at the counter for days on end. This first effort set off a wave of sit-ins to desegregate southern restaurants. Typical were the instructions given in Nashville: "Do show yourself friendly on the counter at all times. Do sit straight and always face the counter. Don't strike back or curse back if attacked." Candie Anderson, one of the students at the Nashville sit-in, recalled: "My friends were determined to be courteous and well-behaved.

... Most of them read or studied while they sat at the counters, for three or four hours. I heard them remind each other not to leave cigarette ashes on the counter, to take off their hats, etc."[6]

To be sure, especially when faced with taunts and violence, tempers were strained. There were breaks in decorum. But especially early in the sixties, leaders worked hard to maintain discipline and spoke out against even relatively mild disturbances. In 1962, when noisy foot stomping by local CORE activists interrupted a school board meeting in Englewood, New Jersey, the national president of CORE publicly declared that under "no condition" would the organization condone such behavior. "We would approve of a sit-in—quiet, peaceful, and orderly, but not a noisy disruption of the proceedings."[7]

The meaning of the polite protests was complicated. Rosa Parks, who refused to move to the back of the bus in Montgomery, Alabama, the students integrating lunch counters in Greensboro, and the marchers at Selma were all not only acting with decorum, they were also all breaking the law, calling attention to the inadequacy of the present system, and violating long-standing white/black custom of the South. The southern caste system was reinforced through an elaborate etiquette. Blacks stepped aside on the street to let whites pass, they averted their eyes from whites, and even adult African Americans were called by a diminutive first name ("Charlie" or "Missie") while addressing all whites with the formal titles of "Sir," "Ma'am," "Mr.," or "Mrs." No distinctions in economic status changed this. Black ministers tipped their hats to white tradesmen.[8] To the overwhelming majority of white southerners, the assertion of civil equality by civil rights protesters was in fact a radical *break* in decorum.

The protest, indeed, highlights some of the complexities of civility itself. On the one hand, politeness is a means of avoiding violence and discord. It is a way of *being nice*. One of sociologist Norbert Elias's great insights was to see that the introduction of civil etiquette in the early modern West was part of an effort to reduce the amount of interpersonal violence prevalent during the Middle Ages.[9] At some time or other, all of us are polite to people we do not like simply because we do not want to live in an overly contentious world. On the other hand, however, civility *also* reaffirms established social boundaries. And when there are huge inequities in the social order, polite custom ratifies them in everyday life.[10]

Direct nonviolent action attempted to undermine southern etiquette. It did so not by attacking civility pure and simple but by using polite behavior to challenge social inequality. More precisely, the first function of politeness (being nice) attacked the second (the caste system). The determined civility of the protesters dramatized the inequities of the South and at the same time signaled to the nation and world the "worthiness" (that is, civility) of African Americans.

Most southern whites did not see it this way. Even those who were called moderates in the early sixties often viewed the polite protests as an attack on civility. Sit-ins, boycotts, and marches openly challenged the caste system and, moderates argued, too easily slipped into violence. To the *Nashville Banner*, the sit-ins were an "incitation to anarchy." Such spokespeople understood civility to necessarily mean discussion instead of protest. In 1960 the *Greensboro Daily News* ran an editorial entitled "Of Civil Rights and Civilities" suggesting that the sit-ins were ill-conceived because civility had to take precedence over civil rights.[11]

Such editorialists, at their best, were genuinely concerned with avoiding violence, even white violence against blacks. Yet in effect they were encouraging—even insisting on—passivity. And they misunderstood the more nuanced functions of the polite protests of SNCC, CORE, and SCLC. Direct action did a number of things at once. It protested the caste system. It also publicly displayed Negro civility. And finally, it demonstrated, again and again, the brutality lurking behind established southern etiquette.

In Greensboro, it was *white* children who were the first to be arrested for disorderly conduct, who harassed blacks at the lunch counter, who got angry. At Selma, it was the white police who waded into crowds of protesters and began clubbing them. Black activists, in fact, had expected this to happen. Martin Luther King was typical, noting that nonviolent resistance forced "the oppressor to commit his brutality openly—in the light of day—with the rest of the world looking on." The net effect, according to King, was that the social conscience of the nation would be stirred. Bob Moses of SNCC spoke of how activists had to bring the South to a "white heat" before change could come. Protest was a form of public drama. In 1962, when officials of Albany, Georgia, refused to beat protesters or make mass arrests, the protest was a bust.[12]

Nonviolent resistance was designed to turn the world upside down. It can perhaps best be described as a bourgeois festival of misrule. Like the old carnivals of Europe, the boycotts, sit-ins, and marches were strategic dramas outside the purview of daily decorum that inverted the social order. Whereas the caste system of the South had been built on the supposed superior "civilization" of whites and the "backwardness" of blacks, the festivals of misrule turned this around. It was the protesters who displayed civility and the whites who did not.

Unlike the old festivals of misrule, however, which were raucous and wild, the sit-ins and boycotts were thoroughly civil and polite. They were utterly bourgeois. In this respect they appear to be directly related to the possibilities opened up by liberal democratic ideology of the nineteenth and twentieth century. Only under regimes where the notion that members of "civil society" should be full-fledged citizens has some weight do such protests make sense. Indeed, outside support for the protests often called attention to the inversion of social roles and the protection that civil protest must be accorded.[13]

While Gandhi, leading thousands of peasants, might convey to British overlords the dignity of simple people, in the United States of America, with no public perception of a peasantry in its midst, mass direct action took on a different meaning. It demonstrated the bourgeois character of the dispossessed. The final goal was to establish an egalitarian civility. For these activists, the etiquette codes of the late 1950s and early 1960s were largely taken for granted. They only wanted them applied equally to African Americans.[14] They were determined to create a truly all-encompassing civil society.

This style of protest was under assault almost as the sixties started. As early as 1961, and certainly by 1964, those partisans of "civil" protest were faced with a growing mass movement that was more assertive, less polite, and more willing to defend itself. A host of reasons explain this shift. The fiercely violent reaction of so many whites made nonviolent decorum extremely hard and dangerous to maintain. Black nationalism, grass roots activism, a growing sense of frustration, and burgeoning antiestablishment sentiment in the culture at large all helped throw bourgeois misrule on the defensive.[15] It would be just a few more steps to the Black Panther party or the calls to violence by people like Stokely Carmichael and H. Rap Brown.

Civil disobedience never died out in the late sixties. And it did have an effect on southern society. By the end of the 1970s, especially in cities, the old etiquette had largely disappeared, although its residues persisted in the countryside and small towns.[16] But nonviolent resistance did disappear from center stage. The rise of a more raucous, incivil disobedience, connected with elaborate attacks on the very idea of a civil society, pushed this peculiarly bourgeois form of carnival to the side.

The Counterculture

One place we can spot the erosion of polite protest is in the Freedom Summer of 1964. Among an important group of young SNCC activists there was a certain skepticism about Martin Luther King. For these civil rights workers, nonviolent resistance was understood to be a strategic tactic rather than a principled commitment. And there was a change in style. As sociologist Robert McAdam has noted, there was a feeling among these civil rights activists that they had to free themselves as much as the southern blacks they worked for. And that meant abandoning middle-class norms. Consequently, more rural dress (blue jeans and work shirt) became the mode. Movement slang also became prominent, as in "three of the white cats who bothered our guys have been picked up by the FBI. You dig it—they are in a Southern jail."[17] While not particularly shocking when compared to what would soon come, these changes were one sign of an emerging attack on prevailing norms of polite behavior.

Another sign was the filthy speech movement at Berkeley. In the fall of 1964, the University of California at Berkeley was rocked by the free speech movement, an effort by students to retain their right to distribute political material on campus. Many of the leaders of the free speech movement had worked for SNCC in the South the summer before and a number of Freedom Summer tactics were adopted at Berkeley. Students used mass civil disobedience and sit-ins to pressure campus officials in November and December. They were generally successful. But the next spring, after the campus had quieted, a new twist came. A nonstudent who hung around in New York beat circles drifted to Berkeley to (in his words) "make the scene." On 3 March he stood on Bancroft and Telegraph and held up a sign that just said "FUCK." When asked to clarify his meaning, he added an exclamation point. His arrest threw the campus into another controversy. Other "dirty speech" protests were held, with other students arrested for obscenity.[18]

The counterculture of the 1960s can be traced back to the beats of the 1950s, earlier still to artistic modernism, and even before that to Rousseau's mid-eighteenth-century attack on politeness.[19] But if there is a long subterranean history, a very visible counterculture began to surface in 1964. The first underground newspapers appeared; they were dominated by countercultural themes.[20] By 1966 the counterculture was a mass media phenomenon. Perhaps its height of popularity were the years 1967 and 1968. And while no precise date marks its end, by the early 1970s it was fading fast at least in its most utopian projections.

From Rousseau through the 1960s, advocates of a counterculture valued authenticity over civility. The command to be polite (that is, to *be nice*) does not encourage personal expression. It suppresses impulsive behavior, relying on established social forms to guarantee comity. As Norbert Elias has put it, the civilizing process is about affect control.[21] Counterculture advocates challenged these presumptions, arguing for the liberation of the self. In the name of personal freedom they attacked the restraints and compromises of civil society. In a phrase introduced to American life by sixties freaks, they were dedicated to "doing their own thing."

This translated into an extraordinarily colorful form of life. Shoulder-length hair on men, Victorian dresses on women, day-glo painted bodies, elaborate slang, and more open sexuality—it was all far removed from "straight" (that is, civil) society. Hippies looked different, acted different, were different. At its best, there was a glorious joy in the freedom of hippie life-styles. The "be-ins" of 1967 celebrated the love that would replace the stilted conformity of the established world. In the 1967 rock musical *Hair*, the music builds to a rousing crescendo to support this playful celebration of counterculture style:

> Let it fly in the breeze
> And get caught in the trees
> Give a home to the fleas
> In my hair
>
> A home for the fleas
> A hive for the bees
> A nest for the birds
> There ain't no words
> For the beauty and splendor
> The wonders of my
> Hair. . . .[22]

It was not only long hair that signaled liberation. Language also had to be freed, as did sex. Hippies are "more tolerant than most people," one hippie told a New York journalist. "Like you can be hung up, say, on eating twat and never want to screw, or I might want to just go to bed with boys, or somebody can be hung up on astrology. But the hippies don't really care." The same was true of psychedelic dress, beads, and long hair: "Basically, it's just a question of freedom. It's your body—you can do with it what you want to."[23]

Drugs too were often defended as a liberating experience. (I myself did so ingenuously in the late sixties.) "It's like seeing the world again through a child's eye," one user noted in 1967. Drugs were "a transcendental glory." "When I first turned on," the owner of a San Francisco head shop reported in 1968, "it pulled the rug out from under me. Suddenly I saw all the bullshit in the whole educational and social system. . . . The problem with our schools is that they are turning out robots to keep the social system going." So "turning on, tuning in, and dropping out means to conduct a revolution against the system."[24]

Intellectuals supportive of the counterculture echoed these themes. For Charles Reich, in *The Greening of America*, the new way of life was profoundly liberating. Straight society, according to Reich, was repressive, committed to "role-playing," to following patterned forms. The new consciousness, on the other hand, began "the moment the individual frees himself from automatic acceptance of the imperatives of society."[25] The psychologist R. D. Laing took it even further, arguing that it was the "normal" people who were the real crazies. In such an insane world, precisely those who knew enough to ignore the rules—schizophrenics— were the sane ones.[26] That was also a theme of Ken Kesey's *One Flew over the Cuckoo's Nest* (1962). The view gained more than a little currency within the counterculture.

To those with no respect for the counterculture, the alternative decorum was gross. There was just too much dirt. Hippies did not have the discipline to hold a job. The sex was too loose. The drugs were destructive. Some critics completely missed the claims to liberation and denounced hippies as simply negative.[27] When *U.S. News & World Report* asked a leading psychiatrist about the changes "beatniks or hippies" might bring to "American manners," he responded by contrasting the thoughtful questioners of the establishment with those "arrogant" kids who "make us more uncomfortable." "They may have long hair and be a little careless in their dress and hygiene," the psychiatrist added. "They may not wear their neckties the way we think they should." He thought them mentally unstable.[28]

Yet while the distance from straight culture was deep, the counterculture might best be seen not so much an attack on politeness as an alternative politeness, one not based on the emotional self-restraint of traditional civility but on the expressive individualism of liberated human beings. It is no surprise that "love" was an important theme running throughout the counterculture. We were, according to *Hair*, at the dawning of the Age of Aquarius, where "peace will guide the planets and love will steer the stars." The vision was explicitly utopian:

> Harmony and understanding
> Sympathy and trust abounding

No more falsehoods or derisions
Golden living dreams of visions
Mystic crystal revelations
And the mind's true liberation[29]

Even some of the behavior that most provoked the straight world was often connected with a new communal sensibility. One typical counterculture youth noted that "smoking grass makes people feel very warm and tender and loving and emotional. This is why, you know, they call it the herb of love."[30] Liberating the self was connected with a new communal culture.

The counterculture, at least in its more utopian moment, did not survive the decade. Already by the end of 1967 hippies in San Francisco were announcing the "death of hippie." The anarchistic Diggers (often called the conscience of the counterculture) were by that time trying to alert newcomers to the ways that some long-haired men preyed on naive young girls who came unsuspecting to the city. The girls were fed drugs they did not understand as a prelude to sex. By 1968 Andy Warhol was noting that the mood had changed in New York, with more distrust and even violence in counterculture circles than during the year before. If the image of Woodstock, with hundreds of thousands of young people coming together and enjoying themselves for three days, signaled the best of the counterculture, that of Altamount, with Hell's Angels beating and killing a fan, conjured up the dark side.

The limits might be found in the vision itself. For communalism and authenticity were harder to combine than one might think. The very lack of roles and restraint, the absence of Elias's affect control, would work only if there was a respect for the group that was not always there. As one more cynical New York hippie put it in 1968: "See, hippie society is a lot more ruthless and a lot more deceptive than straight society. In straight society you have your established rules and regulations, you know; in hippie society anything goes. Some of them will live with you and consume everything you have."[31]

The counterculture, at its most utopian, tried to invent a new civility. It attacked the social roles of straight society and the implied social order contained within it. But it held firm to the other dimension of civility—that of being nice. But in the end, it could not be yoked together as easily as one thought. To some degree, the roles involved in civil etiquette are connected with the avoidance of discord.

To say this, however, is not to condemn the counterculture tout court. It is rather to simply point out the problems in its most utopian dreams and to remind readers in the 1990s how real and prevalent those dreams were in the mid-1960s. For if the counterculture, chastened, fed into the relaxation of mainstream etiquette in the late sixties, it should not be confused with that more moderate, reformist goal. At its most heady, the counterculture thought of itself as a revolution in consciousness, something that could reshape the world. That dream was not realized.

The Political Left

By 1965, as the counterculture was coming to national consciousness, there was another debate going on about the civil society. At least some radical activists had moved beyond the talking stage. Violent behavior became a considered option.

This happened first among black activists, later among whites. African Americans radicals like H. Rap Brown and Stokely Carmichael decisively split with the earlier civil rights movement. Carmichael's 1966 call to let the cities burn, the stream of urban riots after 1965, and the growing militancy in general frightened numerous Americans. To be sure, many whites missed the nuances of the shift. Groups like the Black Panthers conjured violence only as a defensive tactic. Still, the situation was complicated. An activist like Rap Brown loved the effect his talk of violence had on whites. And there was rhetoric that legitimated revolt. Franz Fanon's *Wretched of the Earth* explicitly called for violence, and certain African American radicals did promote it by 1967.[32]

Some white student and antiwar activists were making their own transition. The move from dissent to resistance was accompanied by a shift in rhetoric. "We're now in the business of wholesale disruption and widespread resistance and dislocation of the American society," Jerry Rubin reported in 1967.[33] To be sure, not all white radicals accepted this, but some did, and the thought of disruption scared Middle America, whose more conservative press responded with almost breathless reports about imminent revolution. The heightened rhetoric, on both sides, contributed to the sense that the center might not hold. A string of burned buildings on university campuses as well as a handful of bombings over the next few years contributed as well.

Real violence, against property or person, however, was actually rare. Far more important was the *talk* about violence. The escalation of rhetoric, the easy use of hard words made more centrists very nervous. It reflected, in their eyes, a lack of faith in civil politics.

For these radicals, the hard words were part of their sense that polite society had its priorities backward. There was something grotesquely misguided about a middle-class decorum that masked the profound inequalities of America. The true obscenities, they argued, were the Vietnam War and racial hatred. In fact, some thought, the very idea of obscenity had to be rethought. "The dirtiest word in the English language is not 'fuck' or 'shit' in the mouth of a tragic shaman," one activist wrote, "but the word 'NIGGER' from the sneering lips of a Bull Conner."[34]

Exposing the "real" obscenities of America led to a wave of shock tactics. One of the most provocative was in the May 1967 *Realist*, a monthly partly of the Left, partly just absurdist. The article in question was supposed to be suppressed bits of William Manchester's *Death of a President*, which had been published two years before. In one section of the parody, "Jackie Kennedy" recounted an incident that took place on Air Force One after her husband's assassination. The author has the first lady say that she saw Lyndon B. Johnson "crouching over the corpse" while "breathing hard and moving his body rhythmically." She at first did not understand what was going on, but then "I realized—there is only one way to say this—he was literally fucking my husband in the throat. He reached a climax and dismounted. I froze. The next thing I remember, he was being sworn in as the new President."[35]

The incident, of course, had never occurred. The *Realist*'s editor, Paul Krassner, made it up. It created an enormous stir. The paper was banned in some parts of Boston. Krassner's usual printer, a socialist himself, refused to print it. Subscribers canceled. The Left-oriented journalist Robert Sheer worried that the magazine's real exposés would lose credibility. On the other hand, *Ramparts* editor Warren Hinckle called it a "brilliant dirty issue." One reader raised the question of whether it really was the most obscene thing imaginable: "I don't cancel my subscription to the *Chronicle* because I read every day of the horror, the obscenities, the crimes committed by LBJ. . . . That grisly image was *not* burned children in Vietnam, crying mothers, bombed villages or starving black kids in Oakland."[36]

By the late sixties, then, countercultural politics might mesh with political radicalism. To be sure, the two movements never fit perfectly together. But there were connections. Even long hair could be a threatening statement laden with political overtones. One participant in the Columbia University uprising in 1968 welcomed the "bad vibrations" his long hair brought: "I say great. I want the cops to sneer and the old ladies swear and the businessmen worry. I want everyone to see me and say: 'There goes an enemy of the state,' because that's where I'm at, as we say in the Revolution game."[37]

To the extent that the New Left was connected with more elaborate countercultural themes, it went the way of the counterculture. Even if most did not sell out in the way Jerry Rubin did (going to Wall Street in the 1970s), for thousands there was a scaling down of dress, decorum, and drugs in the ensuing years. This should not be confused with any sort of move to the Right, for despite what some popular retrospectives on the sixties have claimed, like the movie *The Big Chill*, there is good scholarly evidence that the political sympathies of radical activists have remained steady over the decades, whatever the length of their hair.[38]

Nevertheless, as an organized political force the New Left was dead by the mid-1970s. But the New Left's strategic disruption of decorum did not completely fade away. If random bombings stopped, there are still echoes of the New Left's politics of incivility in the verbal assaults on fur wearers in the late 1980s.[39] And more than one commentator has noted that the shock tactics of the late 1980s conservative student newspapers on American campuses aped the tone of the 1960s New Left. In a civil society that relies on the mass media to define public life, one of the best ways to bring attention to your point of view is by strategic acts of incivility.

Informality

The debate in the late sixties was clouded by the polarization of the times. Hippies and violent political radicals were tailor-made for the mass media. But despite the preoccupation with the more extravagant behavior, the nation's manners were changing in more subtle ways. There was a large move toward the informalization of American society.

Informalization is a term invented by sociologists to describe periodic efforts to relax formal etiquette. These periods of informality are then followed by a more conservative "etiquette-prone" reaction.[40] While Americans in the sixties pressed toward more informal social relations, the phenomenon was by no means unique to that period. A significant relaxation of manners took place in Jacksonian America, tied to both egalitarian sentiment and the desire for authenticity.[41] Still another important stage was the 1920s. And as Barbara Ehrenreich has pointed out, sexual mores were becoming less rigid inside mainstream society in the 1950s, a prelude for the next decade.[42]

The counterculture of the mid-1960s was only picking up on debates already under way in mainstream America. Disputes about long hair surfaced not in 1966 with the counterculture but in 1963 when the Beatles first became known in the United States. The *New York Times* first reported on the issue in December 1964, four months after the Beatles began their first full-length tour in the United States. In those early years, the debate over long hair had a very different feel than it would beginning in 1966. The discussion was *not* about basic rottenness of a civilization. Rather, for the boys involved, it was about fun and girls. The look, as it evolved in the United States, was a surfer look. The "mop top," as it was called, was simply a bang swooped over the forehead. The sides were closely and neatly cropped. It was moderate hair by 1966 standards (and by 1994 standards).

Between 1963 and 1965, however, it was controversial. Adults who disliked the bangs claimed they blurred gender lines. Boys looked like girls, something both disquieting and disgusting. Nevertheless, the conservatives on this issue were like the "long hair" kids in not talking about the mop top as a frontal assault on civilization but in the more restricted terms of a threatening relaxation of order.[43] It was only in 1966 that certain forms of male hair became associated with a wholesale attack on what was known as "the American way of life."[44]

Something similar can be said about sexual mores. The urge to liberalize "official" sexual codes was certainly a prominent theme of the counterculture, but it was also a theme of Hugh Heffner's *Playboy*, first published in 1953. And a female variant, Helen Gurley Brown's *Sex and the Single Girl*, was a huge best-seller as early as 1962. By the mid-1960s there were a host of middle-class advocates for a more liberal sexuality, a trend culminating in the early 1970s in books like Alex Comfort's *The Joy of Sex*. The counterculture contributed, but it was neither the beginning nor the end of the change.

The same was true of obscenity. While counterculturalists by 1965 were fighting over "dirty words" at Berkeley, there was a corresponding effort in the mainstream to relax norms. Liberal judges had softened obscenity laws in the 1950s and 1960s. The pornography industry was growing throughout the sixties, with, to take one example, magazines catering to sadists making their appearance early in the decade.[45] In 1965 authorities filed twice as many pornography complaints as in 1959.[46] By the early 1970s, X-rated movie theaters were dotting every city and many towns across the nation. And in 1970 the President's Commission on Obscenity and Pornography "reported" that there was no empirical evidence that exposure to pornography played a significant role in crime, violence, rape, or antisocial behavior of any kind.

In countless ways you could see the mainstream's mores changing. In 1969, for the first time in history, a major dictionary of the English language included the words *fuck* and *cunt*.[47] In August 1971 *Penthouse* magazine first contained pictures of female genitalia. *Playboy* followed five months later.[48] The *New York Times* reported in the fall of 1967 that even doctors and stockbrokers, "traditional squares" the paper called them, were starting to let their hair grow longer.[49] The miniskirt, which first appeared in the mid-1960s, was by no means only worn by girls and women hopelessly alienated from the culture. For its creator, the mini was explicitly tied to sexual liberation.[50] "The old taboos are dead or dying," *Newsweek* reported in 1967. "A new and more permissive society is taking shape."[51]

In the portrayal of violence, as well, mainstream culture was breaking civil taboos. *Night of the Living Dead* (1968) is considered to be a historic turning point in the history of horror films. Its graphic portrayals of splattered brains, dismemberment, cannibalism, and matricide set the stage for later films like *The Texas Chainsaw Massacre* and the *Halloween* series.[52] In 1972 a new type of romance novel, sometimes known in the trade as "sweet savagery," introduced rape to the genre. The first of these novels, Kathleen Woodiwiss's eight-hundred-page *The Flame and the Flower*, sold two and a half million copies by 1978.[53]

The changes touched all sorts of mainstream venues. To trace *Cosmopolitan* magazine between 1964 and 1970 is to chart one variation of the move. In 1964 it ran rather staid articles such as "Catholics and Birth Control" and "Young Americans Facing Life with Dignity and Purpose." By 1969, however, *Cosmo* was reporting on "The Ostentatious Orgasm" and "Pleasures of a Temporary Affair." A piece lauding "hippie capitalists" noted how "loose" and "free form" the new entrepreneur was, not tied to confining restraints of Wall Street. "Nobody, *but nobody*," it observed, "calls the boss by anything except his first name."[54] In 1972 *The Cosmo Girl's Guide to the New Etiquette* was published to provide help for the contemporary world. There was advice about language ("But unless you have been wearing blinders and earmuffs for the last ten years, there is not likely a four-letter expletive a nice girl has never heard or even used."), about "women's lib" ("Coexisting with our militant sisters takes intelligence and tact."), and about household help (Don't be like your mother in the 1950s. Being your maid's "friend" will "probably get you lots farther . . . than being her icky, finicky, stuck-up employer.")[55]

Parallel changes might be found in other magazines with no commitment to the counterculture, as *Esquire*, with its growing respect for sideburns, or *Ebony*, with its increasing tolerance for moderate Afros. This widespread informalization at the center was often missed during the sixties. It lacked the flair of the counterculture or the drama of the Left.

By the early 1970s, however, the changes were becoming apparent. A spate of articles appeared with titles like "Buzz Off, Mrs. Post, It's Time for the New Etiquette" and "Good Manners for Liberated Persons." The old forms were out of date, one writer noted, but that just raised new questions: "The trouble is that the first principle of the way we live now is nonintervention, also known as letting people do their own thing." This *Saturday Review* article included advice about unmarried cohabitation, breast-feeding in public, dress ("Virtually no one tells his guests how to be clad anymore."), even about drugs ("It is the responsibility of the host to provide a roach clip.").[56] Even Amy Vanderbilt tried to update her *Etiquette* to accommodate the changes, although that did not stop partisans of the new from vigorously noting how hopelessly outdated she continued to be.[57]

For writers like Doris Grumbach and Lois Gould, a main point of attack was the older male/female etiquette. If there was one place where the new principle of "nonintervention" was set to the side, it was here. Calling grown women "girls," having men invariably take the lead in dancing, and presuming that men asked women out on dates were mentioned as suspect behavior. These authors introduced to mainstream audiences feminist arguments about the part that male "chivalry" played in female subordination. "If there is to be a new etiquette," Lois Gould wrote in the *New York Times Magazine*, "it ought to be based on honest mutual respect, and responsiveness to each other's real needs."[58]

The two moves—toward informality and toward egalitarian male/female etiquette—indicate the complicated cross-currents of reform. For the informality was rooted in a critique of the "inauthenticity" of the old manners, while complaints about chivalry were connected with the ways that decorum upheld patterns of inequality. To oversimplify, the former was a part of the romantic critique and loosely associated with the same push of the counterculture. The latter was a democratic critique with more in common with the civil protests of black Americans during the decade.

Legalizing an Incivil Society

This shift at the center of American culture did not take place without opposition. There were plaints for the older norms.[59] Nor did the changes take place independent of the law. In fact, they were sanctioned and encouraged through new attitudes toward decorum promulgated by the federal courts, principally the U.S. Supreme Court. A number of decisions, most coming between 1966 and 1973, changed the relationship of the "civilizing process" to the rule of law. This was the legal version of informalization.[60]

In a number of instances, the Court refused to use arguments of bad taste or decorum to uphold a law. In one celebrated case, a young man opposed to the Vietnam War had been arrested in the corridor of the Los Angeles County Courthouse for wearing a jacket with the words "Fuck the Draft" prominently inscribed on it. The Court overturned the conviction, noting that there was no sign of imminent violence at the courthouse and that while the phrase was crude and vulgar to many, the open debate the First Amendment guaranteed necessitated its protection. In a far-reaching departure from earlier decisions, the Court also raised doubts about the possibility of any evaluation of taste: "For, while the particular four-letter word being litigated here is perhaps more distasteful than others of its genre, it is nevertheless true that one man's vulgarity is another's lyric." Since government officials "cannot make principled decisions in this area," it was important to leave "matters of taste and style largely to the individual."[61]

This was a far cry from *Chaplinsky v. New Hampshire* (1942), in which the Court simply asserted that some utterances were of "such slight social value" that the First Amendment did not protect them. In the Chaplinsky case, the defendant was convicted for calling someone a "damned racketeer" and a "damned Fascist." In the next few years, the Court would protect the use of "motherfucker" in public debate. In *Chaplinsky*, the Court also upheld a local ordinance that rather explicitly outlawed incivil behavior: "No person shall address any offensive, derisive, or annoying word to any other person who is lawfully in any street or other public place nor call him by any offensive or dismissive name." In the early 1970s the Court struck down similar ordinances as too broad.[62]

The Supreme Court also addressed differing conceptions of the place of civility in relation to violence. In *Gooding v. Wilson* (1972), it took up an ordinance that made any "opprobrious words or abusive language" a possible misdemeanor. An appellate court had made the case for the older standard: "The term 'breach of peace' is generic, and includes all violations of the public peace or order, or decorum." The Supreme Court, however, rejected this defense of civil society, which made it a crime to "merely speak words offensive to some who hear them, and so sweeps too broadly."[63]

What the Court was doing in these cases was to open up "civil society" to incivil behavior. It was explicitly granting certain "offensive" behavior constitutional protection. In *Gooding*, a protester scuffling with police was arrested for yelling "White son of a bitch, I'll kill you" and "You son of a bitch, I'll choke you to death." In the next couple of years, a number of similar cases came to the Court's attention. In one, a man was arrested at a school board meeting of 150 people (about 40 children) for calling teachers, the school board, and others "motherfuckers." The Court overturned the conviction. In still another decision, a state university student code mandating "generally accepted standards of conduct" and prohibiting "indecent conduct or speech" was struck down. Here, too, decorum was the issue. A graduate student at the university had been expelled for publishing and distributing a paper with a cartoon of a policeman raping the Statue of Liberty and an article entitled "Mother Fucker Acquitted." (This was in reference to the acquittal of a member of a radical student group that called itself "The Motherfuckers.") The Court declared the student code unconstitutional, arguing that a state university had no right to shut off the flow of ideas merely "in the name of the conventions of decency," "no matter how offensive to good taste."[64]

If the Court moved to open up public space to certain sorts of incivil behavior, there were limits. At no time did it accept the legitimacy of violence. The Supreme Court held fast to the notion that the state had a monopoly on the legitimate use of force. What the Court was doing was rewriting the line between behavior and violence, allowing far more space for aggressive words. Earlier laws had defended civil demeanor precisely because "incivil" behavior was thought to *lead* to discord. Now there was to be a toleration of more insulting behavior although it still had to stop short of violence.

At the same time that this whole string of cases opened up room for more "incivil" action in public, there was a parallel set of cases arguing that decorum had to be maintained. These cases all had to do with the functioning of institutions. In courts, schools, even the workplace, the Court upheld the need for civil decorum and left authorities broad discretion in setting standards.

One case, which had to do with a defendant whose "vile and abusive language" disrupted his criminal trial, prompted the Court to argue that "dignity, order, and decorum" must be "the hallmarks of all court proceedings." The "flagrant disregard of elementary standards of proper conduct . . . cannot be tolerated."[65]

In cases like this, the Court explicitly called attention to the decorum of the protest. As it said in *Grayned v. Rockford* (1971), a case on picketing outside a school: "The crucial question is whether the manner of expression is basically incompatible with the normal activity of a particular place at a particular time."[66]

When protest inside an institution was upheld, it was because it was not disruptive. No doubt the most important case of this kind was *Tinker v. Des Moines*, decided in 1969. A handful of students were suspended from a Des Moines high school in 1965 for wearing black arm bands to protest the escalation of the Vietnam War. Prior to this, the school board had voted to forbid the activity. The Court four years later vindicated the students, but precisely because of the civility of their action. The Court noted how the case did not relate "to regulation of the length of skirts or the type of clothing, to hair style or deportment." Nor did it concern "aggressive, disruptive action." There was no evidence "that any of the armbands 'disrupted' the school." The Court, however, added that activity that *did* disrupt a school was *not* protected by the First Amendment.[67]

Debate over institutional decorum also extended to discussion of hair and clothing. In 1975 the Court took up the case of a policeman who had broken the department's dress code by wearing his hair modestly over the collar. While he argued that the code infringed upon his civil rights, the Court's majority disagreed, arguing that the department's need for "discipline, esprit de corps, and uniformity" was sufficient reason for a dress code. Only Justice William O. Douglas dissented, asserting that the policeman should have the right to wear his hair "according to his own taste."[68]

The courts also debated the dress and hair codes of the public schools. Beginning in the late sixties, a number of lawsuits were introduced pitting the dress code of schools against the individual freedom of students and teachers. Although the Supreme Court was reticent to get involved in such cases, preferring to leave them to local authorities, it did say in 1971 that it had no objection to such codes.[69] Lower courts around the country handled a number of these cases. They were split on whether a boy's hair length could be regulated or whether miniskirts and slacks could be forbidden for girls. Blue jeans were also a source of contention. And while the lower courts generally allowed teachers to grow beards, dress codes for employees were routinely upheld. Although these decisions were not uniform, they generally indicate some distance from the old decorum in favor of commitment to the new informality. At the same time, however, state courts almost universally upheld the right of a school board to set some sort of code. For example, even if a court allowed long hair, it often noted that cleanliness could be required. Some institutional authority was sanctioned.[70]

All regimes wind up taking a stand on where decorum can be broken and where it has to be enforced. It is only where there is an abstract commitment to universal equal rights that decorum becomes legally problematic. But, to again repeat, there are different ways that such regimes can handle the issue. In the late 1960s there was a shift in American practice and law. The Supreme Court opened up all sorts of behavior in private life and in public. The Court would do nothing about people yelling "motherfucker" at school board meetings or in street protests. It declared unconstitutionally broad ordinances that outlawed incivil behavior because it "tended" to lead to a breach of the peace. It does not seem inaccurate to suggest that the Court was giving certain leeway to an "incivil society." At the same time, however, the Court also carefully maintained the authority of institutions. The running of a school, a courtroom, or a workplace (for example, a police department) all demanded decorum. Here civil behavior, as defined by authorities, could be enforced by law.

Earlier thought had stressed the continuity between everyday life, public drama, and the avoidance of violence. To keep violence from erupting, the first two had to remain "polite." The new thinking cut that relationship. If one thinks about civil behavior as "affect control," the hiding of emotions, some of these new norms were not civil. The courts might then be interpreted as trying to impose a new level of tolerance by *demanding* that citizens respond to abusive language with restraint. But if one understands the courts as partaking in changes already under way in society at large, then its defense of "Fuck the Draft" or "motherfucker" meant something different. Such words were no longer expected to provoke a violent response, and the Supreme Court was only writing into law the higher state of emotional control in the populace at large.

It should be remembered that the courts only allowed incivil behavior in special settings—in "civil" society.[71] At the same time that they were legalizing certain public incivilities in the name of democratic debate, they were also firmly reinforcing the authority of institutions to maintain order. In schools, courtrooms, and the workplace, some decorum could be imposed.[72] Taken together, the informalization in civic forums and the reaffirmation of institutional authority indicated a strategic response by the Supreme Court to late sixties cultural and social pressures. The two streams of thought on decorum were complementary, defining how the state would give ground to informalizing forces and still shore up the authority of institutions.

The decisions of the Court bear resemblance to the image of social order suggested by Immanuel Kant in his essay, "What Is Enlightenment?" Kant had argued that enlightenment required public freedom so that discussion could take place. On the other hand, he claimed that in our "private" capacities, by which *he* meant basically positions in the civil service (including Protestant ministers, state bureaucrats, and university professors), there was a stronger need for institutional order. In such settings the vigorous use of reason "may often be very narrowly restricted."[73] This is, of course, not to say that Kant would have endorsed the Supreme Court decisions of the late sixties, only that they can be seen as part of one tradition of liberal thought.

By the early 1970s this position had become liberal dogma. John Rawls, in his 1971 neo-Kantian treatise, *A Theory of Justice*, made distinctions very similar to those that contemporary courts were working out. In a just society, Rawls argued, the intolerant must be tolerated. Repression was justifiable only when someone's personal security was threatened or when "the institutions of liberty are in danger."[74] Just as the courts were doing at the very same time, Rawls drew the relevant lines at the point of imminent violence and at the disruption of functioning institutions. Within this frame of reference, the felt need for robust civic discussion would trump any discomfort about the lack of civil etiquette or occasional expressions of irrational bigotry. As the liberal historian C. Vann Woodward put it in 1975, "freedom of expression is a paramount value, more important than civility or rationality."[75]

By 1990 this would be a controversial position within Left and liberal circles. In the late 1980s the notion of "offensiveness" reentered progressive political thought, at this point connected with arguments about the debilitating effect of rude insults and slurs on historically subjugated peoples. Speech codes adopted by a few campuses explicitly used "offensiveness" as a criterion to forbid some forms of expression. Some law professors indicated qualified respect for *Chaplinsky v. New Hampshire*. For them, it was no longer a matter of principle that the intolerant must be tolerated. The other side on this debate continued to argue that the concern for verbal niceties undermined free speech.[76] In 1989 and 1991, cases reviewing campus codes outlawing offensive speech reached the federal courts. In both, the codes were declared unconstitutional.[77] By the early 1990s, these debates not only divided progressives from conservatives but also split the Left-liberal community itself into those defending the "1970 position" and those adhering to arguments developed in the late 1980s.[78] To some, at least, C. Vann Woodward's attitudes about free speech no longer sounded particularly progressive.[79]

Institutional decorum coupled with a relatively unregulated civic forum is one historic way liberal politics has handled the issue of order and freedom. This was the path chosen by U.S. courts in the late 1960s, a legal version of the informalization going on in American society at large. While this perspective was no longer universally accepted on the left of the American spectrum by the early 1990s (perhaps *because* it was no longer universally accepted on the Left), it gained credence at the center and the right. And for the time being, at least, it has remained the law of the land.

NOTES

1. *Chaplinsky v. New Hampshire*, 315 U.S. 568 (1942).

2. Mark C. Rutzick, "Offensive Language and the Evolution of First Amendment Protection," *Harvard Civil Rights–Civil Liberties Law Review* 9 (January 1974): 1–28; Kristen Carol Nelson, "Offensive Speech and the First Amendment," *Boston University Law Review* 53 (July 1973): 834–57.

3. For an insightful discussion about the need to understand the importance of rage and powerful emotions and not to be content with analyzing ritual, see Renalto Rosaldo, *Culture and Truth: The Remaking of Social Analysis* (Boston: Beacon Press, 1989), 1–21.

4. David J. Garrow, *Bearing the Cross: Martin Luther King, Jr., and the Southern Christian Leadership Conference* (New York: William Morrow, 1986), 32, 75. On King's after-the-fact interpretation of Montgomery, see Martin Luther King, Jr., *Stride Toward Freedom: The Montgomery Story* (New York: Harper and Row, 1958); on the SNCC statement of purpose, see Doug

McAdam, *Freedom Summer* (New York: Oxford University Press, 1988), 30.

5. CORE's "Rules for Action" can be found in Inge Powell Bell, *CORE and the Strategy of Nonviolence* (New York: Random House, 1968), 195–96; King, *Stride Toward Freedom*, 63.

6. Miles Wolff, *Lunch at the Five and Ten: The Greensboro Sit-Ins* (New York: Stein and Day, 1970), 11, 31–32; Howard Zinn, *SNCC: The New Abolitionists* (Boston: Beacon Press, 1965), 19–20.

7. Quoted from August Meier and Elliott Rudwick, *CORE: A Study in the Civil Rights Movement, 1942–1968* (New York: Oxford University Press, 1973), 201.

8. David Goldfield, *Black, White, and Southern: Race Relations and Southern Culture, 1940 to the Present* (Baton Rouge: Louisiana State University Press, 1990), 2–6. See also Bertram Wilbur Doyle, *The Etiquette of Race Relations in the South: A Study of Social Control* (Chicago: University of Chicago Press, 1937).

9. Norbert Elias, *The Civilizing Process: The History of Manners* (New York: Urizen Books, 1978), xv–xvi, 191–217, and "Civilization and Violence: On the State Monopoly of Physical Violence and Its Infringements," *Telos* 54 (Winter 1982–83): 134–54.

10. Sociologist Robert Park well understood the dual function of etiquette noted here and how it supported the southern caste system. See Park, "The Bases of Race Prejudice," *Annals of the American Academy of Political and Social Science* 140 (November 1928): 18–19.

11. *Nashville Banner* quoted from Zinn, *SNCC*, 22. On the *Greensboro Daily News*, see William Chafe, *Civilities and Civil Rights: Greensboro, North Carolina, and the Black Struggle for Freedom* (New York: Oxford University Press, 1980), 137.

12. King, *Why We Can't Wait* (New York: Harper and Row, 1963), 27; McAdam, *Freedom Summer*, 186. On Albany, see Garrow, *Bearing the Cross*, 218–19, and Goldfield, *Black, White, and Southern*, 130–32.

13. In 1960 one white Greensboro merchant reacted to the sit-ins by asking whether the town wanted to sit next to "a well-behaved, nicely mannered, cleanly dressed quiet Negro student" or by "a filthy, dirty, . . . disheveled duck tailed, loud mouthed white rowdy" whose "white skin looked as if it hadn't been washed since Christmas." Wolff, *Lunch at the Five and Ten*, 79. Similarly, after Selma police brutally attacked peaceful marchers in 1965, Lyndon Johnson reacted by noting how orderly the protesters had been and how brutal the testers had been and how brutal the

police were. He called for the passing of the Voting Rights Act. *Public Papers of the Presidents of the United States: Lyndon B. Johnson, 1965* (Washington, D.C.: GPO, 1966), 277.

14. Among the demands of the Montgomery bus boycott, for example, was "a guarantee of courteous treatment" for blacks. As King put it, "this is the least that any business can grant to its patrons." See King, *Stride Toward Freedom*, 109–10. Another particularly good example is *Hamilton v. Alabama*, 376 U.S. 650 (1963). Mary Hamilton was a CORE volunteer. When testifying in an Alabama court, she would not answer questions after the lawyer interrogating her refused to call her "Miss Hamilton" and insisted on calling her "Mary." The lawyer was adhering to established southern decorum, where whites called even adult African Americans by their first name. Hamilton insisted on the same sort of civility due to whites. The U.S. Supreme Court sided with Hamilton. For a statement of the facts of the case, see *Ex parte Mary Hamilton*, 156 So.2d 926 (1963). For the best general discussion of this aspect of the civil rights movement, see Goldfield, *Black, White, and Southern*.

15. See, for example, James Farmer, *Freedom—When?* (New York: Random House, 1965).

16. See Goldfield, *Black, White, and Southern*, 207, 272.

17. McAdam, *Freedom Summer*, 137–45 (quotation, p. 143).

18. Max Heirich, *The Beginning: Berkeley, 1964* (New York: Columbia University Press, 1970), 256–70; Hal Draper, *Berkeley: The New Student*

Revolt (New York: Grove Press, 1965), 140–46.

19. For a thoughtful statement bringing some sixties themes back to Rousseau, see Marshall Berman, *The Politics of Authenticity: Radical Individualism and the Emergence of Modern Society* (New York: Atheneum, 1970).

20. See Abe Peck, *Uncovering the Sixties: The Life and Times of the Underground Press* (New York: Pantheon, 1985), and Robert Glessing, *The Underground Press in America* (Bloomington: Indiana University Press, 1970).

21. Elias, *The Civilizing Process*, 140–43, 187–91, 201–2.

22. Gerome Ragni and James Rado, *Hair: The American Tribal Love-Rock Musical* (New York: Pocket Books, 1969), 64.

23. Henry Gross, *Flower People* (New York: Ballantine Books, 1968), 57, 61–62.

24. "Inside the Hippie Revolution," *Look*, 22 August 1967, 64 (1st quotation); Burton H. Wolfe, *The Hippies* (New York: Signet, 1968), 26 (2d quotation).

25. Charles A. Reich, *The Greening of America* (New York: Random House, 1970), 225.

26. R. D. Laing, *The Politics of Experience* (New York: Pantheon Books, 1967).

27. "An Opinion: On the Hippie Put-on," *Mademoiselle*, September 1967, 44.

28. "Hippies and Their Future—A Look Ahead," *U.S. News & World Report*, 17 July 1967, 58–59.

29. Ragni and Rado, *Hair*, 2–3.

30. Gross, *Flower People*, 52.

31. Ibid., 125–26.

32. On Fanon, see Allen Matusow, *The Unraveling of America: A History of Liberalism in the 1960s* (New York: Harper Torchbacks, 1986), 357–58.

33. Quoted from Fred Halstead, *Out Now: A Participant's Account of the American Movement against the Vietnam War* (New York: Monad Press, 1978), 316.

34. Howard Moody, "Toward a New Definition of Obscenity," *Christianity and Crisis*, 25 January 1965, 286–87.

35. Quoted from Peck, *Uncovering the Sixties*, 62.

36. Ibid., 63.

37. James Kunen, *The Strawberry Statement: Notes of a College Revolutionary* (New York: Random House, 1969), 72.

38. On this point, see McAdam, *Freedom Summer*.

39. "The Stink about Mink," *USA Weekend*, 9–11 February 1990, 4–6.

40. The new informality should not be seen as a simple retreat from the emotional control of before. Relaxation of social forms becomes possible, sociologist Cas Wouters has argued, only because there is now "a higher level of self control." According to this argument, reliance on social hierarchy built into established social forms diminishes as people become capable of managing their own emotions. See Wouters, "Formalization and Informalization: Changing Tension Balances in Civilizing Processes," *Theory, Culture, & Society* 3 (1986): 1–18; Wouters, "Informalisation and the Civilizing Process," in *Human Figurations: Essays for Norbert Elias*, edited by Peter R. Gleichmann, Johan

Goudsblom, and Hermann Korte (Amsterdams Sociologisch Tijdschrift, 1977), 437–53; and Wouters, "On Status Competition and Emotion Management," unpublished paper in the author's possession.

41. On egalitarian sentiment, see Kenneth Cmiel, *Democratic Eloquence: The Fight over Popular Language in Nineteenth-Century America* (New York: Morrow, 1990), 55–93; on the drive for authenticity, see Karen Halttunen, *Confidence Men and Painted Women: A Study of Middle-Class Culture in America, 1830–1870* (New Haven: Yale University Press, 1982).

42. Barbara Ehrenreich, *The Hearts of Men: American Dreams and the Flight from Commitment* (Garden City, N.Y.: Anchor Press, 1983).

43. See the string of articles on a boy with a mop top who was excluded from a Connecticut school. *New York Times*, 16–17, 22–23 December 1964. As late as the fall of 1964, the *Times* considered long hair a strictly British phenomenon. See Anthony Carthew, "Shaggy Englishman Story," *New York Times Sunday Magazine*, 6 September 1964. But by the fall of 1965, long hair on boys was an issue at schools across the nation. See *New York Times*, 13 September 1965. The photographs in this article show hair already somewhat "shaggier" than the Connecticut case the year before. Still, it would be quite moderate by 1968. For other discussions of this first wave of long hair, see "Big Sprout-out of Male Mop Top," *Life*, 30 July 1965, 56–58; "The Short & Long of It," *Time*, 1 October 1965, 54.

44. In reading through the *New York Times*, for example, I find nothing before the fall of 1966 that associates long hair on boys with a wholesale attack on civilization. That contention surfaces in the paper for the first time on 22 September 1966, when it reports J. Edgar Hoover arguing that current hair and dress trends were destroying the family. By the next year, however, such claims were common. For example, in the play *Hair* (written and first produced in 1967), long hair is associated with a culture completely alienated from mainstream America.

45. "End of the Boom in Smut," *U.S. News & World Report*, 4 April 1966, 69.

46. Ibid.

47. *The American Heritage Dictionary of the English Language* (Boston: American Heritage, 1969).

48. Edward de Grazia, *Girls Lean Back Everywhere: The Law of Obscenity and the Assault on Genius* (New York: Random House, 1992), 578–79.

49. *New York Times*, 22 September 1967.

50. See John D'Emilio and Estelle B. Freedman, *Intimate Matters: A History of Sexuality in America* (New York: Harper and Row, 1988), 306.

51. *Newsweek*, 13 November 1967, 74.

52. Kim Newman, *Nightmare Movies: A Critical History of the Horror Movie from 1968* (London: Bloomsbury, 1988), 1–11; Gregory A. Waller, Introduction to *American Horrors: Essays on the Modern American Horror Film*, edited by Waller (Urbana: University of Illinois Press, 1987), 2.

53. Beatrice Faust, *Sex and Pornography* (New York: Macmillan, 1980), 146, 149. For a study of how women actually read these scenes, see Janice Radway, *Reading the Romance: Women, Patriarchy, and Popular Literature* (Chapel Hill: University of North Carolina Press, 1984), 71–77, 141–44.

54. "The Turned-on, Tuned-in World of Hippie Capitalists," *Cosmopolitan*, May 1970, 155.

55. *The Cosmo Girl's Guide to the New Etiquette* (New York: Cosmopolitan Books, 1971), 1, 42, 215, 154.

56. R. Sokolov, "Buzz Off Mrs. Post, It's Time for the New Etiquette," *Saturday Review*, 16 December 1972, 33–41; Lois Gould, "Good Manners for Liberated Persons," *New York Times Magazine*, 16 December 1973.

57. *Amy Vanderbilt's Etiquette* (Garden City, N.Y.: Doubleday, 1972), vii. For criticism, see Doris Grumbach, "Black Boots for Fox Hunts," *New Republic*, 29 April 1972, 25–26, and "Amy Vanderbilt's Everyday Etiquette," *New Republic*, 25 May 1974, 30–31.

58. Lois Gould, "Good Manners for Liberated Persons," 67–69, 71 (quotation, p. 68). See also Grumbach, "Black Boots for Fox Hunts," 25–26, and Sokolov, "Buzz Off Mrs. Post," 41.

59. Norman Vincent Peale, "Manners Make a Difference," *Readers' Digest*, March 1974, 99–100. For a more ambiguous statement, see Eleanor Clift, "Is Chivalry Dead?," *McCall's*, June 1974, 35.

60. Norbert Elias has argued that the civilizing process was connected to the creation of the Western nation state. See Norbert Elias, *Power & Civility: The Civilizing Process, Volume II* (New York: Pantheon, 1982). In this section, I want to show how the state is involved in the informalization process as well and point out some of the specific ways that the state both accepted and contained the informality.

61. *Cohen v. California*, 403 U.S. 15, 25 (1971).

62. *Chaplinsky v. New Hampshire*, 572; *Gooding v. Wilson*, 405 U.S. 518 (1972).

63. *Gooding v. Wilson*, 519, 527. The Court insisted that it still upheld *Chaplinsky* (p. 523) as it continued to claim that "fighting words" were unprotected speech. This ignored how far *Gooding* departed from the older decision.

64. *Rosenfeld v. New Jersey*, 408 U.S. 901 (1972) (for a full report of the facts, see 283 A.2d 535); *Papish v. Board of Curators*, 410 U.S. 667, 668 (1973). See also *Lewis v. City of New Orleans*, 408 U.S. 913 (1972).

65. *Illinois v. Allen*, 397 U.S. 337, 341, 343 (1970).

66. *Grayned v. Rockford*, 408 U.S. 104, 116 (1971). See also *Cameron v. Johnson*, 390 U.S. 611 (1968).

67. *Tinker v. Des Moines*, 393 U.S. 503, 508, 513 (1969).

68. *Kelley v. Johnson*, 425 U.S. 238, 246, 250 (1975).

69. *Karr v. Schmidt*, 401 U.S. 1201 (1971), but also see Justice Douglas's dissent on this issue in *Ferrell v. Dallas*, 393 U.S. 856 (1968). Douglas wanted the Court to declare any school-mandated regulation of hair length unconstitutional.

70. For a good review of the law on

school dress and hair codes, see Louis Fischer and David Schimmel, *The Rights of Students and Teachers: Resolving Conflicts in the School Community* (New York: Harper and Row, 1982), 350–88.

71. What the German philospher Jürgen Habermas has referred to as the "public sphere." See Jürgen Habermas, *The Structural Transformation of the Public Sphere: An Inquiry into a Category of Bourgeois Society* (Cambridge: MIT Press, 1989).

72. There is a more theoretical point that I would like to make here. John Murray Cuddihy calls attention to the Supreme Court's support for institutional decorum and suggests that civility precedes civil rights. Cuddihy, *The Ordeal of Civility: Freud, Marx, Levi-Strauss, and the Jewish Struggle with Modernity* (Boston: Beacon Press, 1974), 200. On the other hand, writers like Harvey Mansfield and Walter Berns have noted the Supreme Court's new attitudes toward public informality and connected this to an attack on civil decorum. Harvey C. Mansfield, Jr., "The Forms and Formalities of Liberty," *Public Interest* 70 (Winter 1983): 121–31; Walter Berns, *The First Amendment and the Future of American Democracy* (New York: Basic Books, 1976). I am arguing that both sides are important, and, moreover, that they are part of a single, coherent story. The support for institutional decorum became so important precisely because the law no longer was supporting "civility" as the norm for "civil" society. This, I suggest in the closing paragraphs, follows the image of civil order and freedom presented

by Immanuel Kant in "What Is Enlightenment?"

73. Immanuel Kant, "What is Enlightenment?," in Kant, *Philosophical Writings* (New York: Continuum, 1986), 265.

74. John Rawls, *A Theory of Justice* (Cambridge: Harvard University Press, 1971), 216–21 (quotation, p. 220). I leave aside the knotty problem of how "truly" neo-Kantian *A Theory of Justice* actually was. For here, it is enough to say that Rawls himself in 1971 presented his theory as neo-Kantian (p. 251) and to note the similarity in outlook between his own position and that in "What is Enlightenment?" For Rawls and the Kantian notion of "publicity," see pp. 133, 251–52. For a perceptive article placing Rawls's book in the stream of American political and intellectual history, see Fred Siegel, "Is Archie Bunker Fit to Rule? Or, How Immanuel Kant Became One of the Founding Fathers," *Telos* 69 (Fall 1986): 9–29.

75. Woodward quoted from *Doe v. The University of Michigan*, 721 F.Supp. 852 (E.D. Mich. 1989), 868.

76. The discussion of the campus speech codes has seemed endless in the past couple of years. For a good summary of this debate, see Warren George Sandmann, Jr., "Freedom of Expression and/or Freedom from Racial and Sexual Harassment: College Campuses and 'Hate-Speech' Codes" (Ph.D. dissertation, University of Iowa, May 1992).

Through the 1970s, left-leaning law review articles continued to support the position staked out in the late 1960s. The seminal law review article shifting that debate was Richard Delgado, "Words That Wound: A Tort Action for Racial Insults, Epithets, and Name Calling," *Harvard Civil Rights–Civil Liberties Law Review* 17 (1982): 133–52. This article had little impact until the increase in hate speech incidents on college campuses. Depending on which authority you cite, this upsurge dates from either 1986 or 1987. See Sandmann, "Freedom of Expression," 6–7. In 1989 Mari Matsuda picked up on Delgado's essay in an article that has had a major impact. Unlike Delgado, who called for civil penalties for racist speech, Matsuda advocated criminal sanctions. See Matsuda, "Public Response to Racist Speech: Considering the Victim's Story," *Michigan Law Review* 87 (August 1989): 2320–81. Since this article, there has been a whole literature on the subject.

Matsuda claimed that *Chaplinsky* was still law. Progressives around 1970, on the other hand, were saying that *Chaplinsky* was effectively dead. Still, Matsuda's focus was not on avoiding offensiveness per se, à la *Chaplinsky*, but on outlawing offensive racist speech directed at historically persecuted minorities. In fact, Matsuda argued, epithets directed against whites might be protected because the "dominant group member" would be "more likely to have access to a safe harbor. . . . Retreat and affirmation are more easily attained for historically non-subjugated group members." Matsuda, "Public Response," 2361. For the closest thing to a call for a revival of *Chaplinsky* and the notion that civilities must precede civil rights, see Judith Martin and Gunther Stent, "Say the Right Thing—or Else," *New York Times*, 30 March 1991.

77. *Doe v. University of Michigan*, 721 F.Supp. 852 (E.D. Mich. 1989); *The UMW Post et al. v. Board of Regents of the University of Wisconsin System*, case no. 90-C-328, U.S. District Court for the Eastern District of Wisconsin, LEXIS 14527.

78. For a summary of this debate from a law professor with a sense of history (and who is more sympathetic to the libertarian position), see J. M. Balkin, "Some Realism about Realism: Legal Realist Approaches to the First Amendment," *Duke Law Journal* (June 1990): 375–430.

79. See C. Vann Woodward, "Freedom and the Universities," *New York Review of Books*, 18 July 1991, 32–37; "Illiberal Education: An Exchange," *New York Review of Books*, 26 September 1991), 74–76.

DAVID FARBER*

The Silent Majority and
Talk about Revolution

Slicing, fulminating, crashing through the sixties is the demotic figure of Richard Milhous Nixon. Nixon, as biography after biography reveals, lends himself to a kind of mythopoetic dirge, a haunting melody of midcentury America at war with itself.

The Nixon dirge, verse II—"The Sixties"—goes something like this: Richard Nixon's presidential defeat in 1960 announces the end of the 1950s. Dreams of Camelot and men on the moon replace the modest contentment earned through a tract home of one's own; Jackie Kennedy's leopard-skin glamour overwhelms Pat Nixon's good cloth coat.

Nixon returns to southern California, his base. He runs for governor in

*This essay was made possible by an American Council of Learned Societies fellowship. For comments on drafts of the chapter, I owe special thanks to Stuart Little, Ken Bindas, Mary Sheila McMahon, David Cohen, and Beth Bailey.

1962 and tries to red-bait his Democratic opponent. But the 1950s are over, and the campaign crashes and burns. After his defeat Nixon goes to New York and, like a late entry to a 1950s best-seller, middle-aged but with the energy of a twenty-five-year-old associate, proves he can climb the corporate law ladder with the best of them, wowing Wall Street and the Supreme Court with his legal acumen.

But Nixon knows that it is politics, not the law, that he loves, and he goes back into the arena: he joins the million-mile club, speaking in front of every group of Republicans for every Republican candidate, embracing Barry Goldwater, courting county chairmen, counting courthouse politicians. Nixon does not give up. He takes the 1968 Republican nomination, and the nation, no more in love with him than before, waits for the quieter, whiter, older times he has promised them. The last traces of Camelot fade to black and the age of, let us say, the Camaro, begins.

Between Nixon's electoral defeat and Nixon's talismanic victory his national popularity remains almost constant; in an irony that does not escape him, Nixon's percentage of the vote was higher in his 1960 defeat than in his 1968 victory. In the 1972 presidential election, finally, he gains an electoral mandate, receiving the third largest percentage of votes in American history. But Nixon is pulled down, his great victory turned into humiliating defeat. Faced with sure impeachment for crimes against the nation, he resigns. The interregnum of despair begins. Nixon's failed bid for the presidency begins the sixties, Nixon's failed presidency ends the sixties era.

Nixon the polarizer, Nixon the invader of Cambodia, Nixon unleashing the dogs of war, Nixon who triangulated American foreign policy, Nixon who blasted busing and ordered affirmative action, Nixon indicted, pardoned, Nixon, as he proudly notes in an endless stream of autobiographies, in the arena . . . buried by his sins and ours. The Nixon dirge has its elemental truths but it avoids the larger story of Nixon's success in refashioning his own and his party's political legitimacy. And the conventional story of Nixon's fall and rise and towering smashup perhaps underplays the significance of the strategy he used.

Richard Nixon understood how a great many Americans felt about themselves and their country. He understood in simple terms something about Americans in the post–World War II era that several French intellectuals would enjoy saying in extremely arcane ways throughout the 1970s and 1980s. He understood how a great many Americans in the postwar era were roughly divided and divided themselves into two separate castes (classes?)—those who speak and those who are silent.

French social critic Jean Baudrillard argues that such a divide is paradigmatic of post–World War II advanced capitalist societies. Old Marxist notions of class identities generated through relationship to the production process, he writes, ignore social reality. Thus power and one's relationship to power in advanced capitalist societies are determined "not so much by the ownership of the means of production but by control of the code."[1] Here, Baudrillard means that people who dominate the cultural processes in which shared social meanings are created and marketed possess the means to shape political legitimacy, exercise authority, and get rich.

To some extent, Baudrillard gives theory to what political economist Richard Reich has called the decline of the "routine production services" and the rise of the globally connected, "symbolic-analytic services" sector in which high wages, high status, and power go to highly skilled "symbolic analysts" ("lawyers, investment bankers . . . academics, public relations executives, real estate developers . . . advertising and marketing specialists, art directors, design engineers, architects, writers and editors, musicians, television and film producers").[2] Neither Reich nor Baudrillard asserts that power is in the hands of a new class per se (such as the "new class" bandied about both by right-wingers and left-wingers for many years now).[3] They do argue that ruling elites have become more and more overtly dependent on the manipulation of laws, regulations, texts, pictures, and other symbols as necessary means to gain and maintain power, authority, and wealth.

American elites' manipulation of Americans' cultural codes is, of course, not a recent turn of events. From democracy's advent, politicians have had a formal obligation to make symbolic and practical sense of Americans' feelings and understandings of who they are, what they wish to be, and what they will and will not allow. By the early twentieth century, business corporations and a few of America's wealthiest men had begun to develop sophisticated efforts to manage their public images and political fortunes. Due to the tremendous expansion of the federal government, due to the massive increase in the reach of mass media, and due to the embracing of market-forged consumer life-styles by most Americans, elites have had to pay increasing attention to maintaining or improving their status by controlling for cultural manipulations.[4]

An incident during World War II indicated this change, at least in the minds of some of the most powerful men in the United States at the time. The story represents a bit of a chronological detour but seems worth the risk in that it so well sets up the crisis in political legitimacy that erupted in the sixties.

The story begins with Nelson Rockefeller. In 1941 young Nelson was not only the immensely wealthy grandson of oil billionaire John D. Rockefeller but also the official State Department wartime overlord of U.S. interests in Latin America. Rockefeller ordered Alfred Sloan, head of America's largest corporation, General Motors (GM), to fire several of his Latin American representatives who had close ties to the Nazi and fascist cause. Sloan was furious. He wrote one of his very few peers, Walter Carpenter, chief executive officer of Du Pont, about his desire to tell Rockefeller off. Carpenter, as chief executive officer, represented Du Pont's controlling stock interest in General Motors and thus had the right and duty to lecture Sloan about his attitude, which, in a gingerly fashion, he did: "If we don't listen to the urgings of the State Department in this connection it seems to me just a question of time when there will be a blast of some form from Washington. The effect of this will be to associate General Motors with Nazi or Fascist propaganda against the interests of the United States in South America with the very potent sounding board in the hands of Washington. . . . The effect on the General Motors Corporation might be a very serious matter and the feeling might last for years." Carpenter, unhappily, noted that simple productive efficiency was no longer the corporate leader's only concern. Public perceptions of his corporation's political and cultural legitimacy *had* to be managed.[5]

Sloan bitterly concurred. "In industry today," he wrote back, "the labor leader determines the economics, the public relations department the policies, and the politicians get whatever is left over. Really there is not much use for anybody else in the picture as far as I can see."[6] Now Sloan was indulging himself in a certain amount of lachrymose self-pity, but recent experience—when GM could not get government support to put a stop to the sit-down strike in 1937—clearly indicated that a new era had begun for America's capitalists.

As both communist-hunting Senator Joseph McCarthy and political master Richard Nixon understood well before poststructuralists said that power is the knowledge of desire, mere status as a "capitalist" does not, under advanced capitalism, at least in America, equal power. Democratic politics are too fluid, the governing apparatus is too flexible, and the market is too fickle.[7] Control of the code—the ability to create shared meanings or, put another way, to give value to things—does equal power. Elizabeth Fones-Wolf, in her fascinating history of the 1950s, "Beneath Consensus," demonstrates that many of America's leading corporations and labor unions had learned this lesson after the New Deal. During the 1950s they undertook major efforts to convince politicians, their customers, their employees, and the wider public of the legitimacy of their enterprise. The bottom line alone, they had come to believe, was not enough. They had to create a public that accepted the legitimacy of their operations.[8]

To some extent, this increased reliance on manipulating and forging shared meanings to create political legitimacy meant that old dogs were learning new tricks. But it also meant that new skills and new techniques, as listed by Reich in the passage quoted above, were evermore in demand and rewarded. The same skills and techniques, not incidently, that were so useful for forging political legitimacy were also central to the explosion in consumer goods and services of the post–World War II world. Marketing and advertising goods, as well as reorganizing and franchising and "conglomeratizing" businesses, became wide avenues to big salaries and high status. It is no accident that one of Richard Nixon's first corporate sponsors was Pepsi, whose major product was (and is) a dark brown beverage that was easily duplicated and undersold but that became a corporate superstar in the sixties when a team of brilliant advertising "creatives" and marketing executives reencoded its presentation.[9]

Nixon's great gift was in seeing how this reorientation of both political legitimacy and the global economy (which he caught midstream, before it became the thing of television talk shows) and the relations Americans had with this new economy and new politics changed their feelings about public life and their role in it. In Nixon's first inaugural address, he underscored this national divide and made it perfectly clear on which side of it he meant to stand: "In these difficult years, America has suffered from a fever of words: from inflated rhetoric that promises more than it can deliver; from angry rhetoric that fans discontent into hatreds; from bombastic rhetoric that postures instead of persuading. . . . For its part, government will listen. We strive to listen in new ways—to the voices of quiet anguish, the voices that speak without words, the voices of the heart—to the injured voices, the anxious voices, the voices that have despaired of being heard."[10]

On the surface, Nixon was in this inaugural address attacking all those protesters—black and white—who had disturbed Americans' domestic tranquility. Read somewhat differently, Nixon's words also attacked all the image merchants and word specialists in America—advertisers, public relations specialists, free-talking politicians, flim-flamming lawyers, sanctimonious TV anchormen, know-it-all college professors. Nixon, here and elsewhere, was struggling to change the political fortunes of the presidential Republican party by dressing it up as the congeries for the silent rather than the rich or propertied.

Nixon, son of a small-time, small-town grocer—a dying breed—understood that one sort of social system in America, given blurred political expression in the 1930s and built rhetorically around workers and bosses, had broken down and that political loyalties, as a result, might be recast. A whole range of constituencies that had flocked to the New Deal Democratic party because of its support of "the little man," in status terms, and the working man, in traditional if nonradical terms, could be reencoded and reclassed to Nixon's Republican party.

Nixon, a hyperarticulate man, tried to perform a nearly impossible task. He tried to speak for those who felt themselves silent and who felt, with a rushing urgency, a blind rage for all those people who shattered their domestic tranquility, who forced themselves into their living rooms, blue screen ablaze, with all the endless shouting and yelling, promoting and demanding, pitching and huckstering that told people they were, indeed, living through the sixties.

At the close of the sixties, a machinist tried to explain his sense of frustration. He tried to explain how he divided up the world. He was struggling to say something never expressed in the mass media, never taught at the universities. What he felt was so obvious and in some ways so gross a truth that it escaped most of America's professional observers and commentators. What he felt was that what some people called the establishment and antiestablishment forces were really just two sides to the same coin:

> The way I see it, you've got these people who run the big companies. Then you've got others who run the newspapers and the magazines and the television stations, and they're all full of themselves. . . . They're full of long lectures. . . . They can take anything and make it into what they want. I guess they're just smart talkers. . . . What I don't like about the students, the loudmouthed ones, is that they think they know so much they can speak for everyone, because they're right and the rest of us aren't clever enough and can't talk like they can. . . . There are people in this country who make all the noise and have their hands on most of the money. . . . I have a friend, he and I work together, and he says he wishes they'd get rid of each other, the rich guys and the college radicals.[11]

Many working-class Americans hated the student protesters of the sixties, not because they disagreed with the students' opinions on this issue or that (more working people opposed the war in Vietnam than did people of the upper and middle classes),[12] but because they could not stomach the idea of the nation not only being run by corporate elites but also listening so seriously to the clamorous claims of the corporate elites' privileged children. Richard Nixon tried to take people's resentment against all the "smart talkers" and "loudmouths"—young and old—and turn it into a potent political weapon.

To some extent, he came by his strategy honestly. Nixon had these same feelings of resentment. They were bred into him during his boyhood in the provinces. They were seared home in his post–law school search for a job in New York City, where one elite law firm after another turned him away, his brilliance and ferocious drive not enough, in their sophisticated eyes, to make up for his humble past.

Nixon knew these feelings—of being excluded, of being mocked by those who felt themselves charged with reproducing American culture in their own powerful image. And from the start of his meteoric political career, Nixon knew the political utility of unleashing and directing the angry feelings generated by sociocultural exclusion. Nixon blasted off into the political stratosphere when—in Spring 1948—as an unrefined congressman from provincial southern California, unsure of dress or Washington protocol, almost bereft of cultural capital, he took on a paradigmatic "smart talker," Alger Hiss—Harvard man, State Department snob.

At their very first meeting, Nixon regarded Harvard Man Hiss as suspiciously "too mouthy." Nixon ended Hiss's high-flying government career, a career that at the time promised to be far more glorious than Nixon's own, by calling the man a communist traitor and making the charge stick. Here was a classic example, said Nixon, of a man who used his fancy words to sell out the country that too many quiet, simple folk had just died defending during World War II. Ironically, the major piece of physical evidence against Hiss was not a gun or a record of a cash payment but the marks left by his typewriter.[13]

In part, Nixon was then playing on the raw nerve of American populism. He knew the scorn a great many Americans felt for the well born and the well educated—paradigmatically, the East Coast Ivy league elite. For Nixon, this scorn for the proverbial Harvard Man was not simply a political tool—it coursed through his veins. Early in his presidency he secretly ordered his chief of staff, when looking for young people to bring on board the ship of state, "as far as the universities are concerned, [to] just rule out the east even though there are some good ones here and go to the midwest to try to find some decent people. I consider this new direction as being of the highest priority. I want absolutely no deviation from it."[14] Nixon's populist resentment resonated, and he gained support as he expressed his revulsion for a world of privilege and a network of power that many Americans saw as unearned.

Americans' populist resentment of class privilege was, however, neither a historical constant nor unnuanced. In 1960 Americans had scorned Richard M. Nixon, the hard-trudging "iron-butt" from Whittier, California, for Harvard Man, never-worked-a-day-in-his-life John F. Kennedy. When Barry Goldwater had campaigned on the old virtues in 1964 and snickered about sawing off the eastern seaboard and letting it float out to sea, he had garnered only 38 percent of the vote. A good many Americans' feelings about East Coast privilege, cosmopolitanism, and academic credentials were complicated. What they liked and disliked about the world of the privileged, as well as exactly who they considered privileged and why, was changing. It was open to manipulation.

Shortly after Nixon was sworn in as president, a Justice Department official, whose charge it was to go into polarized communities and mediate between civil rights protesters and their white adversaries, tried to put his finger on what made so many Americans so angry about the swirling protests, demands, and challenges of the sixties: "The values we held so dear are being shot to hell. . . . Everything is being attacked—what you believed in and what you learned in school, in church, from your parents. So the middle class is sort of losing heart. They had their eyes on where they were going and suddenly it's all shifting sand."[15]

Polls and surveys gave credence to the idea that a good many Americans were angry about protesters and their clamorous attacks on what many Americans thought of as the "American way." By the fall of 1969, an astounding 84 percent of white Americans assented to the claim that college demonstrators were treated too leniently. The ayes went up to 85 percent when the statement read, "black militants are treated too leniently." At the close of the 1960s, white Americans overwhelmingly disapproved of the main noisemakers in the United States.[16]

But what exactly did a large majority of white America see as so threatening about student protesters, antiwar demonstrators, and black militants? What "values" were being "shot to hell" by these dissidents? These were questions without sure answers but questions politicians needed to answer in the late 1960s and early 1970s.

Back in 1964, Republican nominee for the presidency, Barry Goldwater, in a case of premature articulation, had run on the "values" question. "We must, and we shall," he orated, "return to proven ways—not because they are old, but because they are true." What exactly those values were, though, even Goldwater seemed unwilling—or perhaps, more interestingly, unable—to state clearly. What he did make clear was that the Democrats had sought to replace bold actions in defense of those values with nothing more than slippery rhetoric: "During four futile years the Administration which we shall replace has distorted and lost the faith. It has talked and talked and talked the words of freedom but it has failed and failed and failed in the works of freedom." Goldwater, without as stark a canvas as would be available to Nixon in the late 1960s and early 1970s, struggled to paint Republicans as the party of "the creative and the productive" and Democrats as a cabal of garrulous politicians who thought America could be built on "bureaucratic make-work," "bread and circuses," "spectacles," and "scandals." Goldwater, in an almost prescient way, wanted to define himself and the Republicans as the party of the work ethic, of industrial capitalism, and the family farm. He attacked the Democrats, to use contemporary terms, as a bunch of postmodern, postindustrial, paper shufflers.[17] In the early 1960s, not enough Americans were willing to accept this rhetorical sleight of hand. By the late 1960s, the divide he sought to picture between those who produced and those who schmoozed would gain greater visceral meaning with the prime-time events all America watched.

There they were, on television and in the papers: hippie visionaries, black power fire-eaters, and New Left revolutionaries. They made fun of Americans' hard work and the ethics that put a man on the line day in and day out. They made fun of the good life, the new-car-in-the-garage life, that the hard work paid for. They rejected "respectability" and "decency," terms that they argued had come to mean little more than buying the right products from the right stores so that you looked like everybody else and smelled like everybody else and mowed your lawn like everybody else. The protesters seemed to give the same "stink eye" to both production and consumption, to the old virtues and the new values.

Yippie activist and mass media manipulator extraordinaire Abbie Hoffman, for example, envisioned a society where the machines would do all the factory work and Americans would devote themselves to community good when not reveling in adolescent fantasies.[18] The New Left and the protesters simply never spoke about work as a locus of political consciousness or radical energies. The black power advocates demanded that white America fork over reparations and good jobs and free housing. No one seemed to pay attention to the hard work, to the daily grind, to the effort it had taken so many Americans to make something from nothing. Nor did they seem to understand the economic breakthrough so many Americans felt themselves living through: suddenly, regular, hard-working Americans could and did command a host of luxurious goods and services. As many Americans saw it, the protesters railed against this and they chanted about that but never did they seem willing to do what was necessary to bring a better life to their families and to themselves. *That is how many heard the protesters.*[19]

As one of Nixon's supporters, a bank worker and part-time security guard, raged: "Every time I used to hear on television those spoiled-brat students singing 'we shall overcome,' I'd think of my dad. *There's* someone who has overcome, let me tell you. . . . His father . . . was killed working in a coal mine. Then his mother died giving birth to a child and there was no money for a doctor. . . . But he got a job in Western Union when he was thirteen, and he's been working for them ever since."[20] What the student protesters seemed not to know and too many black activists failed to acknowledge was that many white working people well remembered a time when they had done without, when they had suffered hard times and unemployment. In 1968 Alabama governor and presidential aspirant George Wallace told cheering crowds that he had grown up in a house without indoor plumbing, he had held the short end of the stick, but he had not gone yelling and demanding this and that, he had not rioted, he had soldiered on.

Protesters paid little to no mind to the history of white working people in the United States—conceding little to their struggle to make ends meet and to create meaningful lives in fast-changing times. They seemed to give no respect to the hard work it had taken and still took most Americans to earn the modestly pleasant life-styles they had chosen for themselves. What protesters seemed to offer in the place of the rewards of hard work, in the minds of many Americans, was talk—the free speech movement, the filthy speech movement, participatory democracy, chanting, singing, dancing, protesting. And, as many nonyoung, nonblack Americans believed, all of the talk was aimed at the television cameras. The cameras' red lights stayed on, often enough, because the young protesters knew the new language of entertainment value—"the whole world is watching," they chanted to the cameras. The protesters meant that the whole world was watching the political battle, but many heard the chant differently— "the whole world is watching . . . Them and not Us."

Social critic Christopher Lasch, in *The True and Only Heaven*, excoriates "the habit of criticism" that gushed forth, he argues, from "the dominant culture" in the 1960s and 1970s. From a lower-middle-class point of view, he writes, "the habit of criticism" appeared to invite people to be endlessly demanding of life, to expect more than anyone had a right to expect." As Lasch notes, many white working people saw this "habit of criticism" as a direct repudiation of the dignity of the limited lives that they had fought to earn and they quietly accepted. He quotes a white Catholic housekeeper's contempt for her privileged employers:

> The house is full of talk. . . . He's read something that's bothered him and she's read something that's bothered her. They're both ready to phone their friends. The kids hear all that and they start complaining about what's bothering them—about school, usually. They're all so *critical*. I tell my kids to obey the teacher and listen to the priest; and their father gives them a whack if they cross him. But it's different when I come to fancy Cambridge. . . . I want to scream sometimes when I hear those brats talking as if they knew everything.[21]

Many Americans felt threatened by a world in which hard work and hard knocks seemed to earn less and less respect and less and less money. They felt threatened by a world in which their labor, they felt, was deemed less praiseworthy than somebody else's angry demands. Barry Goldwater, in the 1964 campaign, tried to bestir these feelings, as protests by black Americans in particular touched many white Americans' fears about losing their places in the economic and social hierarchy, as well as their limited arenas of autonomy.

George Wallace in the 1968 campaign pushed hard at those fears. He understood, more clearly than Goldwater, that a great many white Americans felt caught in a paradox. They felt economically beleaguered in the midst of plenty. Paychecks were shredded by high taxes, homes were mortgaged, cars were paid off a month at a time, mass-produced splendors were bought on credit. Even what they had—and it is crucial to note that they had much more than their parents had had—they did not securely have. They were in thrall to credit companies, banks, corporations, and the Internal Revenue Service. That they had, to a large extent, put themselves in such a position was not something Wallace or his audience dwelt on. Wallace did not point a finger at people's own avarice or the acquisitiveness big business pushed at Americans from all directions. Instead, Wallace told white working men and women, in the basic speech he gave around the country in 1968, that what little there was left to the average American was being challenged by the students, the black activists, the intellectuals, and the liberal federal government. In his rambling, visceral way, he listed for his enthusiastic audiences, what he claimed all the "pointy-heads" and "protesters" meant to "take away": "We're talking about domestic institutions, we're talking about schools, we're talking about hospitals, we're talking about the seniority of a workingman in his labor union, we're talking about the ownership of property. . . . We don't need guidelines to tell us and we don't need half a billion dollars being spent on bureaucrats in Washington of your hard earned tax money to check every school system, every hospital, every seniority list of a labor union . . . let them know that a man's home is still his castle."[22]

Wallace used racism as a unifying subtext in his speeches. But his real power came from his ability to tell his audiences that their racism was justified because racism was one of the few weapons they had standing between them and further loss of control over their lives and the lives of their children. More than 20 percent of Americans said in the fall of 1968, before they reconsidered the utility of voting for a third-party candidate, that they supported Wallace. Wallace, they believed, understood their anger against all the cosmopolitan forces and organized shouters. By 1968 Richard Nixon knew that he had a competitor who meant to rub raw the same angry feelings that he meant to massage.

George Wallace, in 1968, tried to mutate a racist populist politics of the Old South into a national politics of resentment. Richard Nixon, picking up on the cultural politics of Barry Goldwater and then California governor Ronald Reagan, tried to quietly unite the producing classes with the capitalist producers against the "critical" and protesting segments of society. Mayor Richard J. Daley, arguably the most powerful local politician in the United States during the 1960s, more powerfully and accurately reflected the political sensibility of at least white northern working people. Daley truly was a kind of organic intellectual of the silent majority.

Daley was born into an Irish Catholic working-class family. His father had been, at the local level, a union activist and had suffered job loss and discrimination as a result. Much of Daley's political success hinged on union support and the good working relations such support created. Although Daley had sweeping support in Chicago, his base remained the southside neighborhood, Bridgeport. He was born at 3602 Lowe Street and never left; he raised his own family half a block away at 3536 Lowe. While he was host of the 1968 Democratic National Convention and the protests that went with it, Daley's political values and understandings of sixties-style protest were put on national display.

Daley still achingly and very much paradoxically believed in an older productionist model of economy and politics, even as his constituents had begun to embrace and be embraced by a consumerist and therapeutic ethos that privileged buying power and a mutable life-style. As a politician, even a local one, Daley was a dinosaur and he knew it, even as he fought it. He had no respect for sound bites, spin control, photo opportunities. He knew the world was changing and changing away from his world in which personal loyalty overrode any ideology, in which a patronage job meant more for a family than any federal program, and in which a precinct captain's political advice stood ahead of a thirty-second-lie broadcast during prime time. Daley feared the loss of a political world in which what programs you brought to whom was replaced by one in which attitudes you sold in living color determined from whom you got support.

Like many of the people Nixon spoke to with such insight, Daley saw in the protesters simply an extreme version of all those who used language and symbols and the sheer manipulation of desire to override an older world of hard work and concrete acts and the complicated reality of making ends meet. As Daley and his police force made clear during the 1968 Democratic convention, to them the radical protesters appeared as a part of a bigger enemy—a class enemy.

The mass media loomed large in the mayor's list of enemies, just as it did in Richard Nixon's. Daley saw the mass media and the protesters as two sides to the same problem. Daley, in answering a hostile question from a reporter about why he did not give protesters permission to march through his city, impishly turned the question around and expressed the contempt he and others felt: "We are talking to the hippies, the Yippies, and the flippies and everything else. . . . We are talking to the newspapers and some of them are hippies and Yippies. And to the TV and radio, and a lot of them, I guess, are the leaders in these movements."[23] Daley was kidding on the square; the protesters and the mass media were all outsiders in his community. More seriously, Daley tried to express his vision to his fellow Democrats when they assembled in Chicago right before the 1968 convention. He suggested: when the reporters ask you questions that you don't want to answer, just don't. Power, he argued, did not have to stem from the lens of a camera.

A Chicago policeman, questioned a few days later why he and others beat and bloodied news reporters, gave the epigrammatic answer, they "act like they own the street."[24] But, the policeman believed, they did not. They just visited the streets, observed them, reported about them. They did not really do anything on them—they just used them as a backdrop for stories they made up in their heads and then tried to put into everybody else's. For the mayor, the convention was the same thing. Reporters and the networks and the protesters all came to do the same thing—to make of a working meeting a symbol for the nation. The talkers and shouters were most interested in colorful images, blowups, and hard feelings. As Daley saw it, they did not care about, let alone understand, the hard work of lining up votes and making deals. The mass media, like the protesters, talked as if their words meant more than people's deeds, indeed, more than the dead American boys about whom they chanted, who they numbered and flashed on the screen in ten-second images. Mayor Daley was a political dinosaur. And after 1968, in part because of the aesthetically displeasing violence at the 1968 Democratic convention, nobody even made believe that a presidential nominating convention was anything but an extended commercial aimed at marketing certain messages.

When Mayor Daley was confronted by the press about his orders to stop the antiwar protests in Chicago in 1968, over and over, he asked hostile reporters, "What programs do they have, what do they want?" And all along he knew that what they wanted was not what he could even begin to deliver. Daley knew how to make a brokered political deal. The protesters he saw on Michigan Avenue and in Lincoln Park were a part of something postpolitical, something new that spoke to images and feelings and the existential wonder of feeling yourself raging on the streets of "America," where the cameras could flash your soul into everybody's living rooms.[25]

The protesters, Mayor Daley felt, were not his kind of people. Most Americans knew this too. "The world hears those demonstrators making their noise. The world doesn't hear me and it doesn't hear a single person I know. . . . Fancy, fast talking students, gabby they are, gab, gab," said the wife of a fireman and part-time carpenter whose son died in Vietnam.[26]

In the logorrhea of the new world in which words were made to stand for more than deeds and images for more than realities, the fireman's wife knew that her son had died, in a way, because he was not a good talker. He had not used student deferments or psychiatrist reports or clever letters to his draft board or any of the other manipulations of the selective service regulations so many well-educated people called on to keep out. The members of her family were not good talkers, just as the machinist quoted earlier was not. In the new information age, these were people accustomed to, but often no longer making, things. In an age where soft drinks that cost more to market than manufacture earned billions, the old lines of division made little sense. And Americans of all socioeconomic castes felt the change and wondered how to maintain their dignity and their economic viability.[27]

For many Americans whose lives were already torn between a belief that said dignity came in your ability to shape a small piece of reality and a life-style that said pleasure came bundled in purchasable quantities, the kind of political protest practiced by white radicals and even by civil rights leaders like Martin Luther King, Jr., seemed to offer them little chance of improved conditions. Whereas the heartfelt beliefs of a Daley and the manipulations of a Nixon proffered a world in which the real lives they had produced mattered, the world invoked by the protesters seemed like nothing more than an ineffective burned offering simulated by the image merchants that sold them their everyday dreams.

Barry Goldwater's instincts, back in 1964, were sound. For many Americans virtue did still attach itself firmly to the act of production, to the making of something concrete. For many Americans, the manipulation of information, symbols, *and capital* was not real work, was without obvious value. Many Americans in the twentieth century had been participating, even if silently, in a complex debate about the relationship between the virtues of production and the values of consumption.

American labor historians have argued convincingly that in the mid- to late nineteenth century, a strong and self-conscious producing class waxed powerful in the United States and did so as its members created a separate consciousness that was based on their collective preindustrial ways of life but also on the lessons they had learned at the point of production. In the mid-nineteenth century, historians tell us, American workers in New York City, in the National Labor Union, and in the Knights of Labor, as well as farmers involved in the Populist movement, believed in a productionist ethos that at the same time linked them to their production-oriented bosses and yet gave them a pride in their own fundamental role in the political economy.[28]

Even late into the nineteenth century many production workers and farmers valorized the actual making of goods and the cooperation and interdependence that they believed made such enterprise possible. These were men and women who spoke up for their vision of America and who cherished the egalitarianism that they believed gave sustenance to American democracy. As social historians have shown, such political feelings revealed themselves in cultural deeds and political styles of all kinds.

In America through most of the nineteenth century, cultural performances and political campaigns were far from passive events—mere spectacles. They were instead participatory extravaganzas—albeit often racist, sexist, and exclusionary ones—in which workers and plain folks marched and sang, built bonfires, and fought on the streets. When watching others perform they felt no hesitancy in screaming out their criticisms and their accolades. Even the language of Americans had, by the post–Civil War years, become a democratic circus with accents and rhetorical styles driven by a folksy, localized approach. Culture and politics were participatory and productionist activities, with the two modes of activity undergirding one another.[29]

All this, to put it baldly, became more of a mixed, contradictory set of feelings as the democratic ethos of the mid-nineteenth century was overlaid by the increasing status and power of professional-scientific elites. These elites put order, reason, and progress above the peculiarly democratic practices of at least some American workers and their leaders.[30]

Similarly, the emerging managerial elite also did its best to do in the cultural richness and parochial concerns of immigrant cultures with assimilatory pressures. They aimed to turn second-generation immigrants into first-generation Americans of the new national consumer culture who would sustain this new system by being efficient workers and enthusiastic consumers. For the mass of Americans, the workplace and the community would be joined by the department store and the amusement park as the locus of identity.[31] Historians who have begun to push this narrative into the twentieth century have increasingly focused, naturally enough, on the ways in which a consumerist gestalt began to complicate and contest the older production-oriented culture that structured class tensions in the nineteenth century.

Obviously, such a project was rudely disturbed by the Great Depression and World War II. But while labor militancy was given a terrific shot in the arm by economic upheavals of the 1930s and the economic mobilization demanded by World War II, the cultural forces engendered by the emergent mass consumer society were working to shape worker-boss conflicts into a narrower and narrower range.[32] In the workplace, at least at the official level, employees were taught by union leaders and by supervisors to listen to and obey the dual bureaucracy of labor and management.[33] In return, workers would earn high wages and good benefits. According to at least one veteran of 1930s union militancy, the lesson had been well learned by 1961: "Today's attitude is not what we can do together but what is the union and the committeeman doing for my five dollars a month."[34]

This attitude was given expression in a noticeable political absence. In Detroit throughout the 1930s and 1940s, building on a long-standing but revitalized tradition, auto workers and other working men and women took to the streets in celebration, in protest, in honor of their achievements and in response to their needs. Public space in Detroit during those years was workers' space. By the early 1950s, such public claims on the attention of the city, and even the nation, had started to disappear from the collective culture of those who worked with their hands to make America the world's most productive nation.[35] Auto workers' disregard for the public realm generally and party politics specifically became embarrassingly obvious to Democratic party leaders on the eve of the 1968 election campaign.

For the previous several elections, the United Automobile Workers (UAW) had come together, even if under the clear direction of their union leaders, in the tens of thousands in downtown Detroit for a massive presidential campaign kickoff rally for the Democratic candidate. By 1968 even the most prounion presidential candidate in Democratic party history, Hubert H. Humphrey, could not guarantee a crowd large enough to avoid mass media embarrassment. As a UAW leader noted, in evaluating the odds of pulling off a successful weekend political rally, "How can you get anyone downtown when they're all out at their cottages or on their boats?"[36] The rally was canceled. Public life and collective expression had been defeated by the wide open privatized pleasures that high wages had made available to the masses.

Coeval with this change was the general reorientation of the work force itself. More or less steadily, from 1946 on, union membership as a total percentage of the work force fell. A concerted effort by employers, especially beginning in the early 1970s, was in part responsible for this deunionization. But in large part it was caused by the general shift in the work force from industrial workers to service and information workers of the pink, white, and grease-splattered collar variety. One simply cannot walk away from the fierce reorganization of the American work force—by 1988, 65 million of the 116 million people in the work force worked in offices, up from the already impressive 49 million who worked there in 1978.[37] Put another way, from 1950 to 1988 complex services (such as insurance, law, finance, and advertising) nearly doubled as a percentage of gross national product (GNP), reaching 25 percent, while manufacturing as a percentage of GNP slipped to 20 percent.[38]

For more and more Americans, experience itself (especially but not solely for the worker in the workplace) was relegated to new, less traditionally and collectively grounded realms of meaning. Active and equitable participation in work life and community life were exchanged, or at least refigured, for consumption opportunities and demands for more consumption opportunities. The old Bob Dylan line—money doesn't talk, it shouts—amplifies a key truth. Those who had little chance and, to an extent, desire to speak with authority in the new realms of economic, cultural, and political production spoke up in the marketplace with their dollars. Herein, they were free to express themselves until they were all spent out. And it was, indeed, in this realm where they could speak with abandon that their most frequent calls for more power reverberated. As poll after poll showed, masses of Americans at the middle- and lower-middle-income levels did want more and more money; their anger was very much directed at those who kept them from it—who kept them from shouting even louder in their purchases, who issued summons against their dreams of a rich consumer life-style, who called on them to stop talking in a language that did have currency for them.[39]

Already by the 1920s, for more and more Americans, the Hollywood film, not the shop floor, became the signpost for one's desires.[40] And because of wartime and then postwar affluence, such dreams took on a reality that could not be denied by calls for worker militancy. Economic growth and the higher wages it offered to pursue a life-style of one's own would become the answer to most Americans' dream, not worker control, not rising up the job ladder, not starting up a business of one's own.[41]

Few understood better or staked more on this new American dream than Richard Nixon. When Nixon went to a trade fair in Moscow in 1959 and found himself being harangued by Premier Nikita Khrushchev about the Soviet system's superiority to the American, he did his best to trump all of Khrushchev's talk with a simple wave to the American trade fair display—a typical American kitchen, complete with refrigerator, stove, washing machine, hot and cold running water, and easy-to-clean counters and cabinets. This lovely kitchen, Nixon knew better than most, was what America could claim it offered the world.[42]

This complicated story is obviously much simplified here for heuristic purposes. But the changes it suggests are relevant to the anger most Americans felt in the 1960s and early 1970s, when confronted by the demands of blacks and the young for ideational control over the country in which they all lived.

This is not to suggest that all Americans bought the false faith in the dignity of the working man sold by a Nixon or later by a Reagan. A welder put it well: "You can't fool a workingman too long. Nixon isn't fooling me. He's an old Wall Street lawyer, right. . . . My Dad never lets me forget what a struggle the workingman had in this country, to get the unions working."[43] Most union men and women continued to pull the lever for Democrats throughout the Nixon years. But overwhelmingly most Americans did not accept the demonstrators or the demonstrators' supporters or sympathizers—the national Democratic party—as spokespeople for them (and, of course, the demonstrators were not really trying to speak for them). They saw in the protesters just another sector of the elite, less reasonable and less concerned about economic viability, bidding for power and walking a path to power that offered those who could not give orders in the new code of consumption nothing more than they already had. Indeed, in the new activists' loud demands for affirmative action programs and a nonsexist, nonracist society, a good many white men, at least, found only new threats and new diminutions to their already circumscribed world.

In a world divided between those who spoke and those who were silent, many protesters in the sixties shouted and claimed the right to speak for all. They often revealed contempt for working people and showed much ignorance about those people who still wondered if it was not what you said that counted but what you did.[44] During the sixties, many people held on to a kind of anachronistic faith in the importance of production—of being working people—and they half-mourned a world that had never come to be.[45] Unlike Richard Nixon, too many protesters failed to consider the meaning of so many Americans' silence. Instead, the protesters' verbosity allowed them to be set up by savvy politicians as scapegoats for any and all problems that encroached on Americans' tenuous hold on a satisfactory life.

Richard Nixon preyed on the sixties protesters who talked about a revolution that offered most Americans nothing but heartache. In 1972, while he was running against Senator George McGovern of South Dakota, Nixon's campaign strategists reveled in cultural politics. A secret campaign strategy memo paints a vivid picture: "Portray McGovern as the pet radical of Eastern Liberalism, the darling of the *New York Times*, the hero of the Berkeley Hill Jet Set, Mr. Radical Chic. . . . By November he should be postured as the Establishment's fair-haired boy, and RN postured as the Candidate of the Common Man, the working man."[46] Nixon and his campaign team understood what Mayor Daley of Chicago had tried to explain a few years earlier and what working people around the country were quietly feeling; the *New York Times*, the University of California professoriat, student radicals, and the establishment had more in common with each other than any one of them had with most working people. All the talkers, all the "symbolic analysts," as Richard Reich would dub them almost twenty years later, Nixon could argue convincingly, were remaking

America in their own image and leaving little dignity—economic dignity eventually, psychic dignity by the late sixties—for the common folk who were willing to labor in productive ways for the good things that America offered its working people.

Richard Nixon understood how to tap such feelings. He knew how to lure enough working people who felt left out of the cultural code that seemed to be America in the 1960s to put together a winning campaign. He would help to chart a new culture. Like a very different kind of Moses, he would not be allowed to lead his people into this new land. Stopped by Watergate, he would watch from his California exile.

He would watch, however, as others followed his lead. Hollywood listened to the fury that marked liberal McGovern's crushing defeat. New films with truck driver heroes appeared. CB radios that let anyone sing into the airways became a market sensation—"Breaker, Breaker, that's a bear in the air, Good Buddy," the nation would learn to say. Fundamentalist preachers and New Right social conservatives would learn to use new technologies and marketing tools to reach huge audiences that Madison Avenue and the universities and the New Left and the Democratic party had long ignored.[47] The silent majority would gain a voice in the 1970s. Then Ronald Reagan would come and put all of these ducks in a row. The silent majority, Nixon's America, would finish off the sixties. With anger and uncertainty and little charity, led by rich men whose real interests were very different from their own, this no longer so silent majority would be about the business of charting America's course into the twenty-first century.[48]

NOTES

1. Jean Baudrillard, *The Mirror of Production*, translated by Mark Poster (St. Louis, Mo.: Telos Press, 1975), 122.

2. Richard Reich, "As the World Turns," in *A History of Our Time: Readings on Postwar America*, edited by William Chafe and Harvard Sitkoff (New York: Oxford University Press, 1991), 466–67.

3. The "new class" debate is wisely summarized by Christopher Lasch, *The True and Only Heaven: Progress and Its Critics* (New York: Norton, 1991), 509–29.

4. For a rich, if only partial, exploration of this relatively underresearched set of notions, see Richard Tedlow, *Keeping the Corporate Image* (Greenwich, Conn.: JAI Press, 1978), Robert Collins, *The Business Response to Keynes, 1929–1964* (New York: Columbia University Press, 1981), Robert Burk, *The Corporate State and the Broker State: The Du Ponts and American*

National Politics, 1925–1940 (Cambridge: Harvard University Press, 1990), Robert McElvaine, *The Great Depression* (New York: Times Books, 1984), Barry Karl, *The Uneasy State: The United States from 1915 to 1945* (Chicago: University of Chicago Press, 1985), David Farber, *Chicago '68* (Chicago: University of Chicago Press, 1988), Roland Marchand, *Advertising the American Dream* (Berkeley: University of California Press, 1985), Jackson Lears, *No Place of Grace* (New York: Pantheon, 1981), Kenneth Cmiel, *Democratic Eloquence: The Fight over Popular Language in Nineteenth-Century America* (Berkeley: University of California Press, 1990), and Ronald Steel, *Walter Lippman and the American Century* (New York: Vintage, 1981).

5. Walter S. Carpenter, Jr., to Alfred P. Sloan, Jr., 18 April 1941, folder 33A, box 837, Walter S. Carpenter Papers, Hagley Library, Wilmington, Del. Carpenter was more sensitive to these issues than most corporate officers, in part, because his company had been attacked during the 1930s as a war profiteer for its World War I munitions sales.

6. Alfred P. Sloan, Jr., to Walter S. Carpenter, Jr., 24 April 1941, folder 33A, box 837, ibid.

7. This is a rather casual assertion to make about who runs America; for more discussions about elite power, see the other essays in this book, especially those by Robert M. Collins (chap. 1) and Mary Sheila McMahon (chap. 2). For a good overview of business power in America, see David Vogel, *Fluctuating Fortunes: The Political Power of Business in America* (New York: Basic Books, 1989). For a good introduction to the argument that the state is a relatively autonomous actor in American power plays from, in part, a Marxist perspective, see Margaret Weir, Ann Shola Orloff, and Theda Skocpol, eds., *The Politics of Social Policy in the United States* (Princeton: Princeton University Press, 1988).

8. Elizabeth Fones-Wolf, "Beneath Consensus" (Ph.D. dissertation, University of Pennsylvania, 1989). Thanks to Fones-Wolf, I had a chance to read this manuscript as she prepared it for publication.

9. Herbert Parmet, *Richard Nixon and His America* (Boston: Little, Brown, 1990), 398–400, tells of Nixon and Pepsi.

10. Richard Nixon, "Inaugural Address," 20 January 1969, *Inaugural Addresses of the Presidents of the United States* (Washington, D.C.: GPO, 1969), 277.

11. Robert Coles, *The Middle Americans: Proud and Uncertain* (Boston: Little, Brown: 1971), 44–46.

12. For an interesting jab at why so many insisted on the opposite during the 1960s and early 1970s, see Andrew Freely, "New Ethnicity and Blue Collars," in *The World of the Blue Collar Worker*, edited by Irving Howe (New York: Quadrangle Books, 1971), 290.

13. For the "too mouthy" phrase and the Nixons' relative social innocence, see Roger Morris, *Richard Milhous Nixon* (New York: Henry Holt, 1990), 400, 358.

14. *From the President: Richard Nixon's Secret Files*, edited by Bruce Oudes (New York: Harper and Row, 1989), 104.

15. "The Troubled America: A Special Report on the White Majority," *Newsweek*, 6 October 1969, 31.

16. Ibid., 35.

17. Barry Goldwater, "Acceptance Speech 1964," in *America Since 1945*, edited by Robert Marcus and David Burner (New York: St. Martin's, 1991), 220.

18. Or Hoffman argued that one could simply steal whatever one needed rather than earn wages to pay one's way—see Farber, *Chicago '68*.

19. Todd Gitlin in *The Whole World Is Watching: Mass Media in the Making and Unmaking of the New Left* (Berkeley: University of California Press, 1980) speaks of the skewed representations that the mass media gave to the student New Left and how the activists' desire to be publicized affected their rhetoric and actions.

20. Coles, *The Middle Americans*, 90.

21. Lasch, *The True and Only Heaven*, 494. Lasch's own comment is on p. 493.

22. Theodore White, *The Making of the President, 1968* (New York: Pocket Books, 1970), 433.

23. Farber, *Chicago '68*, 160. The material on Daley is drawn from chaps. 5–7, 10.

24. Ibid., 160. The attitudes of the police in America during the sixties are discussed in chaps 5–7, 10.

25. This material on Daley is drawn from Farber, *Chicago '68*, esp. chap. 10. Daley, as surveys and his own mail revealed, won overwhelming public support for his hard line against convention protesters—he received 135,000 letters in favor of his deeds and only 5,000 against them. An SRC poll showed that only 10 percent of white Americans believed too much force had been used. See ibid., 205–6.

26. Coles, *The Middle Americans*, 134.

27. The best description of the contradictions surrounding the identity of working people that I have read is given by David Halle, *America's Working Man* (Chicago: University of Chicago Press, 1988), esp. chap. 10.

28. See, for example, Leon Fink, *Workingmen's Democracy: The Knights of Labor and American Politics* (Urbana: University of Illinois Press, 1983), and Lawrence Goodwyn, *Democratic Promise: The Populist Moment in America* (New York: Oxford University Press, 1976).

29. Of course, blacks and women were excluded, and I am certainly not valorizing this world in its entirety. Neil Harris, in his biography of P. T. Barnum, *Humbug* (Boston: Little, Brown, 1973), masterfully explores both the expectations of democratic cultural participation and active play and its frustration and reconstitution in the nineteenth century. More directly speaking to the decline of political participation around the turn of the century is Michael McGerr, *The Decline of Popular Politics: The American North, 1865–1928* (New York: Oxford University Press, 1986). For a brilliant foray into participatory culture and politics, see David Glassberg, *American Historical Pageantry: The Uses of Tradition in the Early Twentieth Century* (Chapel Hill: University of North Carolina Press, 1990). Alan Trachtenberg, in the *Incorporation of*

America (New York: Hill and Wang, 1982), also explores this issue. The overarching argument about participatory culture is made most forcefully by Lawrence Levine in *Highbrow/Lowbrow: The Emergence of Cultural Hierarchy in America* (New York: Oxford University Press, 1989). For a consideration about American language and its democratic and participatory character, see Cmiel, *Democratic Eloquence*.

30. This scheme is pushed forward by labor historians like Sean Wilentz, Nick Salvatore, and the late Herbert Guttman. It is heatedly debated by others who are uncomfortable with its emphasis on rhetorical declarations and by the lack of deeds—most especially a labor party or a socialist party—that prove that labor leaders of the nineteenth century meant what they said about the glory of the producer and the wonders of cooperation. For an excellent summary of this debate, see *ILWCH* 26 (Fall 1984), which includes Sean Wilentz, "Against Exceptionalism: Class Consciousness and the American Labor Movement," a favorable response by Nick Salvatore, and a critique by European labor historian Michael Hanagan, who writes that "class consciousness cannot be separated from the political structures which give it form and meaning" (p. 33). What is clear is that labor leaders and the artisans of New York in the early and middle parts of the nineteenth century did express different feelings about the nature and purpose of work and the role of the individual in the production process than did their bosses and others fixated on the possibilities of a cash flow polity. The great farm protests of the late nineteenth century carried with them a similar class consciousness and belief in the divide between those who produce and those who capitalize on others' work (Goodwyn, *Democratic Promise*).

31. I am thinking here of Susan Porter Benson's acclaimed work, *Counter Cultures: Saleswomen, Managers, and Customers in American Department Stores, 1890–1940* (Chicago: University of Illinois Press, 1988), which focuses on the creation of women clerks and consumers in the orbit of the department store. See also Lewis Erenberg, *Steppin' Out: New York Nightlife and the Transformation of American Culture, 1890–1930* (Chicago: University of Chicago Press, 1981), which argues that around the turn of the century wealthy urbanites, in the search for new experiences and new justifications for their wealth, began to take over the demimonde world of the dance hall and restaurant. As a result, a culture of public excess and pleasure made accessible by money was given a new patina of respectability or, at least, legitimization. Even Prohibition would not change this. For an interesting overview of this process, see Trachtenberg, *The Incorporation of America*.

Also, I am not arguing that once upon a time there was an America of sweet community and happy workplaces—but along the lines argued by Robert Wiebe in *The Search For Order, 1877–1920* (New York: Hill and Wang, 1967). I do think that before the rise of the national market system in the

United States, the island community played a critical role in individual experience and clearly many Americans were independent farmers. I am not saying either that the new consumer and national culture was without aspects of class segmentation. Lizabeth Cohen has brilliantly shown how production workers in Chicago moved from divisive religious and ethnic identities to a more class-based identity at least in part because of their participation in a national culture (radio shows, in particular) that enforced—if not purposefully—a national working-class consciousness. Cohen, *Making a New Deal: Industrial Workers in Chicago, 1919–1939* (New York: Cambridge University Press, 1990).

32. This point is argued in Ronald Edsforth's fascinating account of the UAW in Flint, Mich., during the first fifty years of this century—an account accurately titled *Class Conflict and Cultural Consensus: The Making of a Mass Consumer Society in Flint, Michigan* (New Brunswick: Rutgers University Press, 1987).

33. I say at the "official level" because unofficially—beyond both union and management oversight, most workers "make life at work more tolerable . . . [by] wresting from management a degree of control over the work situation in order to create time and space for social activities on the job. The rhetoric may be Frederick Taylor's but the practice is different." Halle, *America's Working Man*, 146. But I would say that this unofficial, carefully nonpolitical contest with their bosses reinforces my argument— the workers are not speaking out against the system or talking about their work but are instead simply absenting themselves from it and the world of rules they allow to be made by others. They are acting in official silence, a point Baudrillard makes in general about the antipolitics of the silent majority—Jean Baudrillard, *In the Shadow of the Silent Majorities*, translated by Paul Foss (New York: Semiotexte, 1983); so does Lasch in *The True and Only Heaven*. Nelson Lichtenstein argues that the muting of worker protest in exchange for union recognition and decent labor contracts occurred during World War II and the immediate postwar years. Nelson Lichtenstein, *Labor's War at Home: The CIO in World War II* (New York: Cambridge University Press, 1982) and "From Corporatism to Collective Bargaining," in *The Rise and Fall of the New Deal Order*, edited by Steve Fraser and Gary Gerstle (Princeton: Princeton University Press, 1989), 122–52.

34. Edsforth, *Class Conflict*, 218.

35. I have taken this material from a fascinating article by Robert H. Ziegler, "Showdown at the Rouge," in *History Today*, January 1990, 49–56.

36. Michael Barone, *Our Country: The Shaping of America from Roosevelt to Reagan* (New York: Free Press, 1990), 449.

37. Kathy Shocket, "Redecorating for the Computer Generation," *New York Times*, 29 January 1989, sec F.

38. Robert Reich, "The Future of Work," *Harper's*, April 1989, 26.

39. For a compelling account of the meaning of the middle-class status and ethos enjoyed by many Americans in

the 1950s and 1960s, see Roland Marchand's fascinating essay, "Visions of Classlessness, Quests for Dominion," in *Reshaping America: Society and Institutions, 1945–1960*, edited by Robert Bremner and Gary Reichard (Columbus: Ohio State University Press, 1982), 163–90. Of course, the degree to which most "workers" in America saw and/or see themselves as middle class is a hotly debated question—for a complex understanding that shows that in the world of consumption most working people see themselves as middle class while at the same time at work they recognize themselves as working people, see Halle, *America's Working Man*.

40. For the potency of Hollywood in forming desires, see Edsforth, *Class Conflict*.

41. For a complicating consideration of the role of work in creating identity as well as culture, see Dan Frank, "The Work of Unemployment: Mourning for Work and the Meaning of Job Loss in an Age of Industrial Decline" (Ph.D. dissertation, Department of Behavioral Science, University of Chicago, 1988). Frank's in-depth interviews with dislocated steel workers reveal the degree to which steel workers in Chicago in the 1970s, awash in consumer goods, disassociated themselves from the workplace until their jobs were threatened and then lost. Then they went through a complex process of self-blame for not having worked harder for their huge wages (they called the wages huge) and anger at the company for screwing up. Clearly, as the "monopoly" system Baudrillard identified in the six-

ties gives way to a global system of competition, much of the class divide that I argue animates many Americans in an age of abundance might well give way to something different—both (1) an older style of worker militancy based on justifiable anger over exploitation justified by managers as being necessary to maintain competitiveness and (2) a new style of class conflict between those who leap into information manipulation of one kind or another and those who are caught in the backwashes of a production system that must compete with less developed countries whose workers will accept far lower wages. See Reich, "The Future of Work," 26–31.

42. The kitchen debate is best covered by Stephen Ambrose, *Nixon: The Education of a Politician, 1913–1962* (New York: Simon and Schuster, 1987), 523–26.

43. Coles, *The Middle Americans*, 138.

44. The Diggers, activists in Haight-Ashbury in the late 1960s, argued that the New Left was missing the whole point of the matter with its emphasis on protests and counterclaims—a new America, they argued, would exist only if people left the old society and started their own. They envisioned and tried to build a genuine counterculture, growing their own food and setting up their own stores, worker cooperatives, transportation systems, and other social functions. But the hard work of such a dream and the atmosphere of drugs and "do your own thing" made the realization of Free City a nonhappening. At its most heroic, the counterculture aimed at tran-

scending the power of images with the formation of new social relations. In a funny way, the arguments between much of the New Left and some of the more visionary counterculturists are reminiscent of the divide between Booker T. Washington and W. E. B. Du Bois in the first years of the twentieth century. The communes and the back-to-the-earth movement of the 1970s were a function of the failure of the New Left and the isolationism generally inherent in the protests of the 1960s.

45. Halle, *America's Working Man*, shows this mixed bag of feelings—a pride and valorization in productive work, a resentment against the lack of status such work earns in the United States, and, at the same time, a glee in the good things in life that productive work affords one.

46. *From the President*, 480. The memorandum, titled "Assault Strategy," is from Buchanan/Khachigian, 8 June 1972.

47. How many American history textbooks circa 1975 portrayed the Scopes trial in Tennessee as the last, sad gasp of old-time Christian culture, little realizing the sheer numbers of Americans who still took creationism literally and little realizing the upsurge in Christian fundamentalism—a term few sophisticated Americans knew about at the close of the sixties—that was occurring all around America?

48. To call the divide between those who operate or seek to operate a code of desire (the manipulators of demand) and those who are essentially silent consumers of or resisters to that code the whole story of the conservative resurgence or even of the rise of the so-called silent majority in America is obviously simplistic. As other contributors to this volume show, racial politics are a key part of this story. For a strong overview of the conservative resurgence at the end of the sixties that aims to be more comprehensive than my avowedly more suggestive account, see Jon Reider, "The Rise of the Silent Majority," in *The Rise and Fall of the New Deal Order*, edited by Gary Gerstle and Steve Fraser (Princeton: Princeton University Press, 1989), 243–68.

Contributors

• • • • • •

Terry H. Anderson is Professor of History at Texas A&M University. He has written many articles about the sixties and about the Vietnam War, of which he is a veteran. Author of *The United States, Great Britain, and the Cold War, 1944–1947* (1981) and coauthor of *A Flying Tiger's Diary* (1984), he is completing "The Movement and the Sixties" (scheduled for publication by the Oxford University Press in 1994), a book examining social activism from 1960 to the early 1970s.

Beth Bailey teaches at Barnard College, where she is Director of the American Studies Program. She is the author of *From Front Porch to Back Seat: Courtship in Twentieth-Century America* (1988) and coauthor of *The First Strange Place: Race and Sex in World War II Hawaii* (1992). She is currently writing a history of the sexual revolution.

Kenneth Cmiel is Associate Professor of History at the University of Iowa. He is the author of *Democratic Eloquence: The Fight over Popular Speech in Nineteenth-Century America* (1990).

David R. Colburn is Professor of History at the University of Florida. The author of *Racial Change and Community Crisis* (1985; paperback, 1992), he has recently completed a book with Jane Landers entitled *Race and Society in Florida: The African American Heritage in Florida from Early Contact*

to the Present (1993). Colburn is also President of the Florida Historical Society and a contributing writer to the *Orlando Sentinel* on national and state politics.

Robert M. Collins teaches modern U.S. history at the University of Missouri. He has written *The Business Response to Keynes, 1929–1964* (1981) and is presently working on a study of the relationship between economic growth and U.S. public policy in the twentieth century.

Alice Echols is the author of *Daring to Be Bad: Radical Feminism in America, 1967–75* (1989). She lives in Los Angeles, where she is currently working on "Nobody's Girl: The Life and Times of Janis Joplin," which will be published by Hill and Wang.

David Farber is Assistant Professor of History at Barnard College. He is the author of *Chicago '68* (1988) and *The Age of Great Dreams: America in the 1960s* (1994) and coauthor of *The First Strange Place: Race and Sex in World War II Hawaii* (1992).

George Lipsitz is Professor of Ethnic Studies at the University of California, San Diego. He is the author of *Class and Culture in Cold War America* (1982), *A Life in the Struggle: Ivory Perry and the Culture of Opposition* (1988), and *Time Passages: Collective Memory and American Popular Culture* (1990).

Mary Sheila McMahon studied diplomatic history with Akira Iriye at the University of Chicago. She has taught diplomatic and intellectual and cultural history at the State University of New York at Buffalo. Currently, she is working on an intellectual history of national security in the 1930s and 1940s.

Chester J. Pach, Jr., is Associate Professor of History and Director of the Contemporary History Institute at Ohio University. He is the author of *Arming the Free World: The Origins of the United States Military Assistance Program, 1945–1950* (1991) and *The Presidency of Dwight D. Eisenhower*

(rev. ed., 1991). He is working on a history of war and television from Korea to the Persian Gulf.

George E. Pozzetta is Professor of History at the University of Florida. His research, writing, and teaching have centered on the history of American immigration and ethnicity. His recent publications include *The Immigrant World of Ybor City* (1988), with Gary Mormino; *American Immigration and Ethnicity* (1991); and *The Italian Diaspora: Migration Across the Globe* (1992), with Bruno Ramirez. He is presently completing a study of Italian Americans and World War II.

Index

• • • • • •

Whyte, William H., Jr., 177
Wilkins, Roy, 127
Willis, Ellen, 158
Wilson, Charlie, 177
Wilson, Jackie, 217
Wilson, Sloan, 177
"Wise Men," 33
WITCH, 192
Witco Chemical, 180
Wobblies, 159
Wolfe, Tom, 2
Wolfers, Arnold, 51
Women, 130, 152; female orgasm, 242; in labor force, 152–53, 200; and marriageability, 243; status of, 1; subordination of in family, 157
"Women's community," 160
Women's Equity Action League, 183
Women's movement, 6, 150, 176, 183, 237, 239, 277
Women's Strike for Equality, 183

Wonder, Stevie, 215
Woodiwiss, Kathleen, 277
Woodstock, 196, 209, 215, 225, 272
Woodul, Jennifer, 161
Woodward, C. Vann, 283–84
World War I, 47, 50
World War II, 1, 3, 12, 45, 49, 50, 91, 92, 97, 98, 152, 180, 198, 206, 208, 214, 231, 244–45, 292, 293–95, 297, 306

Yippies, 150, 164, 224, 225, 255, 256, 299, 303
Young, Owen, 48
Young Rascals, 217
Youth culture, 1, 213, 238, 255; revolution of, 238; and rock and roll, 206–31

Zappa, Frank, 222, 226
Ziebarth, Warren, 194